Elementary School Scheduling: Enhancing Instruction for Student Achievement

Robert Lynn Canady and Michael D. Rettig

EYE ON EDUCATION
6 DEPOT WAY WEST, SUITE 106
LARCHMONT, NY 10538
(914) 833–0551
(914) 833–0761 fax
www.eyeoneducation.com

Library of Congress Cataloging-in-Publication Data

Canady, Robert Lynn.
  Elementary school scheduling : enhancing instruction for student achievement / Robert Lynn Canady and Michael D. Rettig.
     p. cm.
  Includes bibliographical references and index.
  ISBN 978-1-59667-080-8 (alk. paper)
  1. Schedules, School—United States. 2. Elementary school administration—United States. I. Rettig, Michael D., 1950- II. Title.
  LB3032.C364 2008
  372.12'42—dc22
                                2008011063

10 9 8 7 6 5 4 3

Also Available from Eye On Education

Family Reading Night
Darcy Hutchins, Marsha Greenfeld and Joyce Epstein

Family Math Night: Math Standards in Action
Jennifer Taylor-Cox

Teach My Kid – I Dare You!
The Educator's Essential Guide to Parent Involvement
Sherrel Bergmann, Judith Brough and David Shepard

Differentiated Instruction for K–8 Math and Science:
Activities and Lesson Plans
Mary Hamm and Dennis Adams

Differentiating by Student Learning Preference:
Strategies and Lesson Plans
Joni Turville

Differentiating by Student Interest:
Strategies and Lesson Plans
Joni Turville

Teaching in the Block: Strategies for Engaging Active Learners
Robert Lynn Canady and Michael D. Rettig

Scheduling Strategies for Middle Schools
Michael D. Rettig and Robert Lynn Canady

Block Scheduling:
A Catalyst for Change in High Schools
Robert Lynn Canady and Michael D. Rettig

Acknowledgements

Because much of the content of this book has been developing over a period of 42 years, the authors are indebted to hundreds of teachers and school administrators throughout the United States who have worked with us in implementing and evaluating the strategies described in detail in this book. As with most change efforts, in schools and districts where the scheduling and instructional ideas described in this text have been sustained for three or more years, there has been consistent and quality leadership that maintained the fidelity of implementation.

Beginning in the early 1960s, one of the authors worked both as a principal and as a central office supervisor in the Chattanooga City Schools in Tennessee under the leadership of Dr. Benjamin E. Carmichael, who was superintendent from 1960 to 1966. He had the vision and philosophy that "all students can and must learn" long before the legislation of *No Child Left Behind*. At the time, the city schools were in the early stages of school integration, and Dr. Carmichael gave the author both opportunities and support in developing various scheduling structures and instructional delivery systems. It was during this time period that eight elementary schools in the Chattanooga City Schools implemented many of the concepts of parallel block scheduling (PBS) described in detail in chapters 6, 7, and 8.

Beginning in the mid-1990s the same author worked in the Troup County, Georgia schools with superintendent Dr. J. Terry Jenkins and associate superintendent Joyce Morgan. Because Troup County personnel were responsible for merging four rather diverse school districts, they, too, saw the advantages of the various grouping and scheduling strategies discussed in this book. Troup County has continued to use parallel block scheduling in all of its elementary schools for more than a decade with the support of Dr. Patricia Barton. Bonnie Dudley, an extension center teacher from Hollis Hand Elementary School, wrote the section in chapter 7 on "managing the extension center." Based on numerous data sources and reports from the Georgia State Department of Education, the Troup County schools have shown sustained achievement gains over time, and personnel there give at least partial credit to the scheduling and grouping concepts described in this book.

During the past nine years all 12 elementary schools in the Augusta County, Virginia, Public Schools have implemented parallel block scheduling, with the support of elementary supervisor Dorothy Donat (now retired), and have made significant gains on the Phonemic Awareness Literacy Screening and Virginia's Standards of Learning assessments. These schools were instrumental in developing the kindergarten and first grade early literacy group schedules and instructional strategies described in chapter 6.

We also are indebted to the administrators and teachers of the Manassas Park City Schools in Virginia, who in 1999, under the leadership of superintendent Dr. Thomas DeBolt and then principal Ritchie Carroll, had the vision to design their new primary school building around an educational program supported by parallel block scheduling. With the assistance of one of the authors of this book, the ground-breaking design of VMDO Architects of Charlottesville, Virginia, and the support of many others, this school's successful program was created and is described in detail at the conclusion of chapter 6. We also thank the current principal of Cougar Elementary School, Patricia Miller, who implemented PBS in 1999 at Conner Elementary School and who has guided the evolution of the program at Cougar over the past five years; she contributes her reflections in chapter 6.

Beginning in 2001 several schools in Prince William County, Virginia began to implement the elementary scheduling model described in detail in chapters 2 to 4. After two years of piloting the program, the decision was made to implement a district-wide elementary school scheduling plan which included agreements on time allocations, the Intervention/Enrichment period, and common planning time for all teachers, as described at the end of chapter 2. We extend our thanks to associate superintendent Pamela K. Gauch, health and physical education supervisor Fred Milbert, and the hardworking elementary school principals of the school district for their continuing leadership in this effort.

We also acknowledge the principals and teachers in hundreds of other elementary schools across this country who have embraced and struggled with the scheduling structures and instructional approaches detailed in this book.

Over the past 15 years, the University of Virginia School of Continuing and Professional Studies has disseminated many of the scheduling ideas found in all of our books by sponsoring informative and interactive workshops that have been attended by thousands of educators. We thank Nancy R. Iverson, assistant dean of K-12 Education, and Martha Ann Toms-Farmer, director of K-12 Education Programs, for their continuing support and assistance.

In addition to those already mentioned, several of our revered colleagues agreed to contribute to this book. Our thanks go to Ruth Short of the University of Milwaukee-Wisconsin and Karen Broaddus of the Woodberry Forest School in Virginia, both recognized practitioners and scholars in literacy development, for their detailed descriptions of literacy instruction in chapters 9 and 10. We also thank our good friend Laura L. McCullough of Waynesboro (Virginia) City Schools for her practical and understandable description of exemplary mathematics instruction in chapter 11. We also acknowledge Susan W. Golder, retired director of curriculum and instruction from the Rose Tree Media School District (PA) and current consultant, for sharing her advice regarding managing the change process found in chapter 12. And, finally, our thanks go to our friend, Harriet J. Hopkins, former elementary principal and coordinator of elementary programs in the Fairfax County (Virginia)

Schools, for her contribution to chapter 6 and the wonderful list of extension activities found in Appendix 2.

In addition, after all these years we still appreciate Robert Sickles, our publisher, for his patience in waiting for the completion of this book and his commitment to ensuring its high quality. Thanks also go to Celia Bohannon, our developmental editor, who makes us appear to be better writers than we are.

Finally, and as always, this effort would not be possible without the continuing support of our patient spouses, Marjorie and Sally. We love you both.

Dedication

For our grandchildren, already born and to be born, and for all grand-children, who deserve the best schools we can provide.

Meet the Authors

Robert Lynn Canady is Professor Emeritus and former chair, Department of Leadership, Foundations and Policy Studies, University of Virginia. He has taught in grades 4 through 12, served as principal of elementary, middle, and junior high schools, and held positions in school district central offices.

Professor Canady has worked extensively with school districts in 45 states. His major presentations have been in the areas of grading practices, active teaching strategies, implementation of programs for at-risk students, and the restructuring of schools through various types of scheduling and instructional strategies.

Professor Canady has received numerous awards for outstanding teaching and service, including the Phi Delta Kappa Distinguished Service Award, the Outstanding Professor Award in the School of Education, University of Virginia, two university-wide awards for distinguished teaching and service, and many others. He has published more than 50 articles on the topics of school scheduling and grading in respected educational journals and has co-authored five books. He and his wife, Marjorie, live in Albemarle County, Virginia, where they reared their four children.

Michael D. Rettig spent 15 years as a professor in the College of Education and Director of the Center for School Leadership at James Madison University (JMU), Harrisonburg, VA. He retired from JMU as Professor Emeritus in June 2006 to work full-time with schools across the country. In addition to his work in higher education, he taught in elementary and middle schools for 10 years and served as a school principal.

Dr. Rettig has served as a consultant on school scheduling issues in 40 states with over 750 school districts nationally and internationally. He also has conducted hundreds of workshops and has authored or co-authored numerous articles and books on school scheduling and related topics.

A past president and current board member of the Virginia Association of Curriculum and Supervision, he has received many awards, including the Service Award from the Shenandoah chapter of Phi Delta Kappa (PDK). He was also named a Madison Scholar at James Madison University and was the recipient of the outstanding graduate student award through PDK at the University of Virginia. He and his wife Sally live in Charlottesville, Virginia. Together they have three children.

Table of Contents

Part III: Instruction and Planning

Preface

*For every complex problem there is an answer
that is clear, simple, and wrong.*

H.L. Mencken

In our combined 80+ years of working in PK–12 schools in 45 states, one factor remains clear to us: School personnel have given far more thought and attention to scheduling middle and high schools than to elementary schools. Elementary schools have escaped much of the national scrutiny and the resultant criticism heaped upon secondary schools in such reports as *A Nation at Risk* (National Commission on Excellence in Education, 1983), *Prisoners of Time: Report of the National Education Commission on Time and Learning* (1994), and *Breaking Ranks: Changing an American Institution* (National Association of Secondary School Principals, 1999). While a proposed change to a high school schedule can bring out the fighting spirit of teachers, parents, students and school board members, the fact that one third grade teacher routinely instructs science far less than other third grade teachers in the same elementary school often goes unnoticed.

Sadly, it is not unusual to find elementary schools that do not even have a master schedule. Yes, most schools have a lunch schedule and schedules for physical education, art, music, and other "specials," but too often the schedule for language arts and reading, mathematics, social studies, science, and the many support programs provided for students is constructed haphazardly by teachers working in isolation—private contractors without the global vision of the school's mission that should guide the allocation of time and resources. Too often teachers with the most power—sometimes based on seniority, parent support of special programs, and assertive personalities—end up with preferred schedules.

Since the mid-1960s, elementary schools have added significant numbers of personnel; in one count we found that staff had increased over 50 percent. In some cases these additional resource and support personnel have been used effectively; however, we also have noted that in schools without well-crafted schedules, resource personnel are not well integrated into the instructional program and often are treated as add-ons. With this situation, support personnel compete with classroom teachers for access to students and rarely achieve their potential positive impact on student achievement.

As we have stated previously in our books on high school scheduling (Canady & Rettig, 1995) and middle school scheduling (Rettig & Canady, 2000), we continue to believe that school scheduling—high, middle, *and* elementary school scheduling—is far more important than the simple mechanical assignment of students to teachers, spaces, and time periods. Within the school schedule resides power: the power to address problems and the power to facilitate the successful implementation of effective instructional practices. As well, those who have the responsibility for the school schedule also have the power to create confusion, to waste resources, and to cause unnecessary stress for all who work in the school.

In no way do we mean to imply that by simply implementing the scheduling strategies offered in this book that higher levels of student achievement automatically will result. Significantly increasing student achievement depends primarily on quality teaching. We can say with confidence, however, that implementation of these scheduling strategies can

- ◆ reduce fragmentation of the school day for both teachers and students;

- ◆ reduce conflict and frustration among core, support and encore teachers;

- ◆ offer equity to *all* students and teachers in the school;

- ◆ capitalize on the potential of time as a variable that can impact student achievement;

- ◆ build efficiency into the school day;

- ◆ harness the power of professional learning communities to support school improvement; and

- ◆ institutionalize generally accepted research-based principles of quality instruction including the following:

  - • increasing the amount of instructional time for some subjects and/or for some students;

  - • reducing class size during key instructional activities;

  - • using formative assessment techniques to monitor students' learning; and

  - • providing team-based, data-driven intervention, enrichment, and tutoring services during the school day.

We believe it is important that principles of quality instruction be institutionalized into practice so they can be evaluated and changed if they are not working successfully. One way to support the institutionalization of a good practice is to build it into the schedule! Nearly all educators agree that raising expectations for students without increasing the support they receive is a recipe for failure. Similarly, increasing expectations for teachers without providing support is a formula for stress and eventual burnout. By implementing many of the scheduling strategies presented in this book we support teachers' efforts; quality instruction for *all* students is left less to chance.

The mission of elementary schools in our society has changed little over the decades; elementary school personnel seek to build basic skills in literacy, numeracy, science, social studies, the arts, wellness, democratic ideals, and civility. What has changed, however, is the realization of the importance of achieving this mission for *all* children. In our work, we have had the opportunity to visit schools across our country at all levels: elementary, middle, and high school. When we witness staggering numbers of high school students failing math and English, giving up on school because they cannot read, write, or think mathematically, we know the roots of these problems were established earlier in their schooling. All of society pays a high price for this failure.

We believe that the elementary school is possibly the most critical institution in our society: the invisible backbone of our democracy. Of all the levels of schooling, the elementary school has the best chance of erasing the quality gap that exists for many children in terms of healthcare, parenting, and readiness to begin school. In essence, elementary schools hold the primary ticket to a better life for millions of children. Today, students who leave the elementary grades without sufficient skills to succeed in future years of schooling pose serious problems for themselves and society. The stakes are too high to allow this to continue. The goal of this book is to make elementary schools more efficient and effective for both teachers and students.

As Mencken's quote to begin this preface suggests, the solutions to the problems facing elementary schools today are complex. For that reason this was not an easy book for us to write; we began more than five years ago. We suspect, too, that a book with more than 100 schedules illustrated and explained will not be an easy book to read. For readers willing to rise to the challenge of that task, we hope you find our efforts worth your effort.

Finally, we invite your comments and suggested improvements. We, too, are still searching for ways to organize and schedule elementary schools so they can become more efficient and successful places for teaching and learning for *all* teachers and *all* students.

Lynn and Mike
May 2008

References

Canady, R. L., & Rettig, M. D. (1995). *Block scheduling: A catalyst for change in high school.* Larchmont, NY: Eye on Education.

Rettig, M. D., & Canady, R. L. (2000). *Scheduling strategies for middle schools.* Larchmont, NY: Eye on Education.

National Association of Secondary School Principals (1999). *Breaking ranks: Changing an American institution.* Reston, VA: Author.

National Commission on Excellence in Education (1983). *A nation at risk.* Cambridge, MA: USA Research.

National Education Commission on Time and Learning. (1994). *Prisoners of time: Report of the National Education Commission on Time and Learning.* Washington, DC: U.S. Government Printing Office.

Note

The figures in this book show the school day divided into 5-minute increments. The printing process does not allow us to print the time in every 5-minute slot clearly. We do print the time each hour; times printed refer to the line to the left. The CD-ROM that accompanies this book, however, does have times printed every 5 minutes. When printed on an ink-jet or laser printer, these charts will be clear. Because many of the full-page figures have been placed at the end of each chapter, we suggest that readers consider reading the text in the book while viewing the figures on a computer to avoid flipping back and forth between text and figures.

1

The Case for Building Master Schedules in Elementary Schools

Educators in elementary schools today are under tremendous pressure to increase student performance, most often measured by test scores in reading and mathematics. In fact, raising test scores has become a prime-time national news item and a topic on the agendas of local, state, and national officeholders alike.

With a major focus on increasing student achievement and the accompanying accountability issues, scheduling strategies that can help elementary teachers maximize both instructional time and resources are critical to major school reform efforts. This book explains and explores our belief that scheduling is an untapped resource for enhancing instructional time and learning in elementary schools. From our 80+ years of study and educational experience, we have drawn the conclusion that a well-crafted elementary schedule that effectively uses time, space, and resources can

◆ improve the quality of school time;

◆ reduce problems associated with various pull-out programs;

◆ decrease class size during critical instructional periods;

◆ allow for temporary, flexible instructional groups based on what and who is being taught; and

◆ provide varying amounts of time for students to learn based on their individual needs.

While simply rearranging the bells in a school will not automatically increase student achievement, the school schedule is a significant factor in determining how successfully teachers work with students between the bells. The school schedule is a powerful tool for addressing problems and for facilitating the institutionalization of effective instructional practices. An ill-crafted schedule often results in fragmented and frequently interrupted instructional time, wasted time and resources, and unnecessary stress for both students and teachers.

In our experience, elementary personnel have not been very concerned with scheduling. Pre-service or potential elementary principals typically spend little time and study related to the topic of scheduling. Principals often delegate the responsibility to a teacher or two (often specialists, such as physical education, art, or music). Although middle and high schools generally spend considerable time and effort creating some type of schedule to guide people through the day, it generally has been assumed that if the elementary teacher had a class of no more than 25 students (now some are saying 20) and if they could get to lunch, PE, art, and music on time, all was right with the world!

We argue otherwise. The creation of an effective school schedule is a key component of every elementary principal's work. Even though many different personnel should be involved in the process, to delegate this responsibility is to abdicate the role of instructional leader.

This chapter briefly outlines several problems we have identified with typical elementary school schedules, ponders the causes of these problems, and suggests several general principles for designing effective elementary school schedules.

Problems with Current Elementary School Schedules

When *Prisoners of Time* (National Education Commission on Time and Learning, 1994) was published, a great deal of attention was focused on how secondary schools used time. The problems and foibles of the high school schedule were put under the microscope. Elementary schools escaped this scrutiny largely because the self-contained classroom with the teacher in control of school time was so pervasive and had been accepted without question. We do not accept this model without question. At least in high schools and middle schools we know where the time goes; there is a school-wide master schedule. When the schedule states that students are in an English class for 45 or 90 minutes (whatever the period or block length), one generally can assume that some kind of instruction in English will occur at that time. No such assumption can be made for the use of time in elementary schools, where individual teachers decide what is appropriate. We believe that accountability for the use of time in elementary schools has been spotty at best, and that this issue warrants careful examination. In the sections that follow, we discuss several common problems, including the following:

- ◆ the inconsistent allocation of time to subjects both within and across grade levels;

- ◆ the fragmentation of instructional time;

- ◆ the difficulty of providing institutionalized time for intervention, remediation, enrichment, and special services;

- ◆ the lack of common planning time for teachers during the school day;

- ◆ the mismatch between needs and resources; and

- ◆ the mismatch between teaching skills and teaching assignments.

Inconsistent Allocation of Time

How should time be allocated in elementary school? How should time be allocated at each grade level? These basic questions rarely are discussed, although they must be answered before an appropriate school schedule can be constructed.

Most decisions regarding the allocation of time in elementary schools (except for lunch and encore[1] classes) are at the discretion of individual teachers, who vary greatly in their philosophies regarding time usage. Some focus much of their efforts on language arts and to a lesser extent on mathematics, with little or no instruction in social studies and/or science. It is not unusual to find one third grade teacher in a school who provides 30 minutes of science *daily,* and another who provides 30 minutes of science *weekly.* Therein lies a major problem with elementary school schedules; the curriculum students receive and how much time is spent on each subject should not depend on the teacher's preference. Thoughtful discussion should guide a school or district to allocate time in accordance with its mission and then guarantee that the same allocation occurs across all similar classes and schools.

Fragmented Instructional Time

Many elementary school schedules are plagued by the fragmentation of core instructional time for classroom teachers, who are confronted with a situation in which students who receive special services come and go all day long and the scheduling of encore classes also chops up the instructional schedule. We heard from one teacher in Arizona who stated that she had 132 separate occasions during the week when students receiving special services either departed from or arrived at her classroom, and only two hours weekly when her entire class was scheduled to be there!

The encore schedule likewise contributes to the fragmentation. We worked in one district in which physical education classes were 45 minutes twice weekly for grades 3–5 and 30 minutes three times weekly in grades K–2, and music was 25 minutes twice a week in grades K–2 and 45 minutes once a week in grades 3–5. The schedule for art classes showed similar variations.

When encore teachers' schedules are combined with special service teachers' schedules, regular classroom teachers become traffic directors, ushering groups from one place to the next—rarely having the entire class in attendance and forced to plan instruction around the remaining fragmented time in the

---

1 We define "encore" as those classes that are taught by a specialist in the field and that all children receive, such as physical education, art, music, library-media, foreign language, computers, and so on. Typically, when these classes meet, the base teacher has a planning period. Often such activities have been called "specials." Many instructors of these classes have objected to this title because it implies something extra and, there-

fore, expendable. We agree; however, encore teachers often have been their own worst enemies by advocating scheduling accommodations that force base teachers to plan core instruction within short, fragmented periods of time. While respecting the preferences of encore teachers, schools still must design schedules that insure that their primary mission is implemented effectively. Such a plan will require compromise.

school day. This frustrating circumstance often results in a diluted sense of accountability and efficacy—teachers rationalize, "If I don't have my kids, I can't very well teach them, can I?"

Even though each self-contained teacher will struggle to plan basic instruction around such a schedule, it becomes nearly impossible to find blocks of time when all teachers at a grade level have concurrent uninterrupted instructional time to allow teaming and regrouping of students. When one teacher has her class, another teacher's group may be in music, or several students from a third teacher's class may be receiving extra reading instruction.

Difficulty of Structuring Time for Intervention, Remediation, Enrichment, Special Services

The recipe for students' successful learning includes a continuous cycle of teaching, assessing, and re-teaching, a challenging task for individual teachers to accomplish on their own with a class of 25 very different students. In fact, it was the difficulty of meeting this challenge that doomed the Mastery Learning and Outcomes-based Education movements of the 1970s and 1980s to the junk-heap of discarded education change efforts. Our current "standards-based" educational environment differs from these past programs only in that high-stakes accountability measures have been added as motivation for making the system work. Consequently, there now is great interest among educators in finding time to remediate long-term learning deficits, to intervene quickly when students don't grasp concepts after initial instruction, and to provide enrichment for those who do. However, the basic problem of providing remediation, intervention, and enrichment remains the same as with these past efforts: How can one teacher possibly address all three modes of instruction at the same time? It was impossible for all but the most gifted teachers in the past; why should it be any easier now?

Perhaps the most critical (and unresolved) time allocation issue is the indisputable fact that some students need more time to learn than others. In this age of accountability, when all students are expected to achieve a high level of content mastery, how do we provide more time for those who need it? In elementary schools, our usual response is to provide individual assignments to those who learn quickly, and to regroup, slow down, and provide pull-out programs for those who need more time. The problems with these accommodations are that sometimes the "individualized" activities are thrown together haphazardly (Renzulli, 1996), students placed in slower groups fall farther behind, and that pull-out programs often are poorly integrated with classroom instruction that also stigmatize students who are involved in them (Hopkins, 1990).

Lack of Common Planning Time for Teachers During the School Day

To accomplish the important work of data analysis, curriculum management, lesson study, instructional improvement, and formative assessment design, in addition to the planning required to support the system of remediation, intervention, and enrichment discussed above, professionals must have time to collaborate. This collaboration is difficult to accomplish before school, when preparing for the day's instruction is the main focus. It is equally difficult to accomplish at the end of a tiring day, when out-of-school family responsibilities await. Professional learning communities of teachers must have common planning time during the school day to engage in this work; many still do not (Dufour & Eaker, 1998).

Mismatch Between Needs and Resources

The primary mission in elementary school is literacy and numeracy. Why, then, do we most often present reading and math instruction with the very same class size as physical education, music, art, or even science and social studies classes? Shouldn't our resources follow our needs? Why is it that in some districts, a school with 400 students will have a full-time art teacher—and so will a school of 200? Shouldn't we distribute resources of time and talent in a pattern that reflects needs rather than tradition and simplicity?

Mismatch Between Professional Teaching Skills and Teaching Assignments

We often have mused that the perfect elementary school schedule would include self-contained classes staffed by Renaissance teachers, knowledgeable and skillful in all areas. If base teachers were all equally talented, we wouldn't need encore and special service teachers, and we could lower class size to 10:1. Until we reach this utopian state, however, why not recognize that different teachers have different strengths and utilize them accordingly? If one of the four first grade teachers has a master's degree in reading and is a superstar literacy teacher whereas another is very strong in math or science,

wouldn't it be wise to expose every child to both instructors? Often principals know a teacher is weak in a particular subject, yet students must be assigned to that teacher for that subject—and suffer through a year of questionable instruction. While we agree that the evaluation system should address the issue of incompetent teachers, we also believe in assigning teachers according to their strengths.

Causes of Elementary School Scheduling Problems

The problems discussed previously spring primarily from one factor: Most elementary schools do not construct a master schedule that delineates when all instruction will occur. Generally, the only classes scheduled on a school-wide basis are encore classes, lunch, and recess. Consequently, much of the school schedule is created by independent contractors (classroom teachers and special service providers), usually with very little consultation with other instructors their decisions might affect. Without a school-wide plan for the use of time, our traditional practices for scheduling encore classes and special services cause a host of problems.

Lack of a Master Schedule

A major problem with elementary school scheduling is that those who construct the schedule do not take a school-wide view. Encore teachers' schedules are built with their needs in mind; individual teachers schedule with their preferences at the forefront. Little thought is given to overall school priorities. The program that students encounter is as fragmented as the decision-making process that created it.

Typically, individual classroom teachers have enormous latitude regarding their use of time. They are told when to go to lunch and when to send students to encore classes; otherwise, they often are free to schedule as much or as little specific instruction as they see fit. Consequently, the distribution of instructional time may vary widely even within the same grade level of a single school.

One of the attention-getters we often use with teachers in a schedule-building workshop involves this very issue. The first question we ask is "What time in the morning does school begin?" Pose this question in your school someday, asking teachers to think silently of their responses. Count to three, and then invite them to respond in chorus. You'll probably hear three or four different times mentioned! Teachers invariably have different notions about when school actually starts, and these differences in opinion regarding time only multiply as you begin to discuss instruction.

To guide teachers in their first experience of building a master schedule, we first establish beginning and ending times, then calculate the number of minutes in the school day (e.g., 8:00 A.M. to 2:30 P.M. is 390 minutes). We post this number on the board. We then choose a particular grade level (say, third grade) and ask a teacher to respond to a few questions. "What is the first activity we should put on the schedule?" Teachers often jokingly call out "Lunch!" or "Planning time!" We then say, "Let's start with our most important activity." Consistently, language arts and reading top the list, but teachers differ greatly in the amount of time to allocate—in third grade, anywhere from 60 minutes to three hours daily. Once a time is agreed upon, we subtract it from the 390-minute total.

Mathematics typically is the next emphasis, and then social studies and science, encore classes, and, finally, lunch and recess. For each activity, we subtract the agreed-upon time allocation. Often we finish with a substantial amount of time left over, and teachers scratch their heads in disbelief, wondering, "Where did it come from?" Or they state, "Oh, that's travel time, bathroom time, rest time, and so forth." Other times, the total isn't enough to cover all subject areas, and then teachers ask, "How am I ever going to fit everything in?"

We consider this to be an essential exercise for every elementary school staff. How should our time be used in school? Does our response differ for different grade levels or students with different needs? We argue for consistency within a grade level and a logical articulation between grade levels. Thus, it may be just fine for first grade teachers to spend more time on language arts and reading and less on social studies and science than fifth grade teachers, as long as they allocate time consistently within the grade level.

Moreover, these allocations should make sense as students move from grade to grade. It seems illogical to provide two-and-a-half hours of language arts instruction in first grade, 90 minutes in second grade, and then back up to two hours in third grade (unless there are idiosyncrasies in the state testing program).

We realize that the consistency we describe cannot and should not be etched in granite. Some students may need more time to learn key skills. For students in the primary grades who are having difficulty learning to read, we would be wise to focus much of their time in school on instruction in this area, while this may not be necessary for other students.

Finally, and perhaps most importantly, the amount of school time allocated to certain subjects is strongly related to student achievement in that area (Marzano, Pickering, & Pollock, 2001). It is important to have a thoughtful school-wide plan for the assignment of time in elementary schools. That is the primary purpose of constructing an elementary school master schedule.

Issues with Scheduling Core Instruction

The predominant elementary school scheduling structure for core instruction over the years has been the *self-contained classroom,* where each teacher was responsible for the instruction of all aspects of language arts, reading, mathematics, science, and social studies. In the self-contained classroom, teachers organized time as they saw fit around their encore, lunch and recess schedules. Again, if all teachers were Renaissance men or women, this would be the best of all worlds. Because all teachers are not skilled in all areas, a number of other scheduling structures have developed.

To address the difficulty of instructing a truly heterogeneous group of students, especially in reading and language arts (and to a lesser extent in mathematics), many schools have adopted some form of regrouping practice. The most common manifestation of this notion is *regrouping among homerooms at the same grade level* for reading and possibly language arts. Based on some criteria (such as basal reading level, test scores, individual reading inventory results, teacher judgment), students from sev-

eral classes at the same grade level are divided into more homogeneous learning groups. Each teacher in the grade level has responsibility for instructing one of these groups during a time block of 60 to 150 minutes, depending on the grade level.

Typically, in a grade level with three teachers and 75 students, one teacher might manage a group of 32 students, all of whom were reading on or above grade level; a second teacher might work with a group of 25 students, all of whom were on grade level; and the third teacher would instruct the remaining 18 below-grade-level readers. The primary purpose of regrouping is to reduce the number of different reading levels in the instructional group, thereby trimming prep time for the teacher. The same practice often is employed for mathematics, during a different time block and (hopefully) with different criteria for regrouping.

Because some students may be reading far above grade level while others remain far below, occasionally the regrouping structure expands to include multiple grade levels. *Regrouping across multiple grade levels,* also known as the Joplin Plan, offers a more precise placement of students on their instructional reading level (Cushenberry, 1967).

In the past decade, as states have developed accountability systems with subject-based assessments and as federal law (Elementary and Secondary Education Act, 2001) has required the implementation of such assessments, the practice of *departmentalization* at the elementary school has become more prevalent. This practice assigns teachers to their instructional strength and reduces the number of preparations required. In its simplest and most common form, two teachers exchange classes for science and social studies. The rest of the day might be self-contained, or this mini-departmentalization could combine with one of the regrouping practices discussed above.

As the number of teachers on a team increases, the variations of departmentalization also multiply. Note that when we decide to departmentalize, whatever subjects we include must receive equal time. Thus, if we have a three-teacher team and we decide to departmentalize for math, social studies, and science, each of these subjects would receive the same amount of time. The pros and cons of these options are discussed in chapter 5.

Similarly, there are a variety of core curriculum programs with specific time requirements. Success for All (Success for All Foundation, 2005) requires 90 minutes of uninterrupted reading time daily using the Joplin grouping plan. The Four-Blocks reading program (Cunningham, Hall, & Sigmon, 1999) requires 120 to 160 minutes daily that can be divided into four different blocks. Everyday Mathematics, developed by the University of Chicago Mathematics Project, requires an hour of time for mathematics daily (McBride et al., 2002).

Regardless of the scheduling option or the program format chosen, without a master schedule that carefully creates the necessary periods for core, encore, and special service instruction, teachers will struggle to implement any of these plans.

Another important scheduling consideration is class size. For the past three decades, researchers have studied the issue of class size and its relationship to student achievement. While lowering the pupil-to-teacher ratio is always welcomed by teachers and frequently touted by politicians, the goal seems always just out of reach. The research on this topic is very specific:

- There is little evidence that reducing class size to any number above 15 has a major impact on student achievement; that is not to say that such a reduction might not offer other benefits, such as a reduction in teacher stress, student stress, discipline infractions, or other factors.

- There is significant evidence that lowering class size to 15 or fewer students does increase students' achievement as measured by standardized tests; this is especially true in the primary grades, with minority and economically disadvantaged students, especially boys (Achilles, 1997; Achilles, Finn, & Pate-Bain, 2002; Robinson, 1990; Smith, Molinar, & Zahorik, 2003; Wenglinsky, 1997).

- There is evidence that achievement benefits persist into later years of schooling if students remain in smaller classes for at least three years (Achilles, Finn, & Pate-Bain, 2002; Finn, 1998; Nye, Fulton, Boyd-Zaharias, & Cain, 1996).

Consequently, lowering class size, especially in the primary grades, has become a major political issue during local, state, and national "save public education" budget debates. Threats of increasing class size can stir up political passions. The issue intuitively makes sense to educators and the general public. We believe, however, that our nation is unwilling to devote the monetary resources necessary to achieve homeroom classes of 15 or smaller.

Reducing class size has what we call a multiplier effect. Because the homeroom remains the primary scheduling unit in elementary schools, smaller class size means hiring more teachers—but that is not all. Each new teacher requires a classroom. Each new classroom group requires scheduled periods in art, music, physical education, and other special activities, which may result in additional hiring and space needs.

Furthermore, we consider it wrong-headed to focus on smaller homeroom classes. If we accept the research, we must accept the fact that this will not automatically boost student achievement. To pursue that goal, elementary schools must give greater attention to varying the size of instructional groups based on what is being taught. Do schools really need (or can they afford?) physical education classes, music classes, recess, and story hours with fewer than 15 students?

What teachers really need are reading and math groups with fewer than 15 students. They need flexible scheduling strategies that enable them to alter the size and composition of instructional groups based on the day's instructional goals and varying student needs. Chapter 6, which addresses parallel block scheduling, offers such a plan.

Issues with Scheduling Special Services

The scheduling of instruction provided by teachers other than the classroom teacher has developed somewhat haphazardly over time. While a considerable number of programs and personnel have been added to elementary schools during the past 35 years, no master plan has governed their inclusion in the school day. At first, these programs were welcomed with eager and open arms. One assistant superintendent, when notified in 1965 that the Elementary and Secondary Education Act would bring federal funds to her school district, remarked, "We finally have an answer to educational problems; now we've got to think about how we are going to spend it." The district decided to use these first Title I funds to provide pull-out programs for disadvantaged students. Someone undoubtedly took the reins of this program and became an advocate for it.

In 1975, when PL 94–142 (Education for All Handicapped Children Act) mandated a free and appropriate education for students with disabilities, another professional had responsibility for implementing the program. These two committed educators each had their own vision; rarely did they work together to determine how best to implement both programs, or how each affected the other. Since then, schools have added programs for bilingual and English as a Second Language (ESL) students, gifted and talented students, and children of migrant workers. Some schools also have offered instrumental music lessons and sundry other special services— all for laudable purposes, but all without a master plan.

Haphazardly scheduled pull-out programs,[2] such as special education and talented and gifted services, can disrupt instruction for all students in the classroom (Achilles, Finn, & Pate-Bain, 2002; Hopkins, 1990; Hopkins & Canady, 1997). Unfortu-

---

2 We define pull-out programs as programs students must qualify for or choose, such as Title I, special education, English as a Second Language, gifted and talented, migrant education, instrumental music, and so on.

nately, many schools still resort to what we call the "When can I have your kids?" model of scheduling for special services programs. All too often, elementary school specialists build their own schedules. Upon receiving her list of eligible students at the start of the school year, the teacher of students with learning disabilities meets with each homeroom teacher to schedule contact time. If—as often happens—she starts with the teachers with whom she already feels comfortable, those teachers get the "preferred" times.

On the surface, building her schedule student by student and class by class seems reasonable, flexible, and highly individualized. But in many cases, the teachers of Title I, speech and language, ESL, gifted and talented, and instrumental music programs follow the same procedure. When all is said and done, the schedule resembles a crazy quilt, with no apparent rhyme or reason.

Issues with Scheduling Encore Instruction

Even if not scheduled independently by their teachers, art, music, PE, and the like may contribute to the fragmentation of instructional time. Problems ensue when different encore classes take periods of different length, when encore teachers insist on consecutive classes for the same grade level, when a school relies totally on a Monday to Friday scheduling format, and when allocations of itinerant teachers from the central office do not fit with the school's needs.

Different Length Class Periods

It is not unusual for an elementary school teacher's class to have physical education three days a week for about 30 minutes, art once a week for 50 minutes, music two days a week for 20 to 40 minutes, and library class for 40 minutes—each in its own time slot. How does this scheduling mess come about?

In a way, it makes sense. Elementary students, some argue, do have a short attention span and need frequent physical activity, as the PE teacher asserts. Art teachers do need time to distribute materials at the start of class and clean up at the end. Principals do want to respect and respond to encore teachers' individual needs. But the pieces of the puzzle don't fit together very well, and core classroom teachers face the impossible task of filling in the gaps with effective core instruction.

Scheduling Classes of the Same Grade Level Consecutively

A music teacher's request to instruct the three grade 1 classes in consecutive half-hour sessions because that makes planning and materials preparation easier seems quite reasonable. An art teacher can logically ask for the same consideration. But scheduling encore classes this way has two negative consequences. First, it becomes impossible to schedule common planning time for base teachers at the same grade level; they simply never have the same encore/planning time. Second, it becomes more difficult to schedule time for regrouping or mini-departmentalization, because one section or another will probably be unavailable.

Scheduling with a Monday-to-Friday Mindset

As a classroom teacher, did you ever have an art class scheduled for Friday or Monday? Not surprisingly, your students had fewer art classes than students scheduled for art on Tuesday, Wednesday, or Thursday. Why? Because more holidays, teacher in-service days, and workdays fall on Friday, and Monday comes in second. This means less planning time for you (art classes are often the longest planning periods for classroom teachers) and less art for your students. Monday-to-Friday schedules are inherently unfair, yet we persist in scheduling art, music, computers, PE, foreign language, and a host of other specialized elementary school classes based on the days of the week.

Similarly, the most common sharing arrangement for itinerant specialists is 50 percent in one school and 50 percent in another. This typically translates into two and one-half days in each school—not only a nightmare to schedule, but also a waste of resources, because instructional time is lost and expenses must be paid for travel between the two schools on the shared day. In chapter 3, we suggest encore teachers' schedules that operate on three-, four-, six-, or eight-day cycles, and even by semesters, which are far more equitable and efficient than the traditional Monday-to-Friday plans.

Allocations of Itinerant Teachers from the Central Office

Have you ever worked in a school where teachers had two planning periods on one day and no break at all on another? Ever wonder why? When smaller schools need less than full-time encore staffing, or when larger schools need some additional

encore staff, a practical solution is to share staff between one or more schools. More often than not, a central office administrator assigns these itinerants. Occasionally, the music supervisor assigns music staff, the physical education supervisor assigns PE staff, the art supervisor assigns art staff, and none of them talks to the others! Little wonder a school ends up with three encore teachers on one day of the week and none on another day, giving the base teachers a lopsided planning schedule.

Six Key Principles of Elementary School Scheduling

We have distilled six principles that should guide elementary school scheduling: focusing on the mission, school-wide scheduling, collaboration, practicality and appropriateness of teaching assignments, fairness, and efficiency.

Focusing on the Mission

Schedule design should be mission driven. Just as a school's mission statement should guide all major decisions regarding budget, program, textbooks, and instruction, so should a school's mission guide the design of the school schedule. Our value for a particular subject or activity is manifested on the schedule in the following ways:

♦ by the amount of time we provide for the activity;

♦ by the time period during the day when we schedule it;

♦ by its relative class size limit; and

♦ by the space we assign for it.

When we look at school schedules from across the country, we can tell what is valued most highly. Elementary schools, especially in the primary grades, spend two to two-and-a-half hours a day on language arts and reading because they regard it as the most important activity. A third grade teacher who allots 30 minutes a week to science evidently considers its value low. First grade teachers fight tooth and nail to instruct reading in the morning, because (whether true or not) they believe morning is the best time to teach reading. Teachers rarely want encore classes first thing in the morning, which says something about the value of encore classes in their minds.

When we schedule five students to work with the teacher of the gifted and put 25 students in the low math group with another, we, too, express our value for these activities. Finally, when we rewire a classroom for the Internet, equip it with 30 state-of-the art computers and then relegate the self-contained special education class to the mobile classroom behind the building, we express our value for the activities that unfold in these spaces. Each individual scheduling decision expresses our values.

We understand that the principal and teachers are not the only ones who influence the schedule; school board policies, state and federal regulations, parental pressures, and even tradition also factor into these decisions. Nevertheless, we argue that the amount of time spent in a subject, its strategic placement in the schedule, the size of the instructional group, and the space assigned to a particular activity should be guided by the school's stated mission.

School-wide Scheduling

School schedules should be designed with the big picture in mind. As previously discussed, core classes, special services, the arts, and PE cannot be scheduled effectively and efficiently independently of each other. This results in fragmented instructional time. Someone, or some group, must look at the school schedule globally, answering the following questions *before* constructing the schedule:

♦ What are the school's instructional priorities?

♦ How much time should be allocated for each core subject at each grade level?

♦ How much time should be allocated to provide programs in the arts, physical education, technology, foreign language and other encore subjects?

♦ When should services (pull-out programs) be provided to students who qualify for or are selected to be involved in special programs? What are the limitations for scheduling these programs (e.g., uniform length, frequency)? What will students miss to attend these programs?

♦ How does the scheduling of core subjects relate to the scheduling of encore subjects and special services? How are they integrated?

The difficulty in this task lies in the fact that just as the different programs cannot be scheduled independently, the questions we ask cannot be answered independently or without general consideration for some basic scheduling model. Otherwise, we end up with a fragmented list of goals and requirements that no schedule can efficiently and effectively meet.

For example, if we insist (as many have) that all students engage in language arts and reading for the first two-and-a-half hours of the day, it becomes very difficult to provide a sensible plan for the provision of encore classes and special services. Better to ask, "Is there a way for our school to provide about two-and-a-half hours of language arts and reading instruction to all students *and* provide a reasonable plan for providing art, music, PE, special education, and the like? What program compromises would have to be made to accomplish both?" We contend that the scheduling team must take a global view of the school and its needs and design a schedule that keeps the mission of the school central, while still addressing issues of practicality, fairness, and efficiency.

Collaboration

School schedules should be designed to facilitate teacher collaboration, both for planning and for instruction. When art (or PE, music, etc.) classes are scheduled one after another for each of the three first grade teachers, common planning time for these teachers becomes less likely. Also, when one first grade class is scheduled into art class while the other two are having language arts, these teachers find it difficult to regroup students among teachers for specific skill instruction. Research supports our belief that teachers need to collaborate with their colleagues for sustained periods of time within the context of their teaching environment (Iverson, 2003; King & Newman, 2000).

Practicality

School schedules should be designed with practicality in mind. What can we reasonably expect typical classroom teachers (not just superstars) to do? If all teachers were superstars, perhaps self-contained classrooms with totally heterogeneous classes would be a reasonable course of action. But given the accountability demands placed upon teachers for student achievement, is it reasonable to expect all teachers to be experts in all subjects? Is it reasonable to expect that they can differentiate curriculum and instruction for the full range of abilities found in a particular grade level group for six hours a day, 180 days a year? Is it reasonable to think that they can slot effective core instruction into the fragments of time left over after encore classes and pull-outs are scheduled?

We believe that it is time to consider a certain degree of specialization among teachers in elementary schools. We also believe that while the majority of the school day can be spent working with heterogeneous groups, homogeneous, skill-based groups are appropriate for part of the day, specifically when students are being instructed in reading and mathematics. We believe that school should be scheduled with its primary mission (literacy and numeracy) at the forefront; other important activities should be scheduled around these classes, not the reverse. Each of these beliefs supports the notion that an elementary teacher's job could be made more doable, and that not only the superstars of our profession should attain success .

Fairness

School schedules should be created with fairness for both students and teachers in mind. Whether students at the same grade level receive equal amounts of science instruction (or time in the computer lab, or time with the teacher in a reading group) should not be left to the preferences of individual teachers. If we decide a particular program or curriculum is desirable for students, then we should guarantee, at the very least, that they have an equal opportunity to learn it. A schedule is a beginning point for this guarantee.

In the past 30 years, many specialized positions have been added to elementary schools to serve students with a variety of needs (special education [SPED], ESL, Title I, etc.) and to provide enrichment activities (e.g., instrumental music lessons). From the vantage point of core classroom teachers, few of these additions have made their jobs any easier, and some have made them more difficult (often because of scheduling).

Furthermore, classroom teachers often see the workload of the school unfairly distributed. They wonder: Why do I work with 25 students at a time and resource teachers with two to five? Why do I begin class the first day of school and they start two weeks later? Why do I teach up to the last day of the year while they stop meeting with students two weeks earlier to do assessments, reports, and other paperwork? On the other hand, resource personnel often feel misunderstood by general education faculty and frequently commiserate together about their paperwork, intransigent parents, looming individual education program (IEP) battles and the ubiquitous threat of the lawsuit. This dysfunctional lack of mutual respect has not helped to integrate the services for students appropriately. Principals must openly discuss workload issues and help to design a schedule that fairly distributes responsibility.

Efficiency

School schedules should be designed with efficiency in mind. Few school leaders would argue with this statement. We also believe, however, that efficiency should not trump all other criteria for judging a school's effectiveness.

For example, this may be the most efficient way to schedule encore classes: Compute the total number of homeroom classes for a school and assign each encore teacher exactly that number of instructional periods (plus lunch and planning) in that school. So, if a school has 18 homerooms and art is 45 minutes long, assign 18 art periods of 45 minutes to the school. This is very "efficient" in the eyes of the central office administrator charged with assigning encore teachers across the entire district.

Unfortunately, this practice violates nearly all of our previously discussed criteria. It is not mission driven, global, or practical. Under this system, principals almost always create a schedule by sending one first grade class to art, followed immediately by the next, and so on. Yes, on the surface it's efficient and the process can be justified as fair, but we have already documented the problems this scheduling strategy causes. In the long run, we find it more efficient to build in some flexibility; the upfront "efficiency" of allocating staff by the numbers fragments the schedule and leads to great inefficiency in delivery of the core program.

Planning Process and Implementation

While one might think that staff would welcome any improvements to the school schedule, the fact is that what one faculty member sees as an improvement, another may view as a disaster. We recommend a year of study and planning before implementing any significant scheduling change. Typically, a school or school district empowers a study committee to analyze the problems of the current schedule, to set goals for improvement, and to investigate potential solutions and alternatives. This committee generally has representatives from every grade level, from the encore teachers and from special service programs, in addition to administrative representatives from schools and the central office. Often, too, it includes several parents. It is essential that the makeup of the committee mirror the composition of the faculty. It also is essential to include union representation. Planning and implementation of proposed schedule changes are addressed in greater detail in chapter 12.

Organization and Structure of This Book

Part I of this book explores the creation of the major aspects of the elementary school schedule: the master schedule (chapter 2), the encore schedules (chapter 3), and special service schedules (chapter 4). Chapter 5 analyzes the more commonly used departmentalization strategies.

Part II develops what we consider to be the optimal scheduling model for elementary schools: parallel block scheduling (PBS). Chapter 6 introduces the rationale and basic plan for PBS and then develops the model with the express purpose of creating an optimal environment for literacy and numeracy acquisition. Chapter 7 addresses staffing, scheduling, managing, and implementing the "extension center," a critical and exciting instructional center used in parallel block scheduling. Chapter 8 is devoted to ideas for scheduling mathematics instruction in both traditional and PBS scheduling formats.

Part III of the book is devoted to quality instruction in reading, language arts, and mathematics—concepts that can be used in either traditional or PBS models. In chapter 9, Ruth Short describes the primary literacy classroom; in chapter 10, Karen Broaddus paints a picture of the intermediate literacy classroom. In chapter 11, Laura L. McCullough describes outstanding elementary school mathematics instructional practices. Finally, in chapter 12, Susan W. Golder outlines planning and implementation at the school and district levels.

References

Achilles, C. M. (1997, October). Small classes, big possibilities. *The School Administrator*, 6–15.

Achilles, C.M., Finn, J. D., & Pate-Bain, H. (2002). Measuring class size: Let me count the ways. *Educational Leadership, 59* (5), 24–26.

Cunningham, P.M., Hall, D.P., & Sigmon, C.M. (1999). *The teacher's guide to the four blocks*. Greensboro, NC: Carson-Dellosa Publishing.

Cushenberry, D.C. (1967). *The Joplin Plan and cross grade grouping*. Paper presented at the International Reading Association Conference (Seattle, May 4–6, 1967) (ERIC Document Reproduction Service No. ED013708).

DuFour, R., & Eaker, B. (1998). *Professional learning communities at work: best practices for enhancing student achievement*. Bloomington, IN: National Educational Service.

Elementary and Secondary Education Act, P.L. 107–110, The No Child Left Behind Act of 2001.

Finn, J. D. (1998). *Class size and students at risk: What is known? What is next?* Washington, DC: U.S. Department of Education, Office of Educational Research and Improvement, National Institute on the Education of At-Risk Students.

Hopkins, H. J. (1990). *A comparison of the effects of pull-out programs in a parallel block scheduled school and a traditionally scheduled school*. Unpublished doctoral dissertation, University of Virginia, Charlottesville.

Hopkins, H. J., & Canady, R. L. (1997). Parallel block scheduling for elementary schools. In *ASCD Curriculum Handbook*, 13.109 –13.130. Alexandria, VA: Association for Supervision and Curriculum Development.

Iverson, N. R. (2003). *Staff development and kindergarten reading achievement*. Unpublished doctoral dissertation, University of Virginia, Charlottesville.

King, M. B., & Newman, F. M. (2000, April). Will teacher learning advance school goals? *Phi Delta Kappan*, 576–580.

Marzano, R. J., Pickering, D. J., & Pollock, J. E. (2001*). Classroom instruction that works: Research-based strategies for increasing student achievement*. Alexandria, VA: Association for Supervision and Curriculum Development.

McBride, J., Bell, M., Bell, J., Bretzlauf, J., Dillard, A., Hartfield, R., Isaacs, A., Pitvorec, K., & Saecker, P. (2002). *Everyday mathematics* (2nd ed.). New York: Wright Group/McGraw Hill.

National Education Commission on Time and Learning. (1994). *Prisoners of time: Report of the national education commission on time and learning*. Washington, DC: U.S. Government Printing Office.

Nye, B., Fulton, B. D., Boyd-Zaharias, J., & Cain, V.A. (1995). *The lasting benefits study: Eighth grade technical report*. Nashville, TN: Center of Excellence for Research in Basic Skills, Tennessee State University.

Renzulli, J. S. (1996). *The Interest-A-Lyzer family of instruments: A manual for teachers*. Mansfield Center, CT: Creative Learning Press.

Robinson, G. L. (1990). Synthesis of research on class size. *Educational Leadership, 47*(7), 80–90.

Smith, P., Molinar, A., & Zahorik, J. (2003, September). Class-size reduction: A fresh look at the data. *Educational Leadership, 51*(4),72–74.

Success for All Foundation (2005). *Success for All Foundation*. Retrieved September 12, 2006 from http://www.successforall.net/

Wenglinsky, H. (1997). When money matters: How educational expenditures improve student performance and how they don't. Princeton, NJ: Educational Testing Service.

Part I

Master Schedules, Encore Schedules, and Special Service Schedules

2

Designing Elementary School Master Schedules

Given the problems and principles outlined in chapter 1, we begin the task of constructing master schedules. Collaboratively constructing a practical, fair and efficient school-wide plan that embodies the mission of the school is not as linear as the end product might suggest. First and foremost, a master schedule serves to answer two important questions:

1. How should we allocate time among a variety of potential subjects/activities?

2. How should we schedule resources shared by several grade levels? These shared resources include encore teachers and their spaces, special service teachers and their spaces, cafeteria personnel and the lunchroom, and playgrounds.

How Should We Allocate Time in Elementary School?

As discussed in chapter 1, elementary schools have largely left it up to individual teachers to determine how to use their time, working around encore classes, lunch, and recess. In this age of high-stakes testing and accountability, however, it increasingly is likely that such decisions will be made at the school or even district level. Some states specify minimum time requirements for core instruction in elementary school. In Virginia, for example, 75 percent of the school day or a minimum of 560 hours annually must be spent instructing in language arts (including reading), mathematics, science, and social studies (Virginia Department of Education, 2006).

Conflicts arise, however, when district-level personnel specify requirements that principals and teachers consider inappropriate for the context of their individual schools or restrictive when it comes to addressing local issues, needs, and problems.

District personnel are likely to issue such mandates (including time allocations) for the following reasons:

- ♦ to rectify poor performance as indicated by high-stakes testing data; or

- ♦ to prevent poor performance when faced with a new requirement for high-stakes testing; or

- ♦ to establish consistency across the district on some factor (the allocation of time, resources, programs, etc.). In our experience, school district leaders like to be able to state categorically that "*All* elementary school students in this school district receive (fill in the blank)," and they are greatly embarrassed when provided with evidence to the contrary (usually to bolster a parent's complaint).

The debate over the allocation of time plays out on a smaller political scale (but with greater impact and participation) between school administrators and teachers when school principals attempt to mandate time use to teachers who can always just close their doors and proceed as they choose.

To address this issue, it is necessary to consider both the district's desire for consistency and the schools' and teachers' needs for some level of autonomy. The best way to navigate this divide is to formally discuss it. We recommend the formation of a district committee that includes central office instructional personnel, principals, representative teachers, and perhaps a school board member and/or parent(s) to discuss openly the allocation of the available time to various subjects and activities.

The committee should include several professionals who have what we call the "scheduling gene"—people who can and will temper with reality the philosophical discussion that inevitably develops. There is nothing more frustrating for a group engaged in such a task than to discover, after agreements already have been made, that the negotiated compromise is impractical from a scheduling standpoint.

The entire group must recognize one of the immutable principles of the "physics" of school scheduling: "Any time you put something into the schedule, you must take something out." All too often, school board members, central office administrators, officials from state departments of education, and even state legislators forget this principle, mandating the inclusion of some pet program (e.g., 30 minutes of PE every day) without specifying how to make room in the schedule for the new initiative.

This scheduling committee should formulate recommendations that answer the following questions:

- ♦ What is the appropriate allocation of available school time to core and encore subjects?

- ♦ Within the core time, what is the appropriate allocation of time among the various subjects (language arts, mathematics, science, and social studies)?

- ♦ What do we want to provide students within the encore block, and how should that time be divided among the selected programs?

- ♦ How should we schedule services provided by learning disabilities (LD), ESL, Title I, and other special service providers?

◆ How should we provide time for intervention, remediation, and enrichment?

The resulting set of guidelines could very well include stipulations that are nonnegotiable from a district standpoint and others that offer site-based choices. In this chapter, we differentiate time only as *core, encore*, and *Intervention/Enrichment* (I/E). In the case study that concludes the chapter, we discuss in greater detail one district's compromise between district consistency and site-based autonomy. For purposes of the example to be developed below, we used the time allocations shown in Table 2.1

Table 2.1 Time Allocations

	K	Gr. 1	Gr. 2	Gr. 3	Gr. 4	Gr. 5
Homeroom	15	15	15	15	15	15
LA/Reading	150	140	140	140	100	100
Math	50	60	60	60	75	75
SS/SC	50	50	50	50	75	75
Encore	50	50	50	50	50	50
Lunch/Recess	50	50	50	50	50	50
Intervention/ Enrichment	50	50	50	50	50	50
Closing	5	5	5	5	5	5
Totals	**420**	**420**	**420**	**420**	**420**	**420**

Note: When the school day has less than 420 minutes, obviously adjustments must be made; for example, lunch/recess and I/E might be shortened to 45 minutes each; homeroom time could be cut to 10 minutes, and so on.

How Should We Share Resources Used by Several Grade Levels?

All grade levels generally are provided the same encore programs, although occasionally the amount of PE, music, or art might differ based on age or program requirements. Obviously then, the personnel and spaces assigned to these programs also must be shared.

Likewise, all grade levels generally are provided the same special services (Title I, special education, etc.), although certain grade levels may require more or less of a particular program. For example, students in kindergarten and first grade tend to be found eligible for speech and language services; by the time these students reach fourth or fifth grade, effective remediation has moved some of them off this list. Conversely, few students are found eligible for LD services in the lower grades, so there generally is a greater need for staff to provide these services in grades 4 and 5. Also, instrumental music programs, if available, usually do not begin until grade 4 or 5.

Finally, most schools have limited space in lunchrooms and in play areas and must stagger classes over time for lunch and recess.

Regardless of the details, one principle does not change: To minimize conflicts over staff and space use, the first step in constructing the schedule is to determine the requirements for all services shared among grade levels.

We have worked in some districts that have issued mandates regarding the scheduling of certain subjects (most notably reading) without considering the impact on the efficient use of resources. For example, a district occasionally will require that all grade levels spend the first 90 minutes of the day in reading instruction. While this policy makes a strong statement about the importance of reading, it ignores the practicalities of efficient scheduling. What are we to do with the art, music, and PE teachers during that time? Give them 90 minutes of planning each day? Have them teach reading, even though they're not trained to do so? Neither option is a wise use of resources. A school, however, could readily comply with a policy requiring 90 minutes of uninterrupted reading sometime during the day, or even during the morning.

From a practical viewpoint, when creating a schedule that is both educationally sound and fiscally efficient, the factors to be considered include the following:

♦ the district's recommendations (if any) for the use of time and the provision of encore and special services;

♦ the special populations or needs of the school;

♦ the number of sections per grade level;

♦ the staffing level for both base and encore teachers;

♦ the length of the school day; and

♦ the available space.

In the sections that follow, we gradually construct a full school schedule that includes a master block schedule built on the time allocations noted in Table 2.1 (p. 21). Each grade level will have designated blocks for encore, Intervention/Enrich-

ment, lunch/recess, language arts, mathematics, science, and social studies.

Creating the Encore Schedule

Because all classes share the spaces and services of encore teachers, we generally start the construction of the schedule with these classes. Our goals here are to construct an encore schedule that

♦ respects the needs of the encore disciplines;

♦ provides common planning time for teams of core teachers;

♦ minimally disrupts the flow of core instruction; and

♦ efficiently uses the school's spaces and other resources.

Encore Period Length

As mentioned in chapter 1, teachers of encore classes sometimes disagree about the optimal length of class periods. Some instructors, typically general music and sometimes PE, prefer shorter periods of 25 to 30 minutes, and others, most notably art teachers, prefer longer classes of 45 to 60 minutes. The construction of an encore schedule that meets our goals nearly always requires compromise among encore staff regarding the length of classes. Generally, the compromise period length is somewhere between 40 and 50 minutes, depending mostly on the length of the school day.

Most elementary schools have six grade levels (K–5), so generally we need to have six periods, one for each grade level, to schedule encore classes. Two additional periods also are required, one for planning for the encore teachers and one for lunch for the encore teachers. Thus, in most elementary schools we begin with an eight-period schedule as the basic template.

The length of the period depends on the length of the school day. A six-hour school day would allow 45-minute class periods ($360 \div 8 = 45$); six hours and 40 minutes would be required for 50-minute class periods ($400 \div 8 = 50$). With time allowed for passing between classes, the effective length of 45-minute classes is more like 41 or 42 minutes, and the effective length of 50-minute classes is more like 46 or 47 minutes (depending on the distance of classrooms from encore rooms).

Occasionally it is possible to create appropriate schedules with periods of different lengths; in this case, one period is usually half of another. For example, we might schedule hour-long art classes and 30-minute PE and music classes; however, for several reasons this type of schedule is used infrequently. First, the length of the school day usually discourages schools from allocating 60 minutes of instructional time for encore. Second, if equal planning time is allocated to encore teachers, we would need seven hour-long periods plus a lunch period, or a minimum of seven hours and 30 minutes to fit such a plan into the school day. Generally this plan is used only in one of two circumstances: either the school has sufficient encore resources to serve more than one grade level at a time, or teachers at each grade level forgo planning time one day per cycle.

Encore Period Placement

Once we have determined the length of the period for encore classes, we must decide when during the school day each grade level has encore. This matter usually engenders great debate, because most elementary school teachers would prefer to schedule their encore classes in the afternoon—an impossible task, if efficiency is to be a consideration at all. Consequently, in the sample school illustrated in Figure 2.1 (p. 30),[1] which is based on a seven-hour day with eight 50-minute periods and 20 minutes for homeroom and closing activities, we have eight possibilities for encore periods.

Our bias generally favors students in the earlier grades, whose teachers insist on morning instruction in reading and language arts; we usually allocate afternoon planning/encore periods to primary classes. We avoid assigning either kindergarten or first grade in the last period of the day because five- and six-year-olds take a great deal of time to get ready to depart in the afternoon, especially when mittens, gloves, boots, and heavy coats are involved. Consequently, it is not unusual to allocate the final period of the day to students and teachers in grade 2.

---

1 A spreadsheet such as Microsoft Excel serves as a useful tool in detailing such decisions. In the template illustrated here, each cell on the timeline represents five minutes; these cells are merged together to form periods of greater length. For example, ten cells are merged to form encore periods of 50 minutes in length. Once one period of this length is created, it can be copied and pasted into different locations on the schedule and relabeled as needed. A variety of Excel templates based on different-length cells (three, four, and five minutes) as well as a host of sample complete schedules are available for purchase from schoolschedulingassociates.com.

As is seen in Figure 2.1 (p. 30), we assigned the next-to-last period to grade 1 and the period before that to kindergarten. In our scheduling format, we enter the encore/planning period in two places: once in the row designated for the grade level (labeled *Plan*) and again in the row labeled *Arts/PE*, where we label the period with the grade level served at that time (e.g., grade 1). This practice makes potential conflicts easy to spot.

We set aside lunch time for the encore teachers in the middle of the day, with encore periods for third, fourth, and fifth grades assigned to the morning. Whenever possible, we tend to assign encore teachers planning time first thing in the morning, not so much because they prefer this time, but to ensure that all students begin the day in their core classes. This plan also provides encore teachers with time to set up for their classes.

In schools with a multipurpose room (or the "cafetorinasium," if you prefer!) used for both lunch and physical education classes and a need for several different lunch periods, it becomes necessary to place the encore teachers' planning period in the middle of the day, adjacent to their lunch period, to ensure that enough time is available to schedule lunch in the multipurpose room. This generally requires that fifth grade sections have encore classes during the first period of the day.

In addition, as discussed in chapter 1, encore teachers usually prefer to meet classes in the same grade level in consecutive periods on the same day (to minimize materials and equipment changes). Because this is incompatible with common grade-level planning time, we at least try to cluster primary classes in adjacent periods and intermediate classes in adjacent periods. In this example, we schedule encore for all primary classes in the afternoon and all intermediate classes in the morning.

Sometimes schools have reasons other than those discussed here for ordering encore periods differently. For example, in some states only specific grade levels are tested, and these grade levels receive preferred scheduling slots. In Virginia, because standards tests have been administered only in grades 3 through 5, we occasionally find schools in which grades 3, 4, and 5 are allocated afternoon encore periods to preserve morning instructional time.

In addition, if a school has a half-day kindergarten program with both A.M. and P.M. sessions, it's necessary to provide two scheduling slots, one for each session. The kindergarten encore schedule can be handled in two ways. We can assign two encore periods to kindergarten, one in the morning and one in the afternoon; these periods would be the same length as all other grade levels. Kindergarten teachers would alternate their planning time, planning one day in the morning when the morning kindergarten is in encore and the next day in the afternoon, when the afternoon kindergarten attends encore classes. Thus, the kindergarten teachers' planning time would alternate every other day with the encore teachers' planning time.

A second option would be to schedule two shorter periods that would meet every day, one for the morning kindergarten and one for the afternoon kindergarten. The kindergarten teachers would have two short breaks daily rather than one longer planning period. Chapter 3 illustrates these exceptions and others.

Encore Rotations

Once we have chosen encore blocks for each group, we must schedule encore classes into these slots. The number of encore classes needed at the same time depends on the number of homerooms that need to have common planning time—usually the entire grade level. For example, if we hope to give grade 5 teachers common planning time and there are four grade 5 teachers, there must be four places for the classes to go. We call the way we schedule classes into encore during a specific period the "encore rotation."

Traditionally, encore classes have been scheduled on a Monday-to-Friday schedule, which only works well when there are five classes per grade level and five different encore classes. For reasons discussed previously, we now recommend that encore classes be offered on rotations of three, four, five, six, or eight days that are independent of the days of the week. So in the example mentioned above, if most of the grade levels in the school had four classes, we might employ a four-day rotation such as the following: day 1, PE; day 2, art; day 3, PE; day 4, music. On day 5 the rotation would begin anew.

Figure 2.2 (p. 31) illustrates a four-day rotation for a school with four sections per grade level. Notice that the rotation is moved up one day for each successive teacher; the P-A-P-M rotation begins on day 2 for teacher B, day 3 for teacher C, and so on. Staffing this rotation requires one art teacher, one music teacher and two PE teachers, designated PE-A and PE-B in Figure 2.2.

To complete the encore rotations for the entire school (illustrated in Figure 2.2, p. 31), we must repeat the P-A-P-M rotation, which begins with grade 5 in the 9:05–9:55 slot, in different time slots for every grade level.

Many different rotations are available; a school's decisions are based in part on what they believe is important to provide students, the number of staff available to provide the classes, and the certifications/abilities of these persons. Chapter 3 discusses various rotations and several exceptions and special circumstances.

Encore Teachers' Schedules

Now that encore periods are scheduled and the encore rotation chosen, we can create schedules for the encore teachers. Referring to the rotation (Figure 2.2, p. 31) and the periods allocated to each grade level for encore classes (Figure 2.1, p. 30), we plot the various classes taught by each encore teacher, which is shown in Figure 2.3 (p. 32). Each encore teacher begins the day planning, then works with a fifth grade class, a fourth grade class, and a third grade class. After lunch, encore teachers instruct kindergarten, then first grade, and finish the day with a second grade class.

Adding I/E, Lunch, and Recess Periods, and Academic Blocks

Now the decision-making process becomes considerably less linear. We begin to take a more customized approach as we carefully place academic blocks and the I/E and lunch/recess periods, working back and forth within and between grade levels to preserve solid instructional time as allocated in Table 2.1 (p. 21). Although we may begin this next step by assigning I/E periods to each grade level (Figure 2.4, p. 33), and follow by suggesting lunch and recess periods (Figure 2.5, p. 34), often we must change the original placement of encore classes in the master schedule to achieve the best result. Figure 2.6 (p. 35) shows the final master block schedule, with time allocations respected and large blocks of core instructional time preserved.

The examples detailed in this sequence are relatively simple compared to the complex requirements of programs in many elementary schools, especially with respect to the scheduling of special services. In chapter 4, we set forth various options for scheduling special services, which, in turn, alter and complicate the development of the master schedule. For now, we move on to a case study of one large school division that implemented many facets of this plan.

Case Study: Prince William County, Virginia Public Schools

In spring 2002, in consultation with one of the authors of this book, the elementary schools of Prince William County, Virginia, set out to implement many of the approaches described above. In the past, all 50 elementary schools had operated somewhat independently. The Prince William County Schools had a long tradition of site-based management, with significant programmatic and financial autonomy for each school. There were minimal recommended time allocations for core and encore classes; basic encore staffing gave each homeroom group one 30-minute period each of physical education and music weekly and one 60-minute period of art every two weeks, but common planning time during the school day was rare, although many schools had an early dismissal every week to allow teachers to collaborate. Other funds for additional staffing were used at the discretion of the individual schools.

After an initial presentation of the ideas discussed above and several visits to schools outside the district with scheduling plans similar to the one under consideration, ten schools in the district decided to pilot new schedules. Schools worked closely with the outside consultant and the central office staff member who assigned encore personnel to develop appropriate encore rotations. Several schools shared encore teachers on new formats, including four-day, six-day, and eight-day rotations. Each of the schools managed to schedule common planning time for all their teachers. Times for various core subjects still were allocated based on individual school preferences. The Intervention/Enrichment period was not part of this pilot.

After two years of the pilot, survey data and reports from the individual schools were so positive that a decision was made to expand the effort to include all elementary schools in the county. Several additional factors had to be considered, though:

♦ The district was moving away from the weekly early dismissal, thereby increasing the need for common planning time during the school day.

♦ There was a desire to increase the amount of physical education, music, and art received by students.

♦ There was a desire to provide an elementary program in both the core and encore classes that was more equitable across all schools.

♦ State and federal accountability programs precipitated a need to provide time for instructional interventions, remediation, and re-teaching.

♦ An elementary strings program had been introduced in the fifth grade, and the scheduling format for the program (rotating pull-outs from all classes) was found to be a new and aggravating source of instructional fragmentation for fifth grade teachers and students.

In the late winter and spring of 2004, a district-wide committee met to plan for implementation of the new scheduling format across the district. The committee included representatives from the ten pilot schools and from many of the additional 40 schools that would be implementing the new format the next fall. School-based representatives, including administrators, guidance counselors, core teachers, encore teachers, and special service providers, were joined by representatives from central office.

Table 2.2 Time Allocations

Grades K–2	Minutes	Grades 3–5	Minutes
LA/R	120	LA/R	90
Math	90	Math	75
SS/SC	45	SS/SC	90
Encore/Plan	45	Encore/Plan	45
I/E	45	I/E	45
Lunch/Recess	45	Lunch/Recess	45
Total	**390**	**Total**	**390**

After reviewing the fundamental ideas of the proposed scheduling format, we addressed the first basic question: How should we allocate time in the school day? After a lively discussion, we agreed on the allocation shown in Table 2.2.

One reason why high school and middle school scheduling is more straightforward (easier) than elementary school scheduling is that all the periods generally are the same length. While we don't advocate forcing elementary schools into such a structure, there are minor changes to time allocations and period length that can make the schedule much easier to construct. Notice that the greatest common factor of all the possible allocated class lengths (45, 75, 90, and 120 minutes) in this example is 15. Similarly, a schedule with suggested periods of 40, 80, and 100 minutes would have a greatest common factor of 20. Our experience scheduling hundreds of schools has led us to formulate the following rule: "The higher the greatest common factor and the closer it approaches a standard period length, the easier it will be to construct a schedule." Thus a schedule with periods having a greatest common factor of 20 is easier to construct than one for which the greatest common factor is 15. Similarly, when the greatest common factor is smaller, say 5 minutes, in the case where suggested periods are 45, 60, and 80 minutes, the scheduling puzzle is more difficult. There must be a balance between the practicalities of a schedule and the mission-driven desire for particular time allocations; period length is one of the practicalities that must be considered.

The second issue to be decided was the allocation of time in the 45-minute encore period. How much physical education, art, music, and other encore classes should students receive? Huge variety existed in the schools of the county. Some schools gave students one PE class per week; others gave three. Innovative encore classes were provided in different schools, including the following: library media, computer lab, foreign language, reading, science lab, math lab, and guidance. Several of these programs were either important to the school or necessary to maintain its identity. To complicate the process of change, schools had acquired staff to meet these varying programmatic emphases. So how could the district attain some level of standardization without undoing programs that were valued and/or needed? After much debate, the committee agreed on the following standard:

> Instructional time in art, music, physical education, and other encore subjects (as determined by the school) for grades 1–5 shall be 45 minutes. Schools shall schedule art, music, and physical education to meet at least once in six days. These classes may meet more frequently, every three, four, or five days. Half-day kindergarten students shall receive instruction in art, music, and physical education as part of the rotation block with half the frequency of grades 1–5. (Prince William County Public Schools, 2004)[2]

This regulation left room for schools to insert other subjects into the rotation to meet the individual needs of their school, as long as they allocated the minimum one day in six to PE, art, and music. This regulation also opened up the door for encore rotations other than the standard Monday-to-Friday schedule, such as four-day, five-day, six-day, eight-day, and even 12-day rotations, so long as at least one day of every six days students had a period of PE, music, and art.

One benefit of four-, six-, and eight-day rotations was that it simplified the sharing of teachers across schools. For example, if two schools with three sections each both operated a six-day rotation, itinerant teachers could be shared more easily, with the art and music teachers switching schools every three days. (In chapter 3 these rotations are discussed in great detail.)

A debate occurred as to how best to implement the strings program at fifth grade. As mentioned previously, the strings teacher would work in the school one or more days a week by pulling out groups on a rotating schedule so that a different class was missed each session. For the grade 5 classroom teachers, this practice resulted in a day or two every week during which small groups left and returned to the classroom all day long—a maddening circumstance, especially since fifth grade is a testing year in language arts, math, science, and social studies.

Our negotiated solution was to designate each elementary school in the district as an "early morning," "midday," or "late afternoon" strings school. We required "early morning" strings schools to schedule encore and I/E consecutively in periods 1 and 2, "late afternoon" schools in periods 7 and 8, and "midday" schools in periods 4 and 5. A strings teacher then visited each school as many days as necessary to serve the number of groups created, but only during the two assigned periods. Strings teachers had to travel midday, but that seemed a small price to pay to minimize interruptions during core fifth grade instruction.

As Figure 2.7 (p. 36) shows, the master schedule for Antietam Elementary School faithfully fulfills the time allocations agreed upon in the district (Table 2.2, p. 27). Note that the sched-

---

2 Effective for the 2006–07 school year, the regulation was changed to require a minimum of two physical education periods every six days (not reflected in the included policy for 2004); one music and one art period still are required every six days. The full text of the original policy is included in Appendix 3.

ule includes no "slivers" of time; the shortest period is 30 minutes. This schedule was negotiated with the principal, with representatives from each grade level, encore, and special services involved in the talks.

The school decided on an eight-day rotation, with PE, music, and art every four days and library and computer lab every eight days (Figure 2.8, p. 37). Notice that the master schedule (Figure 2.7, p. 36) includes separate encore blocks for the morning and afternoon kindergartens; the kindergarten teachers alternate planning in the morning and the afternoon every other day. Half-day kindergarten students receive half as many encore classes as students in grades 1–5.

Figure 2.9 (p. 38) illustrates the encore schedules; note that in addition to their regularly scheduled classes, both the library and the computer lab have large blocks of uninterrupted open time during which other classes could return to these venues accompanied by their homeroom teachers for research, keyboarding, or other appropriate activities.

So far, we only have hinted at the breadth and complexity of designing elementary school schedules. In chapter 3, we explore the many possibilities for encore class scheduling. In chapter 4, we develop a variety of scenarios for providing special services, and in chapter 5 we detail a variety of departmentalized teaming models.

References

Prince William County Public Schools (2004). *Regulation 602.1, instruction: Elementary instructional day.* Manassas, VA: Author.

Virginia Department of Education (2006). *Standards for accrediting public schools in Virginia.* 8 VAC 20-131-80. Richmond, VA: Author.

Figure 2.1 Encore/Planning Time Period Assignment
(School Day Divided into 5-Minute Increments)

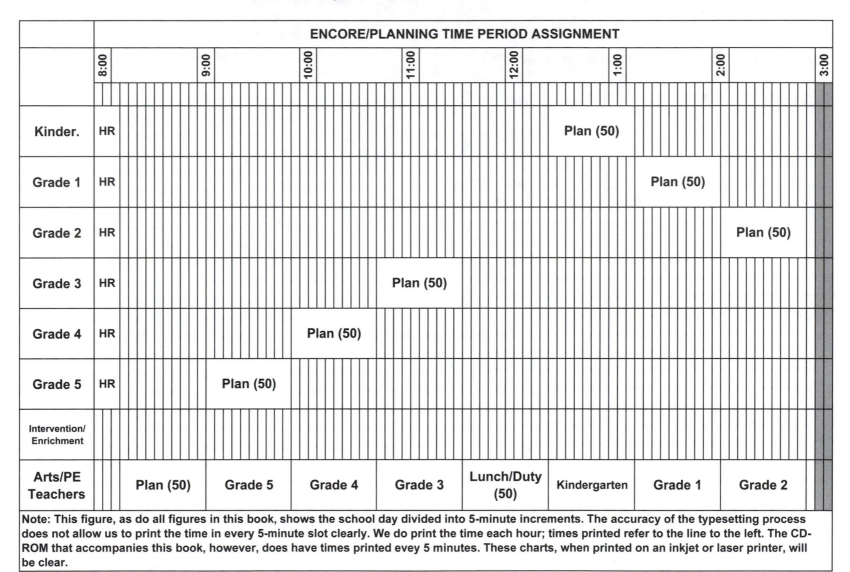

	ENCORE/PLANNING TIME PERIOD ASSIGNMENT							
	8:00	**9:00**	**10:00**	**11:00**	**12:00**	**1:00**	**2:00**	**3:00**
Kinder.	HR					Plan (50)		
Grade 1	HR						Plan (50)	
Grade 2	HR							Plan (50)
Grade 3	HR			Plan (50)				
Grade 4	HR		Plan (50)					
Grade 5	HR	Plan (50)						
Intervention/ Enrichment								
Arts/PE Teachers	Plan (50)	Grade 5	Grade 4	Grade 3	Lunch/Duty (50)	Kindergarten	Grade 1	Grade 2

Note: This figure, as do all figures in this book, shows the school day divided into 5-minute increments. The accuracy of the typesetting process does not allow us to print the time in every 5-minute slot clearly. We do print the time each hour; times printed refer to the line to the left. The CD-ROM that accompanies this book, however, does have times printed evey 5 minutes. These charts, when printed on an inkjet or laser printer, will be clear.

Figure 2.2 Encore Rotations

8:15-9:05		Encore Plan				11:35-12:25		Encore Lunch/Duty			
		Day 1	Day 2	Day 3	Day 4						
9:05-9:55	5A	PE-A	Art	PE-A	Music	12:25-1:15		Day 1	Day 2	Day 3	Day 4
	5B	Music	PE-A	Art	PE-A		KA	PE-A	Art	PE-A	Music
	5C	PE-B	Music	PE-B	Art		KB	Music	PE-A	Art	PE-A
	5D	Art	PE-B	Music	PE-B		KC	PE-B	Music	PE-B	Art
							KD	Art	PE-B	Music	PE-B
		Day 1	Day 2	Day 3	Day 4						
9:55-10:45	4A	PE-A	Art	PE-A	Music	1:15-2:05		Day 1	Day 2	Day 3	Day 4
	4B	Music	PE-A	Art	PE-A		1A	PE-A	Art	PE-A	Music
	4C	PE-B	Music	PE-B	Art		1B	Music	PE-A	Art	PE-A
	4D	Art	PE-B	Music	PE-B		1C	PE-B	Music	PE-B	Art
							1D	Art	PE-B	Music	PE-B
		Day 1	Day 2	Day 3	Day 4						
10:45-11:35	3A	PE-A	Art	PE-A	Music	2:05-2:55		Day 1	Day 2	Day 3	Day 4
	3B	Music	PE-A	Art	PE-A		2A	PE-A	Art	PE-A	Music
	3C	PE-B	Music	PE-B	Art		2B	Music	PE-A	Art	PE-A
	3D	Art	PE-B	Music	PE-B		2C	PE-B	Music	PE-B	Art
							2D	Art	PE-B	Music	PE-B

Figure 2.3 Encore Teacher Schedules

PE Schedule (2 Teachers)

Arts/PE	Plan	Grade 5	Grade 4	Grade 3	Lunch/Duty	Kindergarten	Grade 2	Grade 1
Day 1	Plan	5A, 5C	4A, 4C	3A, 3C	Lunch/Duty	KA, KC	1A, 1C	2A, 2C
Day 2	Plan	5B, 5D	4B, 4D	3B, 3D	Lunch/Duty	KB, KD	1B, 1D	2B, 2D
Day 3	Plan	5A, 5C	4A, 4C	3A, 3C	Lunch/Duty	KA, KC	1A, 1C	2A, 2C
Day 4	Plan	5B, 5D	4B, 4D	3B, 3D	Lunch/Duty	KB, KD	1B, 1D	2B, 2D

Art Schedule

Arts/PE	Plan	Grade 5	Grade 4	Grade 3	Lunch/Duty	Kindergarten	Grade 2	Grade 1
Day 1	Plan	5D	4D	3D	Lunch/Duty	KD	1D	2D
Day 2	Plan	5A	4A	3A	Lunch/Duty	KA	1A	2A
Day 3	Plan	5B	4B	3B	Lunch/Duty	KB	1B	2B
Day 4	Plan	5C	4C	3C	Lunch/Duty	KC	1C	2C

Music Schedule

Arts/PE	Plan	Grade 5	Grade 4	Grade 3	Lunch/Duty	Kindergarten	Grade 2	Grade 1
Day 1	Plan	5B	4B	3B	Lunch/Duty	KB	1B	2B
Day 2	Plan	5C	4C	3C	Lunch/Duty	KC	1C	2C
Day 3	Plan	5D	4D	3D	Lunch/Duty	KD	1D	2D
Day 4	Plan	5A	4A	3A	Lunch/Duty	KA	1A	2A

Figure 2.4 Intervention/Enrichment Period

		Add the Intervention/Enrichment Period							
	8:00	9:00	10:00	11:00	12:00	1:00	2:00	3:00	
Kinder.	HR					Plan (50)	Intervention/ Enrichment (50)		
Grade 1	HR				Intervention/ Enrichment (50)	Plan (50)			
Grade 2	HR			Intervention/ Enrichment (50)			Plan (50)		
Grade 3	HR			Plan (50)			Intervention/ Enrichment (50)		
Grade 4	HR	Intervention/ Enrichment (50)	Plan (50)						
Grade 5	HR	Plan (50)	Intervention/ Enrichment (50)						
Intervention/ Enrichment	Plan (50)	Grade 4	Grade 5	Lunch/ Duty (40)	Grade 2	Grade 1	Kindergarten	Grade 3	
Arts/PE Teachers	Plan (50)	Grade 5	Grade 4	Grade 3	Lunch/Duty (50)	Kindergarten	Grade 2	Grade 1	

Figure 2.5 Lunch and Recess

	8:00	9:00	10:00	11:00	12:00	1:00	2:00	3:00
Kinder.	HR			Lunch/Recess (50)		Plan (50)	Intervention/Enrichment (50)	
Grade 1	HR				Lunch/Recess (50)	Intervention/Enrichment (50)	Plan (50)	
Grade 2	HR			Recess/Lunch (50)	Intervention/Enrichment (50)			Plan (50)
Grade 3	HR			Plan (50)	Recess/Lunch (50)			Intervention/Enrichment (50)
Grade 4	HR		Intervention/Enrichment (50)	Plan (50)		Lunch/Recess (50)		
Grade 5	HR		Plan (50)	Intervention/Enrichment (50)		Recess/Lunch (50)		
Intervention/Enrichment		Plan (50)	Grade 4	Grade 5	Lunch/Duty (40)	Grade 2	Grade 1	Kindergarten	Grade 3
Arts/PE Teachers		Plan (50)	Grade 5	Grade 4	Grade 3	Lunch/Duty (50)	Kindergarten	Grade 2	Grade 1

Figure 2.6 Core Instructional Blocks

		8:00	9:00	10:00	11:00	12:00	1:00	2:00	3:00
Kinder.	HR	Language Arts (150 Minutes)			Lunch/ Recess (50)	Math (50)	Plan (50)	Intervention/ Enrichment (50)	SS/SC (50)
Grade 1	HR	Language Arts (140 Minutes)		Math (60)	Lunch/ Recess (50)	Intervention/ Enrichment (50)	Plan (50)	SS/SC (50)	
Grade 2	HR	Language Arts (140 Minutes)		Recess/ Lunch (50)	Intervention/ Enrichment (50)	Math (60)	SS/SC (50)	Plan (50)	
Grade 3	HR	Language Arts (90 Minutes)	Math (60)	Plan (50)	Recess/ Lunch (50)	LA (50)	SS/SC (50)	Intervention/ Enrichment (50)	
Grade 4	HR	Math (50)	Intervention/ Enrichment (50)	Plan (50)	Language Arts (100 Minutes)	Lunch/ Recess (50)	Math/SS/SC (100)		
Grade 5	HR	Math (50)	Plan (50)	Intervention/ Enrichment (50)	Language Arts (100 Minutes)	Recess/ Lunch (50)	Math/SS/SC (100)		
Intervention/ Enrichment		Plan (50)	Grade 4	Grade 5	Lunch/ Duty (40)	Grade 2	Grade 1	Kindergarten	Grade 3
Arts/PE Teachers		Plan (50)	Grade 5	Grade 4	Grade 3	Lunch/Duty (50)	Kindergarten	Grade 2	Grade 1

Figure 2.7 Antietam Master Schedule

Time markers: 8:45, 9:45, 10:45, 11:45, 12:45, 1:45, 2:45, 3:15

Kinder.	AM Core Instruction 135			Encore/CE 45	Lunch 30	Encore/CE 45	PM Core Instruction 135	
Grade 1	Language Arts 120		Math 90		L/R 45	C/E 45	SS/SC 45	Encore 45
Grade 2	Language Arts 120		Math 30	L/R 45	Math 60	Encore 45	C/E 45	SS/SC 45
Grade 3	Language Arts 90	C/E 45	L/R 45	Math 75		SS/SC 45	Encore 45	SS/SC 45
Grade 4	SS/SC 45	Encore 45	Language Arts 90	L/R 45	Math 75		SS/SC 45	C/E 45
Grade 5	Encore 45	C/E 45	Math 75	L/R 45	Language Arts 90		SS/SC 90	
I/E	Plan 45	5th Grade	3rd Grade	K a.m.	Lunch 30	K p.m.	1st Grade	2nd Grade	4th Grade
Arts/PE	5th Grade	4th Grade	Plan 45	K/Duty	Lunch 30	K/Duty	2nd Grade	3rd Grade	1st Grade

Figure 2.8 Antietam Encore Rotations

		Day 1	Day 2	Day 3	Day 4	Day 5	Day 6	Day 7	Day 8
8:45-9:30	5A	PE	Art	Music	L	PE	Art	Music	CL
	5B	L	PE	Art	Music	CL	PE	Art	Music
	5C	Music	L	PE	Art	Music	CL	PE	Art
		Day 1	Day 2	Day 3	Day 4	Day 5	Day 6	Day 7	Day 8
9:30-10:15	4A	PE	Art	Music	L	PE	Art	Music	CL
	4B	L	PE	Art	Music	CL	PE	Art	Music
	4C	Music	L	PE	Art	Music	CL	PE	Art
	4D	Art	Music	L	PE	Art	Music	CL	PE
10:15-11:00	Specialists' Planning								
		Day 1	Day 2	Day 3	Day 4	Day 5	Day 6	Day 7	Day 8
11:00-11:45	KA	PE		Art		Music		CL/L	
	KB	Art		Music		CL/L		PE	
11:45-12:15	Specialists' Lunch								
		Day 1	Day 2	Day 3	Day 4	Day 5	Day 6	Day 7	Day 8
12:15-1:00	KA		PE		Art		Music		CL/L
	KB		CL/L		PE		Art		Music
1:00-1:45		Day 1	Day 2	Day 3	Day 4	Day 5	Day 6	Day 7	Day 8
	2A	PE	Art	Music	CL	PE	Art	Music	L
	2B	CL	PE	Art	Music	L	PE	Art	Music
	2C	Music	CL	PE	Art	Music	L	PE	Art
	2D	Art	Music	CL	PE	Art	Music	L	PE
1:45-2:30		Day 1	Day 2	Day 3	Day 4	Day 5	Day 6	Day 7	Day 8
	3A	PE	Art	Music	CL	PE	Art	Music	L
	3B	CL	PE	Art	Music	L	PE	Art	Music
	3C	Music	CL	PE	Art	Music	L	PE	Art
	3D	Art	Music	CL	PE	Art	Music	L	PE
2:30-3:15		Day 1	Day 2	Day 3	Day 4	Day 5	Day 6	Day 7	Day 8
	1A	PE	Art	Music	CL	PE	Art	Music	L
	1B	CL	PE	Art	Music	L	PE	Art	Music
	1C	Music	CL	PE	Art	Music	L	PE	Art
	1D	Art	Music	CL	PE	Art	Music	L	PE

Figure 2.9 Encore Schedules

Antietam PE Schedule

	8:45	9:45	10:45		11:45	12:45	1:45	2:45	3:15
Day 1	5A	4A	Plan	KA	Lunch		2A	3A	1A
Day 2	5B	4B	Plan		Lunch	KA	2B	3B	1B
Day 3	5C	4C	Plan		Lunch		2C	3C	1C
Day 4		4D	Plan		Lunch	KB	2D	3D	1D
Day 5	5A	4A	Plan		Lunch		2A	3A	1A
Day 6	5B	4B	Plan		Lunch		2B	3B	1B
Day 7	5C	4C	Plan	KB	Lunch		2C	3C	1C
Day 8		4D	Plan		Lunch		2D	3D	1D

Antietam Art Schedule

	8:45	9:45	10:45		11:45	12:45	1:45	2:45	3:15
Day 1		4D	Plan	KB	Lunch		2D	3D	1D
Day 2	5A	4A	Plan		Lunch		2A	3A	1A
Day 3	5B	4B	Plan	KA	Lunch		2B	3B	1B
Day 4	5C	4C	Plan		Lunch	KA	2C	3C	1C
Day 5		4D	Plan		Lunch		2D	3D	1D
Day 6	5A	4A	Plan		Lunch	KB	2A	3A	1A
Day 7	5B	4B	Plan		Lunch		2B	3B	1B
Day 8	5C	4C	Plan		Lunch		2C	3C	1C

Figure 2.9 Encore Schedules, cont'd

Antietam Library Schedule

	8:45	9:45	10:45		11:45	12:45	1:45	2:45	3:15
Day 1	5B	4B	Plan		Lunch				
Day 2	5C	4C	Plan		Lunch	KB(CI too)			
Day 3		4D	Plan		Lunch				
Day 4	5A	4A	Plan		Lunch				
Day 5			Plan	KB(CI too)	Lunch		2B	3B	1B
Day 6			Plan		Lunch		2C	3C	1C
Day 7			Plan	KA(CLtoo)	Lunch		2D	3D	1D
Day 8			Plan		Lunch		2A	3A	1A

Antietam Computer Lab Schedule

	8:45	9:45	10:45		11:45	12:45	1:45	2:45	3:15
Day 1			Plan		Lunch		2B	3B	1B
Day 2			Plan		Lunch	KB(L too)	2C	3C	1C
Day 3			Plan		Lunch		2D	3D	1D
Day 4			Plan		Lunch		2A	3A	1A
Day 5	5B	4B	Plan	KB(L too)	Lunch				
Day 6	5C	4C	Plan		Lunch				
Day 7		4D	Plan	KA(L too)	Lunch				
Day 8	5A	4A	Plan		Lunch	KA(L too)			

Figure 2.9 Encore Schedules, cont'd

	8:45	9:45	10:45		11:45	12:45	1:45	2:45	3:15
Day 1	5C	4C	Plan		Lunch		2C	3C	1C
Day 2		4D	Plan		Lunch		2D	3D	1D
Day 3	5A	4A	Plan	KB	Lunch		2A	3A	1A
Day 4	5B	4B	Plan		Lunch		2B	3B	1B
Day 5	5C	4C	Plan	KA	Lunch		2C	3C	1C
Day 6		4D	Plan		Lunch	KA	2D	3D	1D
Day 7	5A	4A	Plan		Lunch		2A	3A	1A
Day 8	5B	4B	Plan		Lunch	KB	2B	3B	1B

Antietam Music Schedule

3
Scheduling Encore Classes

In many elementary schools across the nation, the scheduling of art, music, physical education (PE), foreign language, computer, and other "encore" classes is less than ideal. All too often, elementary school encore teachers' schedules are pieced around the assignment of part-time itinerant specialists (based on responses to the question, "When can I have your kids?" asked by encore teachers individually) and/or structured around a variety of individual teacher preferences unrelated to the mission of the school. This practice invariably yields a schedule characterized by haphazard and inefficient personnel assignments and fragmented core instructional time.

This chapter explores the problems we face in scheduling elementary encore classes and offers a variety of options that we believe form the basis of a more rational organizational plan for the delivery of encore programs.

The Effects of Poor Scheduling

We first review the problems created by the current system.

- *Fragmentation*. It is not unusual for an elementary school teacher's class to be assigned physical education two days a week at one time for about 30 minutes, art once a week at another time for 50 minutes, and music two days a week during yet another slot for 20 to 40 minutes. We actually have worked with schools where, in order to provide state-mandated and local option programs, a class received ten separate encore periods during the week, dramatically reducing and fragmenting the time available for core instruction, and virtually ruling out uninterrupted instructional time for teaming, regrouping, or common planning by all teachers at one grade level.

♦ *Unfairness.* Teacher in-service days, parent conferences, and holiday closures tend to fall on Mondays or Fridays. Thus, students with special classes scheduled on these two days often receive significantly less instruction in the program than do other students; teachers with the accompanying planning period receive less planning time. Another fairness issue is the assignment of preferred times within the encore teachers' schedules. It has been our observation that under the "When can I have your kids?" model of scheduling, teachers who are friendly with specific encore teachers receive the preferred times for these classes and planning periods.

♦ *Lack of common planning time.* Teachers involved in school improvement efforts through the creation of learning communities (DuFour & Eaker, 1998) need time together to plan lessons and units, to analyze student performance data, to prepare intervention and enrichment activities, and to participate in staff development. All too often, however, the only time teachers at the same grade level can get together is before school, after school, or during lunch. While many schools attempt to schedule common planning time during the school day, teachers often are fortunate to have one such period weekly.

Factors Contributing to Ineffective Encore Teachers' Schedules

We have found that the following six factors contribute to the aforementioned problems:

♦ Lack of congruence between a school's mission and its schedule

♦ Schedules designed by individual encore teachers

♦ Schedules designed by central office

♦ Periods of variable length

♦ The Monday-to-Friday scheduling format

♦ Unwise arrangement for sharing itinerant faculty

Lack of Congruence Between a School's Mission and Its Schedule

Most elementary school mission statements include a primary emphasis on the core instructional program, most notably the development of students' skills in language arts and mathematics. Yet we almost always schedule these critical subjects around the times when students attend encore teachers' classes and lunch. If mission statements were truly guides for action, schools would schedule encore teachers' schedules around core instruction, not the reverse.

Encore schedules sometimes are constructed to allow the art teacher, for example, to work with classes of the same grade level in consecutive periods on the same day. If one third grade teacher has art from 9 to 10, a second from 10 to 11, and the third from 11 to 12, the result is obvious: no common planning time, no possible cooperation among the three teachers during this three-hour block, and a fragmented morning of core instruction.

Schedules Designed by Individual Encore Teachers

Although this practice happens more often with pull-out programs, it also occurs with encore teachers. No overall plan is conceived. Often, the schedule is designed with the convenience of the encore teacher in mind, rather than in the best interests of the core instructional program, the students, and the overall school mission. We have seen schedules that were planned around the secondary school coaching duties of teachers whose elementary school teaching responsibility was diminished because practice started before the elementary school day ended. We also have seen schedules designed with the childcare needs of the instructor as the governing factor. While we understand the realities of school and the needs of individual teachers, the lack of an overall plan wastes resources and fragments core instructional time.

Schedules Designed by Central Office

Usually a central office administrator is charged with the assignment of encore teachers to individual schools. We have noted two distinct extremes to this responsibility: the benign neglect of the laissez-faire manager and the over-attention to detail of the efficiency expert. Each of these styles has its problems.

When the assignment of encore teachers is laissez faire, schedules evolve over time, sometimes based on noneducational criteria such as the instructors' proximity to home or babysitters. Occasionally, no one in the district seems to know how the schedule was developed, what criteria were used, and where itinerant teachers are at any particular time. These schedules tend to be very inefficient, often wasting a great deal of time on between-school travel and encouraging the "When can I have your kids?" habit of scheduling at the school level.

At the other extreme (and much more prevalent) is the central office administrator who, in the name of efficiency and equality among schools, determines the exact number of grade level sections in each school, multiplies this by the number of weekly minutes to be offered to each class (such as 40 minutes of music), and calculates the number of days every school needs each encore teacher to accomplish this instruction. While this schedule guarantees schools and students equal exposure to these specialized programs, it is so tight and inflexible that all other instructional programs must revolve around it. The allocation chart may look fair and equitable on paper, but the resulting schedules have fragmented core instructional time and provide little continuity for the encore teachers' programs.

Even more problematic is the practice of having individual central office administrators assign personnel in their discipline independently of each other: the physical education supervisor assigns the physical education teachers, the music supervisor assigns the music teachers, the art supervisor assigns the art teachers, and so on. The resulting mishmash of allocations makes the creation of an educationally sound schedule nearly impossible.

Periods of Variable Length

Another bane to the design of encore teachers' schedules is the fact that encore teachers often prefer to offer their programs in periods of different length. It is not unusual to have physical education and classroom music periods between 25 and 45 minutes several times weekly, art classes from 40 to 60 minutes once a week, and library-media classes of anywhere from 25 to 50 minutes weekly. Piecing together an efficient and sensible schedule composed of periods of unequal length is virtually impossible; we see classes of unequal length as the major cause of fragmented core instructional time.

The Monday-to-Friday Schedule

The Monday-to-Friday schedule is inherently unfair because we have more Tuesdays, Wednesdays, and Thursdays during the school year than Mondays and Fridays. Thus if your class has music scheduled on Monday or Friday, you and your students miss this class more frequently than if it were held on Tuesday, Wednesday, or Thursday.

Unwise Arrangement for Sharing Itinerant Faculty

Often, when a school needs less than one full-time equivalent (FTE) teacher[1] to meet program requirements, personnel are assigned for partial days to schools. For example, two schools may be required to share an art teacher; each school has been assigned 0.5 FTE of art. The typical sharing arrangement is 2.5 days per school. It is difficult to use the "half day" in any systematic scheduling plan. Also, because the teacher must travel between buildings, an instructional period often is lost, making the 0.5 FTE on paper somewhat less in reality—not to mention that your school's half-day of service from the art teacher may come at just the wrong time.

Effective Encore Teachers' Schedules

Although the circumstances and staffings for every school vary, we suggest that the scheduling of encore programs should attempt to attain the following goals: (a) quality time for encore programs, (b) common grade-level or team planning time, (c) large blocks of uninterrupted instructional time for core subjects, and (d) fairness to all teachers and students. To accomplish these goals, we suggest that schedulers at the central office and individual schools adhere to the following three principles.

Principle 1

Set a standard period length for all encore classes.

As noted above, encore classes of different lengths make it difficult to create a relatively efficient schedule that supports quality instruction. Opinions about what the standard length

---

1 A "full time equivalent" is a human resources management term to track faculty positions. 1.0 FTE is a full-time teacher; 0.5 FTE is a half-time teacher. A teacher who works one day *per week* (1 of 5 days) is 0.2 FTE; a teacher who works 2 days *of six* is 0.33 (2 of 6) FTE.

should be often differ; most schools seek a compromise. A number of factors enter into the deliberations:

1. How long is the school day, and how much time do we want to allocate to encore activities overall?

We have worked in school divisions with as little as 5 hours and 10 minutes and as much as 6 hours and 30 minutes for instruction (after lunch is subtracted). We also have visited schools with the resources available for as many as ten periods of encore classes weekly. If the instructional day is short, however, are we willing to take that much time from core instruction?

Also, what about half-day kindergarten? Although kindergarten teachers should receive the same amount of planning time as teachers in other grade levels, should the students, who attend half as long (or less), receive the same amount of time in encore? Our general solution to the problem of half-day kindergarten is to give each group of students half as much exposure to the various encore classes, which offers the kindergarten teachers the same amount of planning time as other grade-level teachers.

2. How many grade levels must be served?

You may be asking yourself why the number of grade levels might affect the length of periods for encore classes. The typical elementary school has six grade levels, K–5. Consequently, we would need a total of eight periods to schedule encore appropriately: one for each grade level, one period for encore planning and one for encore lunch. So, if the school has a 6½-hour school day (390 minutes), we could schedule eight 45-minute periods and still have 30 minutes for beginning-of-the-day and end-of-the-day routines, as well as a bit of "wiggle room" between certain classes or around the lunch blocks. A school with fewer grade levels or teams (or a longer school day) may be able to schedule a longer encore period, or it may need to split large grade levels into two teams that receive encore instruction during different periods. A school also may have more than six groupings if two sessions (A.M. and P.M.) of kindergarten receive services from the encore team.

Another consideration is that many schools have one or more self-contained special education programs and/or pre-school classes. If there are pre-school classes, often these part-time programs don't receive the services of encore programs and need not be factored into the schedule. Almost all special education students are integrated back into the mainstream for encore classes, even if they are totally self-contained for their core academic program. If these programs receive services separately, however, they must be factored into the overall plan.

3. What is optimal for each subject offered in encore?

While no research supports one particular period length over another, art teachers generally prefer a longer period than do physical education, library, or music teachers because of materials distribution and cleanup issues. Similarly, PE and general music teachers usually prefer more frequent classes rather than longer meeting times. It is not unusual to have art scheduled for 45 to 60 minutes weekly, while music, PE, and library are scheduled for 30- to 40-minute periods once or twice weekly.

Although it would be possible to create a modular time frame with one hour for art and two 30-minute periods rotated among music, library, and PE, in a typical school with six grades there is not enough time in the day to run this schedule. A minimum of seven and one-half hours would be necessary: six hour-long encore blocks, one hour for each grade; an hour planning for the encore teachers; and 30 minutes for encore lunch. Furthermore, the 30-minute period realistically only allows for about 25 minutes of instruction once time for the class change is subtracted.

Given these considerations, the compromise time frame for a standard encore period generally is somewhere between 40 and 50 minutes, most often 45 minutes—too short in the eyes of the art teacher and too long in the opinion of the music teacher; in other words, a good compromise.

Principle 2

Abandon the Monday-to-Friday scheduling of encore classes in favor of a cycle that repeats every three, four, six, or more days.

The Monday-to-Friday schedule is problematic because we miss more Mondays and Fridays for holidays and teacher in-service than any other days of the week. Consequently, encore programs are delivered unevenly to students. Monday-to-Friday scheduling also is difficult because five is an unwieldy number in encore scheduling; it works well only when there are five sections at a grade level and five encore classes that each meet once a week. Even so, we would prefer a five-day rotation over a Monday-to-Friday schedule. Schedules tend to be easier to design if the number of sections at the grade level is equal to (or has a common factor with) the number of days in the scheduling cycle. If there are two sections per grade level, a four-, six-, or even eight-day rotation will work better than a five-day rotation.

Principle 3

Give all teachers—core, encore, and special service—the same amount of time for lunch and planning.

This is a fairness issue. On occasion, encore teachers have large blocks of unassigned time in their schedules; in other cases, they may be so tightly scheduled that they have nothing but a short break for lunch. This problem also is evident in special service schedules. Schedulers should strive to provide equal planning time and equal duty time for all professional employees. While this statement may seem unnecessary in union states, where contract provisions attempt to ensure such fairness, in many other parts of the country it can be a significant problem.

Steps in the Process of Creating Effective Encore Teachers' Schedules

Once we have decided the amount of time to be allocated to encore classes in total, we must decide how to allocate this time to the various encore class possibilities. Assigning encore teachers is a district-level decision.

District Assignment Principle 1

A district must know what it wants to provide for students in the encore block before it can create a schedule and assign staff.

Deciding which classes to include and with what frequency the classes should meet in the encore rotation usually requires a district-level debate and decision. To illustrate, consider the following example.

Table 3.1 Sample School District Elementary School Organization

School	Typical number of sections per grade
School I	6
School II	5
School III	4
School IV	4
School V	3
School VI	2

The Sample School District has determined that it is willing to allocate 45 minutes daily to the encore block, and the committee discussing the elementary school schedule now begins to discuss how these 45 minutes will be used. Sample School District traditionally has provided physical education, music, art, library media, and classroom guidance instruction taught by specialists, although the latter was provided for only a limited number of weeks during the school year for each grade level.

Sample School District has six elementary schools: School I with six sections at most grade levels, School II with five sections at most grade levels, Schools III and IV with four sections at most grade levels, School V with three sections at most grade levels, and School VI with two sections per grade level.

To begin our discussion, we start with a four-day rotation of encore classes; later in the chapter we explore six-day, eight-day, and twelve-day variations, along with several other variations.

Four-Day Rotation

We can choose from a variety of different allocations of encore time. For example, a school might decide that PE, music, art, and library media should be emphasized equally and that guidance instruction should not be included in the encore block. If so, the most logical choice would be a four-day rotation as illustrated in Figure 3.1. If the 45-minute encore/planning blocks were assigned in a school with four sections, as illustrated in the master schedule for encore blocks in Figure 3.2 (p. 58), the rotation for encore classes would be repeated for each grade level in a different time slot, yielding the full rotation shown in Figure 3.3 (p. 59). Drawing from these two figures, we can write out the encore teachers' schedules, as shown in Figure 3.4 (p. 60).

Figure 3.1 Four-Day Encore Rotation (One Grade)

	Day 1	Day 2	Day 3	Day 4
Teacher A	Music	PE	Art	Lib.
Teacher B	Lib.	Music	PE	Art
Teacher C	Art	Lib.	Music	PE
Teacher D	PE	Art	Lib.	Music

To staff this rotation, schools III and IV would require full-time PE, music, art, and library teachers, for a total of four full-time equivalents (FTEs) each (see Figures 3.5, pp. 61–62, and 3.5a, p. 63). School III uses music teacher A, PE teacher A, art teacher A, and librarian A; school IV uses their B counterparts. The rotation of classes shown for each homeroom teacher would be repeated during different periods of the day in each school.

By rights, school I (six sections per grade level) should receive 1.5 FTEs in each position, and school VI (two sections per grade level) only 0.5 FTEs for each. It would make sense for them to share these part-time teachers. In many districts that assign itinerants based on the Monday-to-Friday week, these half-time positions would be allotted 2½ days to each school, resulting in the problems described previously. This leads us to our second district principle.

District Assignment Principle 2

In general, think of the entire school district as one big school for the purposes of assigning encore staff.

It is much more efficient and schedule-friendly to share the 0.5 FTEs as shown in Figure 3.5 (p. 61). School I must have six encore teachers every day; school VI needs only two. Partnering these two schools, we treat them almost as if they were one large building with eight sections. School I uses the full services of music teacher C, PE teacher C, art teacher C, and librarian C, but still needs two days of each subject to complete the cycle for six sections; these are provided by their D counterparts. School VI uses the remaining two days from each of these teachers. As shown in Figure 3.5, each D teacher spends two days of four in

school I and two days in school VI. So we build these two encore rotations together. Figure 3.5a (p. 63) shows the schools to which teachers are assigned each day; this matches the rotations shown in Figure 3.5.

Similarly, we pair schools II (5 sections) and V (3 sections) to equal eight sections, which requires eight encore positions daily. This lets us efficiently share the services of the F encore teachers, one day in school II and three in school V. In all, Sample School District would need six music, six art, and six physical education teachers, as well as six librarians.

This example leads us to a corollary: district assignment principle 2a.

District Assignment Principle 2a

If at all possible, assign encore specialists to schools for full days only.

If each grade level has a daily block of time set aside for encore classes, an itinerant encore teacher who comes for part of the day can only meet with certain grade levels. For example, if the art teacher is only there for the afternoon, only classes with afternoon encore periods have easy access. The others must then schedule art outside their normal encore block, thus fragmenting the schedule.

In essence, to create an efficient encore schedule that puts grade-level encore classes and core planning time in the same block, a school must have the same number of encore teachers as there are base teachers in each grouping (usually the grade level). In a typical K–5 school, this means encore teachers must be in the building for full days—not necessarily full time, but in each school of their rotation for a full day at a time.

A schedule that follows this principle has two additional benefits. First, because it eliminates or at least greatly reduces midday travel, it preserves midday instructional periods and saves mileage costs. Second, when shared teachers spend full days in schools, there is less reason to worry about proximity. When midday travel is necessary, we try to save travel time and expense by pairing schools that are close to each other. (Proximity may still be a consideration when before- or after-school commitments require travel.)

District Assignment Principle 3

Assign encore teachers to schools based on the typical number of homerooms per grade level (or teaching team) rather than the exact number of periods required for the mandated meetings of a particular encore class.

What if, for example, the number of sections per grade level for school III were as shown in Table 3.2?

Table 3.2 Sample School District Elementary School III

School	Sections Per Grade	Students Per Grade
K	4	85
Grade 1	4	85
Grade 2	4	85
Grade 3	4	90
Grade 4	3	75
Grade 5	3	78

Because grades 4 and 5 have fewer sections per grade level, should school III be allotted proportionally less of each encore teacher? We would argue not. If we subtract periods from each encore teacher for the sake of proportionality, on some days only three encore teachers will be in the building, which means the four-section grade levels will not have common planning time. School III is still basically a four-section school; it needs four encore teachers daily for almost all grade levels. Over the four-day cycle, each encore teacher would simply have two open periods. We recommend identifying ways to fill those slots, such as assisting during the Intervention/Enrichment period or in the extension center in a parallel block schedule, or providing additional encore instruction for more needy or more gifted students.

Similarly, if school I had the configuration shown in Table 3.3, should more staff be assigned to cover the additional sections in grades K and 1? Again, we would argue not. School I is still basically a six-section school, with an "extra" class in grades K and 1.

Table 3.3 Sample School District Elementary School I

School	Sections Per Grade	Students Per Grade
K	7	126
Grade 1	7	125
Grade 2	6	125
Grade 3	6	125
Grade 4	6	125
Grade 5	6	125

Solving the Problem of the "Extra" Class

We realize that schools often have an uneven number of sections per grade level. There are several ways of handling this problem in the encore rotation. First, if two grade levels balance each other out (e.g., if the typical grade has six sections, but one has seven and another has five), we could simply slot the extra section into the space in the five-section rotation. If no grade level has an opening, then we could allow the encore teachers to instruct an extra class every six days during their planning period for additional remuneration. The disadvantage of these options is that they preempt common planning time for the grade with seven teachers.

Second, we could add a seventh encore teacher to the rotation for the seven-section grade level. For example, the librarian might be added, or in some states a teaching assistant could serve the seventh group. Although this plan preserves common planning time, it, too, has disadvantages. The school now has two rotations, a situation that might cause confusion if not handled well. Creating a seven-day rotation also reduces the annual number of PE, music, and art classes for each section in that grade level. In the four-day rotation shown, each section receives 90 PE classes, 45 music classes, and 45 art classes over the course of the 180-day school year. Adding library to the mix reduces those numbers, thus creating inequity.

A third way to address the "extra" section is to bring in itinerant PE, art and music teachers to cover it. In this situation, we would need two additional PE periods and one additional art and music period every four days for each extra section. While we have seen many schools make this choice, we believe it has too many disadvantages. Each of the itinerants must travel midday; space problems often occur when two music or art sections overlap; and the itinerants are loosely connected to the school culture because they spend so little time in the building.

A fourth approach divides the total number of students in the grade level into six sections rather than seven. Almost always, the "extra" homeroom is in a primary grade, often added to reduce class size for literacy instruction, not to make art, music, and PE classes smaller. If we divide that grade level into six sections for encore, average class size in encore classes would grow from 18 to about 21. In our example, about 125 students in first grade could be divided into seven homeroom sections of 18 for core instruction, but six sections of 21 during the encore period. There are two distinctly different ways to do this: (a) divide one section, distributing three to four students to each of the six remaining classes; or (b) divide the entire grade into six new sections, each with students from every homeroom. Each option has pros and cons.

If we distribute one section among the others, the divided class might become the "orphan." We believe this depends on how the split is handled. In the best-case scenario, the principal negotiates the cooperation of an organized and centrally located teacher, then visits the classroom to speak with the students. The question "Do you have friends in other first grade classrooms?" gets a cheerful positive response. "What would you think of going to PE, art, and music with those other friends?" is likewise well received. Then the class is divided based (mostly) on students' friendships.

The option of creating a whole new mix for encore time is often chosen for intermediate classes, for a number of reasons.

For one, mirroring similar plans in middle school, it allows ongoing personality conflicts among students a cooling-off period when they are separated during encore classes.

Six-Day Rotation

Many schools do not allocate encore time equally among physical education, art, music, and library classes. Given the publicity regarding childhood obesity, elementary schools often allocate a larger proportion of time to physical education. The six-day rotation illustrated in Figure 3.6 provides 45 minutes for physical education every other day. In addition, it offers one art period, one music period, and one library period every six days. Figure 3.7 (p. 64) shows the encore rotation for all grade levels, and Figure 3.8 (pp. 65–66) details the encore teachers' schedules for a school with four sections per grade level.

Figure 3.6 Six-Day Encore Rotation (One Grade)

	Day 1	Day 2	Day 3	Day 4	Day 5	Day 6
Teacher A	PE	Art	PE	Music	PE	L
Teacher B	L	PE	Art	PE	Music	PE
Teacher C	PE	L	PE	Art	PE	Music
Teacher D	Music	PE	L	PE	Art	PE

Figure 3.9 (p. 67) illustrates possible sharing arrangements for itinerant encore teachers if the Sample School District implements a six-day rotation. Schools III and IV (with four sections) each would need two full-time PE teachers (2 FTEs) and four days (0.67 FTEs) each from art, music, and library instructors. PE teachers A and B work full-time in school III, C and D in school IV. Art teacher A, music teacher A, and librarian A each work four days of six in school III and two days of six in school IV.

School IV needs two more days each of art, music, and library to complete the schedule; these classes are provided by the three B instructors, who also work two days in school VI (two sections) and school II (two of the five sections). Thus each B instructor (except PE B) works in three schools—two full days each in schools II, IV, and VI. We realize that being assigned to three different schools is less than ideal; the alternative, however, likely is a fragmented schedule for all core teachers in several schools and itinerant schedules that involve midday travel. We also recognize that schools II and IV each have two music teachers, which complicates preparation for musical programs.

Note that the total number of FTEs of district encore staff is the same (24 FTEs), for the six-day rotation (Figure 3.9, p. 67) as the four-day rotation (Figure 3.5, p.p. 61–62), but that the number of positions in each specialty area is different to reflect the different amounts of PE, music, art and library offered by each rotation (Table 3.4).

Table 3.4 Sample School District Encore Staff Requirements for Four- and Six-Day Rotations

School	FTEs Needed for Four-Day Rotation (PE, A, M, L)	FTEs Needed for Six-Day Rotation (PE, A, PE, M, PE, L)
PE	6	12
Art	6	4
Music	6	4
Library	6	4
District Total	24 FTEs	24 FTEs

Eight-Day Rotation

Before moving on to discuss a variety of other options and exceptions for scheduling encore classes, we apply an eight-day rotation to the Sample School District. This rotation provides two PE classes, two music classes, two art classes, one library class, and one computer lab class every eight days (shown for one grade in Figure 3.10). Notice how library and computer lab alternate; this is essentially a four-day rotation with computer and library meeting every eight days. Often we are loath to fully schedule the library, preferring to provide some open time for classroom teachers to come to the media center with their classes for research. Schools also benefit from open time in the computer lab. Having the library and computer lab share a scheduling slot keeps each teacher and facility "open" at least half-time.

Figure 3.10 Eight-Day Encore Rotation (One Grade)

	Day 1	Day 2	Day 3	Day 4	Day 5	Day 6	Day 7	Day 8
A	Music	PE	Art	L	Music	PE	Art	CL
B	L	Music	PE	Art	CL	Music	PE	Art
C	Art	L	Music	PE	Art	CL	Music	PE
D	PE	Art	L	Music	PE	Art	CL	Music

We could schedule all classes into the library for the first four days of the rotation (days 1 to 4) and then into the computer lab on days 5 to 8, but it makes far more sense to schedule both for partial days every day, as shown in Figures 3.11 (p. 69; full school rotations) and 3.12 (pp. 70–72; encore teacher schedules). Library classes are held in the morning on days 1 to 4 for grades 3–5 and during the afternoon on days 5 to 8 for grades K–2. Conversely, computer lab classes meet during the afternoon for grades K–2 on days 1 to 4 and in the morning on days 5 to 8 for grades 3–5. The beneficial result of this flip is illustrated in Figure 3.12, which depicts the encore teachers' schedules for this rotation. Figures 3.12d and 3.12e show that both the library and computer lab never have more than three classes scheduled daily, yielding significant unscheduled open times.

We recommend that whole-class guidance lessons also be scheduled during the encore period, routinely sharing a slot with some other class (typically library). All too often, guidance schedules follow the "When can I have your kids?" pattern, whittling away instructional time from key areas. While we understand that the duties of guidance counselors require some flexibility, especially for dealing with crises, we believe that scheduling as we describe below offers that flexibility.

National standards from the American Counseling Association recommend that between 35 and 45 percent of the counselor's time be devoted to the guidance curriculum (Gysbers & Henderson, 2000).

Twelve-Day Rotation

We recommend limiting classroom guidance lessons to one-fourth to one-third of the counselor's time and making provisions for the real possibility that the counselor might need to be pulled from the schedule to deal with a crisis. We accomplish this by having the counselor share a scheduling slot with another teacher, as we did with library and computer lab in Figure 3.11 (p. 69).

A counselor scheduled one-third of the time would meet with classes once in every three four-day rotations, or once every 12 days. Figure 3.13 (p. 73) illustrates this 12-day rotation. Notice that the counselor works with kindergarten and third grade students on days 1 to 4, first and second grade students on days 5 to 8, and fourth and fifth grade students on days 9 to 12. As illustrated in Figure 3.14e (p. 76), the counselor never works with more than two classes per day, leaving significant open time to work with small groups, conduct individual counseling, and pursue other important duties. Should a crisis occur during one of the counselor's teaching periods, the librarian (Figure 3.14d, p. 75) has an open period and could fill in. The missed guidance lesson could be made up during a future rotation by substituting into the library schedule.

If the decision were made to offer guidance only once every four rotations, then a 16-day schedule could be constructed for both library and guidance; the library media specialist would meet with classes three times every 16 days, while the guidance counselor did so once every 16 days. Admittedly, there are pros and cons to this instructional schedule for counselors. Although once every 16 days does provide contact with students throughout the school year, classes are spaced far apart, making continuity a major concern. As an alternative, guidance instruction could be scheduled for the same proportion of time (25 percent) by offering nine-week units for each grade level, during which students would receive guidance instruction once every four days. The rest of the year (75 percent), students would visit the library during this time slot. If this option were selected, we would recommend scheduling a short (i.e., 20 minutes), book checkout time weekly outside of the encore time slot during the nine weeks when the class was attending guidance.

We have worked in several schools that had guidance, library, and the computer lab sharing the same scheduling slot, each meeting once every 12 days. The encore rotation and encore teachers' schedules are shown in Figures 3.15 (p. 77) and 3.16 (pp. 78–80). Each of the three teachers only instructs two regularly scheduled classes per day (see Figures 3.16d–f, pp. 79–80).

The district allocations shown for the eight-day rotation in Figure 3.17 (p. 81) are the same for PE, art, and music as for the four-day rotation, but (as is often the case) we leave a full-time librarian in each school. The larger schools often have one or two clerical assistants in the library to compensate for the additional teaching load.

In summary, to calculate the staffing needs of a school district that wants to provide common planning time for all elementary school teachers and a consistent and equitable encore rotation across all schools, perform the following steps:

1. *Divide each school into six relatively equal groupings of base teachers.* For a typical K–5 school, the groupings will be by grade level; for a school that only includes grades K–2, we would create two groupings of kindergarten teachers, two groupings for grade 1 teachers and two groupings of grade 2 teachers. We create six groupings to schedule six daily periods of encore; with two additional periods added for encore teachers' lunch and planning, we create an eight-period (as a minimum) scheduling template as described above.

2. *Determine the typical number of base teachers per grouping for each school in the district.* In nearly every case, we can look at the numbers of sections per grade level and state that "School X is basically a five (or some other number)-section-per-grade-level school." This is the number of encore teachers needed in this school every day. Refer to earlier sections in this chapter for strategies for dealing with the "extra" class.

3. *Total the number of groupings needed per school for the entire district.* In a school district with three elementary schools, if one school generally has *five* classes per grade level, another school has *four,* and another has *three,* the total number of groupings in the district is *12; therefore, the total number of encore teachers needed for the district is also 12.* This is true for any rotation used.

4. *Determine the encore rotation to be used throughout the district.* This involves debate as to what students should receive during encore. In one school district in which we have worked, with 12 groupings across three schools, the district decided on a six-day rotation: PE, art, Spanish, PE, music, Spanish.

5. *Determine the number of encore teachers per discipline needed.* Because one-third of the encore time (two of six days) is spent in PE, one-third of the encore teachers must be PE teachers ($12 \div 3 = 4$); because one-third of the encore time is spent in Spanish, four Spanish teachers are needed; and because one-sixth of the encore time is spent in music and art, two music and two art teachers are required, for a total of 12 encore teachers.

6. *Develop the encore sharing arrangements across schools.* Figures included in this chapter detail such sharing arrangements for multiple schools on four-, six-, eight-, and 12-day rotations and the encore rotations that support them.[2]

Designing Extended Planning Blocks to Support Professional Learning Communities

While creating common planning time for all teachers at a grade level goes a long way toward supporting the work of professional learning communities (PLCs), administrators must recognize that in addition to teachers' collaborative efforts during this planning time, they also have individual work to complete. In fact, some union contracts prevent administrators from impinging on teachers' minimum daily planning time at all.

---

2 The CD-ROM that accompanies this book also illustrates a five-day rotation that includes two physical education classes and one class each of art, music, and library.

Thus, it is incumbent on schedulers to try to carve out additional time for teachers to engage in data analysis, curriculum work, analysis of students' work, and instructional improvement (William, 2007/2008) . Some schools and districts provide this time through early dismissal days, on teacher workdays, or after school in place of faculty meetings. The school schedule also could allow extended time for collaboration during the day. Two basic means of creating such schedules are discussed below, along with variations on each.

Creating an Extended Planning Block by Shortening the Typical Planning Period

Figure 3.18 (p. 83) shows a basic master encore schedule built originally from Figure 3.2 (p. 58). In this case, however, we have shortened each encore period, encore planning time, and encore teachers' lunch by 5 minutes, to 40 minutes each. We moved the 40 minutes saved by these cuts to the beginning of the day, forming an 80-minute extended planning block. Once every six days, each grade level is assigned to plan during this 80-minute time slot instead of their normal time block. With a school day of 405 minutes (15 minutes more than that shown in Figure 3.18) we could construct nine, 45-minute periods, which would allow the creation of a 90-minute extended planning block. If the day were 420 minutes we could operate nine, 45-minute periods with 15 minutes for opening and closing homeroom activities.

Students attend two 40-minute encore classes during this time, although occasionally the same encore class appears in both slots, yielding an 80-minute block of that encore class. Figure 3.19 (pp. 84–85) shows the encore rotations that support this schedule for a school with six teachers per grade level on a six-day rotation.

To make sense of this, let's take a look at the grade 3 rotations shown in the 11:00 to 11:40 slot in Figure 3.19 (p. 85). On days 1, 2, 4, 5, and 6, the third grade teachers plan in their normal time slot from 11:00 to 11:40 while their students attend encore classes. On day 3, because day 3 of the rotation is the extended planning block for grade 3, all the third grade teachers plan from 8:20 until 9:40 while their students attend two encore classes. On day 3 the third grade teachers work with their own classes during their normal planning time from 11:00 to 11:40 while the encore teachers have their planning time.

Let's follow teacher 3D's encore schedule. From 11:00 to 11:40 (Figure 3.19, pp. 84–85), class 3D always has music on day 1, PE on day 2, PE on day 4, art on day 5, and PE on day 6. On day 3, the encore block shifts to an earlier time (8:20–9:40) for grade 3; for the first half of the extended planning block (8:20–9:00) teachers always have whatever class they would have had in the six-day rotation. Look in the 8:20 to 9:00 time slot on Figure 3.19, labeled *Extended Planning Blocks—First 40 Minutes*, to see which class teachers begin their extended planning block; 3D always starts with library. The second half of the block, labeled *Extended Planning Blocks-Second 40 Minutes* on Figure 3.19, lasts from 9:00 to 9:40, but the class provided during this time changes over six rotations. To find where class 3D goes for each rotation for the second half of the block, look just below the 9:00 to 9:40 time slot in Figure 3.19 to the table entitled *All grades follow the rotation...* and examine the row labeled *Class D*.

The first time during the year that the third grade has the double planning period (rotation 1), students in homeroom 3D attend music from 9:00 to 9:40 as their second class in the 80-minute block; remember that on each extended planning day the 3D group always has library from 8:20 to 9:00. Six days later, the third grade follows rotation 2, with an additional period of PE for 3D. Six days later (rotation 3), the extra class is library; because 3D always starts with library on day 3, the back-to-back periods form an 80-minute block. Six days later (rotation 4), PE is the second half of the block again. Six days later (rotation 5), art is the second class. Finally, in rotation 6, PE again completes the block. Thus, over six rotations each section receives three additional periods of PE and one each of library, music, and art. Each grade level ends up with the extended planning period once every six days, each on a different day of the cycle.

Table 3.5 summarizes teacher 3D's full encore schedule.

Table 3.5 Summary of Teacher 3D's Encore Classes Taken from Figure 3.19

Day 1 11–11:40	Day 2 11–11:40	Day 3 Double Planning Period	Day 4 11–11:40	Day 5 11–11:40	Day 6 11–11:40
Music	PE	**1st Half** 8:20–9:00 Library **2nd Half** 9–9:40: Rotates Rotation 1: Music Rotation 2: PE Rotation 3: Library Rotation 4: PE Rotation 5: Art Rotation 6: PE	PE	Art	PE

One weakness of this plan is that the only 80-minute class that homeroom 3D receives is library (during rotation 3), because the first half (8:20–9:00) of the extended planning block for homeroom 3D is always library and the second half during rotation 3 also is library. Likewise, homerooms 3A, 3C, and 3E have double periods only in PE, 3B only in art, and 3F only in music, because those are their regularly scheduled classes on day 3, when grade 3 teachers always have their extended planning block. We would prefer to have an occasional double period for all classes in all encore areas. One way to accomplish this feat would be to schedule each grade level for a double planning period once every *seven* days rather than every six (something even we hesitate to try to depict in a chart!). Because this secondary rotation would not match perfectly with the six-day rotation, a different class would be doubled each time. Another benefit of this adaptation is that it would provide all encore teachers with a double planning period on the seventh day, making the schedule equitable for all.

Some schools (Reading First Grants) require all primary grade classrooms to teach reading during the first 90 minutes of the day; the plan outlined above would violate that rule. We address this by placing the double planning block at the end of the day, as shown in Figures 3.20 (p. 86) and 3.21 (pp. 87–88).

Creating an Extended Planning Block by Replacing the I/E Period with a Second Encore Rotation

Another approach to creating the extended planning block is to schedule the I/E periods and encore periods for each grade level back to back, as illustrated in Figure 3.22 (p. 89). We then replace the I/E period for each grade level with a second encore rotation on an occasional basis to provide the double planning period. For example, as shown in Figure 3.23a (p. 90), the normal encore rotation for four classes per grade level is PE, music, art, and library. To provide the double planning period, we insert a second encore rotation—computer lab, science lab, math lab, guidance (Figure 3.23b, p. 90)—into the I/E period. Each time the double planning period comes around, the four classes at each grade level rotate among these four additional offerings.

A variation of this format that provides common planning time for two consecutive grade levels on the double-planning-period day is illustrated in Figures 3.24 (p. 91) and 3.25 (p. 92). In this plan, the kindergarten and grade 1 teachers are able to plan together, as are the grades 2 and 3 and grades 4 and 5 teachers.

A Final Word on Scheduling Encore Classes

As accountability measures in core subjects continue to take center stage in elementary schools, encore subjects may become endangered or—even worse—reduced to make way for additional core learning time or to save money. To prevent this, we must value the encore programs and schedule them in such a way that they do not fragment the school day for teachers and students. This chapter presents numerous examples of elementary school master schedules constructed to avoid many of the past conflicts between core and encore programs. Encore classes enhance and enrich the elementary school curriculum; they should be protected and scheduled so they do not detract from core instruction. To accomplish this feat, scheduling compromises are required by *all* professionals!

References

DuFour, R., & Eaker, B. (1998). *Professional learning communities at work: Best practices for enhancing student achievement*. Bloomington, IN: National Educational Service.

Gysbers, N.C., & Henderson, P. (Eds.). (2000). *Developing and managing your school guidance program* (3rd ed.). Alexandria, VA: American Counseling Association.

William, D. (2007/2008, December/January). Changing classroom practice. *Educational Leadership, 65*(4), 36–42.

Figure 3.2 Master Schedule for Encore Blocks
(School Day Divided into 5-Minute Increments)

	8:00	9:00	10:00	11:00	12:00	1:00	2:00	2:30
Kindergarten	HR (20)				Encore/ Plan (45)			HR (10)
Grade 1	HR (20)					Encore/ Plan (45)		HR (10)
Grade 2	HR (20)						Encore/ Plan (45)	HR (10)
Grade 3	HR (20)			Encore/ Plan (45)				HR (10)
Grade 4	HR (20)		Encore/ Plan (45)					HR (10)
Grade 5	HR (20)	Encore/ Plan (45)						HR (10)
Encore	Duty (20)	Plan (45) · Grade 5	Grade 4 · Grade 3	Lunch (45)	Kinder.	Grade 1	Grade 2	Duty(10)

Note: This figure, as do all figures in this book, shows the school day divided into 5-minute increments. The accuracy of the typesetting process does not allow us to print the time in every 5-minute slot clearly. We do print the time each hour; times printed refer to the line to the left. The CD-ROM that accompanies this book, however, does have times printed evey 5 minutes. These charts, when printed on an inkjet or laser printer, will be clear.

Figure 3.3 Four-Day Encore Rotation (Entire School)

8:00-8:20	Duty			
8:20-9:05	Plan			
9:05-9:50	Day 1	Day 2	Day 3	Day 4
Teacher 5A	Music	PE	Art	Lib.
Teacher 5B	Lib.	Music	PE	Art
Teacher 5C	Art	Lib.	Music	PE
Teacher 5D	PE	Art	Lib.	Music
9:50-10:35	Day 1	Day 2	Day 3	Day 4
Teacher 4A	Music	PE	Art	Lib.
Teacher 4B	Lib.	Music	PE	Art
Teacher 4C	Art	Lib.	Music	PE
Teacher 4D	PE	Art	Lib.	Music
10:35-11:20	Day 1	Day 2	Day 3	Day 4
Teacher 3A	Music	PE	Art	Lib.
Teacher 3B	Lib.	Music	PE	Art
Teacher 3C	Art	Lib.	Music	PE
Teacher 3D	PE	Art	Lib.	Music

11:20-12:05	Lunch			
12:05-12:50	Day 1	Day 2	Day 3	Day 4
Teacher KA	Music	PE	Art	Lib.
Teacher KB	Lib.	Music	PE	Art
Teacher KC	Art	Lib.	Music	PE
Teacher KD	PE	Art	Lib.	Music
12:50-1:35	Day 1	Day 2	Day 3	Day 4
Teacher 1A	Music	PE	Art	Lib.
Teacher 1B	Lib.	Music	PE	Art
Teacher 1C	Art	Lib.	Music	PE
Teacher 1D	PE	Art	Lib.	Music
1:35-2:20	Day 1	Day 2	Day 3	Day 4
Teacher 2A	Music	PE	Art	Lib.
Teacher 2B	Lib.	Music	PE	Art
Teacher 2C	Art	Lib.	Music	PE
Teacher 2D	PE	Art	Lib.	Music
2:20-2:30	Duty			

Figure 3.4 Encore Teachers' Schedules (Four-Day Rotation)

a. Music Schedule

	8:00	9:00	10:00	11:00	12:00	1:00	2:00	2:30
Day 1	Duty	Plan (45)	Teacher 5A	Teacher 4A	Teacher 3A	Lunch/Duty (45)	Teacher KA	Teacher 1A	Teacher 2A	Duty
Day 2	Duty	Plan (45)	Teacher 5B	Teacher 4B	Teacher 3B	Lunch/Duty (45)	Teacher KB	Teacher 1B	Teacher 2B	Duty
Day 3	Duty	Plan (45)	Teacher 5C	Teacher 4C	Teacher 3C	Lunch/Duty (45)	Teacher KC	Teacher 1C	Teacher 2C	Duty
Day 4	Duty	Plan (45)	Teacher 5D	Teacher 4D	Teacher 3D	Lunch/Duty (45)	Teacher KD	Teacher 1D	Teacher 2D	Duty

b. PE Schedule

	8:00	9:00	10:00	11:00	12:00	1:00	2:00	2:30
Day 1	Duty	Plan (45)	Teacher 5D	Teacher 4D	Teacher 3D	Lunch/Duty (45)	Teacher KD	Teacher 1D	Teacher 2D	Duty
Day 2	Duty	Plan (45)	Teacher 5A	Teacher 4A	Teacher 3A	Lunch/Duty (45)	Teacher KA	Teacher 1A	Teacher 2A	Duty
Day 3	Duty	Plan (45)	Teacher 5B	Teacher 4B	Teacher 3B	Lunch/Duty (45)	Teacher KB	Teacher 1B	Teacher 2B	Duty
Day 4	Duty	Plan (45)	Teacher 5C	Teacher 4C	Teacher 3C	Lunch/Duty (45)	Teacher KC	Teacher 1C	Teacher 2C	Duty

c. Art Schedule

	8:00	9:00	10:00	11:00	12:00	1:00	2:00	2:30
Day 1	Duty	Plan (45)	Teacher 5C	Teacher 4C	Teacher 3C	Lunch/Duty (45)	Teacher KC	Teacher 1C	Teacher 2C	Duty
Day 2	Duty	Plan (45)	Teacher 5D	Teacher 4D	Teacher 3D	Lunch/Duty (45)	Teacher KD	Teacher 1D	Teacher 2D	Duty
Day 3	Duty	Plan (45)	Teacher 5A	Teacher 4A	Teacher 3A	Lunch/Duty (45)	Teacher KA	Teacher 1A	Teacher 2A	Duty
Day 4	Duty	Plan (45)	Teacher 5B	Teacher 4B	Teacher 3B	Lunch/Duty (45)	Teacher KB	Teacher 1B	Teacher 2B	Duty

d. Library Media Schedule

	8:00	9:00	10:00	11:00	12:00	1:00	2:00	2:30
Day 1	Duty	Plan (45)	Teacher 5B	Teacher 4B	Teacher 3B	Lunch/Duty (45)	Teacher KB	Teacher 1B	Teacher 2B	Duty
Day 2	Duty	Plan (45)	Teacher 5C	Teacher 4C	Teacher 3C	Lunch/Duty (45)	Teacher KC	Teacher 1C	Teacher 2C	Duty
Day 3	Duty	Plan (45)	Teacher 5D	Teacher 4D	Teacher 3D	Lunch/Duty (45)	Teacher KD	Teacher 1D	Teacher 2D	Duty
Day 4	Duty	Plan (45)	Teacher 5A	Teacher 4A	Teacher 3A	Lunch/Duty (45)	Teacher KA	Teacher 1A	Teacher 2A	Duty

Figure 3.5 District Allocations (Four-Day Rotation)

		Day 1	Day 2	Day 3	Day 4	Music	PE	Art	Library
						FTEs Required			
School III	Homeroom Teacher A	Music Teacher A	PE Teacher A	Art Teacher A	Librarian A				
	Homeroom Teacher B	Librarian A	Music Teacher A	PE Teacher A	Art Teacher A				
	Homeroom Teacher C	Art Teacher A	Librarian A	Music Teacher A	PE Teacher A				
	Homeroom Teacher D	PE Teacher A	Art Teacher A	Librarian A	Music Teacher A	1	1	1	1
		Day 1	Day 2	Day 3	Day 4	Music	PE	Art	Library
						FTEs Required			
School IV	Homeroom Teacher A	Music Teacher B	PE Teacher B	Art Teacher B	Librarian B				
	Homeroom Teacher B	Librarian B	Music Teacher B	PE Teacher B	Art Teacher B				
	Homeroom Teacher C	Art Teacher B	Librarian B	Music Teacher B	PE Teacher B				
	Homeroom Teacher D	PE Teacher B	Art Teacher B	Librarian B	Music Teacher B	1	1	1	1
		Day 1	Day 2	Day 3	Day 4	Music	PE	Art	Library
						FTEs Required			
School I	Homeroom Teacher A	Music Teacher C	PE Teacher C	Art Teacher C	Librarian C				
	Homeroom Teacher B	Librarian C	Music Teacher C	PE Teacher C	Art Teacher C				
	Homeroom Teacher C	Art Teacher C	Librarian C	Music Teacher C	PE Teacher C				
	Homeroom Teacher D	PE Teacher C	Art Teacher C	Librarian C	Music Teacher C				
	Homeroom Teacher E	Music Teacher D	PE Teacher D	Art Teacher D	Librarian D				
	Homeroom Teacher F	Librarian D	Music Teacher D	PE Teacher D	Art Teacher D	1.5	1.5	1.5	1.5

3.4
3.5

Figure 3.5 District Allocations (Four-Day Rotation), cont'd

		Day 1	Day 2	Day 3	Day 4	FTEs Required			
						Music	PE	Art	Library
School VI	Homeroom Teacher A	Art Teacher D	Librarian D	Music Teacher D	PE Teacher D				
	Homeroom Teacher B	PE Teacher D	Art Teacher D	Librarian D	Music Teacher D	0.5	0.5	0.5	0.5
		Day 1	Day 2	Day 3	Day 4	FTEs Required			
						Music	PE	Art	Library
School II	Homeroom Teacher A	Music Teacher E	PE Teacher E	Art Teacher E	Librarian E				
	Homeroom Teacher B	Librarian E	Music Teacher E	PE Teacher E	Art Teacher E				
	Homeroom Teacher C	Art Teacher E	Librarian E	Music Teacher E	PE Teacher E				
	Homeroom Teacher D	PE Teacher E	Art Teacher E	Librarian E	Music Teacher E				
	Homeroom Teacher E	Music Teacher F	PE Teacher F	Art Teacher F	Librarian F	1.25	1.25	1.25	1.25
		Day 1	Day 2	Day 3	Day 4	FTEs Required			
						Music	PE	Art	Library
School V	Homeroom Teacher A	Librarian F	Music Teacher F	PE Teacher F	Art Teacher F				
	Homeroom Teacher B	Art Teacher F	Librarian F	Music Teacher F	PE Teacher F				
	Homeroom Teacher C	PE Teacher F	Art Teacher F	Librarian F	Music Teacher F	0.75	0.75	0.75	0.75
						6	6	6	6
						District Totals			

Figure 3.5a Teacher Assignments (Four-Day Rotation)

		Day 1	Day 2	Day 3	Day 4	FTEs Required
						Physical Education
Physical Education	PE Teacher A	School III	School III	School III	School III	
	PE Teacher B	School IV	School IV	School IV	School IV	
	PE Teacher C	School I	School I	School I	School I	**6**
	PE Teacher D	School VI	School I	School I	School VI	
	PE Teacher E	School II	School II	School II	School II	
	PE Teacher F	School V	School II	School V	School V	
		Day 1	Day 2	Day 3	Day 4	**Music**
Music	Music Teacher A	School III	School III	School III	School III	
	Music Teacher B	School IV	School IV	School IV	School IV	
	Music Teacher C	School I	School I	School I	School I	**6**
	Music Teacher D	School I	School I	School VI	School VI	
	Music Teacher E	School II	School II	School II	School II	
	Music Teacher F	School II	School V	School V	School V	
		Day 1	Day 2	Day 3	Day 4	**Art**
Art	Art Teacher A	School III	School III	School III	School III	
	Art Teacher B	School IV	School IV	School IV	School IV	
	Art Teacher C	School I	School I	School I	School I	**6**
	Art Teacher D	School VI	School VI	School I	School I	
	Art Teacher E	School II	School II	School II	School II	
	Art Teacher F	School V	School V	School II	School V	
		Day 1	Day 2	Day 3	Day 4	**Library Media**
Library Media	Library Teacher A	School III	School III	School III	School III	
	Library Teacher B	School IV	School IV	School IV	School IV	
	Library Teacher C	School I	School I	School I	School I	**6**
	Library Teacher D	School I	School VI	School VI	School I	
	Library Teacher E	School II	School II	School II	School II	
	Library Teacher F	School V	School V	School V	School II	
	Total Encore FTEs Required					**24**

Figure 3.7 Six-Day Encore Rotation (Entire School)

8:00–8:20	Duty					
8:20–9:05	Plan					
9:05–9:50	**Day 1**	**Day 2**	**Day 3**	**Day 4**	**Day 5**	**Day 6**
Teacher 5A	PE	Art	PE	Music	PE	Lib.
Teacher 5B	Lib.	PE	Art	PE	Music	PE
Teacher 5C	PE	Lib.	PE	Art	PE	Music
Teacher 5D	Music	PE	Lib.	PE	Art	PE
9:50–10:35	**Day 1**	**Day 2**	**Day 3**	**Day 4**	**Day 5**	**Day 6**
Teacher 4A	PE	Art	PE	Music	PE	Lib.
Teacher 4B	Lib.	PE	Art	PE	Music	PE
Teacher 4C	PE	Lib.	PE	Art	PE	Music
Teacher 4D	Music	PE	Lib.	PE	Art	PE
10:35–11:20	**Day 1**	**Day 2**	**Day 3**	**Day 4**	**Day 5**	**Day 6**
Teacher 3A	PE	Art	PE	Music	PE	Lib.
Teacher 3B	Lib.	PE	Art	PE	Music	PE
Teacher 3C	PE	Lib.	PE	Art	PE	Music
Teacher 3D	Music	PE	Lib.	PE	Art	PE

11:20–12:05	Lunch					
12:05–12:50	**Day 1**	**Day 2**	**Day 3**	**Day 4**	**Day 5**	**Day 6**
Teacher KA	PE	Art	PE	Music	PE	Lib.
Teacher KB	Lib.	PE	Art	PE	Music	PE
Teacher KC	PE	Lib.	PE	Art	PE	Music
Teacher KD	Music	PE	Lib.	PE	Art	PE
12:50–1:35	**Day 1**	**Day 2**	**Day 3**	**Day 4**	**Day 5**	**Day 6**
Teacher 1A	PE	Art	PE	Music	PE	Lib.
Teacher 1B	Lib.	PE	Art	PE	Music	PE
Teacher 1C	PE	Lib.	PE	Art	PE	Music
Teacher 1D	Music	PE	Lib.	PE	Art	PE
1:35–2:20	**Day 1**	**Day 2**	**Day 3**	**Day 4**	**Day 5**	**Day 6**
Teacher 2A	PE	Art	PE	Music	PE	Lib.
Teacher 2B	Lib.	PE	Art	PE	Music	PE
Teacher 2C	PE	Lib.	PE	Art	PE	Music
Teacher 2D	Music	PE	Lib.	PE	Art	PE
2:20–2:30	Duty					

Figure 3.8 Encore Teachers' Schedules (Six-Day Rotation)

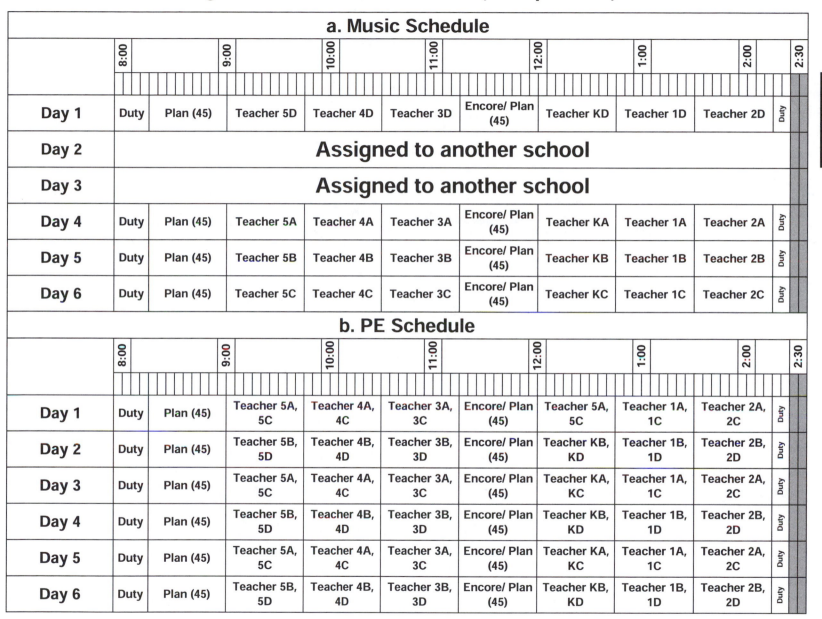

a. Music Schedule

	8:00	9:00	10:00		11:00	12:00		1:00	2:00	2:30
Day 1	Duty	Plan (45)	Teacher 5D	Teacher 4D	Teacher 3D	Encore/ Plan (45)	Teacher KD	Teacher 1D	Teacher 2D	Duty
Day 2	Assigned to another school									
Day 3	Assigned to another school									
Day 4	Duty	Plan (45)	Teacher 5A	Teacher 4A	Teacher 3A	Encore/ Plan (45)	Teacher KA	Teacher 1A	Teacher 2A	Duty
Day 5	Duty	Plan (45)	Teacher 5B	Teacher 4B	Teacher 3B	Encore/ Plan (45)	Teacher KB	Teacher 1B	Teacher 2B	Duty
Day 6	Duty	Plan (45)	Teacher 5C	Teacher 4C	Teacher 3C	Encore/ Plan (45)	Teacher KC	Teacher 1C	Teacher 2C	Duty

b. PE Schedule

	8:00	9:00	10:00		11:00	12:00		1:00	2:00	2:30
Day 1	Duty	Plan (45)	Teacher 5A, 5C	Teacher 4A, 4C	Teacher 3A, 3C	Encore/ Plan (45)	Teacher 5A, 5C	Teacher 1A, 1C	Teacher 2A, 2C	Duty
Day 2	Duty	Plan (45)	Teacher 5B, 5D	Teacher 4B, 4D	Teacher 3B, 3D	Encore/ Plan (45)	Teacher KB, KD	Teacher 1B, 1D	Teacher 2B, 2D	Duty
Day 3	Duty	Plan (45)	Teacher 5A, 5C	Teacher 4A, 4C	Teacher 3A, 3C	Encore/ Plan (45)	Teacher KA, KC	Teacher 1A, 1C	Teacher 2A, 2C	Duty
Day 4	Duty	Plan (45)	Teacher 5B, 5D	Teacher 4B, 4D	Teacher 3B, 3D	Encore/ Plan (45)	Teacher KB, KD	Teacher 1B, 1D	Teacher 2B, 2D	Duty
Day 5	Duty	Plan (45)	Teacher 5A, 5C	Teacher 4A, 4C	Teacher 3A, 3C	Encore/ Plan (45)	Teacher KA, KC	Teacher 1A, 1C	Teacher 2A, 2C	Duty
Day 6	Duty	Plan (45)	Teacher 5B, 5D	Teacher 4B, 4D	Teacher 3B, 3D	Encore/ Plan (45)	Teacher KB, KD	Teacher 1B, 1D	Teacher 2B, 2D	Duty

3.7
3.8

Figure 3.8 Encore Teachers' Schedules (Six-Day Rotation), cont'd

c. Art Schedule

	8:00	9:00	10:00	11:00	12:00	1:00	2:00	2:30
Day 1				Assigned to another school				
Day 2	Duty	Plan (45)	Teacher 5A	Teacher 4A	Teacher 3A	Encore/ Plan (45)	Teacher KA	Teacher 1A	Teacher 2A	Duty
Day 3	Duty	Plan (45)	Teacher 5B	Teacher 4B	Teacher 3B	Encore/ Plan (45)	Teacher KB	Teacher 1B	Teacher 2B	Duty
Day 4	Duty	Plan (45)	Teacher 5C	Teacher 4C	Teacher 3C	Encore/ Plan (45)	Teacher KC	Teacher 1C	Teacher 2C	Duty
Day 5	Duty	Plan (45)	Teacher 5D	Teacher 4D	Teacher 3D	Encore/ Plan (45)	Teacher KD	Teacher 1D	Teacher 2D	Duty
Day 6				Assigned to another school				

d. Library Media Schedule

	8:00	9:00	10:00	11:00	12:00	1:00	2:00	2:30
Day 1	Duty	Plan (45)	Teacher 5B	Teacher 4B	Teacher 3B	Encore/ Plan (45)	Teacher KB	Teacher 1B	Teacher 2B	Duty
Day 2	Duty	Plan (45)	Teacher 5C	Teacher 4C	Teacher 3C	Encore/ Plan (45)	Teacher KC	Teacher 1C	Teacher 2C	Duty
Day 3	Duty	Plan (45)	Teacher 5D	Teacher 4D	Teacher 3D	Encore/ Plan (45)	Teacher KD	Teacher 1D	Teacher 2D	Duty
Day 4				Assigned to another school (or Open Library Time)				
Day 5				Assigned to another school (or Open Library Time)				
Day 6	Duty	Plan (45)	Teacher 5A	Teacher 4A	Teacher 3A	Encore/ Plan (45)	Teacher KA	Teacher 1A	Teacher 2A	Duty

Figure 3.9 District Allocations (Six-Day Rotation)

		Day 1	Day 2	Day 3	Day 4	Day 5	Day 6	FTEs Required			
								Music	PE	Art	Lib.
School III	Homeroom Teacher A	PE Teacher A	Art Teacher A	PE Teacher A	*Music Teacher A*	PE Teacher A	Librarian A	0.68	2.00	0.68	0.68
	Homeroom Teacher B	Librarian A	PE Teacher A	Art Teacher A	PE Teacher A	*Music Teacher A*	PE Teacher A				
	Homeroom Teacher C	PE Teacher B	Librarian A	PE Teacher B	Art Teacher A	PE Teacher B	*Music Teacher A*				
	Homeroom Teacher D	*Music Teacher A*	PE Teacher B	Librarian A	PE Teacher B	Art Teacher A	PE Teacher B				

		Day 1	Day 2	Day 3	Day 4	Day 5	Day 6	FTEs Required			
								Music	PE	Art	Lib.
School IV	Homeroom Teacher A	PE Teacher C	*Music Teacher A*	PE Teacher C	Librarian A	PE Teacher C	Art Teacher A	0.68	2.00	0.68	0.68
	Homeroom Teacher B	Art Teacher A	PE Teacher C	*Music Teacher A*	PE Teacher C	Librarian A	PE Teacher C				
	Homeroom Teacher C	PE Teacher D	Art Teacher B	PE Teacher D	*Music Teacher B*	PE Teacher D	Librarian B				
	Homeroom Teacher D	Librarian B	PE Teacher D	Art Teacher B	PE Teacher D	*Music Teacher B*	PE Teacher D				

		Day 1	Day 2	Day 3	Day 4	Day 5	Day 6	FTEs Required			
								Music	PE	Art	Lib.
School VI	Homeroom Teacher A	PE Teacher E	Librarian B	PE Teacher E	Art Teacher B	PE Teacher E	*Music Teacher B*	0.33	1.00	0.33	0.33
	Homeroom Teacher B	*Music Teacher B*	PE Teacher E	Librarian B	PE Teacher E	Art Teacher B	PE Teacher E				

3.8
3.9

Figure 3.9 District Allocations (Six-Day Rotation), cont'd

		Day 1	Day 2	Day 3	Day 4	Day 5	Day 6	FTEs Required Music	PE	Art	Lib.
School II	Homeroom Teacher A	PE Teacher F	Music Teacher B	PE Teacher F	Librarian B	PE Teacher F	Art Teacher B				
	Homeroom Teacher B	Art Teacher B	PE Teacher F	Music Teacher B	PE Teacher F	Librarian B	PE Teacher F				
	Homeroom Teacher C	PE Teacher G	Art Teacher C	PE Teacher G	Music Teacher C	PE Teacher G	Librarian C	0.82	2.50	0.82	0.82
	Homeroom Teacher D	Librarian C	PE Teacher G	Art Teacher C	PE Teacher G	Music Teacher C	PE Teacher G				
	Homeroom Teacher E	PE Teacher H	Librarian C	PE Teacher H	Art Teacher C	PE Teacher H	Music Teacher C				
		Day 1	Day 2	Day 3	Day 4	Day 5	Day 6	FTEs Required Music	PE	Art	Lib.
School V	Homeroom Teacher A	Music Teacher C	PE Teacher H	Librarian C	PE Teacher H	Art Teacher C	PE Teacher H				
	Homeroom Teacher B	PE Teacher I	Music Teacher C	PE Teacher I	Librarian C	PE Teacher I	Art Teacher C	0.50	1.50	0.50	0.50
	Homeroom Teacher C	Art Teacher C	PE Teacher I	Music Teacher C	PE Teacher I	Librarian C	PE Teacher I				
		Day 1	Day 2	Day 3	Day 4	Day 5	Day 6	FTEs Required Music	PE	Art	Lib.
School I	Homeroom Teacher A	PE Teacher J	Art Teacher D	PE Teacher J	Music Teacher D	PE Teacher J	Librarian D				
	Homeroom Teacher B	Librarian D	PE Teacher J	Art Teacher D	PE Teacher J	Music Teacher D	PE Teacher J				
	Homeroom Teacher C	PE Teacher K	Librarian D	PE Teacher K	Art Teacher D	PE Teacher K	Music Teacher D	1.00	3.00	1.00	1.00
	Homeroom Teacher D	Music Teacher D	PE Teacher K	Librarian D	PE Teacher K	Art Teacher D	PE Teacher K				
	Homeroom Teacher E	PE Teacher L	Music Teacher D	PE Teacher L	Librarian D	PE Teacher L	Art Teacher D				
	Homeroom Teacher F	Art Teacher D	PE Teacher L	Music Teacher D	PE Teacher L	Librarian D	PE Teacher L				
								4.0	12.0	4.0	4.0

Figure 3.11 Eight-Day Encore Rotation (Entire School)

8:00-8:20	Duty

8:20-9:05	Plan

9:05-9:50	Day 1	Day 2	Day 3	Day 4	Day 5	Day 6	Day 7	Day 8
Teacher 5A	Music	PE	Art	L	Music	PE	Art	CL
Teacher 5B	L	Music	PE	Art	CL	Music	PE	Art
Teacher 5C	Art	L	Music	PE	Art	CL	Music	PE
Teacher 5D	PE	Art	L	Music	PE	Art	CL	Music

9:50-10:35	Day 1	Day 2	Day 3	Day 4	Day 5	Day 6	Day 7	Day 8
Teacher 4A	Music	PE	Art	L	Music	PE	Art	CL
Teacher 4B	L	Music	PE	Art	CL	Music	PE	Art
Teacher 4C	Art	L	Music	PE	Art	CL	Music	PE
Teacher 4D	PE	Art	L	Music	PE	Art	CL	Music

10:35-11:20	Day 1	Day 2	Day 3	Day 4	Day 5	Day 6	Day 7	Day 8
Teacher 3A	Music	PE	Art	L	Music	PE	Art	CL
Teacher 3B	L	Music	PE	Art	CL	Music	PE	Art
Teacher 3C	Art	L	Music	PE	Art	CL	Music	PE
Teacher 3D	PE	Art	L	Music	PE	Art	CL	Music

11:20-12:05	Lunch

12:05-12:50	Day 1	Day 2	Day 3	Day 4	Day 5	Day 6	Day 7	Day 8
Teacher KA	Music	PE	Art	CL	Music	PE	Art	L
Teacher KB	CL	Music	PE	Art	L	Music	PE	Art
Teacher KC	Art	CL	Music	PE	Art	L	Music	PE
Teacher KD	PE	Art	CL	Music	PE	Art	L	Music

12:50-1:35	Day 1	Day 2	Day 3	Day 4	Day 5	Day 6	Day 7	Day 8
Teacher 1A	Music	PE	Art	CL	Music	PE	Art	L
Teacher 1B	CL	Music	PE	Art	L	Music	PE	Art
Teacher 1C	Art	CL	Music	PE	Art	L	Music	PE
Teacher 1D	PE	Art	CL	Music	PE	Art	L	Music

1:35-2:20	Day 1	Day 2	Day 3	Day 4	Day 5	Day 6	Day 7	Day 8
Teacher 2A	Music	PE	Art	CL	Music	PE	Art	L
Teacher 2B	CL	Music	PE	Art	L	Music	PE	Art
Teacher 2C	Art	CL	Music	PE	Art	L	Music	PE
Teacher 2D	PE	Art	CL	Music	PE	Art	L	Music

2:20-2:30	Duty

3.9
3.11

Figure 3.12 Encore Teachers' Schedules (Eight-Day Rotation)

a. Music Schedule

	8:00	9:00	10:00	11:00	12:00	1:00	2:00	2:30
Day 1	Duty	Plan (45)	Teacher 5A	Teacher 4A	Teacher 3A	Lunch/Duty (45)	Teacher KA	Teacher 1A	Teacher 2A	Duty
Day 2	Duty	Plan (45)	Teacher 5B	Teacher 4B	Teacher 3B	Lunch/Duty (45)	Teacher KB	Teacher 1B	Teacher 2B	Duty
Day 3	Duty	Plan (45)	Teacher 5C	Teacher 4C	Teacher 3C	Lunch/Duty (45)	Teacher KC	Teacher 1C	Teacher 2C	Duty
Day 4	Duty	Plan (45)	Teacher 5D	Teacher 4D	Teacher 3D	Lunch/Duty (45)	Teacher KD	Teacher 1D	Teacher 2D	Duty
Day 5	Duty	Plan (45)	Teacher 5A	Teacher 4A	Teacher 3A	Lunch/Duty (45)	Teacher KA	Teacher 1A	Teacher 2A	Duty
Day 6	Duty	Plan (45)	Teacher 5B	Teacher 4B	Teacher 3B	Lunch/Duty (45)	Teacher KB	Teacher 1B	Teacher 2B	Duty
Day 7	Duty	Plan (45)	Teacher 5C	Teacher 4C	Teacher 3C	Lunch/Duty (45)	Teacher KC	Teacher 1C	Teacher 2C	Duty
Day 8	Duty	Plan (45)	Teacher 5D	Teacher 4D	Teacher 3D	Lunch/Duty (45)	Teacher KD	Teacher 1D	Teacher 2D	Duty

b. PE Schedule

	8:00	9:00	10:00	11:00	12:00	1:00	2:00	2:30
Day 1	Duty	Plan (45)	Teacher 5D	Teacher 4D	Teacher 3D	Lunch/Duty (45)	Teacher KD	Teacher 1D	Teacher 2D	Duty
Day 2	Duty	Plan (45)	Teacher 5A	Teacher 4A	Teacher 3A	Lunch/Duty (45)	Teacher KA	Teacher 1A	Teacher 2A	Duty
Day 3	Duty	Plan (45)	Teacher 5B	Teacher 4B	Teacher 3B	Lunch/Duty (45)	Teacher KB	Teacher 1B	Teacher 2B	Duty
Day 4	Duty	Plan (45)	Teacher 5C	Teacher 4C	Teacher 3C	Lunch/Duty (45)	Teacher KC	Teacher 1C	Teacher 2C	Duty
Day 5	Duty	Plan (45)	Teacher 5D	Teacher 4D	Teacher 3D	Lunch/Duty (45)	Teacher KD	Teacher 1D	Teacher 2D	Duty
Day 6	Duty	Plan (45)	Teacher 5A	Teacher 4A	Teacher 3A	Lunch/Duty (45)	Teacher KA	Teacher 1A	Teacher 2A	Duty
Day 7	Duty	Plan (45)	Teacher 5B	Teacher 4B	Teacher 3B	Lunch/Duty (45)	Teacher KB	Teacher 1B	Teacher 2B	Duty
Day 8	Duty	Plan (45)	Teacher 5C	Teacher 4C	Teacher 3C	Lunch/Duty (45)	Teacher KC	Teacher 1C	Teacher 2C	Duty

Figure 3.12 Encore Teachers' Schedules (Eight-Day Rotation), cont'd

c. Art Schedule

	8:00	9:00	10:00	11:00	12:00	1:00	2:00	2:30
Day 1	Duty	Plan (45)	Teacher 5C	Teacher 4C	Teacher 3C	Lunch/ Duty (45)	Teacher KC	Teacher 1C	Teacher 2C	Duty
Day 2	Duty	Plan (45)	Teacher 5D	Teacher 4D	Teacher 3D	Lunch/ Duty (45)	Teacher KD	Teacher 1D	Teacher 2D	Duty
Day 3	Duty	Plan (45)	Teacher 5A	Teacher 4A	Teacher 3A	Lunch/ Duty (45)	Teacher KA	Teacher 1A	Teacher 2A	Duty
Day 4	Duty	Plan (45)	Teacher 5B	Teacher 4B	Teacher 3B	Lunch/ Duty (45)	Teacher KB	Teacher 1B	Teacher 2B	Duty
Day 5	Duty	Plan (45)	Teacher 5C	Teacher 4C	Teacher 3C	Lunch/ Duty (45)	Teacher KC	Teacher 1C	Teacher 2C	Duty
Day 6	Duty	Plan (45)	Teacher 5D	Teacher 4D	Teacher 3D	Lunch/ Duty (45)	Teacher KD	Teacher 1D	Teacher 2D	Duty
Day 7	Duty	Plan (45)	Teacher 5A	Teacher 4A	Teacher 3A	Lunch/ Duty (45)	Teacher KA	Teacher 1A	Teacher 2A	Duty
Day 8	Duty	Plan (45)	Teacher 5B	Teacher 4B	Teacher 3B	Lunch/ Duty (45)	Teacher KB	Teacher 1B	Teacher 2B	Duty

d. Library Media Schedule

	8:00	9:00	10:00	11:00	12:00	1:00	2:00	2:30
Day 1	Duty	Plan (45)	Teacher 5B	Teacher 4B	Teacher 3B	Lunch/ Duty (45)				Duty
Day 2	Duty	Plan (45)	Teacher 5C	Teacher 4C	Teacher 3C	Lunch/ Duty (45)				Duty
Day 3	Duty	Plan (45)	Teacher 5D	Teacher 4D	Teacher 3D	Lunch/ Duty (45)				Duty
Day 4	Duty	Plan (45)	Teacher 5A	Teacher 4A	Teacher 3A	Lunch/ Duty (45)				Duty
Day 5	Duty	Plan (45)				Lunch/ Duty (45)	Teacher KB	Teacher 1B	Teacher 2B	Duty
Day 6	Duty	Plan (45)				Lunch/ Duty (45)	Teacher KC	Teacher 1C	Teacher 2C	Duty
Day 7	Duty	Plan (45)				Lunch/ Duty (45)	Teacher KD	Teacher 1D	Teacher 2D	Duty
Day 8	Duty	Plan (45)				Lunch/ Duty (45)	Teacher KA	Teacher 1A	Teacher 2A	Duty

3.12
3.12

Figure 3.12 Encore Teachers' Schedules (Eight-Day Rotation), cont'd

e. Computer Lab Schedule										
	8:00	**9:00**		**10:00**		**11:00**	**12:00**	**1:00**	**2:00**	**2:30**
Day 1	Duty	Plan (45)					Lunch/ Duty (45)	Teacher KB	Teacher 1B	Teacher 2B	Duty
Day 2	Duty	Plan (45)					Lunch/ Duty (45)	Teacher KC	Teacher 1C	Teacher 2C	Duty
Day 3	Duty	Plan (45)					Lunch/ Duty (45)	Teacher KD	Teacher 1D	Teacher 2D	Duty
Day 4	Duty	Plan (45)					Lunch/ Duty (45)	Teacher KA	Teacher 1A	Teacher 2A	Duty
Day 5	Duty	Plan (45)	Teacher 5B	Teacher 4B	Teacher 3B		Lunch/ Duty (45)				Duty
Day 6	Duty	Plan (45)	Teacher 5C	Teacher 4C	Teacher 3C		Lunch/ Duty (45)				Duty
Day 7	Duty	Plan (45)	Teacher 5D	Teacher 4D	Teacher 3D		Lunch/ Duty (45)				Duty
Day 8	Duty	Plan (45)	Teacher 5A	Teacher 4A	Teacher 3A		Lunch/ Duty (45)				Duty

Figure 3.13 12-Day Encore Rotation
(Library and Guidance Share One Scheduling Slot)

8:00-8:20	Duty											

8:20-9:05	Planning											

9:05-9:50	Day 1	Day 2	Day 3	Day 4	Day 5	Day 6	Day 7	Day 8	Day 9	Day 10	Day 11	Day 12
Teacher 5A	Music	PE	Art	L	Music	PE	Art	L	Music	PE	Art	G
Teacher 5B	L	Music	PE	Art	L	Music	PE	Art	G	Music	PE	Art
Teacher 5C	Art	L	Music	PE	Art	L	Music	PE	Art	G	Music	PE
Teacher 5D	PE	Art	L	Music	PE	Art	L	Music	PE	Art	G	Music

9:50-10:35	Day 1	Day 2	Day 3	Day 4	Day 5	Day 6	Day 7	Day 8	Day 9	Day 10	Day 11	Day 12
Teacher 4A	Music	PE	Art	L	Music	PE	Art	L	Music	PE	Art	G
Teacher 4B	L	Music	PE	Art	L	Music	PE	Art	G	Music	PE	Art
Teacher 4C	Art	L	Music	PE	Art	L	Music	PE	Art	G	Music	PE
Teacher 4D	PE	Art	L	Music	PE	Art	L	Music	PE	Art	G	Music

10:35-11:20	Day 1	Day 2	Day 3	Day 4	Day 5	Day 6	Day 7	Day 8	Day 9	Day 10	Day 11	Day 12
Teacher 3A	Music	PE	Art	G	Music	PE	Art	L	Music	PE	Art	L
Teacher 3B	G	Music	PE	Art	L	Music	PE	Art	L	Music	PE	Art
Teacher 3C	Art	G	Music	PE	Art	L	Music	PE	Art	L	Music	PE
Teacher 3D	PE	Art	G	Music	PE	Art	L	Music	PE	Art	L	Music

11:20-12:05	Lunch											

12:05-12:50	Day 1	Day 2	Day 3	Day 4	Day 5	Day 6	Day 7	Day 8	Day 9	Day 10	Day 11	Day 12
Teacher KA	Music	PE	Art	G	Music	PE	Art	L	Music	PE	Art	L
Teacher KB	G	Music	PE	Art	L	Music	PE	Art	L	Music	PE	Art
Teacher KC	Art	G	Music	PE	Art	L	Music	PE	Art	L	Music	PE
Teacher KD	PE	Art	G	Music	PE	Art	L	Music	PE	Art	L	Music

12:50-1:35	Day 1	Day 2	Day 3	Day 4	Day 5	Day 6	Day 7	Day 8	Day 9	Day 10	Day 11	Day 12
Teacher 1A	Music	PE	Art	L	Music	PE	Art	G	Music	PE	Art	L
Teacher 1B	L	Music	PE	Art	G	Music	PE	Art	L	Music	PE	Art
Teacher 1C	Art	L	Music	PE	Art	G	Music	PE	Art	L	Music	PE
Teacher 1D	PE	Art	L	Music	PE	Art	G	Music	PE	Art	L	Music

1:35-2:20	Day 9	Day 10	Day 11	Day 12	Day 1	Day 2	Day 3	Day 4	Day 9	Day 10	Day 11	Day 12
Teacher 2A	Music	PE	Art	L	Music	PE	Art	G	Music	PE	Art	L
Teacher 2B	L	Music	PE	Art	G	Music	PE	Art	L	Music	PE	Art
Teacher 2C	Art	L	Music	PE	Art	G	Music	PE	Art	L	Music	PE
Teacher 2D	PE	Art	L	Music	PE	Art	G	Music	PE	Art	L	Music

2:20-2:30	Duty											

Figure 3.14 Encore Teachers' Schedules (12-Day Rotation)
(Library and Guidance Share One Scheduling Slot)

a. Music Schedule

	8:00	9:00	10:00	11:00		12:00	1:00	2:00	2:30
Day 1	Duty	Plan (45)	Teacher 5A	Teacher 4A	Teacher 3A	Lunch/Duty (45)	Teacher KA	Teacher 1A	Teacher 2A	Duty
Day 2	Duty	Plan (45)	Teacher 5B	Teacher 4B	Teacher 3B	Lunch/Duty (45)	Teacher KB	Teacher 1B	Teacher 2B	Duty
Day 3	Duty	Plan (45)	Teacher 5C	Teacher 4C	Teacher 3C	Lunch/Duty (45)	Teacher KC	Teacher 1C	Teacher 2C	Duty
Day 4	Duty	Plan (45)	Teacher 5D	Teacher 4D	Teacher 3D	Lunch/Duty (45)	Teacher KD	Teacher 1D	Teacher 2D	Duty
Day 5	Duty	Plan (45)	Teacher 5A	Teacher 4A	Teacher 3A	Lunch/Duty (45)	Teacher KA	Teacher 1A	Teacher 2A	Duty
Day 6	Duty	Plan (45)	Teacher 5B	Teacher 4B	Teacher 3B	Lunch/Duty (45)	Teacher KB	Teacher 1B	Teacher 2B	Duty
Day 7	Duty	Plan (45)	Teacher 5C	Teacher 4C	Teacher 3C	Lunch/Duty (45)	Teacher KC	Teacher 1C	Teacher 2C	Duty
Day 8	Duty	Plan (45)	Teacher 5D	Teacher 4D	Teacher 3D	Lunch/Duty (45)	Teacher KD	Teacher 1D	Teacher 2D	Duty
Day 9	Duty	Plan (45)	Teacher 5A	Teacher 4A	Teacher 3A	Lunch/Duty (45)	Teacher KA	Teacher 1A	Teacher 2A	Duty
Day 10	Duty	Plan (45)	Teacher 5B	Teacher 4B	Teacher 3B	Lunch/Duty (45)	Teacher KB	Teacher 1B	Teacher 2B	Duty
Day 11	Duty	Plan (45)	Teacher 5C	Teacher 4C	Teacher 3C	Lunch/Duty (45)	Teacher KC	Teacher 1C	Teacher 2C	Duty
Day 12	Duty	Plan (45)	Teacher 5D	Teacher 4D	Teacher 3D	Lunch/Duty (45)	Teacher KD	Teacher 1D	Teacher 2D	Duty

b. PE Schedule

	8:00	9:00	10:00	11:00		12:00	1:00	2:00	2:30
Day 1	Duty	Plan (45)	Teacher 5D	Teacher 4D	Teacher 3D	Lunch/Duty (45)	Teacher KD	Teacher 1D	Teacher 2D	Duty
Day 2	Duty	Plan (45)	Teacher 5A	Teacher 4A	Teacher 3A	Lunch/Duty (45)	Teacher KA	Teacher 1A	Teacher 2A	Duty
Day 3	Duty	Plan (45)	Teacher 5B	Teacher 4B	Teacher 3B	Lunch/Duty (45)	Teacher KB	Teacher 1B	Teacher 2B	Duty
Day 4	Duty	Plan (45)	Teacher 5C	Teacher 4C	Teacher 3C	Lunch/Duty (45)	Teacher KC	Teacher 1C	Teacher 2C	Duty
Day 5	Duty	Plan (45)	Teacher 5D	Teacher 4D	Teacher 3D	Lunch/Duty (45)	Teacher KD	Teacher 1D	Teacher 2D	Duty
Day 6	Duty	Plan (45)	Teacher 5A	Teacher 4A	Teacher 3A	Lunch/Duty (45)	Teacher KA	Teacher 1A	Teacher 2A	Duty
Day 7	Duty	Plan (45)	Teacher 5B	Teacher 4B	Teacher 3B	Lunch/Duty (45)	Teacher KB	Teacher 1B	Teacher 2B	Duty
Day 8	Duty	Plan (45)	Teacher 5C	Teacher 4C	Teacher 3C	Lunch/Duty (45)	Teacher KC	Teacher 1C	Teacher 2C	Duty
Day 9	Duty	Plan (45)	Teacher 5D	Teacher 4D	Teacher 3D	Lunch/Duty (45)	Teacher KD	Teacher 1D	Teacher 2D	Duty
Day 10	Duty	Plan (45)	Teacher 5A	Teacher 4A	Teacher 3A	Lunch/Duty (45)	Teacher KA	Teacher 1A	Teacher 2A	Duty
Day 11	Duty	Plan (45)	Teacher 5B	Teacher 4B	Teacher 3B	Lunch/Duty (45)	Teacher KB	Teacher 1B	Teacher 2B	Duty
Day 12	Duty	Plan (45)	Teacher 5C	Teacher 4C	Teacher 3C	Lunch/Duty (45)	Teacher KC	Teacher 1C	Teacher 2C	Duty

Figure 3.14 Encore Teachers' Schedules (12-Day Rotation), cont'd
(Library and Guidance Share One Scheduling Slot)

c. Art Schedule

	8:00	9:00	10:00	11:00	12:00	1:00	2:00	2:30
Day 1	Duty	Plan (45)	Teacher 5C	Teacher 4C	Teacher 3C	Lunch/Duty (45)	Teacher KC	Teacher 1C	Teacher 2C	Duty
Day 2	Duty	Plan (45)	Teacher 5D	Teacher 4D	Teacher 3D	Lunch/Duty (45)	Teacher KD	Teacher 1D	Teacher 2D	Duty
Day 3	Duty	Plan (45)	Teacher 5A	Teacher 4A	Teacher 3A	Lunch/Duty (45)	Teacher KA	Teacher 1A	Teacher 2A	Duty
Day 4	Duty	Plan (45)	Teacher 5B	Teacher 4B	Teacher 3B	Lunch/Duty (45)	Teacher KB	Teacher 1B	Teacher 2B	Duty
Day 5	Duty	Plan (45)	Teacher 5C	Teacher 4C	Teacher 3C	Lunch/Duty (45)	Teacher KC	Teacher 1C	Teacher 2C	Duty
Day 6	Duty	Plan (45)	Teacher 5D	Teacher 4D	Teacher 3D	Lunch/Duty (45)	Teacher KD	Teacher 1D	Teacher 2D	Duty
Day 7	Duty	Plan (45)	Teacher 5A	Teacher 4A	Teacher 3A	Lunch/Duty (45)	Teacher KA	Teacher 1A	Teacher 2A	Duty
Day 8	Duty	Plan (45)	Teacher 5B	Teacher 4B	Teacher 3B	Lunch/Duty (45)	Teacher KB	Teacher 1B	Teacher 2B	Duty
Day 9	Duty	Plan (45)	Teacher 5C	Teacher 4C	Teacher 3C	Lunch/Duty (45)	Teacher KC	Teacher 1C	Teacher 2C	Duty
Day 10	Duty	Plan (45)	Teacher 5D	Teacher 4D	Teacher 3D	Lunch/Duty (45)	Teacher KD	Teacher 1D	Teacher 2D	Duty
Day 11	Duty	Plan (45)	Teacher 5A	Teacher 4A	Teacher 3A	Lunch/Duty (45)	Teacher KA	Teacher 1A	Teacher 2A	Duty
Day 12	Duty	Plan (45)	Teacher 5B	Teacher 4B	Teacher 3B	Lunch/Duty (45)	Teacher KB	Teacher 1B	Teacher 2B	Duty

d. Library Media Schedule

	8:00	9:00	10:00	11:00	12:00	1:00	2:00	2:30
Day 1	Duty	Plan (45)	Teacher 5B	Teacher 4B		Lunch/Duty (45)		Teacher 1B	Teacher 2B	Duty
Day 2	Duty	Plan (45)	Teacher 5C	Teacher 4C		Lunch/Duty (45)		Teacher 1C	Teacher 2C	Duty
Day 3	Duty	Plan (45)	Teacher 5D	Teacher 4D		Lunch/Duty (45)		Teacher 1D	Teacher 2D	Duty
Day 4	Duty	Plan (45)	Teacher 5A	Teacher 4A		Lunch/Duty (45)		Teacher 1A	Teacher 2A	Duty
Day 5	Duty	Plan (45)	Teacher 5B	Teacher 4B	Teacher 3B	Lunch/Duty (45)	Teacher KB			Duty
Day 6	Duty	Plan (45)	Teacher 5C	Teacher 4C	Teacher 3C	Lunch/Duty (45)	Teacher KC			Duty
Day 7	Duty	Plan (45)	Teacher 5D	Teacher 4D	Teacher 3D	Lunch/Duty (45)	Teacher KD			Duty
Day 8	Duty	Plan (45)	Teacher 5A	Teacher 4A	Teacher 3A	Lunch/Duty (45)	Teacher KA			Duty
Day 9	Duty	Plan (45)			Teacher 3B	Lunch/Duty (45)	Teacher KB	Teacher 1B	Teacher 2B	Duty
Day 10	Duty	Plan (45)			Teacher 3C	Lunch/Duty (45)	Teacher KC	Teacher 1C	Teacher 2C	Duty
Day 11	Duty	Plan (45)			Teacher 3D	Lunch/Duty (45)	Teacher KD	Teacher 1D	Teacher 2D	Duty
Day 12	Duty	Plan (45)			Teacher 3A	Lunch/Duty (45)	Teacher KA	Teacher 1A	Teacher 2A	Duty

3.14
3.14

Figure 3.14 Encore Teachers' Schedules (12-Day Rotation), cont'd
(Library and Guidance Share One Scheduling Slot)

e. Guidance Schedule

	8:00	9:00	10:00	11:00	12:00	1:00	2:00	2:30
Day 1	Duty	Plan (45)		Teacher 3B	Lunch/Duty (45)	Teacher KB		Duty
Day 2	Duty	Plan (45)		Teacher 3C	Lunch/Duty (45)	Teacher KC		Duty
Day 3	Duty	Plan (45)		Teacher 3D	Lunch/Duty (45)	Teacher KD		Duty
Day 4	Duty	Plan (45)		Teacher 3A	Lunch/Duty (45)	Teacher KA		Duty
Day 5	Duty	Plan (45)			Lunch/Duty (45)	Teacher 1B	Teacher 2B	Duty
Day 6	Duty	Plan (45)			Lunch/Duty (45)	Teacher 1C	Teacher 2C	Duty
Day 7	Duty	Plan (45)			Lunch/Duty (45)	Teacher 1D	Teacher 2D	Duty
Day 8	Duty	Plan (45)			Lunch/Duty (45)	Teacher 1A	Teacher 2A	Duty
Day 9	Duty	Plan (45)	Teacher 5B	Teacher 4B	Lunch/Duty (45)			Duty
Day 10	Duty	Plan (45)	Teacher 5C	Teacher 4C	Lunch/Duty (45)			Duty
Day 11	Duty	Plan (45)	Teacher 5D	Teacher 4D	Lunch/Duty (45)			Duty
Day 12	Duty	Plan (45)	Teacher 5A	Teacher 4A	Lunch/Duty (45)			Duty

Figure 3.15 12-Day Encore Rotation
(Guidance, Library, and Computer Lab Share One Scheduling Slot)

8:00-8:20	Duty											
8:20-9:05	Planning											
9:05-9:50	Day 1	Day 2	Day 3	Day 4	Day 5	Day 6	Day 7	Day 8	Day 9	Day 10	Day 11	Day 12
Teacher 5A	Music	PE	Art	L	Music	PE	Art	CL	Music	PE	Art	G
Teacher 5B	L	Music	PE	Art	CL	Music	PE	Art	G	Music	PE	Art
Teacher 5C	Art	L	Music	PE	Art	CL	Music	PE	Art	G	Music	PE
Teacher 5D	PE	Art	L	Music	PE	Art	CL	Music	PE	Art	G	Music
9:50-10:35	Day 1	Day 2	Day 3	Day 4	Day 5	Day 6	Day 7	Day 8	Day 9	Day 10	Day 11	Day 12
Teacher 4A	Music	PE	Art	L	Music	PE	Art	CL	Music	PE	Art	G
Teacher 4B	L	Music	PE	Art	CL	Music	PE	Art	G	Music	PE	Art
Teacher 4C	Art	L	Music	PE	Art	CL	Music	PE	Art	G	Music	PE
Teacher 4D	PE	Art	L	Music	PE	Art	CL	Music	PE	Art	G	Music
10:35-11:20	Day 1	Day 2	Day 3	Day 4	Day 5	Day 6	Day 7	Day 8	Day 9	Day 10	Day 11	Day 12
Teacher 3A	Music	PE	Art	G	Music	PE	Art	L	Music	PE	Art	CL
Teacher 3B	G	Music	PE	Art	L	Music	PE	Art	CL	Music	PE	Art
Teacher 3C	Art	G	Music	PE	Art	L	Music	PE	Art	CL	Music	PE
Teacher 3D	PE	Art	G	Music	PE	Art	L	Music	PE	Art	CL	Music
11:20-12:05	Lunch											
12:05-12:50	Day 1	Day 2	Day 3	Day 4	Day 5	Day 6	Day 7	Day 8	Day 9	Day 10	Day 11	Day 12
Teacher KA	Music	PE	Art	G	Music	PE	Art	L	Music	PE	Art	CL
Teacher KB	G	Music	PE	Art	L	Music	PE	Art	CL	Music	PE	Art
Teacher KC	Art	G	Music	PE	Art	L	Music	PE	Art	CL	Music	PE
Teacher KD	PE	Art	G	Music	PE	Art	L	Music	PE	Art	CL	Music
12:50-1:35	Day 1	Day 2	Day 3	Day 4	Day 5	Day 6	Day 7	Day 8	Day 9	Day 10	Day 11	Day 12
Teacher 1A	Music	PE	Art	CL	Music	PE	Art	G	Music	PE	Art	L
Teacher 1B	CL	Music	PE	Art	G	Music	PE	Art	L	Music	PE	Art
Teacher 1C	Art	CL	Music	PE	Art	G	Music	PE	Art	L	Music	PE
Teacher 1D	PE	Art	CL	Music	PE	Art	G	Music	PE	Art	L	Music
1:35-2:20	Day 1	Day 2	Day 3	Day 4	Day 5	Day 6	Day 7	Day 8	Day 9	Day 10	Day 11	Day 12
Teacher 2A	Music	PE	Art	CL	Music	PE	Art	G	Music	PE	Art	L
Teacher 2B	CL	Music	PE	Art	G	Music	PE	Art	L	Music	PE	Art
Teacher 2C	Art	CL	Music	PE	Art	G	Music	PE	Art	L	Music	PE
Teacher 2D	PE	Art	CL	Music	PE	Art	G	Music	PE	Art	L	Music
2:20-2:30	Duty											

Figure 3.16 12-Day Encore Rotation Teachers' Schedules
(Guidance, Library, and Computer Lab Share One Scheduling Slot)

a. Music Schedule

	8:00	9:00	10:00	11:00	12:00	1:00	2:00	2:30
Day 1	Duty	Plan (45)	Teacher 5A	Teacher 4A	Teacher 3A	Lunch/Duty	Teacher KA	Teacher 1A	Teacher 2A	D
Day 2	Duty	Plan (45)	Teacher 5B	Teacher 4B	Teacher 3B	Lunch/Duty	Teacher KB	Teacher 1B	Teacher 2B	D
Day 3	Duty	Plan (45)	Teacher 5C	Teacher 4C	Teacher 3C	Lunch/Duty	Teacher KC	Teacher 1C	Teacher 2C	D
Day 4	Duty	Plan (45)	Teacher 5D	Teacher 4D	Teacher 3D	Lunch/Duty	Teacher KD	Teacher 1D	Teacher 2D	D
Day 5	Duty	Plan (45)	Teacher 5A	Teacher 4A	Teacher 3A	Lunch/Duty	Teacher KA	Teacher 1A	Teacher 2A	D
Day 6	Duty	Plan (45)	Teacher 5B	Teacher 4B	Teacher 3B	Lunch/Duty	Teacher KB	Teacher 1B	Teacher 2B	D
Day 7	Duty	Plan (45)	Teacher 5C	Teacher 4C	Teacher 3C	Lunch/Duty	Teacher KC	Teacher 1C	Teacher 2C	D
Day 8	Duty	Plan (45)	Teacher 5D	Teacher 4D	Teacher 3D	Lunch/Duty	Teacher KD	Teacher 1D	Teacher 2D	D
Day 9	Duty	Plan (45)	Teacher 5A	Teacher 4A	Teacher 3A	Lunch/Duty	Teacher KA	Teacher 1A	Teacher 2A	D
Day 10	Duty	Plan (45)	Teacher 5B	Teacher 4B	Teacher 3B	Lunch/Duty	Teacher KB	Teacher 1B	Teacher 2B	D
Day 11	Duty	Plan (45)	Teacher 5C	Teacher 4C	Teacher 3C	Lunch/Duty	Teacher KC	Teacher 1C	Teacher 2C	D
Day 12	Duty	Plan (45)	Teacher 5D	Teacher 4D	Teacher 3D	Lunch/Duty	Teacher KD	Teacher 1D	Teacher 2D	D

b. PE Schedule

	8:00	9:00	10:00	11:00	12:00	1:00	2:00	2:30
Day 1	Duty	Plan (45)	Teacher 5D	Teacher 4D	Teacher 3D	Lunch/Duty	Teacher KD	Teacher 1D	Teacher 2D	D
Day 2	Duty	Plan (45)	Teacher 5A	Teacher 4A	Teacher 3A	Lunch/Duty	Teacher KA	Teacher 1A	Teacher 2A	D
Day 3	Duty	Plan (45)	Teacher 5B	Teacher 4B	Teacher 3B	Lunch/Duty	Teacher KB	Teacher 1B	Teacher 2B	D
Day 4	Duty	Plan (45)	Teacher 5C	Teacher 4C	Teacher 3C	Lunch/Duty	Teacher KC	Teacher 1C	Teacher 2C	D
Day 5	Duty	Plan (45)	Teacher 5D	Teacher 4D	Teacher 3D	Lunch/Duty	Teacher KD	Teacher 1D	Teacher 2D	D
Day 6	Duty	Plan (45)	Teacher 5A	Teacher 4A	Teacher 3A	Lunch/Duty	Teacher KA	Teacher 1A	Teacher 2A	D
Day 7	Duty	Plan (45)	Teacher 5B	Teacher 4B	Teacher 3B	Lunch/Duty	Teacher KB	Teacher 1B	Teacher 2B	D
Day 8	Duty	Plan (45)	Teacher 5C	Teacher 4C	Teacher 3C	Lunch/Duty	Teacher KC	Teacher 1C	Teacher 2C	D
Day 9	Duty	Plan (45)	Teacher 5D	Teacher 4D	Teacher 3D	Lunch/Duty	Teacher KD	Teacher 1D	Teacher 2D	D
Day 10	Duty	Plan (45)	Teacher 5A	Teacher 4A	Teacher 3A	Lunch/Duty	Teacher KA	Teacher 1A	Teacher 2A	D
Day 11	Duty	Plan (45)	Teacher 5B	Teacher 4B	Teacher 3B	Lunch/Duty	Teacher KB	Teacher 1B	Teacher 2B	D
Day 12	Duty	Plan (45)	Teacher 5C	Teacher 4C	Teacher 3C	Lunch/Duty	Teacher KC	Teacher 1C	Teacher 2C	D

Figure 3.16 Encore Teachers' Schedules (12-Day Rotation), cont'd (Guidance, Library, and Computer Lab Share One Scheduling Slot)

c. Art Schedule

	8:00	9:00	10:00		11:00	12:00		1:00	2:00	2:30
Day 1	Duty	Plan (45)	Teacher 5C	Teacher 4C	Teacher 3C	Lunch/Duty	Teacher KC	Teacher 1C	Teacher 2C	D
Day 2	Duty	Plan (45)	Teacher 5D	Teacher 4D	Teacher 3D	Lunch/Duty	Teacher KD	Teacher 1D	Teacher 2D	D
Day 3	Duty	Plan (45)	Teacher 5A	Teacher 4A	Teacher 3A	Lunch/Duty	Teacher KA	Teacher 1A	Teacher 2A	D
Day 4	Duty	Plan (45)	Teacher 5B	Teacher 4B	Teacher 3B	Lunch/Duty	Teacher KB	Teacher 1B	Teacher 2B	D
Day 5	Duty	Plan (45)	Teacher 5C	Teacher 4C	Teacher 3C	Lunch/Duty	Teacher KC	Teacher 1C	Teacher 2C	D
Day 6	Duty	Plan (45)	Teacher 5D	Teacher 4D	Teacher 3D	Lunch/Duty	Teacher KD	Teacher 1D	Teacher 2D	D
Day 7	Duty	Plan (45)	Teacher 5A	Teacher 4A	Teacher 3A	Lunch/Duty	Teacher KA	Teacher 1A	Teacher 2A	D
Day 8	Duty	Plan (45)	Teacher 5B	Teacher 4B	Teacher 3B	Lunch/Duty	Teacher KB	Teacher 1B	Teacher 2B	D
Day 9	Duty	Plan (45)	Teacher 5C	Teacher 4C	Teacher 3C	Lunch/Duty	Teacher KC	Teacher 1C	Teacher 2C	D
Day 10	Duty	Plan (45)	Teacher 5D	Teacher 4D	Teacher 3D	Lunch/Duty	Teacher KD	Teacher 1D	Teacher 2D	D
Day 11	Duty	Plan (45)	Teacher 5A	Teacher 4A	Teacher 3A	Lunch/Duty	Teacher KA	Teacher 1A	Teacher 2A	D
Day 12	Duty	Plan (45)	Teacher 5B	Teacher 4B	Teacher 3B	Lunch/Duty	Teacher KB	Teacher 1B	Teacher 2B	D

d. Library Media Schedule

	8:00	9:00	10:00		11:00	12:00		1:00	2:00	2:30
Day 1	Duty	Plan (45)	Teacher 5B	Teacher 4B		Lunch/Duty				D
Day 2	Duty	Plan (45)	Teacher 5C	Teacher 4C		Lunch/Duty				D
Day 3	Duty	Plan (45)	Teacher 5D	Teacher 4D		Lunch/Duty				D
Day 4	Duty	Plan (45)	Teacher 5A	Teacher 4A		Lunch/Duty				D
Day 5	Duty	Plan (45)			Teacher 3B	Lunch/Duty	Teacher KB			D
Day 6	Duty	Plan (45)			Teacher 3C	Lunch/Duty	Teacher KC			D
Day 7	Duty	Plan (45)			Teacher 3D	Lunch/Duty	Teacher KD			D
Day 8	Duty	Plan (45)			Teacher 3A	Lunch/Duty	Teacher KA			D
Day 9	Duty	Plan (45)				Lunch/Duty		Teacher 1B	Teacher 2B	D
Day 10	Duty	Plan (45)				Lunch/Duty		Teacher 1C	Teacher 2C	D
Day 11	Duty	Plan (45)				Lunch/Duty		Teacher 1D	Teacher 2D	D
Day 12	Duty	Plan (45)				Lunch/Duty		Teacher 1A	Teacher 2A	D

3.16
3.16

Figure 3.16 Encore Teachers' Schedules (12-Day Rotation), cont'd
(Guidance, Library, and Computer Lab Share One Scheduling Slot)

e. Guidance Schedule

	8:00		9:00	10:00	11:00	12:00		1:00	2:00	2:30
Day 1	Duty	Plan (45)			Teacher 3B	Lunch/Duty	Teacher KB			D
Day 2	Duty	Plan (45)			Teacher 3C	Lunch/Duty	Teacher KC			D
Day 3	Duty	Plan (45)			Teacher 3D	Lunch/Duty	Teacher KD			D
Day 4	Duty	Plan (45)			Teacher 3A	Lunch/Duty	Teacher KA			D
Day 5	Duty	Plan (45)				Lunch/Duty		Teacher 1B	Teacher 2B	D
Day 6	Duty	Plan (45)				Lunch/Duty		Teacher 1C	Teacher 2C	D
Day 7	Duty	Plan (45)				Lunch/Duty		Teacher 1D	Teacher 2D	D
Day 8	Duty	Plan (45)				Lunch/Duty		Teacher 1A	Teacher 2A	D
Day 9	Duty	Plan (45)	Teacher 5B	Teacher 4B		Lunch/Duty				D
Day 10	Duty	Plan (45)	Teacher 5C	Teacher 4C		Lunch/Duty				D
Day 11	Duty	Plan (45)	Teacher 5D	Teacher 4D		Lunch/Duty				D
Day 12	Duty	Plan (45)	Teacher 5A	Teacher 4A		Lunch/Duty				D

f. Computer Lab Schedule

	8:00		9:00	10:00	11:00	12:00		1:00	2:00	2:30
Day 1	Duty	Plan (45)				Lunch/Duty		Teacher 1B	Teacher 2B	D
Day 2	Duty	Plan (45)				Lunch/Duty		Teacher 1C	Teacher 2C	D
Day 3	Duty	Plan (45)				Lunch/Duty		Teacher 1D	Teacher 2D	D
Day 4	Duty	Plan (45)				Lunch/Duty		Teacher 1A	Teacher 2A	D
Day 5	Duty	Plan (45)	Teacher 5B	Teacher 4B		Lunch/Duty				D
Day 6	Duty	Plan (45)	Teacher 5C	Teacher 4C		Lunch/Duty				D
Day 7	Duty	Plan (45)	Teacher 5D	Teacher 4D		Lunch/Duty				D
Day 8	Duty	Plan (45)	Teacher 5A	Teacher 4A		Lunch/Duty				D
Day 9	Duty	Plan (45)			Teacher 3B	Lunch/Duty	Teacher KB			D
Day 10	Duty	Plan (45)			Teacher 3C	Lunch/Duty	Teacher KC			D
Day 11	Duty	Plan (45)			Teacher 3D	Lunch/Duty	Teacher KD			D
Day 12	Duty	Plan (45)			Teacher 3A	Lunch/Duty	Teacher KA			D

Figure 3.17 District Allocation for the Eight-Day Rotation

School III

		Day 1	Day 2	Day 3	Day 4	Day 5	Day 6	Day 7	Day 8	Music	PE	Art	Library
											FTEs Required		
	Homeroom Teacher A	Music Teacher A	PE Teacher A	Art Teacher A	Library/ Guidance	Music Teacher A	PE Teacher A	Art Teacher A	Library/ Guidance				
	Homeroom Teacher B	Library/ Guidance	Music Teacher A	PE Teacher A	Art Teacher A	Library/ Guidance	Music Teacher A	PE Teacher A	Art Teacher A				
	Homeroom Teacher C	Art Teacher A	Library/ Guidance	Music Teacher A	PE Teacher A	Art Teacher A	Library/ Guidance	Music Teacher A	PE Teacher A				
	Homeroom Teacher D	PE Teacher A	Art Teacher A	Library/ Guidance	Music Teacher A	PE Teacher A	Art Teacher A	Library/ Guidance	Music Teacher A	1	1	1	1

School IV

		Day 1	Day 2	Day 3	Day 4	Day 5	Day 6	Day 7	Day 8	Music	PE	Art	Library
											FTEs Required		
	Homeroom Teacher A	Music Teacher B	PE Teacher B	Art Teacher B	Library/ Guidance	Music Teacher B	PE Teacher B	Art Teacher B	Library/ Guidance				
	Homeroom Teacher B	Library/ Guidance	Music Teacher B	PE Teacher B	Art Teacher B	Library/ Guidance	Music Teacher B	PE Teacher B	Art Teacher B				
	Homeroom Teacher C	Art Teacher B	Library/ Guidance	Music Teacher B	PE Teacher B	Art Teacher B	Library/ Guidance	Music Teacher B	PE Teacher B				
	Homeroom Teacher D	PE Teacher B	Art Teacher B	Library/ Guidance	Music Teacher B	PE Teacher B	Art Teacher B	Library/ Guidance	Music Teacher B	1	1	1	1

School I

		Day 1	Day 2	Day 3	Day 4	Day 5	Day 6	Day 7	Day 8	Music	PE	Art	Library
											FTEs Required		
	Homeroom Teacher A	Music Teacher C	PE Teacher C	Art Teacher C	Library/ Guidance	Music Teacher C	PE Teacher C	Art Teacher C	Library/ Guidance				
	Homeroom Teacher B	Library/ Guidance	Music Teacher C	PE Teacher C	Art Teacher C	Library/ Guidance	Music Teacher C	PE Teacher C	Art Teacher C				
	Homeroom Teacher C	Art Teacher C	Library/ Guidance	Music Teacher C	PE Teacher C	Art Teacher C	Library/ Guidance	Music Teacher C	PE Teacher C				
	Homeroom Teacher D	PE Teacher C	Art Teacher C	Library/ Guidance	Music Teacher C	PE Teacher C	Art Teacher C	Library/ Guidance	Music Teacher C				
	Homeroom Teacher E	Music Teacher D	PE Teacher D	Art Teacher D	Library/ Guidance	Music Teacher D	PE Teacher D	Art Teacher D	Library/ Guidance				
	Homeroom Teacher F	Library/ Guidance	Music Teacher D	PE Teacher D	Art Teacher D	Library/ Guidance	Music Teacher D	PE Teacher D	Art Teacher D	1.5	1.5	1.5	1

Figure 3.17 District Allocation for the Eight-Day Rotation, cont'd

		Day 1	Day 2	Day 3	Day 4	Day 5	Day 6	Day 7	Day 8	Music	PE	Art	Library
School VI	Homeroom Teacher A	Art Teacher D	Library/ Guidance	Music Teacher D	PE Teacher D	Art Teacher D	Library/ Guidance	Music Teacher D	PE Teacher D				
	Homeroom Teacher B	PE Teacher D	Art Teacher D	Library/ Guidance	Music Teacher D	PE Teacher D	Art Teacher D	Library/ Guidance	Music Teacher D	0.5	0.5	0.5	1

		Day 1	Day 2	Day 3	Day 4	Day 5	Day 6	Day 7	Day 8	Music	PE	Art	Library
School II	Homeroom Teacher A	Music Teacher E	PE Teacher E	Art Teacher E	Library/ Guidance	Music Teacher E	PE Teacher E	Art Teacher E	Library/ Guidance				
	Homeroom Teacher B	Library/ Guidance	Music Teacher E	PE Teacher E	Art Teacher E	Library/ Guidance	Music Teacher E	PE Teacher E	Art Teacher E				
	Homeroom Teacher C	Art Teacher E	Library/ Guidance	Music Teacher E	PE Teacher E	Art Teacher E	Library/ Guidance	Music Teacher E	PE Teacher E				
	Homeroom Teacher D	PE Teacher E	Art Teacher E	Library/ Guidance	Music Teacher E	PE Teacher E	Art Teacher E	Library/ Guidance	Music Teacher E				
	Homeroom Teacher E	Music Teacher F	PE Teacher F	Art Teacher F	Library/ Guidance	Music Teacher F	PE Teacher F	Art Teacher F	Library/ Guidance	1.25	1.25	1.25	1

		Day 1	Day 2	Day 3	Day 4	Day 5	Day 6	Day 7	Day 8	Music	PE	Art	Library
School V	Homeroom Teacher A	Library/ Guidance	Music Teacher F	PE Teacher F	Art Teacher F	Library/ Guidance	Music Teacher F	PE Teacher F	Art Teacher F				
	Homeroom Teacher B	Art Teacher F	Library/ Guidance	Music Teacher F	PE Teacher F	Art Teacher F	Library/ Guidance	Music Teacher F	PE Teacher F				
	Homeroom Teacher C	PE Teacher F	Art Teacher F	Library/ Guidance	Music Teacher F	PE Teacher F	Art Teacher F	Library/ Guidance	Music Teacher F	0.75	0.75	0.75	1
										6	6	6	6

District Totals

Figure 3.18 Master Schedule for Extended A.M. Planning Blocks

	8:00	9:00	10:00	11:00	12:00	1:00	2:00	2:30
Kindergarten	HR (20)				Encore/ Plan (40)			HR (10)
Grade 1	HR (20)					Encore/ Plan (40)		HR (10)
Grade 2	HR (20)						Encore/ Plan (40)	HR (10)
Grade 3	HR (20)			Encore/ Plan (40)				HR (10)
Grade 4	HR (20)		Encore/ Plan (40)					HR (10)
Grade 5	HR (20)	Encore/ Plan (40)						HR (10)
Encore	Duty (20)	Extended Planning Block (80)	Grade 5 / Grade 4	Grade 3	Lunch (40)	Kinder.	Grade 1 / Grade 2	Duty

3.17
3.18

Figure 3.19 Six-Day Encore Rotation with Extended A.M. Planning Period Every Six Days

8:00-8:20	Duty					
8:20-9:00	Extended Planning Blocks-First 40 Minutes					
	Day 1	Day 2	Day 3	Day 4	Day 5	Day 6
	PE-5A	Art-4A	PE-3A	Music-KA	PE-1A	L-2A
	L-5B	PE-4B	Art-3B	PE-KB	Music-1B	PE-2B
	PE-5C	L-4C	PE-3C	Art-KC	PE-1C	Music-2C
	Music-5D	PE-4D	L-3D	PE-KD	Art-1D	PE-2D
	PE-5E	Music-4E	PE-3E	L-KE	PE-1E	Art-2E
	Art-5F	PE-4F	Music-3F	PE-KF	L-1F	PE-2F
9:00-9:40	Extended Planning Blocks-Second 40 Minutes					
	Day 1	Day 2	Day 3	Day 4	Day 5	Day 6
	Grade 5	Grade 4	Grade 3	Grade K	Grade 1	Grade 2
	All grades follow the rotation below for the second 40 minutes of the extended planning block on their scheduled day (immediately above this note).					
All Grades	Rotation 1	Rotation 2	Rotation 3	Rotation 4	Rotation 5	Rotation 6
Class A	PE	Art	PE	Music	PE	L
Class B	L	PE	Art	PE	Music	PE
Class C	PE	L	PE	Art	PE	Music
Class D	Music	PE	L	PE	Art	PE
Class E	PE	Music	PE	L	PE	Art
Class F	Art	PE	Music	PE	L	PE

Figure 3.19 Six-Day Encore Rotation with Extended A.M. Planning Period Every Six Days, cont'd

9:40-10:20	Day 1	Day 2	Day 3	Day 4	Day 5	Day 6
Teacher 5A	Core	Art	PE	Music	PE	L
Teacher 5B	Core	PE	Art	PE	Music	PE
Teacher 5C	Core	L	PE	Art	PE	Music
Teacher 5D	Core	PE	L	PE	Art	PE
Teacher 5E	Core	Music	PE	L	PE	Art
Teacher 5F	Core	PE	Music	PE	L	PE

10:20-11:00	Day 1	Day 2	Day 3	Day 4	Day 5	Day 6
Teacher 4A	PE	Core	PE	Music	PE	L
Teacher 4B	L	Core	Art	PE	Music	PE
Teacher 4C	PE	Core	PE	Art	PE	Music
Teacher 4D	Music	Core	L	PE	Art	PE
Teacher 4E	PE	Core	PE	L	PE	Art
Teacher 4F	Art	Core	Music	PE	L	PE

11:00-11:40	Day 1	Day 2	Day 3	Day 4	Day 5	Day 6
Teacher 3A	PE	Art	Core	Music	PE	L
Teacher 3B	L	PE	Core	PE	Music	PE
Teacher 3C	PE	L	Core	Art	PE	Music
Teacher 3D	Music	PE	Core	PE	Art	PE
Teacher 3E	PE	Music	Core	L	PE	Art
Teacher 3F	Art	PE	Core	PE	L	PE

11:40-12:20	Lunch					

12:20-1:00	Day 1	Day 2	Day 3	Day 4	Day 5	Day 6
Teacher KA	PE	Art	PE	Core	PE	L
Teacher KB	L	PE	Art	Core	Music	PE
Teacher KC	PE	L	PE	Core	PE	Music
Teacher KD	Music	PE	L	Core	Art	PE
Teacher KE	PE	Music	PE	Core	PE	Art
Teacher KF	Art	PE	Music	Core	L	PE

1:00-1:40	Day 1	Day 2	Day 3	Day 4	Day 5	Day 6
Teacher 1A	PE	Art	PE	Music	Core	L
Teacher 1B	L	PE	Art	PE	Core	PE
Teacher 1C	PE	L	PE	Art	Core	Music
Teacher 1D	Music	PE	L	PE	Core	PE
Teacher 1E	PE	Music	PE	L	Core	Art
Teacher 1F	Art	PE	Music	PE	Core	PE

1:40-2:20	Day 1	Day 2	Day 3	Day 4	Day 5	Day 6
Teacher 2A	PE	Art	PE	Music	PE	Core
Teacher 2B	L	PE	Art	PE	Music	Core
Teacher 2C	PE	L	PE	Art	PE	Core
Teacher 2D	Music	PE	L	PE	Art	Core
Teacher 2E	PE	Music	PE	L	PE	Core
Teacher 2F	Art	PE	Music	PE	L	Core

2:20-2:30	Duty					

3.19
3.19

Figure 3.20 Master Schedule for Extended P.M. Planning Blocks

	8:00	9:00	10:00	11:00	12:00	1:00	2:00	2:30
Kindergarten	HR (20)				Encore/ Plan (40)			HR (10)
Grade 1	HR (20)					Encore/ Plan (40)		HR (10)
Grade 2	HR (20)			Encore/ Plan (40)				HR (10)
Grade 3	HR (20)		Encore/ Plan (40)					HR (10)
Grade 4	HR (20)	Encore/ Plan (40)						HR (10)
Grade 5	HR (20)	Encore/ Plan (40)						HR (10)
Encore	Duty (20)	Grade 5	Grade 4	Grade 3	Grade 2	Lunch (40)	Kinder	Grade 1	Extended Planning Block (80)	Duty

Figure 3.21 Six-Day Encore Rotation with Extended P.M. Planning Period Every Six Days

8:00-8:20	Duty					

8:20-9:00	Day 1	Day 2	Day 3	Day 4	Day 5	Day 6
Teacher 5A	Core	Art	PE	Music	PE	L
Teacher 5B	Core	PE	Art	PE	Music	PE
Teacher 5C	Core	L	PE	Art	PE	Music
Teacher 5D	Core	PE	L	PE	Art	PE
Teacher 5E	Core	Music	PE	L	PE	Art
Teacher 5F	Core	PE	Music	PE	L	PE

9:00-9:40	Day 1	Day 2	Day 3	Day 4	Day 5	Day 6
Teacher 4A	PE	Core	PE	Music	PE	L
Teacher 4B	L	Core	Art	PE	Music	PE
Teacher 4C	PE	Core	PE	Art	PE	Music
Teacher 4D	Music	Core	L	PE	Art	PE
Teacher 4E	PE	Core	PE	L	PE	Art
Teacher 4F	Art	Core	Music	PE	L	PE

9:40-10:20	Day 1	Day 2	Day 3	Day 4	Day 5	Day 6
Teacher 3A	PE	Art	Core	Music	PE	L
Teacher 3B	L	PE	Core	PE	Music	PE
Teacher 3C	PE	L	Core	Art	PE	Music
Teacher 3D	Music	PE	Core	PE	Art	PE
Teacher 3E	PE	Music	Core	L	PE	Art
Teacher 3F	Art	PE	Core	PE	L	PE

10:20-11:00	Day 1	Day 2	Day 3	Day 4	Day 5	Day 6
Teacher KA	PE	Art	PE	Core	PE	L
Teacher KB	L	PE	Art	Core	Music	PE
Teacher KC	PE	L	PE	Core	PE	Music
Teacher KD	Music	PE	L	Core	Art	PE
Teacher KE	PE	Music	PE	Core	PE	Art
Teacher KF	Art	PE	Music	Core	L	PE

11:00-11:40	Lunch					

11:40-12:20	Day 1	Day 2	Day 3	Day 4	Day 5	Day 6
Teacher 1A	PE	Art	PE	Music	Core	L
Teacher 1B	L	PE	Art	PE	Core	PE
Teacher 1C	PE	L	PE	Art	Core	Music
Teacher 1D	Music	PE	L	PE	Core	PE
Teacher 1E	PE	Music	PE	L	Core	Art
Teacher 1F	Art	PE	Music	PE	Core	PE

12:20-1:00	Day 1	Day 2	Day 3	Day 4	Day 5	Day 6
Teacher 2A	PE	Art	PE	Music	PE	Core
Teacher 2B	L	PE	Art	PE	Music	Core
Teacher 2C	PE	L	PE	Art	PE	Core
Teacher 2D	Music	PE	L	PE	Art	Core
Teacher 2E	PE	Music	PE	L	PE	Core
Teacher 2F	Art	PE	Music	PE	L	Core

3.20
3.21

Figure 3.21 Six-Day Encore Rotation with Extended P.M. Planning Period Every Six Days, cont'd

1:00-1:40	Extended Planning Blocks-First 40 Minutes					
	Day 1	Day 2	Day 3	Day 4	Day 5	Day 6
	PE-5A	Art-4A	PE-3A	Music-KA	PE-1A	L-2A
	L-5B	PE-4B	Art-3B	PE-KB	Music-1B	PE-2B
	PE-5C	L-4C	PE-3C	Art-KC	PE-1C	Music-2C
	Music-5D	PE-4D	L-3D	PE-KD	Art-1D	PE-2D
	PE-5E	Music-4E	PE-3E	L-KE	PE-1E	Art-2E
	Art-5F	PE-4F	Music-3F	PE-KF	L-1F	PE-2F
1:40-2:20	Extended Planning Blocks-Second 40 Minutes					
	Day 1	Day 2	Day 3	Day 4	Day 5	Day 6
	Grade 5	Grade 4	Grade 3	Grade K	Grade 1	Grade 2
	All grades follow the rotation below for the second 40 minutes of the extended planning block on their scheduled day (immediately above this note).					
All Grades	Rotation 1	Rotation 2	Rotation 3	Rotation 4	Rotation 5	Rotation 6
Class A	PE	Art	PE	Music	PE	L
Class B	L	PE	Art	PE	Music	PE
Class C	PE	L	PE	Art	PE	Music
Class D	Music	PE	L	PE	Art	PE
Class E	PE	Music	PE	L	PE	Art
Class F	Art	PE	Music	PE	L	PE
2:20-2:30	Duty					

Figure 3.22 Master Schedule for Encore 2 Blocks, Option 1

	8:00	9:00	10:00	11:00	12:00	1:00	2:00	2:30
Kindergarten	HR (20)				I/E and Encore 2 (45)	Encore/ Plan (45)		HR (10)
Grade 1	HR (20)					I/E and Encore 2 (45)	Encore/ Plan (45)	HR (10)
Grade 2	HR (20)						I/E and Encore 2 (45) · Encore/ Plan (45)	HR (10)
Grade 3	HR (20)		I/E and Encore 2 (45) · Encore/ Plan (45)					HR (10)
Grade 4	HR (20)	I/E and Encore 2 (45) · Encore/ Plan (45)						HR (10)
Grade 5	HR (20) · I/E and Encore 2 (45) · Encore/ Plan (45)							HR (10)
Encore	Duty (20) · Plan (45)	Grade 5	Grade 4	Grade 3	Lunch (45) · Kinder.	Grade 1	Grade 2	Duty
I/E and Encore 2	Duty (20) · Grade 5	Grade 4	Grade 3	Lunch (45)	Grade K · Grade 1	Grade 2	Plan (45)	Duty

Note: To provide the double-planning period, the I/E period is replaced periodically by a second encore rotation (Encore 2).

3.21
3.22

Figure 3.23 Encore Rotations

a. Four-day Encore Rotation

Time	Day 1	Day 2	Day 3	Day 4
8:00-8:20	Duty			
8:20-9:05	Planning			
9:05-9:50	Day 1	Day 2	Day 3	Day 4
Teacher 5A	Music	PE	Art	L
Teacher 5B	L	Music	PE	Art
Teacher 5C	Art	L	Music	PE
Teacher 5D	PE	Art	L	Music
9:50-10:35	Day 1	Day 2	Day 3	Day 4
Teacher 4A	Music	PE	Art	L
Teacher 4B	L	Music	PE	Art
Teacher 4C	Art	L	Music	PE
Teacher 4D	PE	Art	L	Music
10:35-11:20	Day 1	Day 2	Day 3	Day 4
Teacher 3A	Music	PE	Art	L
Teacher 3B	L	Music	PE	Art
Teacher 3C	Art	L	Music	PE
Teacher 3D	PE	Art	L	Music
10:35-11:20	Day 1	Day 2	Day 3	Day 4
Teacher 3A	Music	PE	Art	L
Teacher 3B	L	Music	PE	Art
Teacher 3C	Art	L	Music	PE
Teacher 3D	PE	Art	L	Music
11:20-12:05	Lunch			
12:05-12:50	Day 1	Day 2	Day 3	Day 4
Teacher KA	Music	PE	Art	L
Teacher KB	L	Music	PE	Art
Teacher KC	Art	L	Music	PE
Teacher KD	PE	Art	L	Music
12:50-1:35	Day 1	Day 2	Day 3	Day 4
Teacher 1A	Music	PE	Art	L
Teacher 1B	L	Music	PE	Art
Teacher 1C	Art	L	Music	PE
Teacher 1D	PE	Art	L	Music
1:35-2:20	Day 1	Day 2	Day 3	Day 4
Teacher 2A	Music	PE	Art	L
Teacher 2B	L	Music	PE	Art
Teacher 2C	Art	L	Music	PE

b. Four-Cycle Encore 2 Rotation

Time	Cycle 1	Cycle 2	Cycle 3	Cycle 4
8:20-9:05	Cycle 1	Cycle 2	Cycle 3	Cycle 4
Teacher 5A	C.Lab	Guid.	Sci. Lab	M.Lab
Teacher 5B	M.Lab	C.Lab	Guid.	Sci. Lab
Teacher 5C	Sci. Lab	M.Lab	C.Lab	Guid.
Teacher 5D	Guid.	Sci. Lab	M.Lab	C.Lab
9:05-9:50	Cycle 1	Cycle 2	Cycle 3	Cycle 4
Teacher 4A	C.Lab	Guid.	Sci. Lab	M.Lab
Teacher 4B	M.Lab	C.Lab	Guid.	Sci. Lab
Teacher 4C	Sci. Lab	M.Lab	C.Lab	Guid.
Teacher 4D	Guid.	Sci. Lab	M.Lab	C.Lab
9:50-10:35	Cycle 1	Cycle 2	Cycle 3	Cycle 4
Teacher 3A	C.Lab	Guid.	Sci. Lab	M.Lab
Teacher 3B	M.Lab	C.Lab	Guid.	Sci. Lab
Teacher 3C	Sci. Lab	M.Lab	C.Lab	Guid.
Teacher 3D	Guid.	Sci. Lab	M.Lab	C.Lab
10:35-11:20	Lunch			
11:20-12:05	Cycle 1	Cycle 2	Cycle 3	Cycle 4
Teacher KA	C.Lab	Guid.	Sci. Lab	M.Lab
Teacher KB	M.Lab	C.Lab	Guid.	Sci. Lab
Teacher KC	Sci. Lab	M.Lab	C.Lab	Guid.
Teacher KD	Guid.	Sci. Lab	M.Lab	C.Lab
12:05-12:50	Cycle 1	Cycle 2	Cycle 3	Cycle 4
Teacher 1A	C.Lab	Guid.	Sci. Lab	M.Lab
Teacher 1B	M.Lab	C.Lab	Guid.	Sci. Lab
Teacher 1C	Sci. Lab	M.Lab	C.Lab	Guid.
Teacher 1D	Guid.	Sci. Lab	M.Lab	C.Lab
12:50-1:35	Cycle 1	Cycle 2	Cycle 3	Cycle 4
Teacher 2A	C.Lab	Guid.	Sci. Lab	M.Lab
Teacher 2B	M.Lab	C.Lab	Guid.	Sci. Lab
Teacher 2C	Sci. Lab	M.Lab	C.Lab	Guid.
Teacher 2D	Guid.	Sci. Lab	M.Lab	C.Lab
1:35-2:20	Plan			

Figure 3.24 Master Schedule for Encore 2 Blocks, Option 2

	8:00	9:00	10:00	11:00	12:00	1:00	2:00	2:30
Kindergarten	HR (20)				Encore/Plan (45)	I/E and Encore 2 (45)			HR (10)
Grade 1	HR (20)				I/E and Encore 2 (45)	Encore/Plan (45)		HR (10)
Grade 2	HR (20)						Encore/Plan (45)	I/E and Encore 2 (45)	HR (10)
Grade 3	HR (20)						I/E and Encore 2 (45)	Encore/Plan (45)	HR (10)
Grade 4	HR (20)	I/E and Encore 2 (45)	Encore/Plan (45)						HR (10)
Grade 5	HR (20)	Encore/Plan (45)	I/E and Encore 2 (45)						HR (10)
Encore	Duty (20)	Grade 5	Grade 4	Plan (45)	Lunch (45)	Grade K	Grade 1	Grade 2	Grade 3	Duty
I/E and Encore 2	Duty (20)	Grade 4	Grade 5	Plan (45)	Lunch (45)	Grade 1	Grade K	Grade 3	Grade 2	Duty

Note: To provide the double-planning period, the I/E period is replaced periodically by a second encore rotation (Encore 2).

3.23
3.24

Figure 3.25 Encore Rotations

a. Four-day Encore Rotation				
8:00-8:20	Duty			
8:20-9:05	Day 1	Day 2	Day 3	Day 4
Teacher 5A	Music	PE	Art	L
Teacher 5B	L	Music	PE	Art
Teacher 5C	Art	L	Music	PE
Teacher 5D	PE	Art	L	Music
9:05-9:50	Day 1	Day 2	Day 3	Day 4
Teacher 4A	Music	PE	Art	L
Teacher 4B	L	Music	PE	Art
Teacher 4C	Art	L	Music	PE
Teacher 4D	PE	Art	L	Music
9:50-10:35	Plan			
10:35-11:20	Lunch			
11:20-12:05	Day 1	Day 2	Day 3	Day 4
Teacher KA	Music	PE	Art	L
Teacher KB	L	Music	PE	Art
Teacher KC	Art	L	Music	PE
Teacher KD	PE	Art	L	Music
12:05-12:50	Day 1	Day 2	Day 3	Day 4
Teacher 1A	Music	PE	Art	L
Teacher 1B	L	Music	PE	Art
Teacher 1C	Art	L	Music	PE
Teacher 1D	PE	Art	L	Music
12:50-1:35	Day 1	Day 2	Day 3	Day 4
Teacher 2A	Music	PE	Art	L
Teacher 2B	L	Music	PE	Art
Teacher 2C	Art	L	Music	PE
Teacher 2D	PE	Art	L	Music
1:35-2:20	Day 1	Day 2	Day 3	Day 4
Teacher 3A	Music	PE	Art	L
Teacher 3B	L	Music	PE	Art
Teacher 3C	Art	L	Music	PE
Teacher 3D	PE	Art	L	Music
2:20-2:30	Duty			

b. Four-Cycle Encore 2 Rotation				
8:00-8:20	Duty			
8:20-9:05	Cycle 1	Cycle 2	Cycle 3	Cycle 4
Teacher 4A	C.Lab	Guid.	Sci. Lab	Story
Teacher 4B	Story	C.Lab	Guid.	Sci. Lab
Teacher 4C	Sci. Lab	Story	C.Lab	Guid.
Teacher 4D	Guid.	Sci. Lab	Story	C.Lab
9:05-9:50	Cycle 1	Cycle 2	Cycle 3	Cycle 4
Teacher 5A	C.Lab	Guid.	Sci. Lab	Story
Teacher 5B	Story	C.Lab	Guid.	Sci. Lab
Teacher 5C	Sci. Lab	Story	C.Lab	Guid.
Teacher 5D	Guid.	Sci. Lab	Story	C.Lab
9:50-10:35	Plan			
10:35-11:20	Lunch			
11:20-12:05	Cycle 1	Cycle 2	Cycle 3	Cycle 4
Teacher 1A	C.Lab	Guid.	Sci. Lab	Story
Teacher 1B	Story	C.Lab	Guid.	Sci. Lab
Teacher 1C	Sci. Lab	Story	C.Lab	Guid.
Teacher 1D	Guid.	Sci. Lab	Story	C.Lab
12:05-12:50	Cycle 1	Cycle 2	Cycle 3	Cycle 4
Teacher KA	C.Lab	Guid.	Sci. Lab	Story
Teacher KB	Story	C.Lab	Guid.	Sci. Lab
Teacher KC	Sci. Lab	Story	C.Lab	Guid.
Teacher KD	Guid.	Sci. Lab	Story	C.Lab
12:50-1:35	Cycle 1	Cycle 2	Cycle 3	Cycle 4
Teacher 3A	C.Lab	Guid.	Sci. Lab	Story
Teacher 3B	Story	C.Lab	Guid.	Sci. Lab
Teacher 3C	Sci. Lab	Story	C.Lab	Guid.
Teacher 3D	Guid.	Sci. Lab	Story	C.Lab
1:35-2:20	Plan			
Teacher 2A	C.Lab	Guid.	Sci. Lab	Story
Teacher 2B	Story	C.Lab	Guid.	Sci. Lab
Teacher 2C	Sci. Lab	Story	C.Lab	Guid.
Teacher 2D	Guid.	Sci. Lab	Story	C.Lab
2:20-2:30	Duty			

4

Scheduling Special Service Personnel in Elementary Schools

During the past 40 years, large numbers of special service[1] personnel have been added to the staffs of elementary schools to provide assistance to specifically identified groups of students. In 1965, with passage of the original Elementary and Secondary Education Act (ESEA), Title I of the act provided federal funds to aid in the instruction of economically disadvantaged students. Several years later, the Bilingual Act of 1968 provided federal assistance to encourage districts to incorporate native-language instructional approaches. In 1975, the Education of All Handicapped Children Act (PL 94–142) required that previously underserved children be provided a "free and appropriate education." This legislation was reauthorized as the Individuals with Disabilities Education Act (IDEA) in 1990 and amended most recently in 2004. Finally, in 2002 President George W. Bush signed into law a sweeping reauthorization of ESEA called the No Child Left Behind Act of 2001.

Elementary instructional positions funded by these federal programs include Title I reading and math specialists, a host of special education teachers serving students with various disabilities, bilingual educators, and teachers of English as a second language (ESL). In addition to federally funded programs that provide additional personnel to elementary schools, a variety of state and local district initiatives have added reading specialists, math specialists, educators of gifted students, instrumental music lessons, and so on. There seems to be no end to the additional personnel who might join the elementary school staff.

These mandates and initiatives have brought valuable resources to schools; but in addition to the new talent, we have

---

1 Recall that we define "special services" as those educational services provided to *some* students who qualify for and/or elect to receive such services. These services include, for example, special education, Title I reading and mathematics, English as a second language, education for gifted learners, instrumental music, and locally funded reading and mathematics assistance.

observed conflict among various staff members, fragmentation of the school day for homeroom teachers, interruptions of the instructional day for both identified and non-identified students, and concerns about how much the special services teachers actually are improving teaching and learning for both teachers and students.

Many of the problems seem to arise from issues related to "turf protection," to lack of clarification of the various roles of all staff members, to conflicts in scheduling (e.g., pull-out vs. push-in models), and to the number of different special services students need. We have observed that in some schools, in order to meet the demands of a few special education teachers, the tail ends up wagging the dog—that is, the basic school schedule is designed to accommodate the needs of a relatively small percentage of a school's students. This practice aggravates the conflicts.

The problem is exacerbated by a scheduling procedure quite prevalent in special education, Title I reading and mathematics, gifted education, and ESL instruction—the model, already much discussed in this book, known as "When can I have your kids?" Carrying their rosters of qualified students with them, individual special service providers approach homeroom teachers one by one and try to negotiate times to serve their students. The core teachers, however, set their own schedules independently. This practice creates a chaotic schedule that fragments the instructional day, dilutes the sense of accountability homeroom teachers have for their students, and heightens the aforesaid conflicts between homeroom teachers and service providers. We contend that schools can forestall these repercussions by carefully crafting the master schedule.

This chapter illustrates two basic methods of scheduling special services and shows how they can be combined to serve the needs of students, to use resources more effectively, and to sidestep conflict. First, we discuss the operation and scheduling of the Intervention/Enrichment (I/E) period, a relatively straightforward means of providing time for special services, short-term interventions, and enrichment activities. Second, we discuss inclusion scheduling and co-teaching models that provide time for two professional educators (one homeroom teacher and one special service provider) to work together in the same classroom. We then describe creating schedules that employ both inclusion and Intervention/Enrichment, pulling the best from each model. We conclude the chapter by whetting the reader's appetite for Part II of the book by briefly illustrating how special services, enrichment, and intervention are addressed in a parallel block schedule.

The Intervention/Enrichment Period: Scheduling, Organizing, and Instructing

The main purpose for the Intervention/Enrichment period is to provide time for short-term instructional interventions, practice, reinforcement, re-teaching, special services, and various forms of enrichment (Brown-Chidsey, 2007). In the sections that follow, we discuss scheduling and organizing of, and instructing in the I/E period.

Scheduling the I/E Period

The I/E period can be scheduled in several different ways:

- One school-wide period (Figure 4.1, p. 111);

- Two periods, one for grades K–2 and one for grades 3–5 (Figure 4.2, p. 112);

- Three periods, one each for grades K–1, 2–3, and 4–5 (Figure 4.3, p. 113);

- Six separate periods, one for each grade level (Figure 4.4, p. 114); and

- Multiple I/E periods all at the same grade level (Figure 4.5, p. 115).

Some schools decide to operate a *single school-wide Intervention/Enrichment period,* as illustrated in Figure 4.1 with the I/E period at the end of the day. This option has several advantages. It maximizes the potential for cross-grade-level grouping; it promotes team spirit and eases administrative oversight because everyone in the school is engaged in the same processes at the same time; it allows more time for special service providers to provide inclusion services during core time; and it permits encore teachers to participate in the I/E period, so long as their planning periods are scheduled at a different time. The major disadvantage of the single school-wide I/E period is that the special services personnel must be shared across all grade levels at the same time, which limits the number of different students they can serve during the period.

This scheduling model works well for a large school with enough support staff to assign each service provider to one grade level only, thereby eliminating conflicts with other grade levels. Often, though, an individual LD teacher assigned to one grade level in a large school cannot cover all the students eligi-

ble to receive services in one I/E period, making it necessary to create multiple I/E periods within the grade level.

To allow for greater coverage by special services personnel, we could design a master schedule that offers *two separate I/E periods,* as illustrated in Figure 4.2 (p. 112). This model allows special services personnel to serve twice as many identified students during the I/E period. Similarly, Figure 4.3 (p. 113) shows a master schedule that creates *three I/E periods,* each with two consecutive grade levels served at a time. Finally, the schedule in Figure 4.4 (p. 114) offers a *separate I/E period for each grade level.* This model is particularly useful if there is only one resource teacher in a field (e.g., gifted education or ESL) who must cover all grade levels.

The choice among these models depends on the interaction of a variety of factors, including

- school size;

- sharing arrangements for special services personnel;

- the mix of inclusion and pull-out services provided;

- the desire for cross-grade-level groupings; and

- the difficulty of monitoring the use of time during this period.

The impact of *school size* on the decision can vary, depending on other factors. Larger schools often are more likely to assign certain specialists (such as LD teachers) to only one grade level, making it seem unnecessary to place Intervention/Enrichment periods in different time slots for each grade level; however, a grade level might need several different I/E periods. For example, most students qualifying for speech/language services are in grades K–1, making it difficult to serve all those students in one I/E period (Figures 4.1 to 4.3, pp. 111–113) or even in two separate periods, one for K and one for grade 1 (Figure 4.4, p. 114). Perhaps only multiple I/E periods within the two grade levels would make this possible (Figure 4.5, p. 115).

Small schools tend to share special services personnel with other schools; in that case, the service provider would be in the building only on certain days or for part of the day. Covering all grade levels would mean creating fewer I/E periods (as shown in Figures 4.1 to 4.3, pp. 111–113) and scheduling them when the special service teacher or teachers are present.

Efficiency is the major reason for combining grades into the same I/E period in small schools. To maximize the support students receive from a limited number of personnel, they must be *grouped and re-grouped across grade levels*. Also, in small schools with only one or two I/E periods, special service personnel have more time to follow their students from I/E to the classroom for inclusion services, or perhaps to be shared with other schools in the district.

Sharing arrangements for special services personnel also may influence the decision of how to schedule I/E periods based on in-school factors. If second and third grade teachers and students share the same LD teacher, it probably would work best to give them separate I/E periods. Similarly, a school that attempts to implement both the inclusion model and the I/E model would have to craft the schedules of shared special education teachers carefully (discussed in the section, "The Inclusion Model: Scheduling, Organizing, and Instructing," p. 105).

Finally, the I/E period is a novel idea in many schools. Structuring its use for maximum effectiveness requires significant leadership from the principal, as well as cooperation among teachers and special services providers. Institutionalizing effective instruction, assessment, diagnosis, and intervention (as described below) with intervention and enrichment scheduled into the I/E period is a challenge for many educators. Therein lies a danger: The I/E period can deteriorate into the elementary school equivalent of "study hall" if not structured and monitored carefully. Consequently, some schools deliberately schedule this period at the same time for all grade levels, regardless of the difficulty this causes for sharing special services personnel across grade levels, simply because a common school-wide period fosters unanimity of purpose, team spirit, and teamwork, and also because it may be *easier to monitor*. Later in this chapter, in the section entitled "Organizing and Teaching the Intervention/Enrichment Period" (p. 99), we discuss the structure and use of the I/E period in great detail.

Scheduling Instrumental Music Lessons During Intervention/Enrichment

Many schools, especially in the Northeast, provide small-group music lessons for band and/or string instruments during the school day. In most situations, the band and/or strings teacher comes to the school one or more full days each week. The typical scheduling format for this enrichment opportunity is to create a rotating schedule that pulls students out of a different class period each week to receive their lessons. For classroom teachers, a scenario like the following might ensue:

8:30–9:00: two flute players miss the first part of reading class

9:00–9:30: three clarinetists miss the second half of reading

10:00–10:30: the oboist misses the first part of the math lesson

10:30–11:00: the saxophonists miss the second half of math

and so on, through the day. Students are supposed to make up what they missed, but in fact, they have missed valuable core instruction.

Before the days of high-stakes testing in the elementary school, the scenario sketched above was simply a maddening inconvenience. Now, with high-stakes testing in the upper elementary grades and the challenges of making Adequate Yearly Progress (AYP) as required by the No Child Left Behind Act of 2001, the fragmentation it causes borders on malpractice. Recognizing this accountability dilemma, the affected classroom teachers begin to resent lessons, rail against the instructors, and occasionally resist letting students leave their classrooms for lessons.

In an effort to protect core instructional time and still provide this wonderful service, some elementary schools have adopted a new scheduling format for lessons that uses the Intervention/Enrichment period (remember—no new instruction allowed). To accomplish this change requires a different way of assigning instrumental music personnel to schools. For example, we could assign the band instructor or strings instructor or both[2] to begin each instructional day in one school (Figure 4.6, p. 116). In the schedule illustrated, every morning music instructors could pull fourth grade students from the I/E period from 8:15 to 9:00 and fifth graders from 9:00 to 9:45. This would permit a maximum of five groupings per grade level (one every day, Monday through Friday).

Depending on the number of students playing each instrument, we might divide the brass into two groups, the woodwinds into two groups, and keep percussion as the fifth group during the 8:15 to 9:00 time slot (Figure 4.6a, p. 117). When a full band needs to rehearse, it might be possible to combine the woodwinds or the brass together as one group, leaving an open period on Friday during the 9:00 to 9:45 time slot (Figure 4.6a). Similar schedules could be created for strings as well (Figure 4.6b, p. 118).

How can a student who receives special services during the I/E period also take music lessons? Here we must confront the prime axiom of school scheduling: "To put something in, you must take something out." If music lessons were only one day a week, we might consider allowing the student to miss special services on music lesson day. But if this were not possible, we could move to the adjoining period and allow the student to take a music lesson during the encore time slot.

---

2 We actually know of a district in Michigan that sends in a music "swat" team of four instructors to teach woodwinds, brass, percussion, and strings all during the same Intervention/Enrichment periods. After completing a period or two of instruction, the "swat" team moves on to another school.

To facilitate this possibility, we have placed encore and I/E periods for grades 4 and 5 in opposite adjoining periods in each of the schools illustrated in Figures 4.6 to 4.9 (pp. 116–121). As a result, students might miss PE or art or some other encore class to take a music lesson. Because we wouldn't want them to always miss PE or art, it would be wise to place music lessons on a Monday-to-Friday schedule while creating a four-day, six-day, eight-day, or other rotational schedule for encore classes, as described in chapter 3.

After the first two periods in school I, the instrumental music personnel would travel to school II and conduct lessons there (Figure 4.7, p. 119); the day would be concluded at school III (Figure 4.8, p. 120). Notice how the Intervention/Enrichment periods for grades four and five are placed in the first two periods of the day for school I, periods four and five for school II, and periods seven and eight for school III.

If travel time is too great to allow time for planning and lunch, it may be necessary to reduce the number of lessons in some grade levels in some schools. As is shown in Figure 4.9 (p. 121), one lesson time has been removed from school I and two lesson times have been removed from schools II and III to allow for additional planning time. It also would be possible to shorten the I/E periods to 30 minutes, more typical for music lessons, and schedule three lessons on days when the teacher is in the building for 90 minutes and two lessons when in the building for only an hour.

In addition, because it is likely that all three schools would prefer the afternoon instrumental music schedule, it would be fair to rotate every 12 weeks, giving each school 12 weeks of morning, 12 weeks of mid-day, and 12 weeks of afternoon I/E

periods. In the event that there is lower participation in the program than described above, it would be possible for the instructors to come to the school just three days a week for the first two periods, one day for brass, one for woodwinds, and one for percussion.

Figure 4.10 (p. 122) is another master schedule designed to provide a logical structure for instrumental music; in this case, however, the school has a large program in grades 3 to 5, staffed by a full-time instrumental music instructor. To provide access to all three grade levels, we have divided each grade level in half, creating two I/E periods per grade. If there were four classes per grade level, we would serve two during each I/E period. As Figure 4.10 shows, lessons could be conducted from 9:05 to 10:45 for grade 5, from 10:45 to 12:25 for grade 4, and from 1:15 to 2:55 for grade 3. We do understand that this format restricts the ease with which students can be grouped together by instrument and performance levels, but with a bit of creative class assignment we believe that the two oboists both can be assigned to the appropriate I/E period. We must be careful, however, to ensure that our plan for instrumental music is designed with the needs of other service providers in mind, so as to avoid significant scheduling conflicts.

In addition, many instrumental music instructors might argue that the number of groups is too few, the frequency insufficient, or the lesson time too long. We realize that the typical instrumental music lesson generally is 30 minutes. In the schedules shown above, we have allocated 50 minutes because other services provided during the I/E period, such as LD Resource support and Title I reading and math assistance, are usually more on the order of 45 to 50 minutes. While it would be possible to divide the allocated 50-minute period in half to provide two shorter lessons, we question the practicality of this shorter period, given the time it takes beginning musicians to put their instruments together, get their music out, tune up, warm up, and pack up.

Obviously, it is not practical to illustrate every eventuality that might impact the music lesson schedule; school size, space for lessons, the number of students involved in the instrumental music program, and the number and specialization of the instrumental music staff make a big difference. One additional reality also must be considered: In today's world of high-stakes testing, we must minimize interruptions of the academic program by instrumental music lessons or risk losing them, especially in schools struggling to meet state and federal requirements.

Organizing and Teaching the Intervention/Enrichment Period

Recall that the primary purpose for the I/E period is to provide time for short-term instructional interventions, practice, reinforcement, re-teaching, special services, and various forms of enrichment. No new basic instruction is permitted during this time, except for pre-teaching to individual students and small groups with special needs. Careful planning is the key to successful implementation. Success of this flexible period in addressing various student needs is enhanced when teachers

- have common planning time to determine those needs;
- create I/E groupings that are data-driven, flexible, and monitored;

- come to planning meetings prepared to discuss the needs of their students;
- regularly collect common formative assessment data; and
- work in a trusting relationship and can openly report the academic strengths and weaknesses of their students and of themselves.

Without careful planning and periodic review and revision, I/E periods can turn into elementary school study halls for long-term homogeneous groupings—not a development we encourage (Brookhart, 2007/2008; Fisher & Frey, 2007; Gusky, 2007/2008; William, 2007/2008).

Scheduling Time to Plan the I/E Period

Because the preparation time required to implement I/E periods is significant, at a very minimum teachers at the same grade level must have 40 to 50 minutes of common planning daily, typically while students are attending encore classes, such as music, art, PE, dance, or computer lab (see chapter 3 for schedules related to encore classes). If at all possible, though, we strongly suggest that administrators provide elementary teachers with longer blocks of time devoted exclusively to planning for the I/E period. Such I/E planning periods can be provided school-wide or even district-wide by (a) building bimonthly early dismissals into the yearly school calendar and/or (b) designating at least portions of certain in-service days within the school year for I/E planning time.

In the absence of school- or district-wide release days or early dismissals, various accommodations in the elementary school schedule can allow teachers extended common planning times by grade level or by multiple grade levels, depending on a school's size and the number and distribution of support personnel available in the building. By tweaking the encore teachers' schedule as illustrated in chapter 3 (Figures 3.18 to 3.25b, pp. 83–92), teachers occasionally can be given common planning periods for grade-level meetings of 70 to 100 minutes. The length of the extended planning blocks generally is double the length of the single planning period provided in the encore schedule.

In Figures 3.18 (p. 83) and 3.19 (pp. 84–85), we show encore classes meeting for 80 minutes[3] on a rotating basis for the first two periods of the school day. In Figures 3.20 (p. 86) and 3.21 (pp. 87–88), we place the 80-minute planning block at the end of the school day. In Figures 3.22 (p. 89) and 3.23 (p. 90), we spread the double planning periods (now 90 minutes in length) throughout the school day by inserting a second encore rotation into the I/E period on an occasional basis. The schedules shown in Figures 3.24 (p. 91) and 3.25 (p. 92) apply the same concept but allow two consecutive grade levels to plan at the same time, thereby providing the opportunity for articulation meetings.

In some schools, it may be possible to combine the extended blocks with lunch periods—but only if lunch periods are duty-free and union contracts permit teachers, on a rotating basis, to combine a working lunch with their planning period once every six to twelve days.

The design of I/E groupings will vary with the number of base teachers at each grade level, academic needs of students, and the number of support teachers (e.g., special education, English as a second language, talented and gifted, speech therapy, media personnel, encore teachers, and Title I math, reading and science specialists) who might be available to instruct students during each of the I/E periods. Once extended planning blocks have been established, it is essential to train teachers to plan effectively for instruction during I/E periods.

Structuring the I/E Period

The Intervention/Enrichment period essentially is a "pool period" during which various resources are pooled to meet the needs of students. No new basic instruction (except pre-teaching) is permitted because students receiving special services may be pulled out during this time. Typical services provided during the I/E period include special education resource services, ESL services, Title I or other reading services, gifted resource services, instrumental music lessons, tutoring,[4] and the like. For many students who only receive resource support services (i.e., about 45 minutes daily), providing those services during the I/E period is sufficient. For students who are receiving multiple services, additional time will need to be found in their schedules. Students who are not eligible for special resource services are scheduled for interventions, practice, rein-

---

3 The schedules in Chapter 3 referred to here are based on a 390-minute day (including 30 minutes of homeroom time split between the morning and afternoon). With the 405-minute day used in this chapter (and less homeroom time), it would be possible to provide double periods 90 minutes in length.

4 We recommend that schools consider providing No Child left Behind tutoring services during this time. Although this may require special approval, tutoring programs under the supervision of schools may provide more accountability and alignment for these services (see *USA Today*, June 20, 2007, p. 12a).

forcement, and enrichment provided by classroom teachers or perhaps other enrichment specialists, such as those listed above.

Even though the I/E period offers a convenient opportunity for special services and enrichment, the fact remains that all students must be engaged in productive activity during the period. Ideally, if all teachers at a grade level pace their instruction similarly during the core time and use common formative assessments at regular intervals, they can work as a team to review the data and regroup students among several teachers during the common I/E period (Tomlinson, 2007/2008). While some special service providers work with their assigned students, several classroom teachers can provide interventions and still others offer enrichment activities for students with no identified weaknesses on the formative assessments (Rettig, McCullough, Santos, & Watson, 2004). Implementing this model successfully across many collaborating teachers requires a significant level of structure and cooperation.

One school in Virginia with three teachers in one grade level organized the I/E period as shown in Table 4.1. One classroom teacher staffed a writing lab serving about one-fourth of the students. The library media specialist instructed another quarter in science and social studies enrichment activities. A second classroom teacher worked daily with small groups focusing on math interventions. The third classroom teacher, the LD teacher, and two reading specialists worked with very small groups of students needing reading assistance. Every ten days or so, the teachers reconfigured groupings based on students' needs.

As an alternative to a team model, classroom teachers may structure I/E time within their own classrooms as "centers" time, preparing a variety of reinforcing and enrichment activities.

Table 4.1 Sample Structure of Intervention/Enrichment Period for One Grade Level

Groups	Activity	Staff
25% of students	Writing lab	One (of three) classroom teachers
25% of students	Science and social studies enrichment activities	Library/media specialist
15% of students	Math interventions	Second classroom teacher or computer lab
35% of students	Reading interventions	Third classroom teacher, LD teacher, two reading specialists

Special service personnel still may pull their students during this time, as no new instruction is being provided. Classroom teachers pull individuals or small groups from centers to provide interventions based on weaknesses identified by formative assessments or during recently taught lessons. This structure supports differentiation of instruction as described by Tomlinson (1999). This model may be thought of as an incremental step toward the more complex, and potentially more beneficial, conceptualization of Intervention/Enrichment described previously.

We have found pre-teaching during the I/E period particularly effective with struggling learners. For this strategy to work well, we recommend that base teachers prepare brief lesson plans for key concepts in language arts and mathematics five or six days in advance of the whole-class lesson and share them with all the relevant special services teachers. These teachers then pre-teach the materials or skills to their identified students during the I/E period. After two or three such sessions, students have a base of knowledge that sets them up for the lesson their classroom teacher presents to the whole group. Teachers who have followed this cycle tell us that the special needs students typically engage more fully in the regular class instruction and that pre-teaching seems to build students' confidence, especially when joining their peers. The I/E period also can be a time for follow-up, with the special service teacher re-teaching some days and pre-teaching other days, as indicated by the students' progress.

Planning and Implementing the I/E Period in One Grade Level: One Example

In this section, we follow a grade 2 team with four base teachers and 92 students as it plans the I/E period for an upcoming ten-day stint. (Note: In small schools with one or two base teachers per grade level, in order to have sufficient staff to provide the typical needed intervention and enrichment groups, we suggest scheduling I/E periods by two or three grade levels (Figure 4.2, p. 112 or 4.3, p. 113) so that the staff and students balance.)

The Planning Meeting

The committee members (all those who will provide services during the I/E period[5]) start by dividing the students to be served into three broad classifications: special categorical services (SPED, ESL, Title I, TAG, etc.), enrichment services, and short-term instructional interventions. Participants bring appropriate types of formative assessment data to the meeting, such as eligibility lists, students' interest inventories (to guide enrichment activities), and individual education programs (IEPs) to guide them in decision-making. The facilitator—possibly the principal, assistant principal, team leader or grade level chair—might begin by compiling student lists for the typical intervention groups, or the planners could establish enrichment groups first and then move to the intervention groupings.

In our example (Table 4.2), students participate in one of six different activities: social studies enrichment, science enrichment, writing lab, special services, math interventions, or reading interventions. The Talented and Gifted (TAG) teacher or media specialist takes 20 students who for the next ten days will be extending their research on special-interest topics for *social studies enrichment*. The science specialist or one of the base teachers serving in that role works with 15 students in *science enrichment*. Potential special services and interventions in math and reading are illustrated in Table 4.2 and the text that follows.

---

5 Personnel available to provide special services, intervention, and enrichment during the I/E period may vary by grade level, school, school district, and/or state.

Table 4.2 Sample Structure of Intervention/ Enrichment Period for One Grade Level with Four Base Teachers and 92 Students

Number of Students	Activity	Staff
20 students	Social studies enrichment	TAG teacher
15 students	Science enrichment	Library/media specialist or classroom teacher
18 students	Writing lab	Title I or reading specialist
12 students	Special services	LD teacher, ESL teacher, speech/language teacher
10 students	Math interventions	Math specialist, classroom teacher, and/or computer lab
17 students	Reading interventions	Title I, reading specialist, SPED teacher, one or more classroom teachers

Special Services

Special education, ESL, and speech/language teachers most likely will be working primarily with qualifying students (12 in this example) assigned to them, although sometimes their students move to enrichment or intervention groups because of a specific identified need and/or interest; this happens quite often with LD students. Also, a special education teacher with a particular skill or talent might work with a reading intervention group or an enrichment science unit for a ten-day stint.

At least one, possibly two *mathematics intervention* groups would be a fixture on the menu, with topics and group composition changing as needed. Historically, systematic "math interventions are much less common for young children than are reading interventions" (Jordan, 2007, p. 65). Typically, a base teacher who is strong in mathematics (and, where possible, a math specialist or Title I teacher) provides math intervention. If a math specialist is not available, computer-assisted instruction might support intervention and enrichment groups in mathematics. The math groups could be larger than the 10 indicated in Table 4.2, if the computer lab were used. Group size can vary based on student needs.

Writing Interventions

A Title I teacher or reading specialist might assume responsibility for 18 students in the writing lab. Some schools have groups rotate through the writing lab for five to 15 days in a row to focus on specific writing skills and/or specific types of writing. A particular group could focus on helping young writers improve at the sentence level, emphasizing language usage, sentence variety, or correctness. For example, students who can form complete sentences might work on combining sentences and then apply those skills to paragraph revision, with the teacher demonstrating, providing guided practice, and monitoring independent practice.

Another rotation could focus on using a frame or skeleton (separate boxes for the introduction, body, and conclusion, with sentence starters in each box) to produce a particular type of writing (see Wray & Lewis, 1998). The teacher would provide simple demonstrations of how to use the frame, as well as how to use a checklist of the elements for a particular type of writing. During shared writing, students gradually provide more input as the teacher constructs a composition; then students practice with the frame on their own. Eventually, the teacher would model how to use the frame flexibly, then how to write in a specific genre without a frame. Students would be encouraged to cease using the frame as needed.[6]

On other days, students could work on making their writing more colorful by appropriately using adjectives, similes, or metaphors to provide rich description. The teacher could begin by reading appropriate books or texts containing clear, simple illustrations of this skill. If the teacher had multiple copies, students could mark those passages with sticky notes, then experiment with adding such colorful descriptions to their own writing (Canady, 2008; National Commission on Writing in America's Schools and Colleges, 2003-4).

Reading Interventions

The remaining 17 students in our example have been identified for reading intervention, provided in the smallest possible groups by a variety of personnel. If the reading intervention team includes at least two of the four classroom teachers; at least one special education, speech, or ESL resource specialist; and one or more teaching assistants (TAs) working under the direction of a Title I or reading specialist, the teachers and TAs could form four to six skill-based literacy groups.

Lessons would include essential components of effective reading instruction (phonemic awareness, phonics, vocabulary, fluency, comprehension); however, through the school year each scheduled intervention rotation should have a primary focus, progressing from phonemic awareness and phonics to fluency and then to comprehension. Vocabulary should be included as an important element of all groups.

For example, an intervention team could determine that all second graders who have not mastered long vowel patterns will participate in decoding groups for a time, then be reassessed. After analyzing a spelling assessment such as the Bear Spelling Assessment (Bear, Invernizzi, Templeton, & Johnston, 2007) or the Ganske Spelling Assessment (Ganske, 2000), teachers may see the need for intervention groups focused on progressive decoding skills: short vowels, blends and digraphs, and long vowel patterns. With consideration of teacher strengths, the reading specialist and a TA would tend to take lower groups focused on hearing speech sounds. Because blend and digraph issues tend to be related to speech issues, a speech teacher who also is trained in reading could offer specific expertise in teaching this group. More intense intervention groups would be smaller (e.g., three to five students) than less-intense groups (e.g., five to seven students).

Based on spelling assessments, classroom teachers might begin by teaching higher-level decoding groups (syllable stress

---

6 See Canady (2008) for a host of other writing ideas.

in multi-syllable words, prefixes, base words, suffixes in multi-syllable words); however, as students progress throughout the year from beginning- to instructional-level readers and writers, their skill groups will need to focus primarily on fluency and then move to comprehension.

Various types of assessments will be needed to determine the specific intervention groups; for example, if some students are emergent readers, the lowest group's primary focus would be phonemic awareness (rhyming, learning beginning sounds, blending sounds together to read a word, segmenting sounds to write a word, tracking print). The next groups would focus primarily on decoding; the next group would focus on fluency (reading with speed, accuracy, and expression); the highest intervention groups would focus on comprehension. Vocabulary could be emphasized at all levels. In each lesson, specific skills would be applied to authentic reading and writing tasks.

By the end of the extended planning block, the grade 2 team has considered the enrichment and intervention needs of all 92 students and determined the instructional assignments for the next ten days of I/E. The instructional leader can print out the composition of each group, along with teacher assignments and meeting locations.

The Inclusion Model: Scheduling, Organizing, and Instructing

There are several ways to institutionalize inclusion models into the master schedule. Full inclusion models tend to occur in schools with large populations of special needs students along with support and resource staff to serve them. Growing demands that higher numbers of special education students be included in the same testing programs as regular students, as well as the requirement to report achievement data by disaggregated groupings, have made inclusion models increasingly important and necessary.

Scheduling Inclusion Teachers

Pairing one special education teacher with one general education teacher is the simplest scenario for inclusion: The two follow the same schedule (for example, one of the class schedules in Figure 4.4, p. 114). The plot thickens when the special education teacher must serve two inclusion classes at one or more grade levels.

When a school has two inclusion classes at the same grade level (because there were too many special education students to cluster in one class), their schedules essentially add an overlay. In Figure 4.11 (p. 123), we show the schedule for teachers 3A and 3B as well as for the inclusion teacher who splits time between the two classrooms.

If the school is fortunate enough to have a teaching assistant who works with the special education inclusion teacher, we would assign the TA to one classroom when the teacher is in the other classroom. Also, we also might consider rotating the inclusion teacher's and TA's schedules every other day, rather than splitting each period as shown. For example, the inclusion teacher might start the day with 90 minutes in 3B's language arts class while the assistant is with 3A's class. Then the inclusion teacher would move to 3A's class for math while the TA aids teacher 3B. This schedule could be reversed the next day. During the I/E period at day's end, both the special education teacher and assistant could work with mixed groups of students from the two classes.

The schedule shown in Figure 4.12 (p. 124) illustrates a special service teacher split between two different grade levels. In this case, the school has decided to use all of her scheduled time for inclusion; therefore, she doesn't work with her students during the I/E period. To begin the day, she works in fourth grade math for 50 minutes, followed by fifth grade math for 50 minutes. After her planning period (which she shares with the fourth grade teacher), she repeats the pattern for 50 minutes of LA in each grade. After lunch, she spends another 50 minutes with each grade level.

We would prefer to have an inclusion teacher shared across two grade levels work with students in the I/E environment as well. This allows pre-teaching, re-teaching, or specific skill instruction during the I/E period and co-teaching during the inclusion periods. Over the course of the day, we see that the 4/5 special education teacher (highlighted in Figure 4.13, p. 125) spends 50 minutes in each grade supporting math instruction, 50 minutes in each grade supporting language arts instruction, and 50 minutes working with each grade in the Intervention/Enrichment period. Although the special education teacher does not have common planning time with either grade level, she occasionally could forgo working with students in the fourth grade I/E time to plan with the fifth grade teacher, and vice versa. In either case, a teaching assistant, if available, could take the special education teacher's place during the I/E periods to allow for common teacher planning time for both grade levels.

Like other teachers, special education instructors have strengths and weaknesses. Increasingly, we find that schools schedule their special education teachers in a focused area of teacher strength. For example, rather than assigning one to each grade level, the school could pair them. One special education teacher might focus on reading support and intervention during the language arts blocks and Intervention/Enrichment periods of two grade levels, while the second works in the mathematics, science and social studies blocks in both grades.

The plan developed for inclusion greatly depends on the requirements of students' Individual Education Programs. Once known, the IEP requirements determine the necessary sharing of special education personnel both within and between grade levels. Because this information is essential to constructing an educationally sound master schedule, we strongly recommend completing annual IEP reviews by mid-spring. We also recommend constructing the grade-level schedules and the special education teachers' schedules concurrently. Typically, the special education schedules are created after the school's master schedule is set; this practice generates either an unsatisfactory schedule for the special education teachers or a master schedule that is disjointed. Either outcome causes frustration.

Co-teaching Models

School personnel have developed inclusion models in an attempt to reduce the number of students pulled from their base classroom for special services—a practice now considered not highly effective, at least for many special needs students. Further catalysts for inclusion are state accountability systems and No Child Left Behind mandates that require including special needs students in testing programs with the general student population. Schools want these students exposed to basic content instruction taught by those most likely to have a firm grasp of that content, usually the general education teachers.

All of the various forms of inclusion involve some form of co-teaching between general classroom or base teachers and special teachers trained to assist students with specific instructional needs. According to Friend and Cook (1996), co-teaching models draw on the unique strengths of both instructors and enable the two teachers to assume complementary roles, which, theoretically, should enhance the growth of all students in the inclusion classroom. Friend and Cook describe five inclusion or co-teaching models used in elementary schools: one teacher teaching, the other supporting; station teaching; parallel teaching; alternative teaching, and team teaching. These formats are underused, they say, and often replaced by an ineffective model with the general education teacher assuming the major teaching responsibilities and the special teacher merely monitoring instruction or assisting as needed.

In the *one-teaching, one-supporting* model, two teachers are present in the same classroom on a daily basis, but one (generally the base teacher) is the primary teacher for a particular group, lesson or subject, doing most of the teaching while the other does most of the support work with *all* the students in the classroom. Support might include individual and small-group instruction, providing accommodations required in certain IEPs, helping students with homework assignments, providing follow-up interventions after formative testing, and supervising selected students while retaking tests. Friend and Cook illustrate this model with the following example: A class is divided into two unequal groups. While the larger group reviews or does an enrichment activity, the smaller group has concepts re-taught, a lesson previewed, or a specific skill reemphasized. The two teachers may work with either group during the day; however, it is important to vary the composition of the groups and to rotate the teachers to avoid stigma.

Although this model has some advantages (chief among them the limited need to plan together), there also are some challenges. A teacher who consistently serves as the support teacher may come to be seen in that role by students and feel more like an aide than an equal; this possibility makes it a good idea for the two teachers to alternate roles occasionally. In an ideal setting, the two teachers would have complementary teaching strengths and determine their roles as primary or support teacher in a way that tapped the strengths of each.

In the model sometimes called *station teaching,* two co-teachers divide their students into three groups that rotate among three stations within the room. Each co-teacher assumes responsibility for instructing a segment of the lesson at one of the stations. They teach concurrently, perhaps differentiating their instruction by scaffolding differently or by teaching to different learning styles. Meanwhile, the students in the third group engage in peer tutoring or work at the third station on modules the co-teachers prepare in advance. These modules might include elements of the traditional "work centers" used by elementary teachers for years, and/or computer-assisted instruction. Students generally rotate through all three stations during a block of classroom time.

For station teaching to succeed, the two co-teachers must plan extensively, and the work at the stations must be well coordinated, integrated, and supervised. A teacher aide or paraprofessional, if available, most likely would supervise the third station.

In *parallel teaching,* the classroom is divided into two subgroups, and the teachers jointly plan instruction. The major goals of this model are to share teacher strengths in designing lesson plans and to deliver instruction to students in smaller groups. This model requires teachers to coordinate their planning and teaching so that the students essentially receive the same instruction. As in station teaching, teachers must closely regulate noise and activity levels in the classroom. In a classroom with a large enrollment and/or a disproportionate number of severe student behavioral problems, another co-teaching model may be more suitable.

The major advantage of *alternative teaching* is that students with special learning needs sometimes benefit from pre-teaching or re-teaching the instructional content. In this model, one teacher works with a small group of students to pre-teach or re-teach while the co-teacher instructs the larger group. The goal is to provide all students in the classroom opportunities to interact with a teacher in a small group at various times during the day; however, the plan also can stigmatize students with special needs by repeatedly grouping them together for pre-teaching or re-teaching. Ways to avoid this include varying the composition of the groupings, alternating the teacher who works with the smaller group, and doing some enrichment work in the small group.

In *team teaching,* two teachers share the planning and delivery of instruction. The teachers might change roles in leading discussions, demonstrating concepts, modeling note-taking, or leading in a total classroom presentation. This model works best when teachers are committed to team teaching, are compatible in classroom management and philosophy, and respect each other as professionals. Under ideal conditions, it can be wonderful for all concerned. Problems can arise if one teacher perceives the other as weaker professionally or as not carrying a fair share of the workload.

Another model of inclusion, the *blended classroom,* has merit in selected circumstances. Although not described by Friend and Cook (1996), the blended classroom contains elements of all five of their models. Some educators view the blended classroom as one of the most extreme forms of inclusion. In one example, 15 to 18 regular or even TAG students share a classroom with 15 to 18 Title I or low-achieving students (but typically not special education or ESL students). Two teachers, assigned full-time to this blended classroom, provide a grade-level or accelerated curriculum to *all* students in the classroom. They pour their combined efforts into helping each student reach higher levels of achievement. For the blended classroom to work, parents of every student need to understand and agree with the plan. Members of the blended classroom, along with their teachers, tend to loop for a minimum of two years; most remain for three years.

Schools can use the inclusion schedules and co-teaching models described in this chapter with a variety of special service teachers, including special education teachers, Title I or district-funded reading instructors, and ESL staff. For example, in a school with a large population of students experiencing low levels of reading achievement, we might assign two distinct reading groups to the homeroom—one below-grade-level group and one above-grade-level group (see chapter 6 for grouping suggestions). A highly trained reading resource teacher serves as a temporary co-teacher for the students in the lower group during reading instructional time. This model not only allows specialized reading assistance but also contributes to staff development; observant base teachers can improve their strategies for instructing lower-achieving students. Because the reading specialist works in various classrooms throughout the day, students are not stigmatized by pull-out programs, nor are classrooms disrupted by the comings and goings of students during instructional time. As an added benefit, the base teachers maintain contact with all their students.

Providing Special Services in a Parallel Block Schedule

In Part II of this book, we detail a different kind of scheduling model for elementary schools called parallel block scheduling (PBS). In this model, teachers work with one half of the class during part of their language arts and mathematics instructional time. Meanwhile, the other half travels to the extension center and receives practice, reinforcement, enrichment, and/or special services if so required; then the two groups exchange places. The extension center concept, coupled with smaller instructional groupings, offers a host of possibilities for meeting the needs of students with different learning needs.

Conclusion

Like most debates in education, the one between supporters of the inclusion model for providing special services and propo-

nents of the pull-out model can become too polemic. We don't think it needs to be all one or the other. Inclusion programs will not meet every student's needs; pull-out programs are not all bad. Special service providers often see the need for both. The scheduling options illustrated in this chapter enable schools to choose among inclusion, pull-out, and combination programs.

References

Bear, D. H., Invernizzi, M., Templeton, S., & Johnston, F. (2004). *Words their way: Word study for phonics, vocabulary, and spelling instruction.* (3rd ed.). Upper Saddle River, NJ: Merrill.

Brookhart, S.M. (2007/2008, December/January). Feedback that fits. *Educational Leadership, 65*(4), 54–59.

Brown-Chidsey, R. (2007, October). No more "Waiting to Fail." *Educational Leadership, 65*(2), 40–46.

Canady, C. E. (2008). The effects of models, writing frames, and sentence combining on second grade writing quality. Unpublished dissertation, University of Virginia, Charlottesville, VA.

Fisher, D. & Frey, N. (2007). *Checking for understanding: Formative assessment techniques for your classroom.* Alexandria, VA: Association of Supervision and Curriculum Development.

Friend, M. & Cook, L. (1996). *Interactions: Collaboration skills for school professionals.* White Plains, NY: Longman Publishers.

Ganske, K. (2000). *Word journeys: Assessment-guided phonics, spelling, and vocabulary instruction.* New York: Guilford Press.

Guskey, T. R. (2007/2008, December/January). The rest of the story. *Educational Leadership, 65*(4), 28–35.

Jordan, N.C. (2007, October). The need for number sense. *Educational Leadership, 65*(2), 63–66.

National Commission on Writing in America's Schools and Colleges (2003-4). *The neglected "R": The need for writing revolution.* Report of the National Commission on Writing in America's Schools and Colleges (ERIC Document Reproduction Service No. ED475856).

Rettig, M. D., McCullough, L. L., Santos, K. E., & Watson, C. R. (2004). *From rigorous standards to student achievement: A practical process.* Larchmont, NY: Eye On Education.

Tomlinson, C. (1999). *The differentiated classroom: Responding to the needs of all learners.* Alexandria, VA: Association for Supervision and Curriculum Development.

Tomlinson, C. (2007/2008, December/January). Learning to love assessment. *Educational Leadership, 65*(4), 8–13.

William, D. (2007/2008, December/January). Changing classroom practice. *Educational Leadership, 65*(4), 36–42.

Wray, D., & Lewis, M. (1998) An approach to factual writing: An invited article. Newark, DE: International Reading Association. Retrieved July 20, 2007 from http://www.readingonline.org.

Figure 4.1 One School-wide I/E Period
(School Day Divided into 5-Minute Increments)

		8:00	9:00	10:00	11:00	12:00	1:00	2:00	3:00
Kinder.	HR	Language Arts (150 Minutes)			Lunch/ Recess (50)	Plan (50)	Math (50)	SS/SC (50)	Intervention/ Enrichment (50)
Grade 1	HR	Language Arts (140 Minutes)		Math (60)	Lunch/ Recess (50)	Plan (50)	SS/SC (50)		Intervention/ Enrichment (50)
Grade 2	HR	Language Arts (140 Minutes)		Lunch/ Recess (50)	Math (60)	SS/SC (50)	Plan (50)		Intervention/ Enrichment (50)
Grade 3	HR	Language Arts (100 Minutes)	Plan (50)	LA (40)	Lunch/ Recess (50)	Math (60)	SS/SC (50)		Intervention/ Enrichment (50)
Grade 4	HR	Plan (50)	Language Arts (100 Minutes)	Math (75)		Lunch/ Recess (50)	SS/SC (75)		Intervention/ Enrichment (50)
Grade 5	HR	LA (50)	Plan (50)	Math (75)	SS/SC (75)		Lunch/ Recess (50)	LA (50)	Intervention/ Enrichment (50)
Intervention/ Enrichment Teachers		Schedule for Inclusion, Planning, and Lunch							Grades K-5
Arts/PE Teachers		Grade 4	Grade 5	Grade 3	Lunch/Duty (50)	Kinder.	Grade 1	Grade 2	Plan (50)

Note: This figure, as do all figures in this book, shows the school day divided into 5-minute increments. The accuracy of the typesetting does not allow us to print the time in every 5-minute slot clearly. We do print the time each hour; times printed refer to the line to the left. The CD-ROM that accompanies this book, however, does have times printed evey five minutes. These charts, when printed on an ink jet or laser printer, will be clear.

4.1

Figure 4.2 Two I/E Periods

		8:00 – 3:00							
Kinder.	HR	Language Arts (150 Minutes)	Lunch/ Recess (50)	Plan (50)	Math (50)	**Intervention/ Enrichment (50)**	SS/SC (50)		
Grade 1	HR	Language Arts (140 Minutes)	Math (60)	Lunch/ Recess (50)	Plan (50)	**Intervention/ Enrichment (50)**	SS/SC (50)		
Grade 2	HR	Language Arts (140 Minutes)	Recess/ Lunch (50)	Math (60)	SS/SC (50)	**Intervention/ Enrichment (50)**	Plan (50)		
Grade 3	HR	Language Arts (140 Minutes)	Math (60)	Recess/ Lunch (50)	SS/SC (50)	Plan (50)	**Intervention/ Enrichment (50)**		
Grade 4	HR	Language Arts (100 Minutes)	Plan (50)	Math (75)	Recess/ Lunch (50)	SS/SC (75)	**Intervention/ Enrichment (50)**		
Grade 5	HR	LA (50)	Plan (50)	Math (75)	SS/SC (75)	Recess/ Lunch (50)	LA (50)	**Intervention/ Enrichment (50)**	
Intervention/ Enrichment Teachers		Schedule for Inclusion, Planning, and Lunch					**Grades K, 1 & 2**	**Grades 3,4 & 5**	
Arts/PE Teachers		Plan (50)	Grade 5	Grade 4	Lunch/Duty (50)	Kinder.	Grade 1	Grade 3	Grade 2

Figure 4.3 Three I/E Periods

		8:00	9:00	10:00	11:00	12:00	1:00	2:00	3:00
Kinder.	HR	Language Arts (150 Minutes)			Lunch/ Recess (50)	Math (50)	Plan (50)	Intervention/ Enrichment (50)	SS/SC (50)
Grade 1	HR	Language Arts (140 Minutes)		Math (60)	Lunch/ Recess (50)	SS/SC (50)	Intervention/ Enrichment (50)	Plan (50)	
Grade 2	HR	Language Arts (140 Minutes)		Recess/ Lunch (50)	Math (60)	SS/SC (50)	Plan (50)	Intervention/ Enrichment (50)	
Grade 3	HR	Language Arts (90 Minutes)	Math (60)	Plan (50)	Recess/ Lunch (50)	LA (50)	SS/SC (50)	Intervention/ Enrichment (50)	
Grade 4	HR	Language Arts (100 Minutes)	Plan (50)	Math (50)	Intervention/ Enrichment (50)	Recess/ Lunch (50)	Math/SS/SC (100)		
Grade 5	HR	Math (50)	Plan (50)	Language Arts (100 Minutes)	Intervention/ Enrichment (50)	Recess/ Lunch (50)	Math/SS/SC (100)		
Intervention/ Enrichment Teachers		Schedule for Inclusion and Planning			Grades 4 & 5	Lunch/Duty (50)	Grades K & 1	Grades 2 & 3	
Arts/PE Teachers		Plan (50)	Grade 5	Grade 4	Grade 3	Lunch/Duty (50)	Kinder.	Grade 2	Grade 1

4.2
4.3

Figure 4.4 An I/E Period for Each Grade Level

	8:00	9:00	10:00	11:00	12:00	1:00	2:00	3:00
Kinder.	HR	Language Arts (150 Minutes)		Lunch/Recess (50)	Math (50)	Plan (50)	Intervention/Enrichment (50)	SS/SC (50)
Grade 1	HR	Language Arts (140 Minutes)		Math (60)	Lunch/Recess (50)	Intervention/Enrichment (50)	Plan (50)	SS/SC (50)
Grade 2	HR	Language Arts (140 Minutes)		Lunch/Recess (50)	Intervention/Enrichment (50)	Math (60)	SS/SC (50)	Plan (50)
Grade 3	HR	Language Arts (90 Minutes)	Math (60)	Plan (50)	Lunch/Recess (50)	LA (50)	SS/SC (50)	Intervention/Enrichment (50)
Grade 4	HR	Math (50)	Intervention/Enrichment (50)	Plan (50)	Language Arts (100 Minutes)	Lunch/Recess (50)	Math/SS/SC (100)	
Grade 5	HR	Math (50)	Plan (50)	Intervention/Enrichment (50)	Language Arts (100 Minutes)	Lunch/Recess (50)	Math/SS/SC (100)	
Intervention/Enrichment Teachers	Plan (50)	Grade 4	Grade 5	Lunch/Duty (40)	Grade 2	Grade 1	Kinder.	Grade 3
Arts/PE Teachers	Plan (50)	Grade 5	Grade 4	Grade 3	Lunch/Duty (50)	Kinder.	Grade 1	Grade 2

Figure 4.5 Speech/Language and Reading Support Services

Multiple Speech/Language or Reading Support Intervention/Enrichment Periods in One Grade Level

Time scale: 8:00 – 9:00 – 10:00 – 11:00 – 12:00 – 1:00 – 2:00 – 3:00

Teacher KA	HR	Language Arts (150 Minutes)		Lunch/Recess (50)	Math (50)	Plan (50)	SS/SC (50)	Intervention/Enrichment (50)
Teacher KB	HR	Language Arts (150 Minutes)		Lunch/Recess (50)	Math (50)	Plan (50)	Intervention/Enrichment (50)	SS/SC (50)
Teacher KC	HR	Language Arts (150 Minutes)		Lunch/Recess (50)	Intervention/Enrichment (50)	Plan (50)	Math (50)	SS/SC (50)
Teacher 1A	HR	Language Arts (140 Minutes)		Math (60)	Lunch/Recess (50)	Intervention/Enrichment (50)	Plan (50)	SS/SC (50)
Teacher 1B	HR	Language Arts (90 Minutes)	Intervention/Enrichment (50)	Math (60)	Lunch/Recess (50)	LA (50)	Plan (50)	SS/SC (50)
Teacher 1C	HR	Intervention/Enrichment (50)	Language Arts (90 Minutes)	Math (60)	Lunch/Recess (50)	LA (50)	Plan (50)	SS/SC (50)
Speech/Language	Duty	1C	Plan (40)	1B	Lunch/Duty/Plan (60)	KC	1A	KB	KA

4.4
4.5

Figure 4.6 Master Schedule

		School #1 Master Schedule with Separate Intervention/Enrichment Periods for Each Grade Level with Morning Instrumental Music Lessons for Grades 4 and 5											
		8:00	9:00	10:00	11:00	12:00	1:00	2:00	3:00				
Kinder.	HR	Language Arts (150 Minutes)			Lunch/ Recess (50)	Math (50)	Plan (50)	Intervention/ Enrichment (50)	SS/SC (50)				
Grade 1	HR	Language Arts (140 Minutes)		Math (60)	Lunch/ Recess (50)	Intervention/ Enrichment (50)	Plan (50)	SS/SC (50)					
Grade 2	HR	Language Arts (140 Minutes)		Recess/ Lunch (50)	Intervention/ Enrichment (50)	Math (60)	SS/SC (50)	Plan (50)					
Grade 3	HR	Language Arts (90 Minutes)	Math (60)	Plan (50)	Recess/ Lunch (50)	LA (50)	SS/SC (50)	Intervention/ Enrichment (50)					
Grade 4	HR	Intervention/ Enrichment (50)	Plan (50)	Math (50)	Language Arts (100 Minutes)		Lunch/ Recess (50)	Math/SS/SC (100)					
Grade 5	HR	Plan (50)	Intervention/ Enrichment (50)	Math (50)	Language Arts (100 Minutes)		Recess/ Lunch (50)	Math/SS/SC (100)					
Intervention/ Enrichment Teachers		Grade 4	Grade 5	Plan (50)	Lunch/ Duty (40)	Grade 2	Grade 1	Kindergarten	Grade 3				
Instrumental Music Teacher(s)		Grade 4 (50) (Grade 5 alternate*)	Grade 5 (50) (Grade 4 alternate*)	Planning/ Travel (50)	School #2 (100)		Planning/ Travel (50)	School #3 (100)					
Arts/PE Teachers		Grade 5	Grade 4	Plan (50)	Grade 3	Lunch/Duty (50)	Kinder.	Grade 1	Grade 2				

* If a student cannot receive a music lesson during the typical period assigned for his/her grade level because some other special service is provided, the lesson could be provided during the student's encore class.

Figure 4.6a Band Lesson Schedule

		School #I Band Lesson Schedule for Grades 4 and 5							
		8:00 / 9:00		10:00	11:00 / 12:00		1:00	2:00	3:00
Grade 4	HR	Intervention/ Enrichment (50)	Plan (50)	Math (50)	Language Arts (100 Minutes)		Lunch/ Recess (50)	Math/SS/SC (100)	
Grade 5	HR	Plan (50)	Intervention/ Enrichment (50)	Math (50)	Language Arts (100 Minutes)		Lunch/ Recess (50)	Math/SS/SC (100)	
Intervention/ Enrichment Teachers		Grade 4 (50)	Grade 5 (50)	Plan (50)	Lunch/ Duty	Grade 2 (50)	Grade 1 (50)	Kinder. (50)	Grade 3 (50)
Band Instructor	M	Grade 4 Brass I	Grade 5 Brass I	Planning/ Travel/ Lunch (50)	School #2 (100)		Planning/ Travel/ Lunch (50)	School #3 (100)	
	T	Grade 4 Woodwinds I	Grade 5 Woodwinds	Planning/ Travel/ Lunch (50)	School #2 (100)		Planning/ Travel/ Lunch (50)	School #3 (100)	
	W	Grade 4 Brass II	Grade 5 Brass II	Planning/ Travel/ Lunch (50)	School #2 (100)		Planning/ Travel/ Lunch (50)	School #3 (100)	
	R	Grade 4 Percussion	Grade 5 Percussion	Planning/ Travel/ Lunch (50)	School #2 (100)		Planning/ Travel/ Lunch (50)	School #3 (100)	
	F	Grade 4 Woodwinds II	Grade 5 Full Band	Planning/ Travel/ Lunch (50)	School #2 (100)		Planning/ Travel/ Lunch (50)	School #3 (100)	
Arts/PE Teachers		Grade 5	Grade 4	Plan (50)	Grade 3	Lunch/Duty (50)	Kinder.	Grade 1	Grade 2

4.6
4.6a

Figure 4.6b Strings Lesson Schedule

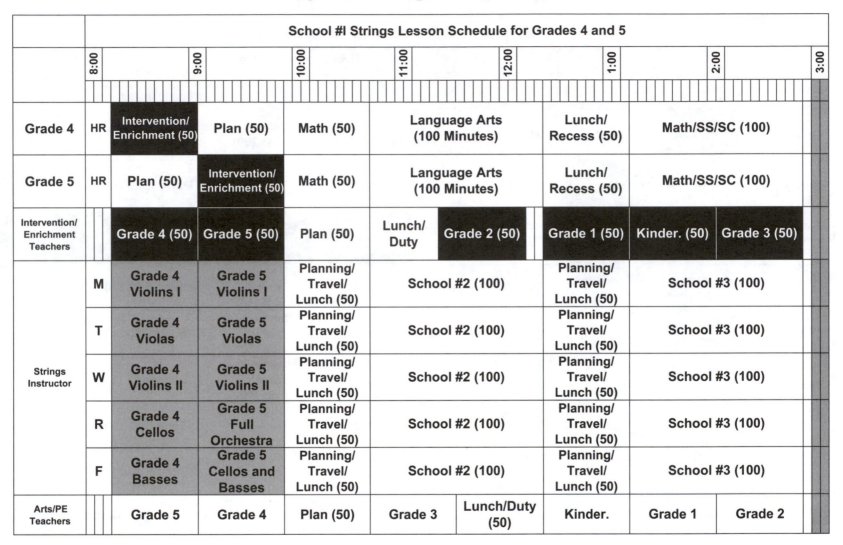

		8:00	9:00	10:00	11:00	12:00	1:00	2:00	3:00
		School #I Strings Lesson Schedule for Grades 4 and 5							
Grade 4	HR	Intervention/ Enrichment (50)	Plan (50)	Math (50)	Language Arts (100 Minutes)		Lunch/ Recess (50)	Math/SS/SC (100)	
Grade 5	HR	Plan (50)	Intervention/ Enrichment (50)	Math (50)	Language Arts (100 Minutes)		Lunch/ Recess (50)	Math/SS/SC (100)	
Intervention/ Enrichment Teachers		Grade 4 (50)	Grade 5 (50)	Plan (50)	Lunch/ Duty	Grade 2 (50)	Grade 1 (50)	Kinder. (50)	Grade 3 (50)
Strings Instructor	M	Grade 4 Violins I	Grade 5 Violins I	Planning/ Travel/ Lunch (50)	School #2 (100)		Planning/ Travel/ Lunch (50)	School #3 (100)	
	T	Grade 4 Violas	Grade 5 Violas	Planning/ Travel/ Lunch (50)	School #2 (100)		Planning/ Travel/ Lunch (50)	School #3 (100)	
	W	Grade 4 Violins II	Grade 5 Violins II	Planning/ Travel/ Lunch (50)	School #2 (100)		Planning/ Travel/ Lunch (50)	School #3 (100)	
	R	Grade 4 Cellos	Grade 5 Full Orchestra	Planning/ Travel/ Lunch (50)	School #2 (100)		Planning/ Travel/ Lunch (50)	School #3 (100)	
	F	Grade 4 Basses	Grade 5 Cellos and Basses	Planning/ Travel/ Lunch (50)	School #2 (100)		Planning/ Travel/ Lunch (50)	School #3 (100)	
Arts/PE Teachers		Grade 5	Grade 4	Plan (50)	Grade 3	Lunch/Duty (50)	Kinder.	Grade 1	Grade 2

Figure 4.7 Master Schedule: Mid-Day Music

		School #II Master Schedule with Separate Intervention/Enrichment Periods for Each Grade Level with MID-DAY Instrumental Music Lessons for Grades 4 and 5								
		8:00	9:00	10:00	11:00	12:00	1:00	2:00	3:00	
Kinder.	HR	LA (40)	Intervention/ Enrichment (50)	LA (60)	Lunch/ Recess (50)	Math (50)	LA (50)	Plan (50)	SS/SC (50)	
Grade 1	HR	Language Arts (90 Minutes)		Intervention/ Enrichment (50)	Math (60)	Lunch/ Recess (50)	LA (50)	SS/SC (50)	Plan (50)	
Grade 2	HR	Language Arts (90 Minutes)		Plan (50)	Recess/ Lunch (50)	Math (60)	LA (50)	Intervention/ Enrichment (50)	SS/SC (50)	
Grade 3	HR	Plan (50)	Language Arts (90 Minutes)		Math (60)	Recess/ Lunch (50)	LA (50)	SS/SC (50)	Intervention/ Enrichment (50)	
Grade 4	HR	Language Arts (100 Minutes)		Math (50)	Intervention/ Enrichment (50)	Plan	Lunch/ Recess (50)	Math/SS/SC (100)		
Grade 5	HR	Language Arts (100 Minutes)		Math (50)	Plan (50)	Intervention/ Enrichment (50)	Recess/ Lunch (50)	Math/SS/SC (100)		
Intervention/ Enrichment Teachers		Plan (50)	Kindergarten	Grade 1	Grade 4	Grade 5	Lunch/Duty (50)	Grade 2	Grade 3	
Instrumental Music Teacher(s)		School #1 (100)		Planning/ Travel (50)	Grade 4 (Grade 5 alternate*)	Grade 5 (Grade 4 alternate*)	Lunch/ Travel (50)	School #3 (100)		
Arts/PE Teachers		Grade 3	Plan (40)	Grade 2	Grade 5	Grade 4	Lunch/Plan (50)	Kinder.	Grade 1	

* If a student cannot receive a music lesson during the typical period assigned for his/her grade level because some other special service is provided, the lesson could be provided during the student's encore class.

4.6b
4.7

Figure 4.8 Master Schedule: Afternoon Music

		School #III Master Schedule with Separate Intervention/Enrichment Periods for Each Grade Level with AFTERNOON Instrumental Music Lessons for Grades 4 and 5								
		8:00	9:00	10:00	11:00	12:00	1:00	2:00	3:00	
Kinder.	HR	Language Arts (150 Minutes)			Lunch/Recess (50)	Intervention/Enrichment (50)	Plan (50)	Math (50)	SS/SC (50)	
Grade 1	HR	Language Arts (90 Minutes)		Plan (50)	Math (60)	Lunch/Recess (50)	Intervention/Enrichment (50)	LA (50)	SS/SC (50)	
Grade 2	HR	Language Arts (100 Minutes)		Intervention/Enrichment (50)	Recess/Lunch (50)	Plan (50)	LA (40)	Math (60)	SS/SC (50)	
Grade 3	HR	Plan (50)	Intervention/Enrichment (50)	Language Arts (100 Minutes)		Lunch/Recess (50)	Math (60)	LA/SS/SC (90)		
Grade 4	HR	Language Arts (100 Minutes)		Math (50)	Math/SS/SC (100)		Lunch/Recess (50)	Intervention/Enrichment (50)	Plan (50)	
Grade 5	HR	Language Arts (100 Minutes)		Math (50)	Math/SS/SC (100)		Lunch/Recess (50)	Plan (50)	Intervention/Enrichment (50)	
Intervention/Enrichment Teachers		Plan (50)	Grade 3	Grade 2	Lunch/Plan (50)	Grade K	Grade 1	Grade 4	Grade 5	
Instrumental Music Teacher(s)		School #1 (100)		Planning/Travel (50)	School #2 (100)		Planning/Travel (50)	Grade 4 (Grade 5 alternate*)	Grade 5 (Grade 4 alternate*)	
Arts/PE Teachers		Grade 3	Plan (40)	Grade 1	Lunch/Plan (60)	Grade 2	Kinder.	Grade 5	Grade 4	

* If a student cannot receive a music lesson during the typical period assigned for his/her grade level because some other special service is provided, the lesson could be provided during the student's encore class.

Figure 4.9 Band Lesson Schedule

		Band Lesson Schedule for Grades 4 and 5 in Schools #I, #II, & #III							
		8:00 — 9:00 — 10:00		11:00 — 12:00		1:00 — 2:00 — 3:00			
		School #1 (100)		Planning/ Travel/Lunch (50)	School #2 (100)		Planning/ Travel/Lunch (50)	School #3 (100)	
Band Instructor	M	Grade 4 Brass I	Grade 5 Brass	Planning/ Travel/Lunch (50)	Grade 4 Brass I	Grade 5 Brass I	Planning/ Travel/Lunch (50)	Grade 4 Brass I	Plan (50)
	T	Grade 4 Woodwinds I	Grade 5 Woodwinds	Planning/ Travel/Lunch (50)	Grade 4 Woodwinds I	Plan (50)	Planning/ Travel/Lunch (50)	Grade 4 Woodwinds I	Grade 5 Woodwinds
	W	Grade 4 Brass II	Plan (50)	Planning/ Travel/Lunch (50)	Grade 4 Brass II	Grade 5 Woodwinds	Planning/ Travel/Lunch (50)	Grade 4 Woodwinds II	Grade 5 Brass I
	R	Grade 4 Percussion	Grade 5 Percussion	Planning/ Travel/Lunch (50)	Grade 4 Percussion	Grade 5 Percussion	Planning/ Travel/Lunch (50)	Plan (50)	Grade 5 Percussion
	F	Grade 4 Woodwinds II	Grade 5 Full Band	Planning/ Travel/Lunch (50)	Plan (50)	Grade 5 Full Band	Planning/ Travel/Lunch (50)	Grade 4 Percussion	Grade 5 Full Band

4.8
4.9

Figure 4.10 Master Schedule with Full-Time Teacher

		School #1 Master Schedule with Full-time Instrumental Music Teacher for Grades 3-5							
		8:00 — 9:00 — 10:00 — 11:00 — 12:00 — 1:00 — 2:00 — 3:00							
Kinder.	HR	Language Arts (150 Minutes)		Lunch/ Recess (50)	Math (50)	Plan (50)	Intervention/ Enrichment (50)	SS/SC (50)	
Grade 1	HR	Language Arts (140 Minutes)		Math (60)	Lunch/ Recess (50)	Intervention/ Enrichment (50)	Plan (50)	SS/SC (50)	
Grade 2	HR	Language Arts (140 Minutes)		Lunch/ Recess (50)	Intervention/ Enrichment (50)	Math (60)	SS/SC (50)	Plan (50)	
1/2 of Grade 3	HR	Language Arts (90 Minutes)	Math (60)	Plan (50)	Lunch/ Recess (50)	LA (50)	SS/SC (50)	Intervention/ Enrichment (50)	
1/2 of Grade 3	HR	Language Arts (90 Minutes)	Math (60)	Plan (50)	Lunch/ Recess (50)	LA (50)	Intervention/ Enrichment (50)	SS/SC (50)	
1/2 of Grade 4	HR	Math (50)	Plan (50)	LA (100)	Intervention/ Enrichment (50)	Lunch/ Recess (50)	Math/SS/SC (100)		
1/2 of Grade 4	HR	Math (50)	Plan (50)	LA (50)	Intervention/ Enrichment (50)	LA (50)	Lunch/ Recess (50)	Math/SS/SC (100)	
1/2 of Grade 5	HR	Plan (50)	Math (50)	Intervention/ Enrichment (50)	LA (100)		Lunch/ Recess (50)	Math/SS/SC (100)	
1/2 of Grade 5	HR	Plan (50)	Intervention/ Enrichment (50)	Math (50)	LA (100)		Lunch/ Recess (50)	Math/SS/SC (100)	
Intervention/ Enrichment Teachers Grades K-2		Inclusion			Lunch/Duty (50)	Grade 2	Grade 1	Grade K	Plan (50)
Intervention/ Enrichment Teachers Grades 3-5		Plan (50)	Grade 5	Grade 5	Grade 4	Grade 4	Lunch/Duty (50)	Grade 3	Grade 3
Instrumental Music Teacher(s)		Plan (50)	Grade 5	Grade 5	Grade 4	Grade 4	Lunch/Duty (50)	Grade 3	Grade 3
Arts/PE Teachers		Grade 5	Grade 4	Plan (50)	Grade 3	Lunch/Duty (50)	Kinder.	Grade 1	Grade 2

Figure 4.11 Master Schedule with Separate I/E Periods for Each Grade Level with Grade 3 Inclusion Teacher

		8:00	9:00	10:00	11:00	12:00	1:00	2:00	3:00
Kinder.	HR	Language Arts (150 Minutes)			Lunch/ Recess (50)	Math (50)	Plan (50)	Intervention/ Enrichment (50)	SS/SC (50)
Grade 1	HR	Language Arts (140 Minutes)			Math (60)	Lunch/ Recess (50)	Intervention/ Enrichment (50)	Plan (50)	SS/SC (50)
Grade 2	HR	Language Arts (140 Minutes)			Lunch/ Recess (50)	Intervention/ Enrichment (50)	Math (60)	SS/SC (50)	Plan (50)
Teacher 3A	HR	Language Arts (90 Minutes)		Math (60)	Plan (50)	Lunch/ Recess (50)	SS/SC (50)	LA (50)	Intervention/ Enrichment (50)
Grade 3 Inclusion		LA 3B (45)	LA 3A (45)	Math 3A (30)	Math 3B (30)	Plan (50)	Recess/ Lunch (50)	LA 3B (50)	LA 3A (50)	Intervention/ Enrichment (50)
Teacher 3B	HR	Language Arts (90 Minutes)		Math (60)	Plan (50)	Lunch/ Recess (50)	LA (50)	SS/SC (50)	Intervention/ Enrichment (50)
Grade 4	HR	Math (50)	Intervention/ Enrichment (50)	Plan (50)	Language Arts (100 Minutes)		Lunch/ Recess (50)	Math/SS/SC (100)	
Grade 5	HR	Math (50)	Plan (50)	Intervention/ Enrichment (50)	Language Arts (100 Minutes)		Lunch/ Recess (50)	Math/SS/SC (100)	
Intervention/ Enrichment Teachers		Plan (50)	Grade 4	Grade 5	Lunch/ Duty (40)	Grade 2	Grade 1	Grade K	Grade 3
Arts/PE Teachers		Plan (50)	Grade 5	Grade 4	Grade 3	Lunch/Duty (50)	Kinder.	Grade 1	Grade 2

4.10
4.11

Figure 4.12 Master Schedule with Separate I/E Periods for Each Grade Level with Grade 4/5 Inclusion Teacher Who Does not Provide I/E Services

		8:00	9:00	10:00	11:00	12:00	1:00	2:00	3:00
Kinder.	HR	Language Arts (150 Minutes)			Lunch/ Recess (50)	Math (50)	Plan (50)	Intervention/ Enrichment (50)	SS/SC (50)
Grade 1	HR	Language Arts (140 Minutes)			Math (60)	Lunch/ Recess (50)	Intervention/ Enrichment (50)	Plan (50)	SS/SC (50)
Grade 2	HR	Language Arts (140 Minutes)			Lunch/ Recess (50)	Intervention/ Enrichment (50)	Math (60)	SS/SC (50)	Plan (50)
Grade 3	HR	Language Arts (90 Minutes)		Math (60)	Plan (50)	Lunch/ Recess (50)	LA (50)	SS/SC (50)	Intervention/ Enrichment (50)
Grade 4	HR	Math (50)	Intervention/ Enrichment (50)	Plan (50)	Language Arts (100 Minutes)		Lunch/ Recess (50)	Math/SS/SC (100)	
Grade 4/5 SPED		Math 4 (50)	Math 5 (50)	Plan (50)	LA 4 (50)	LA 5 (50)	Lunch (50)	SS/SC/M 5 (50)	SS/SC/M 4 (50)
Grade 5	HR	Plan (50)	Math (50)	Intervention/ Enrichment (50)	Language Arts (100 Minutes)		Recess/ Lunch (50)	Math/SS/SC (100)	
Intervention/ Enrichment Teachers		Plan (50)	Grade 4	Grade 5	Lunch/ Duty (40)	Grade 2	Grade 1	Kindergarten	Grade 3
Arts/PE Teachers		Grade 5	Plan (50)	Grade 4	Grade 3	Lunch/Duty (50)	Kindergarten	Grade 1	Grade 2

Figure 4.13 Master Schedule with Separate I/E Periods for Each Grade Level with Grade 4/5 Inclusion Teacher Who Provides I/E Services

		8:00 – 3:00 (time blocks)							
Kinder.	HR	Language Arts (150 Minutes)			Lunch/Recess (50)	Math (50)	Plan (50)	Intervention/Enrichment (50)	SS/SC (50)
Grade 1	HR	Language Arts (140 Minutes)		Math (60)	Lunch/Recess (50)	Intervention/Enrichment (50)	Plan (50)		SS/SC (50)
Grade 2	HR	Language Arts (140 Minutes)		Lunch/Recess (50)	Intervention/Enrichment (50)	Math (60)	SS/SC (50)		Plan (50)
Grade 3	HR	Language Arts (90 Minutes)	Math (60)	Plan (50)	Lunch/Recess (50)	LA (50)	SS/SC (50)		Intervention/Enrichment (50)
Grade 4	HR	Math (50)	Intervention/Enrichment (50)	Plan (50)	Language Arts (100 Minutes)		Lunch/Recess (50)	Math/SS/SC (100)	
Grade 4/5 SPED		Math 4 (50)	Intervention/Enrichment 4 (50)	Intervention/Enrichment 5 (50)	LA 4 (50)	LA 5 (50)	Lunch (50)	Math 5 (50)	Plan
Grade 5	HR	Math (50)	Plan (50)	Intervention/Enrichment (50)	Language Arts (100 Minutes)		Lunch/Recess (50)	Math/SS/SC (100)	
Intervention/Enrichment Teachers		Plan (50)	Grade 4	Grade 5	Lunch/Duty (40)	Grade 2	Grade 1	Kindergarten	Grade 3
Arts/PE Teachers		Plan (50)	Grade 5	Grade 4	Grade 3	Lunch/Duty (50)	Kindergarten	Grade 1	Grade 2

4.12
4.13

5
Departmentalized Team Schedules for Intermediate Grades

This chapter illustrates and discusses the various forms of teaming and departmentalization typically found in elementary schools. A decade or two ago, there was very little departmentalization in the elementary grades; most teachers were expected to teach all subjects, regardless of their teaching strengths, weaknesses, or interests. It was not unusual for elementary teachers to spend more time on subjects they liked than on those with which they felt less comfortable. The self-contained classroom was accepted as the norm; in fact, some would argue, that was the way elementary schools were supposed to be organized!

Given ideal circumstances, that is, teachers who have strong content knowledge and pedagogical skills in all subject areas, deep understanding of child development, a caring soul, and an abiding belief that all children can learn, we might even favor the self-contained classroom. Certainly, we can recite all the typical arguments for maintaining it, such as the need for young children to have the security and support of one competent, caring adult; but we also must admit that not all self-contained classrooms operated according to the textbook ideal. In the team scheduling models described in this chapter, we attempt to preserve many of the benefits of the self-contained classroom, but we also try to capitalize on the strengths of individual teachers and, in all honesty, to minimize students' exposure to teachers' weaknesses. Elementary school content expectations and accompanying accountability measures have risen significantly in the past 20 years, especially in grades 3–5, and it may be unreasonable to expect all teachers to be experts in all subject areas in the upper elementary grades.

Regardless of the logical arguments for departmentalization, undoubtedly the most significant driving force behind the increased use of the practice is the intense focus today on accountability, instigated by state requirements and the mandates of No Child Left Behind. High-stakes testing requirements in grades 3–5 are the norm in most states. Public announcement of test results by district, school, and grade level are common; such scrutiny produces intense pressure on schools and individual teachers. So, when one of the teachers at a grade level in which science is tested loves science, knows the content, and wants to teach science, it makes a great deal of sense to have that teacher instruct more than one homeroom group in that area.[1]

The Master Schedule

All of the teaming examples in this chapter are based on a basic master schedule constructed from a school day of 405 minutes. Before scheduling departmentalized teams of varying size in grades 3–5, time allocations for various subjects in each grade level must be established; examples of possible time allocations are shown in Table 5.1 (p. 140). As is common, the time varies for subjects in different grades. For example, more minutes often are allocated for reading and language arts in grade 3 than in grades 4 and 5. We believe we have selected allocations typical of most elementary schools today, although some differences may occur within school districts and among states.

As described in chapter 2, we create the master schedule (Figure 5.1, p. 142) by addressing shared resources first: encore (planning) periods, intervention/enrichment periods (I/E), and lunch and recess periods (shown as L/R or R/L in the figures). Although we establish this basic template, when we begin scheduling the core content classes, we may shift one of these three "given" periods to create a larger block of time for a partic-

ular subject at a particular grade level or to minimize the occurrence of short (difficult to utilize) time segments.

Our experience suggests that when elementary teachers end up with less than 20 minutes between activities, the time tends to leak away. Some teachers use short time slots effectively; some do not. Primary teachers may do better at this than upper elementary teachers. For example, a primary teacher might engage students in a short writing activity, or read them a story. Such activities seem to be more difficult for intermediate teachers. We prefer a minimum period of 40 minutes, but we certainly try never to schedule less than 20 minutes.

After placing the encore, intervention/enrichment, lunch/recess periods, we have 270 minutes remaining to schedule all core classes and to generate our various departmentalization schemes. We must emphasize here the importance of building the master schedule with the departmentalization schemes in mind, creating appropriate equal time blocks for the part of the schedule in which teachers exchange students.

In the following sections, we detail the structure of two-, three-, four-, and six-person teams, as enumerated in Table 5.2 (p. 141). While these teaming structures do not constitute all possibilities, we believe they represent the most common departmentalization schemes used in elementary schools today.

---

[1] Readers who notice that all teaming examples are for grades 3–5 may assume we do not support departmentalization in grades K–2. Generally, that's true. Also, while we illustrate a variety of common teaming plans, our inclusion of a plan does not constitute an endorsement. We comment so where appropriate.

Two-Teacher Teams

In Figures 5.2 to 5.6 (pp. 129–132), we show how two-teacher teams in grades 3–5 might be scheduled in our sample master schedule, following the time allocations shown in Table 5.1 (p. 142). The schedule lines for grades K–2 remain the same for all the schedules; however, some changes must be made in the structure of the master schedule lines for grades 3–5 to provide the time allocations within the various of departmentalization plans offered below. We think the schedules offered for grades K–2 are fair, reasonable, and mostly consistent with the scheduling principles we offered in chapter 1.

In *Plan 2A* (Figure 5.2) , the only subjects not taught by both teachers are science and social studies. After they teach their homeroom groups language arts and mathematics, one teacher instructs social studies for both classes during a 45-minute period, while the other instructs science. They exchange classes on some rotating basis within that period: every other day, by quarter or semester, or (much more likely) by unit, with each teaching a 15-day unit to one group and then exchanging classes to instruct the other group in the same content for 15 days. Plans 2A to 2D fit into the grade 3 line on the master schedule shown in Figure 5.1 (p. 142).

In *Plan 2B* (Figure 5.3), both teachers instruct their own homerooms in language arts and reading for 130 minutes (85 in the morning, 45 in the afternoon). One takes responsibility for teaching mathematics (70 minutes) to both groups, while the other instructs science and social studies (70 minutes) to both groups.

Figure 5.2 Plan 2A

Teacher I LA/R/M/ SS	Language Arts and Reading Group A 150	Math Group A 75	Plan 45	L/R 45	SS Gp. A/B 45	I/E 45
Teacher II LA/R/M/ SC	Language Arts and Reading Group B 150	Math Group B 75	Plan 45	L/R 45	SC Gp. B/A 45	I/E 45

Figure 5.3 Plan 2B

Teacher I LA/R/M	Language Arts and Reading Group A 85	Math Gp. A 70	Math Gp. B 70	Plan 45	L/R 45	LA Gp.A 45	I/E 45
Teacher II LA/R/SS/ SC	Language Arts and Reading Group B 85	SS/SC Gp. B 70	SS/SC Gp. A 70	Plan 45	L/R 45	LA Gp.B 45	I/E 45

In *Plan 2C* (Figure 5.4, p. 130), both teachers instruct their own homerooms in just reading for an hour. Then one teaches both groups the remainder of the language arts program and social studies (105 minutes), while the second teacher instructs both groups in mathematics and science (105 minutes). Note that when teacher I works with group B and teacher II works with group A, the instructional time is divided by planning time and lunch into a 60-minute period and a 45-minute period for a total of 105 minutes.

Figure 5.4 Plan 2C

Teacher I R/LA/SS	Reading Gp. A 60	LA/SS Group A 105	LA/SS Gp. B 60	Plan 45	L/R 45	LA/SS Gp. B 45	I/E 45
Teacher II R/M/SC	Reading Gp. B 60	M/SC Group B 105	M/SC Gp. A 60	Plan 45	L/R 45	M/SC Gp. A 45	I/E 45

Many language arts and reading instructors strongly object to the separation of reading from language arts instruction. In *Plan 2D* (Figure 5.5), both teachers instruct their own classes in only social studies for 45 minutes; one instructor teaches all of the language arts and reading to both groups for 110 minutes, while the other instructs the math and science for 110 minutes.

Figure 5.5 Plan 2D

Teacher I LA/R/SS	Language Arts and Reading Group A 110	Language Arts and Reading Group B 110	Plan 45	L/R 45	SS Gp.A 45	I/E 45
Teacher II M/SC/SS	Math and Science Group B 110	Math and Science Group A 110	Plan 45	L/R 45	SS Gp.B 45	I/E 45

In *Plan 2E* (Figure 5.6), instructional time during the day is divided in half (135 minutes for each group). One teacher instructs both groups in language arts and reading; the second teacher instructs mathematics, science, and social studies. This plan fits easily into the grade 5 line in the master schedule (Figure 5.1, p. 142).

Figure 5.6 Plan 2E

Teacher I LA/R/SS	LA/Reading Group A 135	Plan 45	LA/R Gp. B 45	L/R 45	I/E 45	LA/R Gp. B 90
Teacher II M/SC	M/SC/SS Group B 135	Plan 45	M/SC/SS Gp. A 45	L/R 45	I/E 45	M/SC/SS Gp.A 90

Figure 5.7 (p. 131) illustrates three versions of *Plan 2F,* in which the available core instructional time is divided into three 90-minute blocks. In *Version 1,* which follows the grade 4 line on Figure 5.1 (p. 142), the language arts/reading/social studies (LA/R/SS) teacher instructs group A in language arts for 90 minutes while the math/science instructor works with group B in mathematics. At 9:30 A.M., the teachers exchange groups. This second 90-minute block is split by the encore/planning time, although if this were the grade 4 line in Figure 5.1, we could exchange the second half of Core 2 with the planning time to bring the block together. (This would move the encore teachers' lunch period earlier.) After lunch and the I/E period, the LA/SS teacher dons the social studies hat and works with half the students for 90 minutes, while the math/science teacher instructs the others in science.

Again, social studies and science instruction alternates between the two groups on some routine basis. For example, the last block could be configured as two single periods, with each teacher instructing each group in each subject for 42 minutes daily. The instructors could decide to alternate every other day for the entire block, or teach one group for a quarter or semester and then exchange groups. Finally, the alternation could be structured around units of equal length within marking periods; they might exchange groups at the end of three- or four-and-a-

Figure 5.7 Plan 2F

Version 1

Teacher I LA/R/SS	LA Group A 90	LA Gp. B 45	Plan 45	LA Gp.B 45	R/L 45	I/E 45	SS Gp. A/B 90
Teacher II M/SC	Math Group B 90	Ma Gp. A 45	Plan 45	Ma Gp.A 45	R/L 45	I/E 45	SC Gp. B/A 90

Version 2

Teacher I LA/R/SS	LA Gp. A 90	Plan 45	LA Gp. B 90	I/E 45	R/L 45	SS Gp.A/B 90
Teacher II M/SC	Math Group B 90	Plan 45	Math Group A 90	I/E 45	R/L 45	SC Gp. B/A 90

Version 3

Teacher I LA/R/SS	LA/R/SS Group A 90	Plan 45	LA/R/SS Gp.A 45	LA/R /SS Gp.B 45	I/E 45	R/L 45	LA/R/SS Group B 90
Teacher II M/SC	M/SC Group B 90	Plan 45	M/SC Gp.B 45	M/SC Gp.A 45	I/E 45	R/L 45	M/SC Group A 90

half-week units, depending on whether the school has six-week or nine-week grading periods. All students then receive a grade in both science and social studies for each grading period.

We tend to recommend alternations that reduce the workload for both students and teachers; consequently, we prefer quarter-, semester- or unit-based exchanges because teachers work with fewer students, and students take fewer subjects at a time. When either social studies or science mastery is assessed by a high-stakes state examination, we prefer quarter- or unit-

based alternations that reserve some time before the examination to revert to daily or every-other-day instruction for review in both subjects.

Version 2 of *Plan 2F* follows the grade 5 line on Figure 5.1 (p. 142); again, the two teachers instruct either language arts and social studies or math and science, alternating the groups in 90-minute blocks.

Finally, in *Version 3,* the 270 minutes of academic time is divided equally so that each teacher spends 135 minutes of instructional time working with both groups in either language arts and social studies or math and science.

Three-Teacher Teams

Because there are four core subjects, when elementary schools use three-teacher teams generally all of the teachers specialize in one discipline and also teach their own homerooms in a second discipline. In the most common three-person team, all three instructors teach language arts and reading and then specialize in math, science or social studies. Several other possibilities appear in the figures that follow.

In Figure 5.8 (p. 132; which for grade 3 would require an alteration of the master schedule shown in Figure 5.1, p. 142), *Plan 3A* teachers I, II, and III each begin the day teaching reading for 60 minutes, most likely to their homeroom group. Then teacher I instructs group B for 70 minutes in language arts, while teacher II works with group C in mathematics and teacher III teaches group A both science and social studies.

Figure 5.8 Plan 3A

	8:00-9:00	9:00-10:10	10:10-11:20	11:20-12:05	12:05-12:50	12:50-2:00	2:00-2:45
Teacher I LA/R	Read Gp. A 60	LA Gp. B 70	LA Gp. C 70	Plan 45	L/R 45	LA Gp. A 70	I/E 45
Teacher II Math/R	Read Gp. B 60	Math Gp. C 70	Math Gp. A 70	Plan 45	L/R 45	Math Gp. B 70	I/E 45
Teacher III S/SC/R	Read Gp. C 60	SS/SC Gp. A 70	SS/SC Gp. B 70	Plan 45	L/R 45	SS/SC Gp. C 70	I/E 45

At 10:10, student groups change. Teacher I instructs group C for 70 minutes in language arts, while teacher II instructs mathematics to group A and teacher III instructs group B in science/social studies.

At 11:20, the three team members have a common planning time while all students attend their encore classes, as described in chapter 3. Following planning time, all teachers and students have 45 minutes for lunch/recess or recess/lunch.

At 12:50, teachers complete their core instruction with their homeroom groups—teacher I instructing group A in language arts for 70 minutes, teacher II teaching mathematics to group B, and teacher III instructing group C in both science and social studies. They conclude the day with the I/E period, structured as described in chapter 4.

At least four issues need to be addressed before deciding to adopt the departmentalization model shown in Plan 3A (Figure 5.8):

♦ Is it appropriate to separate reading from the full language arts block of instruction, particularly at grade 3? Many reading educators would argue that it is not.

♦ How will the teachers manage parent–teacher conferences? Must all three attend every conference? If homeroom teachers meet with parents alone, how can they expedite planning with colleagues beforehand?

♦ With students assigned to all three teachers and reading and language arts separated, as shown, who is responsible for coordinating support services?

♦ How do the three teachers plan integration in their subjects? For example, are reading, writing and other facets of the language arts program taught separately? Should at least some of the science and mathematics be integrated? Are these issues still important to the teachers, parents and students?

Again, these are issues to be considered carefully before choosing this model.

In *Plan 3B* (Figure 5.9), language arts and reading are integrated and taught by all three team teachers for 90 minutes to begin the day. After the language arts/reading block is completed, each teacher specializes (in mathematics, social studies, or science). The three homerooms rotate among the three teachers, spending 60 minutes in each of these subjects.

Figure 5.9 Plan 3B

Teacher	LA/R	Math	Math	Plan	L/R	Math	I/E
Teacher I LA/R/Math	LA/R Gp. A 90	Math Gp. C 60	Math Gp. B 60	Plan 45	L/R 45	Math Gp. A 60	I/E 45
Teacher II LA/R/SS	LA/R Gp. B 90	SS Gp. A 60	SS Gp. C 60	Plan 45	L/R 45	SS Gp. B 60	I/E 45
Teacher III LA/R/SC	LA/R Gp. C 90	SC Gp. B 60	SC Gp. A 60	Plan 45	L/R 45	SC Gp. C 60	I/E 45

Figure 5.10 Plan 3C

Teacher	Math	Plan	Read	LA	R/L	I/E	LA	LA
Teacher I LA/M/R	Math Gp. A 90	Plan 45	Read Gp. A 45	LA Gp.C 45	R/L 45	I/E 45	LA Gp.B 45	LA Gp.A 45
Teacher II LA/M/SS	Math Gp. B 90	Plan 45	Read Gp. B 45	SS Gp.A 45	R/L 45	I/E 45	SS Gp.C 45	SS Gp.B 45
Teacher III LA/M/SC	Math Gp. C 90	Plan 45	Read Gp. C 45	SC Gp.B 45	R/L 45	I/E 45	SC Gp.A 45	SC Gp.C 45

Figure 5.11 Plan 3D

Teacher	LA	Plan	LA	R/L	I/E	LA
Teacher I LA	LA Gp. A 90	Plan 45	LA Gp. B 90	R/L 45	I/E 45	LA Gp. C 90
Teacher II Math	Math Gp. C 90	Plan 45	Math Gp. A 90	R/L 45	I/E 45	Math Gp. B 90
Teacher III SS/SC	SS/SC Gp. B 90	Plan 45	SS/SC Gp. C 90	R/L 45	I/E 45	SS/SC Gp. A 90

In comparison to Plan 3A, Plan 3B increases the time allocated for social studies and science and decreases the time allocated to language arts and mathematics. Care must be taken not to let departmentalization schemes dictate time allocation. Many educators might consider 60 minutes too little time for mathematics at some grade levels.

In *Plan 3C* (Figure 5.10), we increase the daily allotment of time for mathematics to 90 minutes, taught by all teachers. Each also teaches 45 minutes of reading daily, and then specializes (in language arts, social studies, or science). Students spend 45 minutes in each of these subjects.

Plan 3D (Figure 5.11) shows a three-teacher team using the grade 5 schedule line from Figure 5.1 (p. 142), with three 90-minute blocks of time for all core content. Teacher I (reading and language arts) has group A for 90 minutes, 45 minutes of common planning time, group B for 90 minutes, and then closes the day with group C for 90 minutes. Teacher II (mathematics) and teacher III (science and social studies) follow the same schedule, but with the groups in different order.

The three-teacher team structure illustrated by Plan 3D seems to work better in grades 4 and 5 than in grade 3, primarily because grades 4 and 5 typically spend less time than grade 3 on reading and language arts, and more time on mathematics, science, and social studies. This makes it relatively simple to keep the scheduling blocks equal, with one teacher responsible for science and social studies, one for mathematics, and the third for reading and language arts.

With all of these arrangements, the issues of preparing for parent–teacher conferences and the integration of subjects remain. Also, in states where both science and social studies are tested, the teacher responsible for both science and social studies may feel overworked compared with the mathematics teacher. Some might argue that in the upper grades, these require more time for preparation and for grading papers. Given this perception, and to create at least the illusion of balance, some school leaders ask the mathematics teacher to teach health, if that discipline is part of the core program and not taught by a specialist. Finally, one would hope that both the mathematics and the science/social studies teachers include appropriate writing activities in their classes.

Four-Teacher Teams

Figure 5.12 illustrates how four-teacher teams in grades 3–5 might work in the master schedule shown in Figure 5.1 (p. 142). As we have stated before, either the number of rotating subjects must equal the number of team members (in this case four), or two or more team members must teach sections of the same subject.

In *Plan 4A*, all four teachers instruct 50 minutes of reading to begin the day. Then each teacher specializes (in language arts, mathematics, social studies, or science), with these classes meeting for 55 minutes daily. Notice how all teachers start and end the day instructing their homeroom groups.

The separation of the reading class from the language arts class is a strong disadvantage of this plan. And again, many educators would consider 55 minutes inadequate for daily mathematics instruction. Also, in our experience 110 minutes for social studies and science would be unusually high.

Figure 5.12 Plan 4A

Teacher I R/LA	Read. Gp. A 50	LA Gp. B 55	LA Gp. C 55	LA Gp. D 55	Plan 45	L/R 45	LA Gp. A 55	I/E 45
Teacher II R/Math	Read. Gp. B 50	Math Gp. C 55	Math Gp. D 55	Math Gp. A 55	Plan 45	L/R 45	Math Gp. B 55	I/E 45
Teacher III R/SS	Read. Gp. C 50	SS Gp. D 55	SS Gp. A 55	SS Gp. B 55	Plan 45	L/R 45	SS Gp. C 55	I/E 45
Teacher IV R/SC	Read. Gp. D 50	SC Gp. A 55	SC Gp. B 55	SC Gp. C 55	Plan 45	L/R 45	SC Gp. D 55	I/E 45

Plan 4B (Figure 5.13) is similar to Plan 4A except that the commonly taught subject becomes social studies rather than reading. As shown, the day begins with all four teachers instructing their homerooms in their specialty areas (reading, language arts, mathematics, or science). Each of these classes is taught 55 minutes daily. The day ends with teachers instructing their homerooms for 50 minutes of social studies. While significant time is spent in language arts and reading, the two are still not integrated. Again, many teachers might argue that the schedule allows insufficient time for mathematics and too much time for science and social studies.

In *Plan 4C* (Figure 5.14), the time allocations remain the same as in Plan 4B, but we remedy the language arts/reading disconnection by having teacher I instruct two groups (A and C) in both reading and language arts and teacher II instruct two groups (B and D) as well. Teachers III and IV specialize in math-

Figure 5.13 Plan 4B

Teacher I R/SS	Read. Gp. A 55	Read. Gp. B 55	Read Gp. C 55	Read. Gp. D 55	Plan 45	L/R 45	SS Gp. A 50	I/E 45
Teacher II LA/SS	LA Gp. B 55	LA Gp. C 55	LA Gp. D 55	LA Gp. A 55	Plan 45	L/R 45	SS Gp. B 50	I/E 45
Teacher III Math/SS	Math Gp. C 55	Math Gp. D 55	Math Gp. A 55	Math Gp. B 55	Plan 45	L/R 45	SS Gp. C 50	I/E 45
Teacher IV SC/SS	SC Gp. D 55	SC Gp. A 55	SC Gp. B 55	SC Gp. C 55	Plan 45	L/R 45	SS Gp. D 50	I/E 45

Figure 5.14 Plan 4C

Teacher I R/LA/SS	LA/Reading Gp. A 110		LA/Reading Gp. C 110		Plan 45	L/R 45	SS Gp. A 50	I/E 45
Teacher II R/LA SS	LA/Reading Gp. B 110		LA/Reading Gp. D 110		Plan 45	L/R 45	SS Gp. B 50	I/E 45
Teacher III Math/SS	Math Gp. C 55	Math Gp. D 55	Math Gp. A 55	Math Gp. B 55	Plan 45	L/R 45	SS Gp. C 50	I/E 45
Teacher IV SC/SS	SC Gp. D 55	SC Gp. C 55	SC Gp. B 55	SC Gp. A 55	Plan 45	L/R 45	SS Gp. D 50	I/E 45

ematics and science respectively; all four teachers instruct social studies. Again, we would question whether the amount of time scheduled for mathematics is sufficient.

For *Plan 4D* (Figure 5.15), we remove the commonly taught subject. All teachers now specialize—two in language arts/read-ing (teachers I and II), one in mathematics (teacher III), and one in both social studies and science (teacher IV). Students receive 130 to 135 minutes daily of integrated language arts and read-ing, 65 minutes of mathematics, and 65 minutes of social studies and science.

Figure 5.15 Plan 4D

Teacher I LA/R	LA/Reading Group A 135		LA/R Group C 65	Plan 45	L/R 45	LA/R Group C 65	I/E 45
Teacher II LA/R	LA/Reading Group B 135		LA/R Group D 65	Plan 45	L/R 45	LA/R Group D 65	I/E 45
Teacher III Math	Math Group C 65	Math Gp. D 65	Math Group A 65	Plan 45	L/R 45	Math Group B 65	I/E 45
Teacher IV SS/SC	SS/SC Gp. D 65	SS/SC Gp. C 65	SS/SC Gp. B 65	Plan 45	L/R 45	SS/SC Group A 65	I/E 45

In this plan, teachers I and II instruct groups A and B for 135 minutes. Then they work with groups C and D for 65 minutes before having common planning for 45 minutes while students attend their encore classes. Next they go to lunch/recess for 45 minutes, then return to continue work with groups C and D for 65 minutes to complete the language arts and reading block.

While groups A and B are in reading and language arts, group C is in mathematics for 65 minutes with teacher III and group D works with teacher IV in science and social studies. In this plan, teacher IV could schedule science and social studies instruction on a day 1/day 2 rotation; on a quarter-on, quarter-off basis; on a semester-semester basis; or on the unit teaching format described earlier in this chapter.

After 65 minutes of instruction, teachers III and IV exchange groups and repeat. At 10:15, they dismiss groups C and D and welcome groups A and B, who now have completed their reading and language arts block. At 11:20, the four base teachers have common planning time while their students attend encore classes. At 12:05, all teachers and students have a lunch/recess period of 45 minutes. After lunch/recess, teachers I and II resume with groups C and D for another 65 minutes to complete their instructional time in language arts and reading. Meanwhile, teacher III works with group B in mathematics and teacher IV has group A for science and social studies. Everyone closes the day with a 45-minute I/E period.

Because of the limited time this plan allocates to science and social studies, it is probably more appropriate for grade 3 than either grades 4 or 5, although social studies and science enrichment, which could continue year-long in the I/E period (see chapter 4), might provide additional time for some students.

Finally, in *Plan 4E* (Figure 5.16), we allocate equal time to language arts/reading, mathematics, and science/social studies by dividing the 270 minutes of core instructional time into three 90-minute blocks. These are spread across the day, with a 45-minute planning period between the first and second and 90 minutes of lunch/recess and I/E time before the third.

Because there are four groups of students on the team, and teacher I has time to instruct only three language arts/reading blocks (A, B, and D), teacher III (social studies) must pick up the fourth group for language arts (C). Similarly, teacher IV (science) instructs the fourth group of mathematics (D). During the first and last blocks of the day, teachers III and IV instruct social studies and science respectively.

Figure 5.16 Plan 4E

Teacher I LA/R	LA/R Group A 90	Plan 45	LA/R Group B 90	R/L 45	I/E 45	LA/R Group D 90
Teacher II Math	Math Group C 90	Plan 45	Math Group A 90	R/L 45	I/E 45	Math Group B 90
Teacher III LA/R/SS	SS Gps. B/D 90	Plan 45	LA/R Group C 90	R/L 45	I/E 45	SS Gps. A/C 90
Teacher IV M/SC	SC Gps. D/B 90	Plan 45	Math Group D 90	R/L 45	I/E 45	SC Gps. C/A 90

In this plan, one teacher has responsibility for all the science instruction, the other all the social studies. This scenario is very likely in states that have mandated testing in the two subjects in fifth grade. Figure 5.16 shows groups B/D in the morning blocks for both teachers and groups A/C in their afternoon blocks. We would recommend that one group stay with each teacher for nine weeks and then switch, at least during the fall semester. If testing occurs during late spring, they might alternate day by day during the spring semester. The teachers also could choose to schedule the groups in a quarter-on, quarter-off format or by units, as described previously for other grade levels.

Larger Teams

We recognize that many schools implementing some form of departmentalization have more than four teachers per grade level. Generally, they can combine two or more of the models described above to accommodate the team sizes required.

For example, a school that chooses to allocate 90 minutes daily to language arts/reading, mathematics, and science/social studies at grade 5 with five teachers could combine a three-person team (Plan 3D) and a two-person team (Plan 2F); both of these plans provide the same time allocations.

If there were six teachers, we might form two teams of three (Plan 3D) or three teams of two (Plan 2F). With seven teachers, we could choose to combine a four-person team (Plan 4E) and a three-person team (Plan 3D), or two sets of two (Plan 2F) and one of three (Plan 3D). Both of these staffing arrangements require seven teachers and provide 90 minutes of instruction in language arts/reading, mathematics, and science/social studies daily to all students.

Because of its ubiquity in many middle schools across the nation, especially at the seventh and eighth grade levels, one additional teaming structure that likewise provides 90 minutes of language arts/reading, 90 minutes of mathematics, and 90 minutes of social studies and science is worth mentioning here. In Figure 5.17 we show *Plan 6,* designed for six core teachers. In this plan, every teacher instructs in only one discipline. As shown, there are two language arts/reading instructors (I and V), two mathematics instructors (II and VI), one social studies teacher (III) and one science teacher (IV). The plan may be

thought of as two teams of three that share the social studies and science teachers.

Figure 5.17 Plan 6

Teacher I LA/R	Plan 45	LA/R Group A 90	LA/R Group B 90	I/E 45	R/L 45	LA/R Group C 90
Teacher II Math	Plan 45	Math Group B 90	Math Group C 90	I/E 45	R/L 45	Math Group A 90
Teacher III SS	Plan 45	SS Gps. C/D 90	SS Gps. A/E 90	I/E 45	R/L 45	SS Gps. B/F 90
Teacher IV SC	Plan 45	SC Gps. D/C 90	SC Gps. E/A 90	I/E 45	R/L 45	SC Gps. F/B 90
Teacher V LA/R	Plan 45	LA/R Group E 90	LA/R Group F 90	I/E 45	R/L 45	LA/R Group D 90
Teacher VI Math	Plan 45	Math Group F 90	Math Group D 90	I/E 45	R/L 45	Math Group E 90

Let's follow the schedule of Buster Brown, a student assigned to teacher II's homeroom (group B). Buster starts the day by traveling with group B to attend encore classes while his teacher plans with the others on the team. Next, he returns to teacher II's classroom for 90 minutes of mathematics, followed by 90 minutes of language arts and reading instruction with teacher I. After 45 minutes of Intervention/Enrichment (see chapter 4) and 45 minutes of recess and lunch, Buster completes the day in either social studies (with teacher III) or science (with teacher IV).

As already mentioned, social studies and science classes could alternate in a variety of ways: by period, day, quarter, semester, or unit. Because this team serves six groups of students, we recommend alternating by quarter, semester, or unit—and here's why. The other teachers each meet with three groups daily, all year long. Science and social studies teachers must instruct six groups over the course of the year. If they were to alternate by period or by day, they would meet with all six all year—a much greater student load than their colleagues manage. Alternating groups by quarter, semester, or unit spreads out the workload. What's more, it eases the academic burden on students, who can focus on one subject or the other during any rotation.

Of course, as mentioned before, teachers must choose an option that supports students' ability to recall content on tests at the end of the term or year. The state of Virginia, for example, offers science and social studies assessments every semester in high school and middle school but administers the elementary school tests only at year's end. Thus, teachers must plan for students to have recent contact with material and appropriate review before testing dates.

Rotating the Periods

We also can apply one more scheduling twist to any of the departmentalization schemes presented in this chapter. Teachers who instruct in teams occasionally complain that they always have the same group first thing in the morning, last period of the day, or right after lunch. We all know that some students learn better at different times of the day, and conversely that some teachers are at their best at different times of the day. With a team plan that features periods of equal length, we can vary the routine by rotating the periods.

For example, in Plan 6 (Figure 5.17, p. 137) we could rotate the three core instructional blocks every 12 weeks. Teacher I might work with group A during the first morning block at the start of school, with group B at midyear, and with group C for the final 12 weeks. Encore periods, the I/E period, and lunch can remain stable as the core blocks rotate around them. Core class rotations, however, are possible only if special services schedules can be aligned and rotated similarly.

A Final Word on Elementary School Teaming/Departmentalization

Departmentalization in elementary schools is expanding in popularity and in controversy. On its surface, the practice flies in the face of two values that many elementary educators hold dear: the care, understanding, and safe haven of the self-contained classroom, which they consider necessary for a young child's social and emotional development, and the desire to integrate curriculum across many disciplines.

On the other hand, many schools have opted for departmentalization because state assessments are discipline-based, and administrators and teachers alike believe that slotting instructors into one discipline in which they are most knowledgeable, with one daily lesson preparation, makes the goals for student learning more achievable. We believe that the reality of schools precludes any one pat answer to the question "departmentalized or self-contained?" Rather, as with many issues in education, we believe that a variety of highly contextual factors must be considered.

- What are the strengths and weaknesses of the teachers at a particular grade level? With clearly identified faculty weaknesses or strengths in the disciplines, we lean toward departmentalization.

- How rigorous are the standards in each discipline? The more rigorous the standards, the more we tend to favor specialists over generalists.

- What is the general familial and community climate? While we realize that this is difficult to generalize, we are more likely to support departmentalization when the social emotional needs of the majority of the student body are being well met, and more inclined toward self-contained classrooms when significant numbers of students come to school from difficult family and community circumstances.

- What grade levels are we considering? In general, we prefer more departmentalization in grades 3–5 than in grades K–2.

- What teaming/departmentalization arrangements will students encounter in the first year of middle school? We look more favorably on departmentalization in fifth grade when it mirrors the teaming structures in sixth.

- What communication structures are created to lessen the potential negative impact of departmentalization on our understanding of the whole child and our communications with parents and guardians? Again, we are more inclined to support departmentalization when schools take great care to ensure that parents are well informed about their children's progress and that colleagues regularly share information about the students with whom they work in common.

- What programs and/or resources are available to counter any negative effects of departmentalization? Is there a mentoring or advisory program to give each student a strong link to an individual adult? Can we find a way to use the I/E period to help build relationships? Can technology assist us in the generation of reports?

We hope that these questions can help guide elementary personnel to make the best decisions for their schools regarding the various teaming structures presented above. Absent significant research regarding student achievement in departmentalized versus self-contained scheduling models, we believe these factors form a reasonable framework for our choice of a structural model.

Table 5.1 Time Allocations by Departmentalization Plan

Subject	Plan	2A	2B	2C	2D	2E	2F	3A	3B	3C	3D	4A	4B	4C	4D	4E	6
	Pg. #	129	129	130	130	130	131	132	133	133	133	134	135	135	135	136	137
LA / Reading		150	130	165	110	135	90	130	90	90	90	105	110	110	135	90	90
SS		45	70		45	135	90	70	60	90	90	55	50	50	65	90	90
SC				105	110				60			55	55	55		90	90
Math		75	70				90	70	60	90	90	55	55	55	65	90	90
Encore		45	45	45	45	45	45	45	45	45	45	45	45	45	45	45	45
Lunch/Recess		45	45	45	45	45	45	45	45	45	45	45	45	45	45	45	45
Inter./Enrich.		45	45	45	45	45	45	45	45	45	45	45	45	45	45	45	45
Wiggle Room					5										5		
Totals		**405**	**405**	**405**	**405**	**405**	**405**	**405**	**405**	**405**	**405**	**405**	**405**	**405**	**405**	**405**	**405**

Key: 2E denotes "Two-Person Team-Plan E;" 3D means "Three-Person Team-Plan D," etc.

Note: When the school day has less than 405 minutes, obviously adjustments must be made in the time allocations.

Table 5.2 Typical Elementary School Departmentalization Schemes

Scheme	Number of Teachers on Team	Subjects Taught by All Team Teachers in Self-Contained or Regrouped Classes	Departmentalized Subjects; Groups Rotate to Teachers in Equal Time Blocks
2A	2	Reading, language arts (LA), mathematics	Social studies and science
2B	2	Reading and LA	Math opposite social studies/science
2C	2	Reading	LA/social studies, math/science
2D	2	Social studies	LA/reading, math/science
2E	2	None	LA/reading, math/social studies/science
2F	2	None	LA/reading/social studies, math/science
3A	3	Reading	Math, LA, social studies/science
3B	3	Reading and LA	Math, social studies, science
3C	3	Reading and math	Science, social studies, LA (usually writing)
3D	3	None	Reading/LA, math, science/social studies
4A	4	Reading	LA (usually writing), math, social studies, science
4B	4	Social studies	Reading, LA (usually writing), math, science
4C	4	Social studies	Reading/LA (2 teachers), math (1 teacher), science (1 teacher)
4D	4	None	Reading/LA (2 teachers), math (1 teacher), science/social studies (1 teacher)
4E	4	None	Reading/LA, math, social studies/reading/LA, science/math
6	6	None	2 Reading/LA, 2 math, social studies, science

**Tables
5.1
5.2**

Figure 5.1 Master Schedule for Two-Teacher Teams in Grades 3–5
(School Day Divided into 5-Minute Increments)

	8:00	9:00	10:00	11:00	12:00	1:00	2:00	2:45
Kindergarten	LA (45)	I/E	LA (90)	L/R	Math 75	Plan	SS/SC (45)	
Grade 1	LA (105)		Math 75	LA (45)	L/R	Plan	I/E	SS/SC (45)
Grade 2	LA (90)	I/E	LA (45)	R/L	Math 75	SS/SC (60)	Plan	
Grade 3	Reading (60)	Core 1 (105)	Core 2 (60)	Plan	L/R	Core 2 (45)	I/E	
Grade 4	Core 1 (90)	Core 2 (45)	Plan	Core 2 (45)	R/L	I/E	Core 3 (90)	
Grade 5	Core 1 (90)	Plan	Core 1 (45)	Core 2 (45)	I/E	R/L	Core 2 (90)	
Encore	Plan/PD Period	5th	4th	Lunch	3rd	1	K	2nd
I/E	Plan/Duty	K	2nd	2nd	Lunch/Duty	5th	4th	1st	3rd

Part II
Parallel Block Scheduling

6

An Introduction to Parallel Block Scheduling

Over the past 30 years, we have worked with elementary schools across the country to implement a novel model of elementary school organization called parallel block scheduling (PBS). This model embraces all the principles of scheduling developed in chapters 1 to 5; however, it adds several new elements:

♦ The reduction of class size during key instructional periods, including reading and, when possible, mathematics;

♦ A grouping procedure that reduces the range of achievement in each classroom and provides for a

mix of homogeneous and heterogeneous instruction during the day; and

♦ A new instructional venue, the extension center, in which students receive practice, reinforcement, enrichment, instructional interventions, and/or special services.

To begin this chapter, we build a case for implementing this model to accelerate literacy acquisition in kindergarten and perhaps grade 1. We further develop the model to apply to literacy and numeracy for all primary grades. Finally, we adapt it for use in the intermediate grades.[1]

---

1 Because there are so many variations of parallel block scheduling, we have created Table 6.4, p. 174, to classify the various forms of PBS by feature.

Parallel Block Scheduling: Scheduling Early Literacy Instruction in Grades K–3

Since the advent of high-stakes testing and school accountability, elementary school personnel have begun to scrutinize school-related factors over which they have control and the relationship of such factors in improving student achievement. The factors most often studied in elementary schools are the use of instructional time, the size of instructional groups, the curriculum, and the instructional strategies that teachers use in small groups. Because of universal agreement that strong skills in reading and mathematics underpin future school success, time usage and class size in grades K–3 come under particular scrutiny. Given the poor educational prognosis for students performing a year or more below grade level, especially in reading by the end of grade 3, elementary personnel are searching for strategies not only to improve student achievement but also to accelerate early literacy acquisition for many students who enter kindergarten with serious literacy deficits.

When educators seek ways to accelerate early literacy skills in reading and mathematics, class size becomes a critical issue. In addition to the push for accelerating early literacy acquisition, the "standards movement has encouraged a resurgence in the class size and school size debates" (Wasley, 2002, p. 10). First, we discuss the issue of class size and its relationship to student achievement in primary (K–3) grades; then we illustrate how instructional group size can be managed to help meet the instructional needs of students by using PBS strategies.

The Relationship of Class Size and Student Achievement in Grades K–3

Before we offer a case for reduced instructional groups during critical instructional times in grades K–3 (e.g., reading and mathematics), we briefly review definition of terms used throughout this book. Too often, we find terms such as homeroom group, class size, instructional group and pupil–teacher ratio used interchangeably. Such imprecise language presents problems in interpreting the relationship of student achievement and class size and in explaining "class size" in school budgets to the public. For example, sometimes when educators refer to class size they mean the homeroom class, and other times the term implies a pupil–teacher ratio; the two represent vastly different numbers.

In this chapter, we define "homeroom class" as a group of students that is likely to remain with a single teacher for at least one school year. Except for those students who transfer in and out of the school during the school year, a homeroom class tends to remain fixed throughout the year; also, homeroom classes typically are assigned to a base teacher and to a particular space, such as Room 203. We normally build from a combination of homeroom classes to develop schedules for additional school functions, such as lunch, physical education, music, and art.

We accept the term "pupil–teacher ratio" as "an administrative statistic that helps account for the distribution of resources" (Achilles, Finn, & Pate-Bain, 2002, p. 24). Generally, pupil–teacher ratio is computed by dividing the total number of students in a school by the total number of certificated staff. In addition to classroom teachers, certificated staff may include resource personnel, encore staff, guidance counselors, library media specialists, and sometimes administrators. It is misleading to describe the number of students any one teacher may be responsible for teaching using a school's pupil–teacher ratio. For example, Achilles and other authors have pointed out that the difference between pupil–teacher ratio and class size in U.S. schools is approximately 10. Thus, if the pupil–teacher ratio is 17 to 1, most teachers will have an average class size of 27 students (Achilles & Sharp, 1998).

In this chapter and throughout this book, we often talk about instructional groups, particularly instructional groups in reading and mathematics. We define an instructional group as a group of students, generally ranging in size from 1 to 35 or so, assembled for an identified instructional need; the size and membership of the group is fluid and subject to change based on performance of the group members and the nature of the planned instruction.

We contend that 30 students may be a manageable instructional group if a second grade teacher is reading a story, but for best results, nine students may be too many for a kindergarten teacher instructing a phonemic awareness skill to a group of five-year-olds who have spent very few hours being read to on a parent's lap. Although 30 in a PE class at times may be satisfactory, safety considerations make six to eight preferable when teaching students to use a trampoline. Again, we believe that the size of an instructional group should be based on the age of the group members, the nature of the group, and what the teacher is trying to teach. In chapters 6–11, we refer to five different types of instructional groups: early literacy groups (ELGs), reading/writing groups (RWGs), math groups (MGs), the homeroom class, and the "extension" class.

Although class size in elementary schools traditionally has been defined as the number of students in a self-contained homeroom, we define class size as any group or combination of groups an elementary teacher has the responsibility for instructing and/or supervising at any given time. For example, if a teacher has 24 third graders in the classroom from 10:30 until 11:30 every morning, the class size during this time is 24. If a kindergarten teacher has six students for 35 minutes for an early literacy group, with no other students in the room, the class size is six.

Why Reduce the Size of Instructional Groups in Grades K–3?

The issue of class size and its relationship to student achievement has been studied for at least three decades. When all the studies are reviewed collectively, and when the variable is class size rather than pupil–teacher ratio, a growing pattern shows benefits for students in the primary grades who receive early instruction in small groups; it also can be noted that those benefits are not distributed equally. For example, students of lower socioeconomic status and minority students receive greater benefits from smaller classes than their more affluent majority peers (Finn & Achilles, 1990; Robinson, 1990; Wenglinsky, 1997).

The following is a summary of what Biddle and Berliner (2002) report as the major benefits of small classes for students:

♦ When planned thoughtfully and funded adequately, small classes in the early grades generate substantial gains for students, and those extra gains are greater the longer students are exposed to those classes.

♦ Extra gains from small classes in the early grades are larger when the class has fewer than 20 students.

♦ Extra gains from small classes in the early grades occur in a variety of academic disciplines and for both traditional measures of student achievement and other indicators of student success.

♦ Students whose classes are small in the early grades retain their gains in standard size classrooms and in the upper grades, middle school, and high school.

♦ All types of students gain from small classes in the early grades, but gains are greater for students who have traditionally been disadvantaged in education.

♦ Initial results indicate that students who have traditionally been disadvantaged in education carry greater small-class, early-grade gains forward into the upper grades and beyond.

♦ The extra gains associated with small classes in the early grades seem to apply equally to boys and girls.

♦ Evidence for the possible advantages of small classes in the upper grades and high school is inconclusive (p. 20).

Biddle and Berliner offer two theories as to why small classes are beneficial to students in the early grades. One is that "because the small class context improves interactions between the teacher and individual students," teachers are more likely to teach students "the rules of standard classroom culture" that are so critical for school success. Being able to cope with these expectations seems to be especially challenging for students coming from "impoverished homes, ethnic groups that have suffered from discrimination or are unfamiliar with U.S. classroom culture, or urban communities where home and community problems interfere with education" (p. 20).

"A second group of theories designed to account for class size effects focuses on the classroom environment and student conduct rather than on the teacher." Supporters of these beliefs argue that classroom management problems interfere with student learning and that these problems are less evident in small classes. They further contend that students in small classes are more likely to be engaged in learning and to receive greater support from the teacher. There also is evidence that "small instructional groups can create supportive contexts where learning is less competitive and students are encouraged to form supportive relationships with one another" (p. 21).

In summary, people who argue for small instructional groups contend that in such groups, "less time is spent on management and more time is spent on instruction, students participate at higher levels, teachers are able to provide more support for learning, and students have more positive relationships" (p. 21). Consequently, a key aspect of our scheduling models in this chapter includes frequent, accelerated small-group literacy instruction for K–3 students.

Two Kindergarten Models

In this adaptation of parallel block scheduling (see Canady & Rettig, 1995; Canady & Rettig, 2000; Canady & Rettig, 2001;

Delany, Toburen, Hooton, & Dozier, 1997/1998; Hopkins & Canady, 1997; Rettig & Canady, 2000, chapters 7 and 8; and Rettig & Canady, 1995), we initially describe two potential models for kindergarten: one plan designed for two classes of 20 to 25 students, two teachers and two teaching assistants (Figure 6.1, p. 175), and a second model created for four kindergarten teachers and two or three assistants working with a total of 80 to 100 students (Figure 6.2, p. 176).

Two Kindergarten Teachers

In the model with two teachers and two teaching assistants[2] (Figure 6.1, p. 175), during the first hour of the day students meet with their homeroom teachers for traditional kindergarten opening activities and unit time. This would be an appropriate time for calendar, show and tell, chart stories, mathematics, and other types of interdisciplinary activities. For the next 105 minutes, students are divided into six small early literacy groups (ELGs). Literacy groups are constructed and reconstituted throughout the year based on students' level of reading readiness and performance, as determined from informal teacher assessments and screening instruments such as the Phonological Awareness Literacy Screening (PALS), an instrument used in many schools in Virginia (Invernizzi & Meier, 2000a, 2000b). The lower numbered ELGs in each homeroom (1 and 2 in Figure

6.1) include students initially at the lowest readiness level; the higher numbered ELGs (5 and 6 in Figure 6.1) include students at the highest level. Generally we prefer to construct ELGs in kindergarten within homerooms rather than across homerooms. If it is necessary to change a student's group during the year, we move the child to a different group *within* the homeroom. We believe this method is preferable for maintaining a caring teacher-student relationship with younger children. Occasionally though, we have needed to move a student to another teacher's ELG for placement accuracy. Each literacy group includes six to 12 students.

Early literacy groups meet for 35 minutes in the morning and again during the afternoon with the same literacy teacher. To provide time for the reduced-size literacy groups free of distractions for both the teacher and students, the six groups rotate through a morning schedule. The classroom teachers stay put while other school personnel—an instructional aide, parent volunteer, or other designated person—supervise transitions.

For example (Figure 6.1, p. 175), students in ELGs 1, 3, and 5 remain in homeroom with teacher A from 8:00 to 9:00. Then groups 3 and 5 are escorted from the room while ELG 1 settles in for 35 minutes of small-group literacy instruction. At 9:35, ELG 1 is escorted to 35 minutes in extension centers, and then from 10:10 to 10:45 the group either listens to a story or is supervised

---

2 In classrooms where no teaching assistants are available or in districts where assistants may not be permitted to perform the duties suggested, school administrators should check to see if any of the following personnel are available to help kindergarten teachers spend more time in small instructional groups: the media specialist, a Title I teacher or specially trained assistant, Book Buddies or other parent volunteers working under

the reading specialist, high-school teacher cadets, and/or university practicum students. If teachers truly believe that the small groups are critical for the success of young children in kindergarten, we find that in most schools, creative ways can be found to implement a schedule at least similar to what we propose in Figure 6.1 (p. 175).

in independent reading. One of the two teaching assistants accompanies students in each setting.

After lunch and teacher planning time (when students attend PE, art, music, etc.), the schedule repeats the rotation. Students receive a second small-group literacy lesson with the same teacher as in the morning, a second period of centers, and time for supervised free play; some schools might also offer time in the media center or computer writing lab during this rotation. In this model, the two kindergarten teachers provide the small-group literacy instruction to the six groups, while the two teaching assistants supervise the extension center and rotational activities, possibly under the supervision of a Title I teacher in the building. Students spend the last 45 minutes of the day with their assigned homeroom teacher.

Four Kindergarten Teachers

The four-teacher model (Figure 6.2, p.176) follows a similar schedule. In this example, we suggest using one of the four teachers to organize and supervise the extension center program and the teaching assistants who supervise the rotational activities. When one teacher is assigned duties parallel to the literacy instructional periods, each of the remaining three is assigned three of the nine ELGs, which again should range between 6 and 12 students. In many schools it may not be necessary to use the fourth teacher in this manner, especially if a Title I teacher or reading specialist is available to direct the extension center. We then would divide students into 12 smaller ELGs; we prefer this model.

To understand this model it may be helpful to follow a student throughout the day. Andrea, who is in ELG 3 (Figure 6.2,

p. 176), stays with teacher C, her assigned homeroom teacher, from 8:00 to 9:00 for opening activities, math instruction, and/or unit time. A few minutes before 9:00, a teaching assistant arrives to escort Andrea and the other students in ELG 3 to a quiet corner of the library for story time. At 9:35, the TA delivers Andrea and her group to teacher D's room for extension center activities. The students in ELG 3 are brought to teacher C at 10:10 for literacy instruction. Andrea and her classmates travel to lunch and recess from 10:50 until 11:40. The kindergarten teachers plan from 11:40 to 12:30 while their students attend encore classes, such as physical education, art, music, and computers. Then, repeating the morning rotation, Andrea and her group are supervised on the playground from 12:30 to 1:05, engage in center activities from 1:05 to 1:40, and receive a second small-group, teacher-directed literacy lesson from 1:40 to 2:15, again from teacher C. They spend the last 45 minutes of the day with their homeroom teacher.

Other Support Services

Time when students are assigned to extension activities, such as centers, story, or play, may also be earmarked to provide identified students with special services such as LD resource, speech therapy, ESL, and so on. These specialists meet with the principal and the extension center teacher to decide which of the rotational activities each student who receives services should miss. In the examples illustrated in Figures 6.1 (p. 175) and 6.2 (p. 176), each student attends centers twice a day, story once, and supervised free play once. Typically, if a student's IEP specifies daily speech and language services, that student would work with the speech teacher in place of one of the two center times scheduled. Students who also receive LD resource services probably would miss playtime to attend LD resource services, because they would have recess at lunchtime. No students would be pulled from their small ELG classes.

Elementary schools serving a large at-risk population often have access to additional funding. They frequently spend it to employ reading specialists to work with small groups of students throughout the day. For schools having such specialists and employing the PBS model of scheduling, we suggest partnering the reading specialist with each of the base teachers when the lowest ELGs (1, 2, and 3) are receiving direct instruction. Now these two teachers can divide the ELG for literacy instruction.

Thus, in the example illustrated in Figure 6.2 (p. 176), the reading specialist would split ELG 1 with teacher A from 9:00 to 9:35, ELG 2 with teacher B from 9:35 to 10:10, and ELG 3 with teacher C from 10:10 to 10:45. This plan generally reduces each ELG to four or five students, and it gives the two teachers flexibility in grouping and regrouping the subgroups. It also makes it possible for one of the two teachers to work occasionally with just two or three students in the ELG who may have been absent from school several days and need intensive catch-up work.

Now is an appropriate time to comment on the placement of the groups in the schedule shown in Figure 6.2 (p. 176). Note that while teacher A is working with her lowest group (ELG 1) from 9:00 to 9:35, teacher B is instructing her highest group (ELG 8), and teacher C is working with her middle group (ELG 6). This assignment serves two important purposes. The remaining groups who attend the extension center form a heterogeneous mix. If each of the teachers worked with high groups at the same time, the remaining students would form a more homogeneous extension group, not the preferred choice in many schools. The schedule also allows the services of specialists, who work with only a few selected students, to be spread over several periods during the day.

Constructing Kindergarten Homerooms and Early Literacy Groups

At the kindergarten level, we recommend constructing heterogeneous homerooms and balancing all classes by using data regarding students' gender, race, socioeconomic status, and any achievement information available from preschool teachers or readiness assessments.

There are two basic ways to create ELGs from homeroom groups: within homerooms or across homerooms. If, as in the example shown in Figure 6.2 (p. 176), one of the kindergarten homeroom teachers (teacher D) must be used as the extension teacher, it will be necessary to create the ELGs across homerooms. This means that after all kindergarten students are assessed, ELGs are constructed by forming groups of students who have the same approximate level of literacy acquisition, without regard to homeroom. So, teacher A's students could end up in an ELG taught by teacher A, B, or C.

There are two main advantages to this arrangement: Students assigned to each group would be very similar in literacy skill, and no additional teacher would be required to organize extension. There also are two disadvantages to this system: Students may not have their homeroom teacher for literacy instruction, and groups are larger because a teacher has been removed to staff the extension center. In a school with a very diverse population, this may be the preferred option for constructing ELGs because of the importance of students receiving literacy instruction on their appropriate level.

If there were no need to pull one of the teachers to organize extension, the teachers could construct ELGs from within homerooms. In this case, they would use assessment information to create three ELGs from each homeroom, and homeroom teachers would teach their own groups separately during the periods provided for small-group literacy instruction. The two main advantages of this arrangement are that the groups would be smaller and students would travel to fewer teachers. The major disadvantage is that students' skill levels would not be as tightly matched.

It would have been possible to schedule one longer (70-minute) time block for literacy instruction for each ELG; however, to take advantage of the learning benefits of spaced practice, we have scheduled two shorter periods. Obviously, in schools with half-day kindergarten programs or fewer resources, teachers could work with each ELG only once a day, either morning or afternoon.

Instructional Practices in ELGs

During ELGs, teachers provide a variety of phonemic awareness activities by using manipulatives—*not* workbooks and worksheets. Rather than teach one letter name a week for 26 weeks, as has been the practice in some schools, teachers focus their instruction on letter sounds. Initially, students are not introduced to upper-case letters. Early focus is on lower-case letters.

Acceleration is the goal of this model; therefore, teachers choose instruction with the greatest potential for accelerating student progress. Early in the year, after introducing five or so consonant sounds, they present the first vowel. Students begin blending sounds into words shortly thereafter. Word families arrive to appropriate fanfare. As soon as students can blend sounds into words, they begin reading sentence strips and books. Teachers incorporate comprehension strategies throughout the instructional process and include some form of writing every day.[3]

During extension time, students participate in centers twice daily, morning and afternoon. Located in one of the teacher's rooms (teacher D's for Figure 6.2, p. 176), the kindergarten centers include traditional kindergarten activities such as sand table, water table, housekeeping, blocks, crafts, paint, and so forth, as well as centers that support the literacy program. In addition, students have story time and play time once a day, supervised by an instructional assistant or other designated person. If a student receives any special service, such as LD, ESL, speech and/or language instruction, these sessions are scheduled during extension time.

Parallel Block Scheduling Grades 1–3

In Figure 6.3 (p. 177), we illustrate how teachers in grade 2 (or 1, or 3) may work with reduced instructional groups during

---

3 Activities adapted from *Reading Their Way: A Balance of Phonics and Whole Language* by Dorothy J. Donat (2003), retired curriculum supervisor of the Augusta County Public Schools, where 12 schools currently are using the model described above.

the reading/language arts/social studies and mathematics/science blocks. Reduced-size reading groups are labeled reading/writing groups (RWGs), and their math counterparts are shown as math groups (MGs). The schedule is similar to that designed for kindergarten students, except that homeroom teachers work with two small half-class groups instead of three small groups that are about one-third of a class. This plan extends the time blocks to 50 minutes. Before we take a detailed look at this schedule, we examine possible grouping arrangements for the construction of the three homerooms shown in Figure 6.3.

Constructing Homerooms and Instructional Groups for Grades 1–5[4]

In most schools, planners first create homerooms and then construct reading groups from each homeroom. We recommend creating the reading groups first, then pairing two groups to form each homeroom. In this example, choosing from a variety of methods, we establish six reading/writing groups (RWGs) and assign two to each teacher. Data informing the decisions usually include some or all of the following: Individual Reading Inventories (IRIs), running records, standardized test scores, teacher recommendations, individualized education programs (IEPs), English language proficiency, gender, and race. In the section that follows, we offer three different ways to form reading/writing groups and several ways of combining groups to form homeroom groups.

Grouping Plan A

All Groups Heterogeneous by Achievement Level, Race, and Gender					
RWG 1	RWG 2	RWG 3	RWG 4	RWG 5	RWG 6

For example, in Plan A, we create six groups balanced by achievement level, race, and gender. Because all the RWGs are heterogeneous, pairing any two groups yields a heterogeneous homeroom. Constructing totally heterogeneous homerooms may seem fair and egalitarian, but it does present classroom teachers with a challenge—instructing the full range of achievement levels day after day. While we believe in the tenets of differentiation of instruction, we also know that not all teachers are able to achieve the goal of meeting students' individual needs. In several of the plans that follow, we create homerooms with relatively heterogeneous mixings but a more manageable instructional situation.

Grouping Plan B

Homogeneous Groups Ordered by Achievement Level					
Lower		⟶			Higher
RWG 1	RWG 2	RWG 3	RWG 4	RWG 5	RWG 6

In Plan B, we establish six ordered homogeneous groups based on students' performance in language arts, with RWG 6 the highest-achieving group and RWG 1 the lowest-achieving

---

4 Adapted from Rettig and Canady (2000).

group. While group makeup predominantly reflects literacy level, we also kept in mind the need to carefully place any students with significant learning problems and severe behavior problems.

Pairing Plans

After determining the composition of the instructional groups, we can choose from a variety of pairing plans to create homerooms.

Pairing Plan I

For example, we could pair groups 1 and 2, 3 and 4, 5 and 6, and so on to create homerooms. These pairings obviously would result in severely tracked homerooms, with the 5/6 combination at the top of the scale and the 1/2 combination at the low end. While this grouping practice has been used in a variety of states for many years, it creates an economic and racial caste system, which in our opinion is unethical. In fact, many schools that have grouped in this manner have found themselves facing complaints from the Office of Civil Rights.

Pairing Plan II

Another possible format for combining RWGs to create homerooms would be to pair groups 1 and 6, 2 and 5, and 3 and 4. We could justify this pairing in a number of ways. First, the pairing of groups 1 and 6, which seems counterintuitive, does provide several benefits. Typically, the students who compose group 6 have parents who write letters to the principal requesting their placement with the perceived "best" teacher at the grade level. The students in group 1 have parents who rarely participate in their children's education; these students need the "best" teacher. By assigning each of these groups to the perceived "best," we keep the parents of one group happy while serving the needs of the other group. We also could argue that this pairing provides a set of role models for group 1 to follow.

Similarly, the pairing of groups 3 and 4, the most "average" groups of the ranking, may be the perfect assignment for a new teacher; few problem students and few "problem parents" likely would fall into these middle groups. While this discussion is largely tongue-in-cheek, it does touch upon issues educators often feel uncomfortable discussing, and suggests the complexity of the grouping process and the need for careful planning and thought.

Pairing Plan III

Another more realistic possibility would be to pair groups 1 and 4, 2 and 5, and 3 and 6. In this arrangement, before we create any pairs, we suggest spreading all identified special education students among the lowest three RWGs (unless they place in a higher group) and distributing all students exhibiting severe behavior problems across all six groups. Plan III creates homerooms that are relatively heterogeneous in overall composition, yet comprise two fairly distinct groups of students having similar instructional needs; we refer to this pairing as "controlled heterogeneity."

Our goal is to create homerooms that are diverse in gender, race, instructional needs, special education assignments, and behavior; we hope that no teacher would have a homeroom group without at least one of the two groups being able to work at or above grade level. In this pairing, although the homeroom created from RWGs 1 and 4 reflects a lower observed performance level than the homeroom composed of RWGs 3 and 6, the differences among homerooms are not nearly as great as in Plan I.

Keep in mind that in PBS, teachers have at least one daily period to work alone with each reduced-size instructional group. To assist the homeroom teachers assigned RWGs 1, 4 and 2, 5, some schools operate an inclusion model in which a special education resource teacher or a reading specialist works with the base teacher when both groups are in the classroom; others prefer to have the co-teaching occur when RWGs 1, 2, and possibly 3, have their small group instruction, dividing these groups in half.

Although some elementary school personnel in Georgia and Virginia have used the Plan III format successfully for more than 20 years, people occasionally oppose the plan because they feel it has elements of tracking. We understand their concern. We have observed, however, that if a school has a large number of students with disabilities, and the state's accountability system calls for testing the majority of these students, greater student gains occur when classrooms are organized so that special needs students receive more focused attention within the regular classroom. Today it is critical that special needs students receive the "full curriculum" on which they will be tested.

We contend that Plan III does this. Special needs students have opportunities to work with peers, their base teacher, and various support personnel without being stigmatized by being pulled out of their classroom environment. If a school uses the Intervention/Enrichment period discussed in chapter 4, special needs students can receive both pre-teaching and interventions by various types of special service teachers during that period

without missing instruction from their base teacher. Furthermore, when sufficient special service personnel are available, their support teacher can follow them and co-teach with the base teacher during the reduced reading and/or math groups, the large-group instructional time, or both. Pairing Plan III offers much more support than other plans that spread special needs students more broadly.

Grouping Plan C

Homogeneous Groups Ordered by Achievement Level			Heterogeneous Higher Groups		
Lower →→		Higher			
RWG 1	RWG 2	RWG 3	RWG 4	RWG 5	RWG 6

It is not necessary to strictly rank all groups as shown in the previous section. In Plan C, the top half of the grade level, groups 4 to 6, is divided into three *equal* groups balanced by achievement level, race, and gender. Students in these groups likely would be on or above grade level. The bottom half of the grade level is divided into three *ranked* groups. For example, if we were preparing homerooms for grade three, RWGs 4 to 6 might include students reading on a 3^1 level or higher, while RWG 3 and RWG 2 might be reading at the 2^2 level, and RWG 1 at 2^1 or lower.

Now when we pair groups, each homeroom would have one of the higher groups, 4 to 6, containing on- or above-grade-level students, and one of the lower groups that falls below grade level. All homerooms would have a few stars and would be relatively heterogeneous. Regardless of the grouping strategy, we believe it wise to distribute students with behavior problems evenly among classes, and we always try to ensure that all students have at least one friend in their homeroom.

Because we have constructed homerooms by reading level, when transfer students register, it is important to assess their reading level *before* placing them into homerooms. Traditionally, when a third grade student transfers in, the student is placed in homeroom with the fewest number of students; in PBS a transfer student must be placed in the correct reading group, even if it means class sizes are a bit unequal.

Benefits of Controlled Heterogeneous Grouping[5]

♦ Ensures the creation of instructional groups by analyzing data in the following order of individual student performance: reading, spelling, writing, behavior, and IEP information. After all these factors have been used to determine initial placements, tweaking can occur by considering such factors as gender, race, social needs (friendships) and parental issues.

♦ Ensures both homogeneous groupings (which at least reduce the range of diverse needs) and heterogeneous groupings as needed throughout the school day; when implemented fully, also can allow groupings based on students' interests and preferences, particularly during various times in social studies, science, and extension centers.

♦ Ensures greater knowledge of each child's reading level when instructing in word study, science, social studies, and mathematics.

♦ Allows various groupings for Gifted and Talented, ESL, or SPED students during reading and/or math, if those students are not already assigned to the homeroom; the plan also makes it easier to implement co-teaching with students' IEP support teachers during either/or the combined or reduced grouped instructional periods.

♦ Facilitates parent conferences because parents do not have to confer with multiple teachers in various content areas.

♦ Eases completion of reporting instruments because teachers do not have to determine grades (marks) for students from another homeroom group. Teachers have a more complete picture of students, because they are not working with students from other homerooms unless they have departmentalized, as may happen in the upper grades.

Parallel Block Scheduling in the Primary Grades

Now we return to the schedule designed for grade 2 with three homeroom classes illustrated in Figure 6.3 (p. 177).

---

5 We thank Dorothy J. Donat, retired elementary supervisor from the Augusta County (VA) Schools, for her contribution to this list of benefits.

The Augusta County Schools have 12 elementary schools which, over a period of eight years, have been involved in implementing PBS.

Language Arts and Language Arts Extension

After homeroom, students in RWG 5 remain with teacher 2B for 50 minutes of small-group reading and writing instruction. At 9:10, students from teacher 2B's second group (RWG 2) rejoin the class for 50 minutes of whole-group language arts instruction. Social studies also may be included during this time if the extension center does not provide this instruction in the afternoon (shown later in Figure 6.4, p. 178). At 10:00, RWG 5 is escorted to the extension center for activities that practice, reinforce, and/or enrich the regular classroom program. Teachers providing special programs, such as LD, ESL, speech, or gifted resource, may work with their students during extension time, without interrupting regular classroom instruction. (See chapter 7 for ideas on structuring activities during extension time for students not assigned some special service.)

During whole-group language arts time, teachers may read a story to the larger heterogeneous group, have students journaling or responding to a writing prompt, work with vocabulary, supervise students in independent reading, or engage students in spelling, possibly by using some of the same activities but different lists of words. During RWG periods, teachers may conduct a directed-reading/thinking lesson, a guided writing activity, a writers' workshop, and/or perhaps conference with individual students. Best practices in reading and language arts instruction are detailed in chapters 9 and 10.

Mathematics and Mathematics Extension

After lunch and recess, students are regrouped within homerooms based upon math data, and the schedule is repeated for mathematics (Figure 6.3, p. 177). Students receive small-group instruction and large-group instruction in mathematics/science, as well as traveling to mathematics extension for practice, reinforcement, and/or enrichment. Students receiving additional special services also could be served at this time. In the afternoon, grade 2 teachers plan during period 7 (1:20–2:10), while their students attend encore classes such as PE, art, and music. Specialized mathematics schedules are detailed in chapter 8; best practices in mathematics instruction are addressed in chapter 11.

A Practitioner's View of the Extension Center[6]

In the traditional three-group, self-contained elementary classroom, two groups of students generally work independently on paper-and-pencil tasks while the teacher instructs the third. The chore of finding, organizing, and grading quality independent seatwork activities becomes a significant planning challenge for the classroom teacher and often results in reams of worksheets just to keep the independent groups busy. In schools with extension centers, however, while the classroom teacher instructs one group, the other travels to the extension center classroom, where the extension center teacher plans and directs their work. Many

---

6 Harriet J. Hopkins, former elementary principal and coordinator of elementary programs, Fairfax County Schools, Fairfax, VA.

homeroom teachers applaud this practice because they can now plan for instruction rather than for "busy work."

Extension center teachers collaborate with grade-level teachers to develop activities that meet varying student needs. Whether the activities reinforce concepts taught in the homeroom or provide enrichment, extension center teachers can be very creative, unhampered by many of the constraints found in textbook-driven regular classrooms. The difference is that while the classroom teacher is responsible for teaching the basic curriculum to students, the extension center teacher has responsibility for enriching and extending the learning that occurs in the classroom. Thus, the extension center activities allow students to practice skills and apply their learning in a different setting. The extension center program becomes a place where every child can experience a "gifted-quality" education. The planned activities address students' different learning needs and learning styles and focus on reinforcement through application—the heart of the extension center philosophy.

There are many sources for activities to support the extension center program. Parallel block scheduling (PBS) is a perfect platform for implementing differentiated instruction (Tomlinson, 1999). We know that students learn at different rates. Differentiation builds on core teaching and learning practices, refining them to meet individual student needs (whether for remedial or enriched learning activities). This is particularly important in a diverse classroom with a wide range of student achievement. Thus, the classroom teacher teaches initial concepts to the entire homeroom and then plans activities to meet the needs of small, homogeneous

groups of students during small-group time. The extension center teacher also plans activities to support the group. Both teachers, thereby, increase their capacity to differentiate instruction.

Some elementary schools use Howard Gardner's (1997) theory of multiple intelligences as a basis for their extension center program, planning activities that focus on the eight intelligences. In other schools, extension center teachers apply Bernice McCarthy's 4MAT (2000) system of learning. When planning the program, the extension center teacher identifies activities that support the classroom instructional program and address the students' different learning styles and intelligences. Occasionally, students may choose among activities, and their preferences usually support their learning styles. Through use of centers and a system of rotation, teachers can provide students with a variety of instructional activities to reinforce learning concepts and skills. [See Appendix 2 for a host of extension center activities.]

One extension center teacher recently expressed a sentiment heard in many PBS schools: "At last I feel like a professional teacher. I design the Extension Center curriculum based solely on the academic needs and interests of my students. You would be astonished to see how much more they are reading. And the creative writing is the best my children have ever produced! Please, never take me out of my extension center!"

Science and Social Studies Extension

Alternatively, as shown in Figure 6.4 (p. 178), the extension teacher could provide language arts extension services during the morning and then become the science and social studies teacher in the afternoon. This teacher often alternates units in social studies and science, teaching three weeks of one, then three weeks of the other. See Table 6.1 for a list of pros and cons regarding these two uses of the extension center.

Table 6.1 Mathematics Extension or Social Studies and Science Extension?

	Mathematics Extension	Social Studies and Science Extension
Pros	1. Provides for another view of mathematics.	1. Limits preparations for each teacher: language arts and math for the base teacher; extension, science and social studies for the extension teacher.
	2. Allocates a second time slot for special services if necessary.	2. Delineates clear lines of accountability.
	3. Allows for easier integration of LA/SS.	3. Reduces the need for multiple science kits because one person instructs all of the science.
	4. Allows for easier integration of M/SC.	4. Takes advantage of good elementary science instructors (If you can find them, use them!).
Cons	1. Requires many preparations for each teacher	1. Creates more difficulty in integrating LA/SS and M/SC.
	2. Offers less accountability for science and social studies.	2. Provides fewer convenient slots for special services because students should not miss SS/SC.

Four Homerooms Per Grade Level

When a grade level has four homeroom classes, there are two predominant ways to implement parallel block scheduling. It is important to consider both homeroom size and the number of pull-outs when choosing a model. If homeroom classes are small, or if a significant number of students are pulled for special services, the schedules illustrated in Figures 6.5 (p. 179) and 6.6 (p. 180) are possible. Schools having larger homerooms and/or fewer pull-outs are more likely to employ the schedules illustrated in Figures 6.7 (p. 181), 6.8 (p. 182), and 6.8a (p. 183).

Because eight instructional groups are formed from four homeroom classes and scheduled in a three-period instructional block, three groups must be assigned to the extension center for several periods each day, which could overload the center. In the schedule shown in Figure 6.5 (p. 179), RWGs 3, 5, and 8 are assigned to the extension room from 9:10 to 10:00 and RWGs 1, 4, and 6 are there from 10:00 to 10:50. Similarly, MGs 3, 5, and 8 (12:30–1:20) and MGs 1, 4, and 6 (2:10–3:00) are assigned to math extension in the afternoon.

If only 20 students are assigned to each homeroom, then the average RWG (and MG) would have 10 students. Consequently, because three groups are assigned to the extension center during these periods, one would expect approximately 30 students there. Given a couple of students pulled out in each of these periods and the help of a teacher assistant, this class size might be acceptable.

However, if the homeroom class size is 26, the average RWG would have 13 students; therefore, when three RWGs are assigned to the extension center, nearly 40 students would be in attendance. This number might be acceptable—but only under very special circumstances. First, if a large classroom were available and two teachers or one teacher and two assistants could staff the extension center, 40 students could be served. (For example, Cougar Elementary School in Manassas Park, Virginia, has three technology centers with 50 computer stations in each. A technology instructor and one or two teaching assistants staff each center.) Second, if there were a significant number of special service pull-outs (10 or more) every day from each of these overloaded periods, the model shown in Figure 6.5 (p. 179) also could work.

Finally, a pull-out could be created to reduce extension class size. We know of one school where the library-media specialist took 10 students every day from fourth and fifth grade extension classes on a rotating basis to teach research and study skills; this reduced extension class size to an acceptable level. Similarly, on a rotating basis eight students might leave extension class once or twice each week to provide peer tutoring to younger students.

If in the example shown in Figure 6.5 (p. 179) the afternoon extension periods are used for science and social studies instruction, then class size could not be reduced by pull-outs, because all students must take these core subjects. Consequently, if there were only 20 students per homeroom, two of the social studies/science classes would have approximately 30 students, while one had an enrollment of 20. However, we could manipulate group size to make these classes more equal. By assigning MGs 2 and 7 approximately 13 students each, we could lower the class size for the remaining math groups to 9 each; therefore, the three afternoon science and social studies classes would contain 26, 27, and 27 students, respectively.

However, if class size pushed much higher than 20, this manipulation would not work during the social studies and science time, although we still might be able to lower class size during the morning language extension classes with special service pull-outs. Figure 6.6 illustrates just such a case. We provide only three language arts extension classes in the morning because pull-outs reduce class size to an acceptable level. In the afternoon, however, we must add a fourth period for science and social studies because students are not pulled from these classes. This class is taught from 2:10 to 3:00 for MGs 3 and 6 by extension center teacher F. One period of additional staff would be needed to cover this class, which might be provided by an extension teacher assigned to a grade level with fewer classes (who has a free period) or by a special education teacher who works closely with extension center teacher E.

If there are not enough pull-outs to reduce extension class size sufficiently to maintain three morning LA/SS blocks, we could move to four blocks of time for these programs. While this will solve our extension-class-size problems, it creates a new dilemma. If we keep eight 50-minute periods with four periods allocated to language arts and social studies, one to lunch/recess, and one to encore classes, there will be only two periods left for mathematics and science. In Figures 6.7 (p. 181), 6.8 (p. 182), and 6.8a (p. 183), we illustrate two ways to schedule within these constraints.

First a few comments about scheduling LA/SS over four periods. By spreading extension over four periods of time instead of the three periods available in earlier schedules, we reduce class size in extension. As illustrated in Figure 6.7 (p. 181), only two groups are assigned to extension each morning extension period. If homeroom size is about 25, group size will average 12 to 13, and extension classes will average about 25 students each, minus any pull-outs.

Notice how each teacher is given a long block of uninterrupted time for language arts and social studies with the entire class. This 100-minute block is either preceded or followed by two 50-minute periods of RWGs. Teachers 3A and 3B have their long block from 8:20 to 10:00; their RWGs follow in the next two periods. Teachers 3C and 3D have their two small group RWGs in periods 1 and 2 respectively, followed by their language arts and social studies classes in periods 3 and 4 from 10:00 to 11:40.

After we schedule period 5 for lunch/recess and period 6 for encore classes and teacher planning, we have only two periods remaining to schedule math and science. Periods 7 and 8 of Figure 6.7 (p. 181) illustrate one way to meet this challenge. Teacher 3A divides her homeroom class into two math groups (MGs 1 and 5) based on students' current mastery levels in mathematics. In the schedule shown in Figure 6.7, she works with the entire class every day during period 7, and the two math groups meet with teacher 3A every other day in period 8.

During period 7, she works with her class teaching either mathematics or science. During period 8, on day 1 (D1) she works with MG 1 while her other group (MG 5) has math extension. On day 2 (D2), the groups switch. This gives students whole-group math or science instruction every day and small-group mathematics every other day, alternating with math extension. As a variation, we could replace math extension with a science class. In the primary grades, we also could combine science with social studies in the morning.

In a second variation (Figures 6.8, p. 182, and 6.8a, p. 183), we combine periods 7 and 8 to form a 100-minute-long instructional block devoted to mathematics and science. As illustrated in Figure 6.8a, we have created a four-day cycle. On days 1, 2, and 3 of the cycle, teacher 3A works with her entire class in mathematics and science. On day 3, she administers a math quiz; based on the results, she forms students into two groups, an enrichment group and an intervention group.

On day 4, the intervention group (MG A-I) goes to the computer lab during period 7 to work on areas of identified weaknesses. The enrichment group (MG A-E) stays with teacher A for enrichment activities. During period 8 (2:10–3:00), the groups switch places; now MG A-I works with their teacher and MG A-E students travel to the computer lab for enrichment. All students receive small-group instruction one day out of every four. This scheduling plan can be helpful especially in schools using one of the mastery learning models described in detail in chapter 8.

Another adaptation of the basic schedule format is worth mentioning here. A school with many students receiving special services could cluster these pull-outs into two extension center periods, thus permitting the language arts schedule to be completed in three periods. We illustrate such a situation in Figure 6.9 (p. 184). If approximately 10 students were pulled to receive special services in each of periods 2 and 3 (when three groups have been scheduled into the extension center), extension class size could be maintained below 30 students. For example, if we assume homerooms of 25 and instructional groups of no more than 13, an extension class with three groups of 13 minus 10 pull-outs would leave 29 students.

In this situation, there likely would be fewer pull-outs during math/science/social studies time for a couple of reasons. First, if we were providing science and social studies during afternoon extension time, we wouldn't pull students from this core subject. Also, even if we allocated time for math extension and permitted pull-outs, there would be fewer pull-outs because most students had been served during LA extension time.

We also could allocate four periods for the math/science/social studies schedule if we created a nine-period master schedule. To accomplish this within the seven-hour school day, we shorten the periods to 45 minutes and reduce homeroom by 5 minutes.

Let's follow teacher 1A's mathematics/science/social studies schedule, which is illustrated in Figure 6.9 (p. 184). After lunch he keeps his entire homeroom for a two-period (5 and 6) block. If extension time during mathematics is used for math extension, it is likely that three different kinds of activities would be scheduled during this block. Some of the time would be devoted to whole-group mathematics, some would be devoted to science, and some time would be added to the language arts program. If extension time were used for science and social studies, this whole-group time most likely would be split between mathematics and additional whole-class language arts.

After planning during period 7 (when students attend encore classes), teacher 1A works with MG 1 for 45 minutes during period 8, while MG 5 visits the extension center for either mathematics extension or science and social studies. MGs 1 and 5 switch places for period 9.

It is important to keep the division of time among subjects congruent with the school's mission. For example, a student in a class following the schedule illustrated in Figure 6.4 (p. 178) would receive 300 minutes of core instruction daily, including 150 minutes of LA/R (50 LA, 50 RWG, 50 LA ext.), 100 minutes of math (50 whole-group, 50 MG), and 50 minutes of science and social studies. One-half of the time would be spent in LA/R, one-third in math, and one-sixth in science and social studies.

To achieve a relatively equivalent proportion of the core subjects in the schedule shown in Figure 6.9 (p. 184) would require some adjustments. Only three of seven core periods are devoted to LA/R—less than half the core time. Consequently, to maintain a similar proportion, some of the afternoon time block (periods 5 and 6) would need to include language arts. The focus here could be reading and writing in the content areas, with an emphasis on comprehension strategies specific to the content (see chapters 9 and 10).

Finally, we suppose it would be possible—although we think not advisable—to divide the day into ten 40-minute periods, allocating four to LA/R, four to M/SC/SS, one to encore, and one to lunch recess. The schedule illustrated in Figure 6.10 (p. 185) shows this possibility. We consider 40 minutes quite short for most classes and hesitate to suggest periods of this length.

Three Master Schedules

Figure 6.11 (p. 186) shows the master schedule of eight 50-minute periods (six core periods) that underpins the schedules we have presented for kindergarten (Figures 6.1, p. 175, and 6.2, p. 176) and for grade 2 (Figures 6.3 to 6.6, pp. 177–180). If it were necessary to create four M/SS/SC blocks to reduce class size, we could build a master schedule of nine 45-minute periods (seven core periods), as illustrated in Figure 6.12 (p. 187). Similarly, the grade 1 schedule illustrated in Figure 6.10 (p. 185) was developed from the master schedule of ten 40-minute periods (eight core periods) shown in Figure 6.13 (p. 188).

PBS Models for the Intermediate Grades

In chapter 5, we developed a variety of departmentalized models for grades 3–5 based on traditional elementary scheduling principles. So far in this chapter, we have applied principles of PBS to grades K–3. Now we blend elements of departmentalization with the principles of PBS to create departmentalized parallel block schedules for grades 4–5. Especially in districts and states with mandated high-stakes testing programs, the plan that follows allows teachers to specialize in a subject area in which they have the most interest and competency.

In this section, we offer three variations of PBS that we consider appropriate for grades 4 and 5. In the first option, illustrated in Figure 6.14 (p. 189), language arts extension is replaced by social studies and the math extension or social studies/science extension is replaced by science. The extension teacher has become the social studies and science teacher, providing 50 minutes of both social studies and science daily to students. If we follow a student in RWG 5–2 (Figure 6.14),[7] we discover that after 15 minutes of homeroom with teacher B the student joins group 5–6 in social studies class with teacher D. From 9:05 to 9:55, the student attends whole-group language arts class with teacher B, followed by encore classes. Group 5–2 then has small-group reading and writing from 10:45 to 11:35, followed by lunch and recess. If we assume that the student also was in MG 5–2 (not necessarily the case), the afternoon would begin with science class with teacher D, followed by whole-group math class with teacher B. The day would end with small-group math class from 2:05 to 2:55.

In Figure 6.15 (p. 190), we illustrate how grade 5 students in a large elementary school assigned to eight teachers with an average class size of 18–20 students per teacher might be scheduled in a departmentalized, parallel block format. In Figure 6.16 (p. 191), we show a similar schedule for a smaller elementary school with four teachers at grade 4 and four teachers at grade 5. In both schedules, we have based the periods on the assumption that the school has 420 minutes for all school activities—including homeroom, lunch, recess, support services, and a common planning time for teachers.

For a school with only 380 minutes in the school day, the eight 50-minute periods could be reduced to 45 minutes each. With a typical 5-minute passing time, each period would allow 40–45 minutes of instruction. Another way to gain additional instructional time in a shorter working day would be to trim the homeroom time to five or ten minutes and schedule it as part of period 1, so no change or student movement would need to

---

7 Grouping strategies for the creation of Reading Writing Groups and homerooms were detailed earlier in this chapter.

occur. Also, in some schools lunch and recess may not need to be a full 45 or 50 minutes.

In Figure 6.15 (p. 190), three of the eight grade 5 teachers (A, B, and C) teach reading and language arts to two different groups of students; three teachers (D, E and F) instruct mathematics to two groups. The seventh (G) teaches social studies to all of the grade 5 students, spread over six of the eight periods scheduled in the school day, while the eighth teacher (H) does the same for science. All grade 5 students are scheduled for core instruction during periods 1, 2, 4, 6, 7, and 8. Teachers have common planning time during period 3 when the students are in their encore classes (as described in detail in chapter 3). Fifth graders and their teachers are in lunch and recess during period 5. In some schools, approximately one-half of the grade 5 students might have recess for the first 20 to 25 minutes and then eat lunch, while the rest do the reverse. Teachers have either a partial or full duty-free lunch period, depending on policies and practices that vary with local school districts.

During the first period of Figure 6.15 (p. 190), teacher A works with RWG groups 1 and 7, which likely would be the homeroom group. Meanwhile, teacher B has RWG 8 and C has RWG 3; teacher D works with combined groups 4 and 10, teacher E has reduced math group 11, and F has reduced MG 6.

At the same time, RWGs 2 and 9 attend social studies with teacher G, and MGs 5 and 12 attend science with teacher H. In most elementary schools, teachers G and H would have some teaching assistance, at least in periods where they have students from RWGs l and 2 (and possibly 3). This might be provided by a teaching assistant (TA) or a special education, ESL, or Title I teacher. In some schools, the science teacher might work in a co-teaching format with a technology teacher in a computer lab (CL).

During period 2, the various groups are assigned in a similar pattern, this time sending RWGs 3 and 7 to teacher G for social studies and RWGs 6 and 10 to teacher H for science. To check that all groups (RWGs 1 through 12) are assigned, one can count down the column representing each of the periods.

During period 3, all eight core teachers have a common planning period while their students attend various encore classes on a rotating basis. Most days, teachers are free to use the planning period for their own individual planning and personal needs. Typically, however, at least one day out of six all the core teachers, along with any support teachers and/or teaching assistants who work with them, attend a common planning time (unless double periods have been provided on a rotating basis for common grade-level planning time, as described in chapters 3 and 4).

In Figure 6.16 (p. 191), we show a departmentalized parallel block schedule that might operate in an elementary school with four base teachers in each grade level. Again, we have scheduled an eight-period format similar to that shown in Figure 6.14 (p. 189). Each of the periods is 50 minutes; however, if the school day does not allow for 50-minute periods, 45-minute periods would also work, with other adaptations as explained previously.

With four base teachers assigned to each grade level, two teachers (B and D) must teach students from two levels (here, grades 4 and 5), although not in mixed grade level classes. In Figure 6.16 (p. 191), teachers A, B and F teach reading/language arts; A has fourth graders, F has fifth graders, and B teaches fourth grade in the morning and fifth grade in the afternoon. Math instruction (teachers C, E, and D) follows a similar format—C in grade 4, E in grade 5, and D in both (mornings with fifth grade and afternoons with fourth grade).

Teacher G teaches social studies to all students in grades 4 and 5, and H does the same for science. In this format, these two teachers would most likely be assigned some type of co-teaching assistance, such as a TA or a special education, ESL, or Title I teacher.

Although the schedules illustrated in Figures 6.14 to 6.16 (pp. 189–191) provide more time for science and social studies than schedules previously described in this chapter, they have one major drawback: There is no true extension period, without which there is no convenient time during the day to provide students with special needs any pull-out services. To provide such special services, therefore, would require a total commitment to the inclusion model and collaborative teaching. As an alternative, we could add a scheduling feature that was detailed in chapter 4, the Intervention/Enrichment (I/E) period, to the schedule. By shortening the 50-minute periods used in Figure 6.14 to 45 minutes and by shortening homeroom to 10 minutes, we can create an additional 45-minute period for intervention and enrichment activities. A sample schedule is shown in Figure 6.17 (p. 192), in which we have scheduled the I/E period for grade 5 from 10:25 to 11:10 and the I/E period for grade 4 from 11:10 to 11:55. It might be more appropriate for all teachers who work with fourth and fifth grade students to be available during I/E time. This would work if both grade levels had the same I/E period, as shown in Figure 6.18 (p. 193).

The Manassas Park Story

In July 1998, one of the authors was invited by the president of VMDO Architects of Charlottesville, Virginia, and the superintendent of Manassas Park City Schools to take part in a series of meetings of educators and architects for the purpose of writing the educational program for a new primary school to be built in Manassas Park. At the time, this small school division in northern Virginia had a newly built high school (opened in 1999), a middle school, and three elementary schools (pre-K and kindergarten in one school, grades 1–3 in another building, and grades 4 and 5 at a third site). The middle school and two elementary schools were housed in wooden modular trailers, the third in an outdated 1956 school building. School division leaders had decided to build a new elementary school to house grades pre-K–3, a building to be designed for 1,000 students including 100 pre-school children.

The committee included the superintendent of schools, curriculum specialists from the central office, the principal of the new building, teachers from each grade level and specialty areas, architects from VMDO, and three consultants—a college professor with expertise in school scheduling from James Madison University in Harrisonburg, Virginia; another who was director of the Thomas Jefferson Center for Educational Design at the University of Virginia in Charlottesville; and the president of an educational technology company that had worked extensively with Manassas Park City Schools.

Dr. Thomas DeBolt, the superintendent, gave the group free rein to dream and plan an educational program that would meet the needs of a student population that was growing in numbers and diversity.[8] The committee charged into the task.

No one in the group was excited about the size of the school; a primary school of 1,000 students defied everyone's beliefs about "developmental appropriateness" for young children. Thus, the first decision was to cut the school down in size from the students' viewpoint. Three K–3 "communities" were envisioned, each with a maximum of 300 students, approximately 75 per grade level. Each community would be housed in a separate wing of the building with separate staff. Absent any severe personality clashes or major space problems, students would remain in the same community for four years, and when younger siblings entered school, they also would be slotted into that community. A separate, smaller pre-school community (and building wing) also was to be created.

During that August meeting, discussions identified the needs of the students of Manassas Park and the instructional desires of the school personnel—strong among them were the need for outstanding instruction in language arts, math, science, and social studies, as well as the goal of ramping up both faculty and students' use of technology. At the conclusion of that meeting, the co-author of this book was asked to propose a practical elementary school master schedule that captured the essence of these discussions that could be used to help design the building. The schedule that follows is based on the staffing levels shown in Table 6.2.

Pre-school, special education, English as Second Language, counseling, and administrative staff were in addition to the general education staff shown in Table 6.2.

Table 6.2 Cougar Elementary School Instructional Staffing

	Community 1	Community 2	Community 3
Kinder. (9 sections)	KA, KB, KC	KD, KE, KF	KG, KH, KI
Grade 1 (9 sections)	1A, 1B, 1C	1D, 1E, 1F	1G, 1H, 1I
Grade 2 (9 sections)	2A, 2B, 2C	2D, 2E, 2F	2G, 2H, 2I
Grade 3 (9 sections)	3A, 3B, 3C	3D, 3E, 3F	3G, 3H, 3I
Social Studies and Science Teachers	2	2	2
Technology Teacher	1	1	1
Technology Aide	1	1	1
School-wide Instructional Staff (General Education Only)			
PE/Health	3		
Art	1		
Music	1		
Library/Media	1		
Library/Media Assist.	1		

---

8 The Manassas Park City Schools have changed demographically during the past seven years. During the 1999–2000 school year, 29% of the student body qualified for free or reduced lunch; in 2007–2008, 41% did. During the same time period, the percentage of English Language Learners grew from 16.3% to 31%; the Latino population increased from 15.3% to 50%.

Figure 6.19 (p. 194) illustrates the master schedule developed for the entire school. As shown, half of each community plans together. Thus the six grade K and 1 teachers from a community plan together while their students are in encore classes, and the six grades 2 and 3 teachers plan together. The encore rotation (see Figure 6.22, p. 198) is a six-day cycle: PE–Art–PE –Music–PE–Library. The physical education, art, music, and library media schedules are shown in Figure 6.21 (pp. 196–197).

In Figure 6.20 (p. 195), we follow one community's academic schedule. Teacher 1A, for example, has 15 minutes with her homeroom class of about 22 students (RWGs 1–1 and 1–4) to start the day. At 8:15, they embark on 50 minutes of uninterrupted whole-group language arts. From 9:05 to 9:55, her homeroom goes to an encore class while she has planning time with the other K–1 teachers from Community I. At 9:55, the technology aide arrives at her room to escort RWG 1–4 to the technology center for 50 minutes of practice, reinforcement, or enrichment. Any students needing special services or instructional interventions are served at this time in place of the technology class. Meanwhile, teacher 1A works with RWG 1–1 (11 students) providing direct instruction in reading and writing. If RWG 1–1 includes a cluster of students who receive special education services, teacher 1A may divide this group with a co-teacher to provide more individual attention.

At 10:45, the technology aide drops off RWG 1–4 for their small group instruction and takes RWG 1–1 to the technology center. The two groups come back together at 11:35 for 50 minutes of whole-group mathematics instruction. After lunch and recess, the social studies and science teacher picks up Math Group 1–4 (MG 1–4), leaving MG 1–1 with teacher 1A for 50

minutes of small-group mathematics instruction. The two groups exchange places at 2:05.

Upon receiving the committee's approval, the proposed schedule was presented to the combined PK–3 staff. There was broad consensus that the features of the schedule were appropriate for the age level and needs of their students and offered the following benefits:

♦ Clearly delineated time allocations for language arts (100 minutes daily), mathematics (100 minutes daily), science and social studies (50 minutes daily), technology-based reinforcement and extension (50 minutes daily), encore (50 minutes daily), and lunch/recess (50 minutes daily);

♦ Reduced-sized groups (average 11) in language arts (RWGs) and mathematics (MGs);

♦ Specially-trained and assigned science/social studies teachers;

♦ Technology centers for each community to provide reinforcement and enrichment (students requiring pull-out special services often served during this time); and

♦ An encore rotation that included three physical education classes, one music class, one art class, and one trip to the library every six days.

The eventual result of this comprehensive process of gathering input was the writing of the final Education Program Advisory. This document contains a clear description of Manassas Park City Schools' educational philosophy, educational program and curricular initiative. Part of the document is dedicated to describing specific requirements for the architectural program, including information about the types, quantity and quality of space, furnishings, equipment and fixtures. For example, the new building that opened in January 2001 facilitated the implementation of the educational program in many ways. Each community occupies a single three-story wing of the building. Kindergarten and first grade classrooms were placed on the ground floor; second and third grade classrooms occupy the third floor. Instructional and support spaces shared by all grade levels within the community were slotted for the second floor; thus the technology center (designed for 50 stations), the science and social studies rooms, several smaller rooms for the provision of special services, the counselor's office, and the teacher workroom are all on the second level, just one flight of stairs away from all homeroom classrooms (pictures and floor plans of Cougar Elementary School are available at the VMDO Architects website: http://www.vmdo. com/).

Each community is attached to the central hub of the building, which houses the music and art rooms, the media center, the gymnasium, the cafeteria and kitchen, and administrative offices.

A Word from the Principal[9]

The utility of Cougar's building design supports our instructional focus and time on task. Just as the Pentagon was designed to facilitate quick access to all parts of the building, Cougar's division into small contained instructional communities allows students to access all instructional areas (except library) by moving up or down a single level. The rear stairwells keep student movement within the instructional core of the building while funneling lunch and encore classes to the front stairs. This plan keeps students moving through smaller, more contained areas along with their grade-appropriate community peers and minimizes noise and other hallway distractions.

The classrooms on the second floor that initially were designed for resource special education instruction have transitioned nicely to support ESL instruction. The different sizes of resource rooms allow for both self-contained and resource special education programs and occasional use by special educators who provide inclusive and consultative services. Special educators work side by side with general education teachers in teacher planning stations, providing informal mentoring and coaching for classroom teachers.

Both the schedule and the building design allow for flexible scheduling to meet student needs. Special education students and English Language Learners benefit from personalized instructional programs to meet their individual needs. At this time, in addition to receiving "pull-out" services, about 3 percent of Cougar students follow an individual schedule. Individual schedules may include cross-grade instruction, double reading instruction, hybrid inclusion and resource special education support.

---

9 Patricia Miller, Principal, Cougar Elementary School, Manassas Park, VA.

The three serving lines in the cafeteria allow six classes to access lunch simultaneously rather than on a staggered basis, allowing the schedule to be divided evenly into 50-minute blocks. (As we talk with other school administrators, single cafeteria serving lines and staggered lunches appear to be the main impediment to older school buildings implementing block schedules.)

Finally, the combination of changing classes and easy movement throughout the building keep both students and teachers focused on instruction. Students (especially our boys) enjoy the activity included in changing classes, going up or down steps and being seated in different furniture. Discipline issues and "in-school field trips" are greatly reduced. Parents report that prior discipline issues are diminished. Parents who move away from Cougar also report that discipline issues increase for their children once they move from Cougar and return to a traditional schedule.[10]

By all accounts, Cougar Elementary School is achieving remarkably; results on Virginia's Standards of Learning Assessments show pass rates dramatically increasing in all areas between spring 1998 and spring 2007.

The school is fully accredited by the Commonwealth of Virginia and achieved Adequate Yearly Progress under No Child Left Behind in the 2005–6, 2006–7, and 2007–8 school years.

Table 6.3 Standards of Learning Pass Rates at Cougar Elementary School

Three-Year Averages 1998–2000 and 2005–2007				
	English/ Reading	Mathematics	History/ SS	Science
Three-year average 1998–2000	51%	61.5%	54%	60.5%
Three-year average 2005–2007	84%	91.7%	89.8%	90.5%

The other Manassas Park elementary school, which houses fourth and fifth grades, operates a schedule very similar to the one described above, with three notable differences:

♦ A technology center is not used as the extension center; instead, students attend daily periods of social studies and science;

♦ Because students cannot be pulled from social studies and science to provide special services, periods have been shortened and an Intervention/Enrichment period has been added to the schedule;

♦ The school has made a commitment to instrumental music; consequently, all fifth grade students take music lessons (instruments provided at no cost to students) as part of the encore rotation, which has

10 Although the description of the building may lead readers to assume that Cougar Elementary School is a "Cadillac" school building, sparing no expense, in fact when it opened in 2001 it was the second-least-expensive elementary school building constructed in the Commonwealth of Virginia.

been changed to provide two lessons, two physical education classes, one art class, and one general music class every six days.

With a process very similar to that which guided the educational program and building design of Cougar Elementary School now complete, the new Cougar Upper Elementary School, which will house grades 3–5, is projected to be completed in November 2008.

Conclusion

We believe that the unique schedules and programs described in this chapter can provide elementary school personnel with the small groups and the critical time necessary to accelerate reading for primary students in a developmentally appropriate manner and to maintain the development of young readers and writers throughout their elementary years. The later educational success of students rests on such a foundation. As we continue to examine numerous reports, it becomes quite clear that students who have not become fluent readers and writers by the end of grade 3 often continue to experience serious educational deficits and failures during their future school years and, too often, into life. Chapters 9 and 10 detail best practices in literacy instruction that are facilitated by PBS.

PBS also has the possibility of preparing stronger elementary mathematics students. This is most important when we look at the high failure rate of students in Algebra I throughout the United States and the low test scores in mathematics in many school districts. Parallel block schedules include both large group and reduced groupings for math instruction. In chapter 8, we discuss three different models for providing intervention, enrichment, and acceleration for elementary students in mathematics, and in chapter 11, Laura McCullough provides numerous teaching strategies for teachers so students can gain greater meaning and understanding in mathematics. PBS can be a valuable scheduling model for implementing many of the ideas presented in chapters 8 and 11.

During its initial development over 40 years ago by one of the authors of this book, PBS was designed primarily (a) to enable elementary teachers to spend some time each day instructing reduced groups without having at the same time to manage (police) other groups in the classroom by providing extensive amounts of independent seatwork that mostly required students to be passive and quiet; and (b) to provide enrichment activities in reading/language arts and mathematics so elementary students could be more active and engaged in their learning. Over time, PBS has been modified in various ways; those design changes are summarized in Table 6.4 (p. 174), which lists the many features of all the parallel block schedules presented in this chapter.

Essentially, when all elements of the PBS model are implemented correctly, it offers these advantages:

◆ Elementary schools achieve the major instructional benefits of flexible, small groups with very few, if any, additional expenditures. PBS designs the schedule for grades 1–5 primarily around half-class instructional groups (no larger than 15) in reading and mathematics. Kindergarten classes may be based on either one-half or one-third-class early literacy groups, depending on the number of resources present in the individual school.

◆ In PBS, teachers have the benefits of small groups for direct instruction at least four periods each day, but students still have their homeroom teacher for all core classes. This plan makes it easier to complete reporting instruments and to conduct parent-teacher conferences; elementary students essentially have one teacher as their anchor and advocate.

◆ Because students in PBS spend time in reduced size groups each day in reading and mathematics, there is a significant increase in the number of minutes students are engaged in direct instruction, which can be most desirable for students who are not strong, well-managed, well-organized, well-behaved independent learners (Fogliani, 1990).

◆ For reasons given above, schools using parallel block scheduling typically experience fewer student behavior problems and office referrals.

◆ If principles of controlled heterogeneous groupings have been followed in establishing the homerooms, the wide range of achievement found in most elementary classrooms today is reduced dramatically; yet, the two groups combined create a good mix of students based on almost any factor schools need to consider—socioeconomic status, race, gender, behavior, special needs, and so forth. It can be very advantageous to elementary teachers always to have at least one group that can work at grade level or above grade level. Good teachers can use such groupings for various instructional pairings during

the two daily periods in PBS when the whole group is present for instruction.

◆ Planning for co-teaching either for reduced groups or combined groups becomes easier.

◆ PBS permits groupings and re-groupings to occur in a systematic manner because all teachers in a particular team or grade level are following the same schedule as outlined in the master schedule, and all support programs have been scheduled with such a plan in mind. Greater integration of content and various programs is most likely to occur when PBS is used.

◆ The need for traditional seatwork activities essentially is eliminated in PBS through the institution of the extension center. For classroom management purposes, traditionally elementary teachers spent much of any planning time they might have had in planning activities for the groups they were not teaching so they could direct instruction to a particular group at any one time. PBS creates a situation (the extension center) where such planning is not needed; hence, all teacher planning can and should focus on each of the two groups being taught alone (see chapter 7 for a detailed discussion regarding the staffing, scheduling, and management of the extension center).

◆ Because of the systematic way PBS schools are scheduled, there is a reduction in the fragmentation of the school day and programs. If, for example, any students must be pulled for support services, those pull-outs most likely occur during extension time at specific scheduled times—*not* throughout the day with numerous interruptions with base teachers and core instruction.

♦ When support programs are blended with regular programs, as highly recommended with PBS, stigmatization of students is reduced.

♦ When extension is used primarily for enrichment in reading/language arts and mathematics, which was the original concept of PBS, then *all* students—including special education and ESL students—have access to the enrichment activities, which in some schools are available only to advanced and gifted students. If PBS is combined with an I/E period, explained in chapter 4, students needing support have even more opportunities for enrichment in addition to their support groups.

♦ The PBS model makes it easy to earmark one or two of the scheduled extension periods as a specialized time for teaching science and social studies. This particular format can be followed in some grades and not in other grades without making any major changes in the master schedule. For example, it may be best for extension time in the primary grades continue to be used primarily for extending, supporting, accelerating, and enriching reading, language arts, and mathematics. Because of accountability mandates, in the upper grades it may be best to schedule science and social studies during one or more of the extension periods, taught by a subject specialist or, as a minimum, by a teacher who enjoys teaching those subjects. Replacing an extension period with social studies and science necessitates the inclusion of an I/E period in the schedule to provide time for intervention, enrichment and/or special services.

♦ In schools with many additional resources and specialists, such as foreign language, science, instrumental music and technology teachers, it is easy to schedule those special programs through the extension classes so they do not fragment the school day or core program. By following the PBS format, such additional programs make it possible for core teachers to have reduced groups; therefore, instead of thinking "No, not another program to take away my core instructional time," in PBS teachers see benefits—not headaches!

References

Achilles, C.M., Finn, J. D., & Pate-Bain, H. (2002). Measuring class size: Let me count the ways. *Educational Leadership, 59*(5), 24–26.

Achilles, C. M., & Sharp, M. (1998, Fall). Solve your puzzles using class size and pupil-teacher ratio (PTR) differences. *Catalyst for Change, 28*(1), 5–10.

Biddle, B.J., & Berliner, D.C. (February, 2002). Small class size and its effects. *Educational Leadership, 59*(5), 12–23.

Canady, R. L., & Rettig, M. D. (1995). The power of innovative scheduling. *Educational Leadership, 53*(3), 4–10.

Canady, R. L., & Rettig, M. D. (2000). Block scheduling: What have we learned? Chapter 13 in Wraga, W. G., & Hlebowitsh, P. S. (Eds.) *Research Review for School Leaders*. Vol. III. Mahway, NJ: Lawrence Erlbaum Associates.

Canady, R.L. & Rettig, M.D. (2001, January). Block scheduling: The key to quality learning time. *Principal, 80*(3), 30–34.

Delany, M., Toburen, L., Hooton, B., & Dozier, A. (December 1997/January 1998). Parallel block scheduling spells success. *Educational Leadership, 55,* 61–63.

Donat, D. J. (2003). *Reading their way: A balance of phonics and whole language.* Lanham, Maryland: Rowman & Littlefield Publishers, Inc.

Finn, J. D,. & Achilles, C.M. (1990). Answers and questions about class size: A statewide experiment. *American Educational Research Journal, 27*(3), 557–577.

Fogliani, A. E. (1990). *A case study of parallel block scheduling: An instructional management study.* Unpublished dissertation, University of Virginia, Charlottesville, VA.

Gardner, H. (1997). *Frames of mind: The theory of multiple intelligences.* Englewood Cliffs, NJ: Basic Books.

Hopkins, H. J., & Canady, R. L. (1997). Parallel block scheduling for elementary schools. In *ASCD Curriculum Handbook,* 13.109 – 13.130. Alexandria, VA: Association for Supervision and Curriculum Development.

Invernizzi, M., & Meier, J. (2000a). *PALS 1–3: Phonological Awareness Literacy Screening 2000–2001 teacher's manual.* Charlottesville, VA: University Press.

Invernizzi, M., & Meier, J. (2000b). *PALS K: Phonological Awareness Literacy Screening 2000–2001 teacher's manual.* Charlottesville, VA: University Press.

McCarthy, B. (2000). *About teaching: 4MAT in the classroom.* Wauconda, IL: About Learning.

Rettig, M. D., & Canady, R. L. (1995, December). When can I have your kids? Scheduling elementary specialists. *Here's How 14*(2).

Rettig, M. D. & Canady, R. L. (2000). *Scheduling strategies for middle schools.* Larchmont, NY: Eye On Education.

Robinson, G. L. (1990). Synthesis of research on class size. *Educational Leadership, 47*(7), 80–90.

Tomlinson, C. (1999). *The differentiated classroom: Responding to the needs of all learners.* Alexandria, VA: Association for Supervision and Curriculum Development.

Wasley, P. A. (2002). Small classes, small schools: The time is now. *Educational Leadership, 59*(5), 6–10.

Wenglinsky, H. (1997). *When money matters: How educational expenditures improve student performance and how they don't.* Princeton, NJ: Educational Testing Service.

Table 6.4 Features of Chapter 6 Parallel Block Schedules

	6.3	6.4	6.5	6.6	6.7	6.8 & 6.8a	6.9	6.10	6.14	6.15	6.16	6.17
Primary or Intermediate?	P	P	P	P	P or I	P or I	P	P	I	I	I	I
Whole Group LA		Y	Y	Y			Y	Y	Y	Y	Y	Y
Whole Group LA/SS	Y				Y	Y						
RWGs	Y	Y	Y	Y	Y	Y	Y	Y	Y	Y	Y	Y
Whole Group M/SC/SS							C	C				
Whole Group Math/SC	Y		C	C	C	Y						
Whole Group Math		Y	C	C	C		C	C	Y	Y	Y	Y
MGs	Y	Y	Y	Y	Y (EOD)	Y (1 day of 4)	Y	Y	Y	Y	Y	Y
LA Extension	Y		Y	Y	Y		Y	Y				
Math Extension	Y		C	C	C (EOD)	Y-CL (1 day of 4)	C	C				
Generic Extension		Y	C	C	C (EOD)							
SS/SC Extension		Y	C	C			C	C				
SS Extension									Y	Y	Y	Y
SC Extension					C (EOD)				Y	Y	Y	Y
Departmentalized										Y	Y	C
I/E Period												Y

Key: Y = feature included; P = primary; I = intermediate; C = choice; EOD = every other day.

Figure 6.1 Parallel Block Schedule for Two Kindergarten Teachers and Two Teaching Assistants (School Day Divided into 5-Minute Increments)

	8:00	9:00	10:00	11:00	12:00	1:00	2:00	3:00
Teacher KA ELGs 1,3,5	Homeroom Activities, Mathematics, and Unit Time (60)	ELG 1 (35) · ELG 3 (35) · ELG 5 (35)		Lunch/ Recess (50)	Encore/ Plan (50)	ELG 1 (35) · ELG 3 (35) · ELG 5 (35)		Homeroom Activities, Mathematics, and Unit Time (45)
Teacher KB ELGs 2,4,6		ELG 4 (35) · ELG 6 (35) · ELG 2 (35)		Lunch/ Recess (50)	Encore/ Plan (50)	ELG 4 (35) · ELG 6 (35) · ELG 2 (35)		
Teaching Assistant A a.m. Story p.m. Play		Story ELGs 3,6 (35) · Story ELGs 2,5 (35) · Story ELGs 1,4 (35)		Lunch/ Recess (50)	Encore/ Plan (50)	Play ELGs 3,6 (35) · Play ELGs 2,5 (35) · Play ELGs 1,4 (35)		
Teaching Assistant B Centers Supervision		Centers ELGs 2,5 (35) · Centers ELGs 1,4 (35) · Centers ELGs 3,6 (35)		Lunch/ Recess (50)	Encore/ Plan (50)	Centers ELGs 2,5 (35) · Centers ELGs 1,4 (35) · Centers ELGs 3,6 (35)		

Notes: 1. ELG-early literacy group 2. Extension center activities also could include any of the following: Title I, special services, media center, PALs intervention, Writing-to-Read, computer lab, etc.

Table 6.4 6.1

Figure 6.2 Parallel Block Schedule for Four Kindergarten Teachers and Extension Center

	8:00	9:00		10:00	11:00	12:00	1:00		2:00	3:00
Teacher KA ELGs 1,4,7	Homeroom Activities, Mathematics, and Unit Time (60)	ELG 1 (35)	ELG 4 (35)	ELG 7 (35)	Lunch/ Recess (50)	Encore/Plan (50)	ELG 1 (35)	ELG 4 (35)	ELG 7 (35)	Homeroom Activities, Mathematics, and Unit Time (45)
Teacher KB ELGs 2,5,8		ELG 8 (35)	ELG 2 (35)	ELG 5 (35)	Lunch/ Recess (50)	Encore/Plan (50)	ELG 8 (35)	ELG 2 (35)	ELG 5 (35)	
Teacher KC ELGs 3,6,9		ELG 6 (35)	ELG 9 (35)	ELG 3 (35)	Lunch/ Recess (50)	Encore/Plan (50)	ELG 6 (35)	ELG 9 (35)	ELG 3 (35)	
Teacher KD & 2 or 3 Teaching Assistants Organize and Supervise Extension Center Activities		Centers ELGs 2,4,9 (35)	Centers ELGs 3,5,7 (35)	Centers ELGs 1,6,8 (35)	Lunch/ Recess (50)	Encore/Plan (50)	Centers ELGs 2,4,9 (35)	Centers ELGs 3,5,7 (35)	Centers ELGs 1,6,8 (35)	
		Play ELG 7 (35)	Play ELG 1 (35)	Play ELG 4 (35)	Lunch/ Recess (50)	Encore/Plan (50)	Play ELGs 3,5 (35)	Play ELGs 6,8 (35)	Play ELGs 2,9 (35)	
		Story ELGs 3,5 (35)	Story ELGs 6,8 (35)	Story ELGs 2,9 (35)	Lunch/ Recess (50)	Encore/Plan (50)	Story ELG 7 (35)	Story ELG 1 (35)	Story ELG 4 (35)	

* ELG: early literacy group
Note: Although this chart shows ELGs "platooning" (staying together as a group) throughout the day, we don't recommend this practice. Instead, we suggest that the groups be mixed when students are assigned to centers, playground, and story time.

Figure 6.3 Parallel Block Schedule for Three Grade 2 Homeroom Teachers and Extension Center (Option 1: Language Arts and Math Extensions)

Periods		Period 1	Period 2	Period 3	Period 4	Period 5	Period 6	Period 7	Period 8
Teacher 2A RWGs 1,4	Homeroom Activities (20)	LA/SS RWGs 1,4 (50)	RWG 1 (50)	RWG 4 (50)	Lunch/ Recess (50)	Math/SC MGs 1,4 (50)	MG 1 (50)	Encore Classes and Teacher Planning Time (50)	MG 4 (50)
Teacher 2B RWGs 2,5		RWG 5 (50)	LA/SS RWGs 2,5 (50)	RWG 2 (50)		MG 5 (50)	Math/SC MGs 2,5 (50)		MG 2 (50)
Teacher 2C RWGs 3,6		RWG 3 (50)	RWG 6 (50)	LA/SS RWGs 3,6 (50)		MG 3 (50)	MG 6 (50)		Math/SC MGs 3,6 (50)
Extension Center*		LA Extension				Math Extension			Math Ext.
		RWGs 2,6 (50)	RWGs 3,4 (50)	RWGs 1,5 (50)		MGs 2,6 (50)	MGs 3,4 (50)		MGs 1,5 (50)

* For language arts extension, the center could be staffed by a Title I teacher and one or more resource teachers, such as LD, reading, ESL, or technology. In the afternoon the center staff focuses on math extension activities and instruction.

6.2
6.3

Figure 6.4 Parallel Block Schedule for Three Grade 2 Homeroom Teachers and Extension Center (Option 2: Language Arts and Science/Social Studies Extensions)

Periods	Homeroom Activities	Period 1	Period 2	Period 3	Period 4	Period 5	Period 6	Period 7	Period 8
Teacher 2A RWGs 1,4		LA RWGs 1,4 (50)	RWG 1 (50)	RWG 4 (50)		Math MGs 1,4 (50)	MG 1 (50)		MG 4 (50)
Teacher 2B RWGs 2,5		RWG 5 (50)	LA RWGs 2,5 (50)	RWG 2 (50)	Lunch/ Recess (50)	MG 5 (50)	Math MGs 2,5 (50)	Encore Classes and Teacher Planning Time	MG 2 (50)
Teacher 2C RWGs 3,6		RWG 3 (50)	RWG 6 (50)	LA RWGs 3,6 (50)		MG 3 (50)	MG 6 (50)		Math MGs 3,6 (50)
Extension Center*		LA Extension				SS/SC Extension			SS/SC Ext.
		RWGs 2,6 (50)	RWGs 3,4 (50)	RWGs 1,5 (50)		MGs 2,6 (50)	MGs 3,4 (50)		MGs 1,5 (50)

Time scale across top: 8:00, 9:00, 10:00, 11:00, 12:00, 1:00, 2:00, 3:00

* For language arts extension, the center could be staffed by a Title I teacher and one or more resource teachers, such as LD, reading, ESL, or technology. In the afternoon the center is devoted to science and social studies.

Figure 6.5 Parallel Block Schedule for Four Grade 2 Homeroom Teachers and Extension Center (Small Classes or Many Pull-Outs Required)

Periods	Homeroom Activities (20)	Period 1	Period 2	Period 3	Period 4	Period 5	Period 6	Period 7	Period 8
Teacher 2A RWGs 1,5		LA RWGs 1,5 (50)	RWG 1 (50)	RWG 5 (50)		Math MGs 1,5 (50)	MG 1 (50)		MG 5 (50)
Teacher 2B RWGs 2,6		RWG 6 (50)	LA RWGs 2,6 (50)	RWG 2 (50)		MG 6 (50)	Math MGs 2,6 (50)		MG 2 (50)
Teacher 2C RWGs 3,7		RWG 3 (50)	RWG 7 (50)	LA RWGs 3,7 (50)	Lunch/ Recess (50)	MG 3 (50)	MG 7 (50)	Encore Classes and Teacher Planning Time	Math MGs 3,7 (50)
Teacher 2D RWGs 4,8		LA RWGs 4,8 (50)	RWG 4 (50)	RWG 8 (50)		Math MGs 4,8 (50)	MG 4 (50)		MG 8 (50)
Extension Center*		LA Extension				SS/SC (or Math Extension)			SS/SC (or Math Ext.)
		RWGs 2,7 (50)	RWGs 3,5,8 (50)	RWGs 1,4,6 (50)		MGs 2,7 (50)	MGs 3,5,8 (50)		MGs 1,4,6 (50)

* For language arts extension, the center could be staffed by a Title I teacher and one or more resource teachers, such as LD, reading, ESL, or technology. In the afternoon the center is devoted to science and social studies or math extension.

6.4
6.5

Figure 6.6 Parallel Block Schedule for Four Grade 2 Homeroom Teachers and Extension Center
(Language Arts Extension and Social Studies/Science Extension; Many Pull-Outs Required During LA Extension)

Periods		Period 1	Period 2	Period 3	Period 4	Period 5	Period 6	Period 7	Period 8
Teacher 2A RWGs 1,5	Homeroom Activities (20)	LA RWGs 1,5 (50)	RWG 1 (50)	RWG 5 (50)	Lunch/ Recess (50)	Math MGs 1,5 (50)	MG 1 (50)	Encore Classes and Teacher Planning Time (50)	MG 5 (50)
Teacher 2B RWGs 2,6		RWG 6 (50)	LA RWGs 2,6 (50)	RWG 2 (50)		MG 6 (50)	Math MGs 2,6 (50)		MG 2 (50)
Teacher 2C RWGs 3,7		RWG 3 (50)	RWG 7 (50)	LA RWGs 3,7 (50)		MG 3 (50)	Math MGs 3,7 (50)		MG 7 (50)
Teacher 2D RWGs 4,8		LA RWGs 4,8 (50)	RWG 4 (50)	RWG 8 (50)		Math MGs 4,8 (50)	MG 4 (50)		MG 8 (50)
Extension Center* Teacher E		LA Extension				SS/SC (or Math Extension)			SS/SC (or Math Ext.)
		RWGs 2,7 (50)	RWGs 3,5,8 (50)	RWGs 1,4,6 (50)		SS/SC MGs 2,7 (50)	SS/SC MGs 5,8 (50)		SS/SC MGs 1,4 (50)
Extension Center* Teacher F		Other Grade Levels							SS/SC MGs 3,6 (50)

* For language arts extension, the center could be staffed by a Title I teacher and one or more resource teachers, such as LD, reading, ESL, or technology. In the afternoon the center is devoted to science and social studies or math extension.

Figure 6.7 Parallel Block Schedule for Four Grade 3 Homeroom Teachers and Extension Center (Every-Other-Day Math Extension or Science)

Periods		Period 1	Period 2	Period 3	Period 4	Period 5	Period 6	Period 7	Period 8
Teacher 3A RWGs 1,5	Homeroom Activities (20)	LA/SS RWGs 1,5 (100)		RWG 5 (50)	RWG 1 (50)	Lunch/ Recess (50)	Encore Classes and Teacher Planning Time (50)	Math/SC MGs 1,5 (50)	Day 1 MG 1 (50)
									Day 2 MG 5 (50)
Teacher 3B RWGs 2,6		LA/SS RWGs 2,6 (100)		RWG 2 (50)	RWG 6 (50)			Math/SC MGs 2,6 (50)	Day 1 MG 6 (50)
									Day 2 MG 2 (50)
Teacher 3C RWGs 3,7		RWG 3 (50)	RWG 7 (50)	LA/SS RWGs 3,7 (100)				Day 1 MG 3 (50)	Math/SC MGs 3,7 (50)
								Day 2 MG 7 (50)	
Teacher 3D RWGs 4,8		RWG 8 (50)	RWG 4 (50)	LA/SS RWGs 4,8 (100)				Day 1 MG 8 (50)	Math/SC MGs 4,8 (50)
								Day 2 MG 4 (50)	
Extension Center* Teacher		LA Extension						Math Extension (or Science)	
		RWGs 4,7 (50)	RWGs 3,8 (50)	RWGs 1,6 (50)	RWGs 2,5 (50)			Day 1 MGs 4,7 (50)	Day 1 MGs 2,5 (50)
								Day 2 MGs 3,8 (50)	Day 2 MGs 1,6 (50)

* For language arts extension, the center could be staffed by a Title I teacher and one or more resource teachers, such as LD, reading, ESL, or Technology. In the afternoon the center is devoted either to math extension or science. This model works well for schools having specialists in science and/or technology, who can staff the extension center on a rotational basis during Periods 7 and 8.

6.6
6.7

Figure 6.8 Parallel Block Schedule for Four Grade 3 Homeroom Teachers and Extension Center (Four-Day Rotation for Math Extension Using Computer Lab; see Figure 6.8a)

Periods		Period 1	Period 2	Period 3	Period 4	Period 5	Period 6	Period 7	Period 8
Teacher 3A RWGs 1,5	Homeroom Activities (20)	LA/SS RWGs 1,5 (100)		RWG 5 (50)	RWG 1 (50)	Lunch/ Recess (50)	Encore Classes and Teacher Planning Time (50)	Math/Science Computer Lab Rotation (See Figure 6.8a) (100)	
Teacher 3B RWGs 2,6		LA/SS RWGs 2,6 (100)		RWG 2 (50)	RWG 6 (50)				
Teacher 3C RWGs 3,7		RWG 3 (50)	RWG 7 (50)	LA/SS RWGs 3,7 (100)					
Teacher 3D RWGs 4,8		RWG 8 (50)	RWG 4 (50)	LA/SS RWGs 4,8 (100)					
Extension Center* Teacher		LA Extension							
		RWGs 4,7 (50)	RWGs 3,8 (50)	RWGs 1,6 (50)	RWGs 2,5 (50)				

* For language arts extension, the center could be staffed by a Title I teacher and one or more resource teachers, such as LD, reading, ESL, or Technology. In the afternoon the computer lab is utilized as the extension center to support the rotation shown in Figure 6.8a

Figure 6.8a Intervention/Enrichment Math Schedule with Computer Lab as Extension Center

Teacher/Block	Day 1 1:20-3:00		Day 2 1:20-3:00		Day 3		Day 4	
					1:20-2:10	2:10-3:00	1:20-2:10	2:10-3:00
Periods	Period 7	Period 8	Period 7	Period 8	Period 7	Period 8	Period 7	Period 8
Teacher 3A	M/SC A Total Group		M/SC A Total Group		M/SC A Total Group		MG A-E Enrichment (50 mins.)	MG A-I Intervention (50 mins.)
Teacher 3B	M/SC B Total Group		M/SC B Total Group		M/SC B Total Group		MG B-I Intervention (50 mins.)	MG B-E Enrichment (50 mins.)
Teacher 3C	M/SC C Total Group		M/SC C Total Group		MG C-E Enrichment (50 mins.)	MG C-I Intervention (50 mins.)	M/SC C Total Group	
Teacher 3D	M/SC D Total Group		M/SC D Total Group		MG D-I Intervention (50 mins.)	MG D-E Enrichment (50 mins.)	M/SC D Total Group	
Computer Lab	Other Grades				MG C-I MG D-E (50 mins.)	MG C-E MG D-I (50 mins.)	MG A-I MG B-E (50 mins.)	MG A-E MG B-I (50 mins.)

Note: This rotation fits into the 1:20–3:00 M/SC slot shown in Figure 6.8.
Key: MG = math group; I = intervention; E = enrichment.

6.8
6.8a

Figure 6.9 Parallel Block Schedule for Four Grade 1 Homeroom Teachers and Extension Center (Many Pull-Outs Required During Language Arts)

Periods		Period 1	Period 2	Period 3	Period 4	Period 5	Period 6	Period 7	Period 8	Period 9
Teacher 1A RWGs 1,5	Homeroom Activities (15)	LA RWGs 1,5 (45)	RWG 1 (45)	RWG 5 (45)	Lunch and Recess (45)	Math or Math/SC/SS MGs 1,5 (90)		Encore Classes and Teacher Planning (45)	MG 1 (45)	MG 5 (45)
Teacher 1B RWGs 2,6		RWG 6 (45)	LA RWGs 2,6 (45)	RWG 2 (45)		Math or Math/SC/SS MGs 2,6 (90)			MG 6 (45)	MG 2 (45)
Teacher 1C RWGs 3,7		RWG 3 (45)	RWG 7 (45)	LA RWGs 3,7 (45)		MG 3 (45)	MG 7 (45)		Math or Math/SC/SS MGs 3,7 (90)	
Teacher 1D RWGs 4,8		LA RWGs 4,8 (45)	RWG 4 (45)	RWG 8 (45)		MG 8 (45)	MG 4 (45)		Math or Math/SC/SS MGs 4,8 (90)	
Extension Center* Teacher		LA Extension				SS/SC or Math Ext.			SS/SC or Math Ext.	
		RWGs 2,7 (45)	RWGs 3,5,8 (45)	RWGs 1,4,6 (45)		MGs 4,7 (45)	MGs 3,8 (45)		MGs 2,5 (45)	MGs 1,6 (45)

* For language arts extension, the center could be staffed by a Title I teacher and one or more resource teachers, such as LD, reading, ESL, or Technology. In the afternoon the center is devoted either to science and social studies or math extension.

Figure 6.10 Parallel Block Schedule for Four Grade 1 Homeroom Teachers and Extension Center (Ten-Period Schedule)

Periods	Homeroom Activities (20)	Period 1	Period 2	Period 3	Period 4	Period 5	Period 6	Period 7	Period 8	Period 9	Period 10
Teacher 1A RWGs 1,5		LA RWGs 1,5 (80)		RWG 1 (40)	RWG 5 (40)	Lunch and Recess (40)	Math MGs 1,5 (80)		Encore Classes and Teacher Planning (40)	MG 1 (40)	MG 5 (40)
Teacher 1B RWGs 2,6		LA RWGs 2,6 (80)		RWG 6 (40)	RWG 2 (40)		Math MGs 2,6 (80)			MG 6 (40)	MG 2 (40)
Teacher 1C RWGs 3,7		RWG 3 (40)	RWG 7 (40)	LA RWGs 3,7 (80)			MG 3 (40)	MG 7 (40)		Math MGs 3,7 (80)	
Teacher 1D RWGs 4,8		RWG 8 (40)	RWG 4 (40)	LA RWGs 4,8 (80)			MG 8 (40)	MG 4 (40)		Math MGs 4,8 (80)	
Extension Center* Teacher		Language Arts Extension					SS/SC or Math Ext.			SS/SC or Math Ext.	
		RWGs 4,7 (40)	RWGs 3,8 (40)	RWGs 2,5 (40)	RWGs 1,6 (40)		MGs 4,7 (40)	MGs 3,8 (40)		MGs 2,5 (40)	MGs 1,6 (40)

* For language arts extension, the center could be staffed by a Title I teacher and one or more resource teachers, such as LD, reading, ESL, or Technology. In the afternoon the center is devoted either to science and social studies or math extension.

Figure 6.11 Parallel Block Master Schedule for Eight Periods

	8:00	9:00		10:00	11:00	12:00	1:00	2:00	3:00
Kinder.	HR Activities, Math and Unit Time (60)	ELG I (35)	ELG II (35)	ELG III (35)	Lunch/ Recess (50)	Plan/ Encore (50)	ELG I (35)	ELG II (35) ELG III (35)	HR Activities, Math and Unit Time (45)

Periods	Homeroom Activities (20)	Period 1	Period 2	Period 3	Period 4	Period 5	Period 6	Period 7	Period 8
Grade 1		Core I (50)	Core II (50)	Core III (50)	Lunch/ Recess (50)	Core IV (50)	Core V (50)	Core VI (50)	Plan/ Encore (50)
Grade 2		Core I (50)	Core II (50)	Core III (50)	Lunch/ Recess (50)	Core IV (50)	Core V (50)	Plan/ Encore (50)	Core VI (50)
Grade 3		Core I (50)	Core II (50)	Core III (50)	Core IV (50)	Lunch/ Recess (50)	Plan/ Encore (50)	Core V (50)	Core VI (50)
Grade 4		Core I (50)	Core II (50)	Plan/ Encore (50)	Core III (50)	Lunch/ Recess (50)	Core IV (50)	Core V (50)	Core VI (50)
Grade 5		Core I (50)	Plan/ Encore (50)	Core II (50)	Core III (50)	Core IV (50)	Lunch/ Recess (50)	Core V (50)	Core VI (50)
Encore		Plan (50)	Grade 5 (50)	Grade 4 (50)	Lunch/ Duty (50)	Kinder. (50)	Grade 3 (50)	Grade 2 (50)	Grade 1 (50)

Figure 6.12 Parallel Block Master Schedule for Nine Periods

Periods		Period 1	Period 2	Period 3	Period 4	Period 5	Period 6	Period 7	Period 8	Period 9
Kinder.	Homeroom Activities (15)	Core I (45)	Core II (45)	Core III (45)	Lunch/ Recess (45)	Core IV (45)	Core V (45)	Core VI (45)	Encore/ Plan (45)	Core VII (45)
Grade 1		Core I (45)	Core II (45)	Core III (45)	Lunch/ Recess (45)	Core IV (45)	Core V (45)	Encore/ Plan (45)	Core VI (45)	Core VII (45)
Grade 2		Core I (45)	Core II (45)	Core III (45)	Core IV (45)	Lunch/ Recess (45)	Core V (45)	Core V (45)	Core VI (45)	Encore/ Plan (45)
Grade 3		Core I (45)	Core II (45)	Core III (45)	Core IV (45)	Lunch/ Recess (45)	Encore/ Plan (45)	Core V (45)	Core VI (45)	Core VII (45)
Grade 4		Core I (45)	Core II (45)	Core III (45)	Encore/ Plan (45)	Core IV (45)	Lunch/ Recess (45)	Core V (45)	Core VI (45)	Core VII (45)
Grade 5		Core I (45)	Core II (45)	Encore/ Plan (45)	Core III (45)	Core IV (45)	Lunch/ Recess (45)	Core V (45)	Core VI (45)	Core VII (45)
Encore		Plan (45)	Other Classes or Extension (45)	Grade 5 (45)	Grade 4 (45)	Lunch/ Duty (45)	Grade 3 (45)	Grade 1 (45)	Kinder. (45)	Grade 2 (45)

6.11
6.12

Figure 6.13 Parallel Block Master Schedule for Ten Periods

Periods	Homeroom Activities (20)	Period 1	Period 2	Period 3	Period 4	Period 5	Period 6	Period 7	Period 8	Period 9	Period 10
Kinder.		Core I (40)	Core II (40)	Core III (40)	Core IV (40)	Lunch/ Recess (40)	Core V (40)	Core VI (40)	Core VII (40)	Encore/ Plan (40)	Core VIII (40)
Grade 1		Core I (40)	Core II (40)	Core III (40)	Core IV (40)	Lunch/ Recess (40)	Core V (40)	Core VI (40)	Encore/ Plan (40)	Core VII (40)	Core VIII (40)
Grade 2		Core I (40)	Core II (40)	Core III (40)	Core IV (40)	Core V (40)	Lunch/ Recess (40)	Core VI (40)	Core VII (40)	Core VIII (40)	Encore/ Plan (40)
Grade 3		Core I (40)	Core II (40)	Core III (40)	Core IV (40)	Core V (40)	Lunch/ Recess (40)	Encore/ Plan (40)	Core VI (40)	Core VII (40)	Core VIII (40)
Grade 4		Core I (40)	Core II (40)	Core III (40)	Core IV (40)	Encore/ Plan (40)	Core V (40)	Lunch/ Recess (40)	Core VI (40)	Core VII (40)	Core VIII (40)
Grade 5		Core I (40)	Core II (40)	Core III (40)	Encore/ Plan (40)	Core IV (40)	Core V (40)	Lunch/ Recess (40)	Core VI (40)	Core VII (40)	Core VIII (40)
Encore		Plan (40)	Other Classes or Extension (80)		Grade 5 (40)	Grade 4 (40)	Lunch/ Duty (40)	Grade 3 (40)	Grade 1 (40)	Kinder. (40)	Grade 2 (40)

Timeline markers: 8:00, 9:00, 10:00, 11:00, 12:00, 1:00, 2:00, 3:00

Figure 6.14 Parallel Block Schedule with Social Studies/Science Extension Grade 5

Periods	HR	Period 1	Period 2	Period 3	Period 4	Period 5	Period 6	Period 7	Period 8
Teacher A LA/Math	HR (15)	LA RWGs 5-1 & 5-4 (50)	RWG 5-1 (50)	Plan (50)	RWG 5-4 (50)	Lunch/ Recess (50)	Math MGs 5-1 & 5-4 (50)	MG 5-1 (50)	MG 5-4 (50)
Teacher B LA/Math	HR (15)	RWG 5-5 (50)	LA RWGs 5-2 & 5-5 (50)	Plan (50)	RWG 5-2 (50)	Lunch/ Recess (50)	MG 5-5 (50)	Math MGs 5-2 & 5-5 (50)	MG 5-2 (50)
Teacher C LA/Math	HR (15)	RWG 5-3 (50)	RWG 5-6 (50)	Plan (50)	LA RWGs 5-3 & 5-6 (50)	Lunch/ Recess (50)	MG 5-3 (50)	MG 5-6 (50)	Math MGs 5-3 & 5-6 (50)
Extension Teacher D SS/SC	HR (15)	SS RWGs 5-2 & 5-6 (50)	SS RWGs 5-3 & 5-4 (50)	Plan (50)	SS RWGs 5-1 & 5-5 (50)	Lunch/ Recess (50)	SC MGs 5-2 & 5-6 (50)	SC MGs 5-3 & 5-4 (50)	SC MGs 5-1 & 5-5 (50)

Time markers: 8:00, 9:00, 10:00, 11:00, 12:00, 1:00, 2:00, 3:00

6.13
6.14

Figure 6.15 Departmentalized Parallel Block Schedule Grade 5

Periods	HR	Period 1	Period 2	Period 3	Period 4	Period 5	Period 6	Period 7	Period 8
Teacher A LA/R	HR (15)	LA RWGs 5-1 & 5-7 (50)	RWG 5-1 (50)	Plan (50)	RWG 5-7 (50)	Lunch/ Recess (50)	LA RWGs 5-4 & 5-10 (50)	RWG 5-4 (50)	RWG 5-10 (50)
Teacher B LA/R	HR (15)	RWG 5-8 (50)	LA RWGs 5-2 & 5-8 (50)	Plan (50)	RWG 5-2 (50)	Lunch/ Recess (50)	RWG 5-11 (50)	LA RWGs 5-5 & 5-11 (50)	RWG 5-5 (50)
Teacher C LA/R	HR (15)	RWG 5-3 (50)	RWG 5-9 (50)	Plan (50)	LA RWGs 5-3 & 5-9 (50)	Lunch/ Recess (50)	RWG 5-6 (50)	RWG 5-12 (50)	LA RWGs 5-6 & 5-12 (50)
Teacher D Math	HR (15)	Math MGs 5-4 & 5-10 (50)	MG 5-4 (50)	Plan (50)	MG 5-10 (50)	Lunch/ Recess (50)	Math MGs 5-1 & 5-7 (50)	MG 5-1 (50)	MG 5-7 (50)
Teacher E Math	HR (15)	MG 5-11 (50)	Math MGs 5-5 & 5-11 (50)	Plan (50)	MG 5-5 (50)	Lunch/ Recess (50)	MG 5-8 (50)	Math MGs 5-2 & 5-8 (50)	MG 5-2 (50)
Teacher F Math	HR (15)	MG 5-6 (50)	MG 5-12 (50)	Plan (50)	Math MGs 5-6 & 5-12 (50)	Lunch/ Recess (50)	MG 5-3 (50)	MG 5-9 (50)	Math MGs 5-3 & 5-9 (50)
Teacher G SS	HR (15)	SS RWGs 5-2 & 5-9 (50)	SS RWGs 5-3 & 5-7 (50)	Plan (50)	SS RWGs 5-1 & 5-8 (50)	Lunch/ Recess (50)	SS RWGs 5-5 & 5-12 (50)	SS RWGs 5-6 & 5-10 (50)	SS RWGs 5-4 & 5-11 (50)
Teacher H SC	HR (15)	SC MGs 5-5 & 5-12 (50)	SC MGs 5-6 & 5-10 (50)	Plan (50)	SC MGs 5-4 & 5-11 (50)	Lunch/ Recess (50)	SC MGs 5-2 & 5-9 (50)	SC MGs 5-3 & 5-7 (50)	SC MGs 5-1 & 5-8 (50)

Figure 6.16 Departmentalized Parallel Block Schedule Grades 4 and 5

Periods	HR	Period 1	Period 2	Period 3	Period 4	Period 5	Period 6	Period 7	Period 8
Teacher A Grade 4 LA	HR (15)	LA RWGs 4-1 & 4-4 (50)	RWG 4-1 (50)	Plan (50)	RWG 4-4 (50)	Lunch/ Recess (50)	RWG 4-3 (50)	RWG 4-6 (50)	LA RWGs 4-3 & 4-6 (50)
Teacher B Grade 4/5 LA	HR (15)	RWG 4-5 (50)	LA RWGs 4-2 & 4-5 (50)	Plan (50)	RWG 4-2 (50)	Lunch/ Recess (50)	LA RWGs 5-1 & 5-4 (50)	RWG 5-1 (50)	RWG 5-4 (50)
Teacher C Grade 4 Math	HR (15)	MG 4-3 (50)	MG 4-6 (50)	Plan (50)	Math MGs 4-3 & 4-6 (50)	Lunch/ Recess (50)	Math MGs 4-1 & 4-4 (50)	MG 4-1 (50)	MG 4-4 (50)
Teacher D Grade 4/5 Math	HR (15)	Math MGs 5-1 & 5-4 (50)	MG 5-1 (50)	MG 5-4 (50)	Plan (50)	Lunch/ Recess (50)	MG 4-5 (50)	Math MGs 4-2 & 4-5 (50)	MG 4-2 (50)
Teacher E Grade 5 Math	HR (15)	MG 5-5 (50)	Math MGs 5-2 & 5-5 (50)	MG 5-2 (50)	Plan (50)	Lunch/ Recess (50)	MG 5-3 (50)	MG 5-6 (50)	Math MGs 5-3 & 5-6 (50)
Teacher F Grade 5 LA	HR (15)	RWG 5-3 (50)	RWG 5-6 (50)	LA RWGs 5-3 & 5-6 (50)	Plan (50)	Lunch/ Recess (50)	RWG 5-5 (50)	LA RWGs 5-2 & 5-5 (50)	RWG 5-2 (50)
Teacher G Grade 4/5 SS	HR (15)	SS RWGs 4-2 & 4-6 (50)	SS RWGs 4-3 & 4-4 (50)	Plan (50)	SS RWGs 4-1 & 4-5 (50)	Lunch/ Recess (50)	SS RWGs 5-2 & 5-6 (50)	SS RWGs 5-3 & 5-4 (50)	SS RWGs 5-1 & 5-5 (50)
Teacher H Grade 4/5 SC	HR (15)	SC MGs 5-2 & 5-6 (50)	SC MGs 5-3 & 5-4 (50)	SC MGs 5-1 & 5-5 (50)	Plan (50)	Lunch/ Recess (50)	SC MGs 4-2 & 4-6 (50)	SC MGs 4-3 & 4-4 (50)	SC MGs 4-1 & 4-5 (50)

6.15
6.16

Figure 6.17 Departmentalized Parallel Block Schedule Grades 4 and 5 with Two Intervention/Enrichment Periods

Periods	HR	Period 1	Period 2	Period 3	Period 4	Period 5	Period 6	Period 7	Period 8	Period 9
Teacher A Grade 4 LA	HR (10)	LA RWGs 4-1 & 4-4 (45)	RWG 4-1 (45)	Plan (45)	RWG 4-4 (45)	Intervention/Enrichment (45)	Lunch/Recess (45)	RWG 4-3 (45)	RWG 4-6 (45)	LA RWGs 4-3 & 4-6 (45)
Teacher B Grade 4/5 LA	HR (10)	RWG 4-5 (45)	LA RWGs 4-2 & 4-5 (45)	Plan (45)	RWG 4-2 (45)	Intervention/Enrichment (45)	Lunch/Recess (45)	LA RWGs 5-1 & 5-4 (45)	RWG 5-1 (45)	RWG 5-4 (45)
Teacher C Grade 4 Math	HR (10)	MG 4-3 (45)	MG 4-6 (45)	Plan (45)	Math MGs 4-3 & 4-6 (45)	Intervention/Enrichment (45)	Lunch/Recess (45)	Math MGs 4-1 & 4-4 (45)	MG 4-1 (45)	MG 4-4 (45)
Teacher D Grade 4/5 Math	HR (10)	Math MGs 5-1 & 5-4 (45)	MG 5-1 (45)	MG 5-4 (45)	Intervention/Enrichment (45)	Plan (45)	Lunch/Recess (45)	MG 4-5 (45)	Math MGs 4-2 & 4-5 (45)	MG 4-2 (45)
Teacher E Grade 5 Math	HR (10)	MG 5-5 (45)	Math MGs 5-2 & 5-5 (45)	MG 5-2 (45)	Intervention/Enrichment (45)	Plan (45)	Lunch/Recess (45)	MG 5-3 (45)	MG 5-6 (45)	Math MGs 5-3 & 5-6 (45)
Teacher F Grade 5 LA	HR (10)	RWG 5-3 (45)	RWG 5-6 (45)	LA RWGs 5-3 & 5-6 (45)	Intervention/Enrichment (45)	Plan (45)	Lunch/Recess (45)	RWG 5-5 (45)	LA RWGs 5-2 & 5-5 (45)	RWG 5-2 (45)
Teacher G Grade 4/5 SS	HR (10)	SS RWGs 4-2 & 4-6 (45)	SS RWGs 4-3 & 4-4 (45)	Plan (45)	Intervention/Enrichment (45)	SS RWGs 4-1 & 4-5 (45)	Lunch/Recess (45)	SS RWGs 5-2 & 5-6 (45)	SS RWGs 5-3 & 5-4 (45)	SS RWGs 5-1 & 5-5 (45)
Teacher H Grade 4/5 SC	HR (10)	SC MGs 5-2 & 5-6 (45)	SC MGs 5-3 & 5-4 (45)	SC MGs 5-1 & 5-5 (45)	Plan (45)	Intervention/Enrichment (45)	Lunch/Recess (45)	SC MGs 4-2 & 4-6 (45)	SC MGs 4-3 & 4-4 (45)	SC MGs 4-1 & 4-5 (45)

Figure 6.18 Departmentalized Parallel Block Schedule Grades 4 and 5 with One Intervention/Enrichment Period

Periods	HR	Period 1	Period 2	Period 3	Period 4	Period 5	Period 6	Period 7	Period 8	Period 9
Teacher A Grade 4 LA	HR (10)	LA RWGs 4-1 & 4-4 (45)	RWG 4-1 (45)	Plan (45)	RWG 4-4 (45)	Intervention/ Enrichment (45)	Lunch/ Recess (45)	RWG 4-3 (45)	RWG 4-6 (45)	LA RWGs 4-3 & 4-6 (45)
Teacher B Grade 4/5 LA	HR (10)	RWG 4-5 (45)	LA RWGs 4-2 & 4-5 (45)	Plan (45)	RWG 4-2 (45)	Intervention/ Enrichment (45)	Lunch/ Recess (45)	LA RWGs 5-1 & 5-4 (45)	RWG 5-1 (45)	RWG 5-4 (45)
Teacher C Grade 4 Math	HR (10)	MG 4-3 (45)	MG 4-6 (45)	Plan (45)	Math MGs 4-3 & 4-6 (45)	Intervention/ Enrichment (45)	Lunch/ Recess (45)	Math MGs 4-1 & 4-4 (45)	MG 4-1 (45)	MG 4-4 (45)
Teacher D Grade 4/5 Math	HR (10)	Math MGs 5-1 & 5-4 (45)	MG 5-1 (45)	MG 5-4 (45)	Plan (45)	Intervention/ Enrichment (45)	Lunch/ Recess (45)	MG 4-5 (45)	Math MGs 4-2 & 4-5 (45)	MG 4-2 (45)
Teacher E Grade 5 Math	HR (10)	MG 5-5 (45)	Math MGs 5-2 & 5-5 (45)	MG 5-2 (45)	Plan (45)	Intervention/ Enrichment (45)	Lunch/ Recess (45)	MG 5-3 (45)	MG 5-6 (45)	Math MGs 5-3 & 5-6 (45)
Teacher F Grade 5 LA	HR (10)	RWG 5-3 (45)	RWG 5-6 (45)	LA RWGs 5-3 & 5-6 (45)	Plan (45)	Intervention/ Enrichment (45)	Lunch/ Recess (45)	RWG 5-5 (45)	LA RWGs 5-2 & 5-5 (45)	RWG 5-2 (45)
Teacher G Grade 4/5 SS	HR (10)	SS RWGs 4-2 & 4-6 (45)	SS RWGs 4-3 & 4-4 (45)	Plan (45)	SS RWGs 4-1 & 4-5 (45)	Intervention/ Enrichment (45)	Lunch/ Recess (45)	SS RWGs 5-2 & 5-6 (45)	SS RWGs 5-3 & 5-4 (45)	SS RWGs 5-1 & 5-5 (45)
Teacher H Grade 4/5 SC	HR (10)	SC MGs 5-2 & 5-6 (45)	SC MGs 5-3 & 5-4 (45)	SC MGs 5-1 & 5-5 (45)	Plan (45)	Intervention/ Enrichment (45)	Lunch/ Recess (45)	SC MGs 4-2 & 4-6 (45)	SC MGs 4-3 & 4-4 (45)	SC MGs 4-1 & 4-5 (45)

Note: Both grade levels could plan together if there were sufficient encore staff to cover all six homerooms during one period.

6.17
6.18

Figure 6.19 Cougar Elementary School Master Schedule

		8:00	9:00	10:00	11:00	12:00	1:00	2:00	3:00
Community I K-1 (6)	HR (15)	LA/Tech. I (50)	LA/Tech. II (50)	LA/Tech. III (50)	Lunch/ Recess (50)	Math/SC/SS I (50)	Math/SC/SS II (50)	Encore/ Plan (50)	Math/SC/SS III (50)
Community I 2-3 (6)	HR (15)	LA/Tech. I (50)	LA/Tech. II (50)	LA/Tech. III (50)	Recess/ Lunch (50)	Math/SC/SS I (50)	Math/SC/SS II (50)	Math/SC/SS III (50)	Encore/ Plan (50)
Community II K-1 (6)	HR (15)	LA/Tech. I (50)	LA/Tech. II (50)	LA/Tech. III (50)	Math/SC/SS I (50)	Lunch/ Recess (50)	Encore/ Plan (50)	Math/SC/SS II (50)	Math/SC/SS III (50)
Community II 2-3 (6)	HR (15)	LA/Tech. I (50)	LA/Tech. II (50)	LA/Tech. III (50)	Encore/ Plan (50)	Recess/ Lunch (50)	Math/SC/SS I (50)	Math/SC/SS II (50)	Math/SC/SS III (50)
Community III K-1 (6)	HR (15)	LA/Tech. I (50)	LA/Tech. II (50)	Encore/ Plan (50)	LA/Tech. III (50)	Math/SC/SS I (50)	Lunch/ Recess (50)	Math/SC/SS II (50)	Math/SC/SS III (50)
Community III 2-3 (6)	HR (15)	LA/Tech. I (50)	Encore/ Plan (50)	LA/Tech. II (50)	LA/Tech. III (50)	Math/SC/SS I (50)	Recess/ Lunch (50)	Math/SC/SS II (50)	Math/SC/SS III (50)
Encore	HR (15)	Planning (50)	Community III (Gr. 2-3)	Community III (Gr. K-1)	Community II (Gr. 2-3)	Lunch/Duty (50)	Community II (Gr. K-1)	Community I (Gr. K-1)	Community I (Gr. 2-3)

Figure 6.20 Cougar Elementary School Community I Grades K–1 Schedule

		8:00	9:00	10:00	11:00	12:00	1:00	2:00	3:00
Teacher KA	HR (15)	LA RWGs K-1, K-4 (50)	Encore/Plan (50)	RWG K-1 (50)	RWG K-4 (50)	Math MGs K-1, K-4 (50)	Lunch/ Recess (50)	MG K-1 (50)	MG K-4 (50)
Teacher KB	HR (15)	RWG K-5 (50)	Encore/Plan (50)	LA RWGs K-2, K-5 (50)	RWG K-2 (50)	MG K-5 (50)	Lunch/ Recess (50)	Math MGs K-2, K-5 (50)	MG K-2 (50)
Teacher KC	HR (15)	RWG K-3 (50)	Encore/Plan (50)	RWG K-6 (50)	LA RWGs K-3, K-6 (50)	MG K-3 (50)	Lunch/ Recess (50)	MG K-6 (50)	Math MGs K-3, K-6 (50)
Teacher 1A	HR (15)	LA RWGs 1-1, 1-4 (50)	Encore/Plan (50)	RWG 1-1 (50)	RWG 1-4 (50)	Math MGs 1-1, 1-4 (50)	Lunch/ Recess (50)	MG 1-1 (50)	MG 1-4 (50)
Teacher 1B	HR (15)	RWG 1-5 (50)	Encore/Plan (50)	LA RWGs 1-2, 1-5 (50)	RWG 1-2 (50)	MG 1-5 (50)	Lunch/ Recess (50)	Math MGs 1-2, 1-5 (50)	MG 1-2 (50)
Teacher 1C	HR (15)	RWG 1-3 (50)	Encore/Plan (50)	RWG 1-6 (50)	LA RWGs 1-3, 1-6 (50)	MG 1-3 (50)	Lunch/ Recess (50)	MG 1-6 (50)	Math MGs 1-3, 1-6 (50)
Technology Center	HR (15)	Tech. RWGs 1-2,1-6 (50)	Encore/Plan (50)	Tech. RWGs 1-3,1-4 (50)	Tech. RWGs 1-1,1-5 (50)	Tech. MGs K-2, K-6 (50)	Lunch/ Recess (50)	Tech. MGs K-3, K-4 (50)	Tech. MGs K-1, K-5 (50)
SS/SC Teacher	HR (15)	SS/SC RWGs K-2, K-6 (50)	Encore/Plan (50)	SS/SC RWGs K-3, K-4 (50)	SS/SC RWGs K-1, K-5 (50)	SS/SC MGs 1-2,1-6 (50)	Lunch/ Recess (50)	SS/SC MGs 1-3,1-4 (50)	SS/SC MGs 1-1, 1-5 (50)

6.19
6.20

Figure 6.21 Cougar Elementary School Schedules

a. PE Schedule

		8:00	9:00	10:00	11:00	12:00	1:00	2:00	3:00
Day 1	HR (15)	Planning (50)	2G,2H,2I (50)	KG,KH,KI (50)	2D,2E,2F (50)	Lunch/Duty (50)	KD,KE,KF (50)	2A,2B,2C (50)	KA,KB,KC (50)
Day 2	HR (15)	Planning (50)	3G,3H,3I (50)	1G,1H,1I (50)	3D,3E,3F (50)	Lunch/Duty (50)	1D,1E,1F (50)	3A,3B,3C (50)	1A,1B,1C (50)
Day 3	HR (15)	Planning (50)	2G,2H,2I (50)	KG,KH,KI (50)	2D,2E,2F (50)	Lunch/Duty (50)	KD,KE,KF (50)	2A,2B,2C (50)	KA,KB,KC (50)
Day 4	HR (15)	Planning (50)	3G,3H,3I (50)	1G,1H,1I (50)	3D,3E,3F (50)	Lunch/Duty (50)	1D,1E,1F (50)	3A,3B,3C (50)	1A,1B,1C (50)
Day 5	HR (15)	Planning (50)	2G,2H,2I (50)	KG,KH,KI (50)	2D,2E,2F (50)	Lunch/Duty (50)	KD,KE,KF (50)	2A,2B,2C (50)	KA,KB,KC (50)
Day 6	HR (15)	Planning (50)	3G,3H,3I (50)	1G,1H,1I (50)	3D,3E,3F (50)	Lunch/Duty (50)	1D,1E,1F (50)	3A,3B,3C (50)	1A,1B,1C (50)

b. Art Schedule

		8:00	9:00	10:00	11:00	12:00	1:00	2:00	3:00
Day 1	HR (15)	Planning (50)	3G (50)	1G (50)	3D (50)	Lunch/Duty (50)	1D (50)	3A (50)	1A (50)
Day 2	HR (15)	Planning (50)	2G (50)	KG (50)	2D (50)	Lunch/Duty (50)	KD (50)	2A (50)	KA (50)
Day 3	HR (15)	Planning (50)	3I (50)	1I (50)	3F (50)	Lunch/Duty (50)	1F (50)	3C (50)	1C (50)
Day 4	HR (15)	Planning (50)	2I (50)	KI (50)	2F (50)	Lunch/Duty (50)	KF (50)	2C (50)	KC (50)
Day 5	HR (15)	Planning (50)	3H (50)	1H (50)	3E (50)	Lunch/Duty (50)	1E (50)	3B (50)	1B (50)
Day 6	HR (15)	Planning (50)	2H (50)	KH (50)	2E (50)	Lunch/Duty (50)	KE (50)	2B (50)	KB (50)

Figure 6.21 Cougar Elementary School Schedules, cont'd

c. Music Schedule

	8:00	9:00	10:00	11:00	12:00	1:00	2:00	3:00
Day 1	HR (15)	Planning (50)	3H (50)	1H (50)	3E (50)	Lunch/Duty (50)	1E (50)	3B (50)	1B (50)
Day 2	HR (15)	Planning (50)	2H (50)	KH (50)	2E (50)	Lunch/Duty (50)	KE (50)	2B (50)	KB (50)
Day 3	HR (15)	Planning (50)	3G (50)	1G (50)	3D (50)	Lunch/Duty (50)	1D (50)	3A (50)	1A (50)
Day 4	HR (15)	Planning (50)	2G (50)	KG (50)	2D (50)	Lunch/Duty (50)	KD (50)	2A (50)	KA (50)
Day 5	HR (15)	Planning (50)	3I (50)	1I (50)	3F (50)	Lunch/Duty (50)	1F (50)	3C (50)	1C (50)
Day 6	HR (15)	Planning (50)	2I (50)	KI (50)	2F (50)	Lunch/Duty (50)	KF (50)	2C (50)	KC (50)

d. Library Schedule

	8:00	9:00	10:00	11:00	12:00	1:00	2:00	3:00
Day 1	HR (15)	Planning (50)	3I (50)	1I (50)	3F (50)	Lunch/Duty (50)	1F (50)	3C (50)	1C (50)
Day 2	HR (15)	Planning (50)	2I (50)	KI (50)	2F (50)	Lunch/Duty (50)	KF (50)	2C (50)	KC (50)
Day 3	HR (15)	Planning (50)	3H (50)	1H (50)	3E (50)	Lunch/Duty (50)	1E (50)	3B (50)	1B (50)
Day 4	HR (15)	Planning (50)	2H (50)	KH (50)	2E (50)	Lunch/Duty (50)	KE (50)	2B (50)	KB (50)
Day 5	HR (15)	Planning (50)	3G (50)	1G (50)	3D (50)	Lunch/Duty (50)	1D (50)	3A (50)	1A (50)
Day 6	HR (15)	Planning (50)	2G (50)	KG (50)	2D (50)	Lunch/Duty (50)	KD (50)	2A (50)	KA (50)

6.21

Figure 6.22 Cougar Elementary School Six-Day Encore Rotation

8:00-8:15	Duty
8:15-9:05	Plan

9:05-9:55	Day 1	Day 2	Day 3	Day 4	Day 5	Day 6
Teacher 2G	PE	Art	PE	Music	PE	L
Teacher 2H	PE	Music	PE	L	PE	Art
Teacher 2I	PE	L	PE	Art	PE	Music
Teacher 3G	Art	PE	Music	PE	L	PE
Teacher 3H	Music	PE	L	PE	Art	PE
Teacher 3I	L	PE	Art	PE	Music	PE

9:55-10:45	Day 1	Day 2	Day 3	Day 4	Day 5	Day 6
Teacher KG	PE	Art	PE	Music	PE	L
Teacher KH	PE	Music	PE	L	PE	Art
Teacher KI	PE	L	PE	Art	PE	Music
Teacher 1G	Art	PE	Music	PE	L	PE
Teacher 1H	Music	PE	L	PE	Art	PE
Teacher 1I	L	PE	Art	PE	Music	PE

10:45-11:35	Day 1	Day 2	Day 3	Day 4	Day 5	Day 6
Teacher 2D	PE	Art	PE	Music	PE	L
Teacher 2E	PE	Music	PE	L	PE	Art
Teacher 2F	PE	L	PE	Art	PE	Music
Teacher 3D	Art	PE	Music	PE	L	PE
Teacher 3E	Music	PE	L	PE	Art	PE
Teacher 3F	L	PE	Art	PE	Music	PE

11:35-12:25	Lunch

12:25-1:15	Day 1	Day 2	Day 3	Day 4	Day 5	Day 6
Teacher KD	PE	Art	PE	Music	PE	L
Teacher KE	PE	Music	PE	L	PE	Art
Teacher KF	PE	L	PE	Art	PE	Music
Teacher 1D	Art	PE	Music	PE	L	PE
Teacher 1E	Music	PE	L	PE	Art	PE
Teacher 1F	L	PE	Art	PE	Music	PE

1:15-2:05	Day 1	Day 2	Day 3	Day 4	Day 5	Day 6
Teacher 2A	PE	Art	PE	Music	PE	L
Teacher 2B	PE	Music	PE	L	PE	Art
Teacher 2C	PE	L	PE	Art	PE	Music
Teacher 3A	Art	PE	Music	PE	L	PE
Teacher 3B	Music	PE	L	PE	Art	PE
Teacher 3C	L	PE	Art	PE	Music	PE

2:05-2:55	Day 1	Day 2	Day 3	Day 4	Day 5	Day 6
Teacher KA	PE	Art	PE	Music	PE	L
Teacher KB	PE	Music	PE	L	PE	Art
Teacher KC	PE	L	PE	Art	PE	Music
Teacher 1A	Art	PE	Music	PE	L	PE
Teacher 1B	Music	PE	L	PE	Art	PE
Teacher 1C	L	PE	Art	PE	Music	PE

7

Staffing, Scheduling, and Managing the Extension Center in Schools Using Parallel Block Scheduling

When elementary school personnel initially investigate the possibility of developing a parallel block schedule (PBS), they invariably ask, "Don't we need additional teachers to staff the extension center room(s)?" We typically respond, "Not necessarily." For example, we find that elementary schools, especially schools with a large number of special needs students and programs, often already have several types of support teachers and staff; designing a PBS for those schools sometimes simply requires using positions in different ways. By developing a parallel block schedule in schools having numerous support personnel, we very often end up with schedules that provide fewer interruptions for both teachers and students and less fragmentation in the school day. Greater inclusion and integration of content also can occur in such schools, and students with special needs are not isolated or stigmatized when receiving the required services because both the students and the support personnel are integrated more fully into the general education program.

The "extension center" is both a place and a program. Typically the extension center needs to be located in a space that can hold at least a normal-sized class; sometimes it is helpful to have a larger space, such as two classrooms with the accordion door open, depending on the programs provided. The programs of the extension center can vary greatly with student needs and school staffing. For example, the extension center can offer

♦ enrichment, including activities delivered by the extension center teacher/assistants, or by others such as the instrumental music teacher, an artist-in-residence, or various volunteers;

♦ special services to qualifying students, such as students with disabilities, English Language Learners, students receiving Title I services, students receiving gifted and talented services;

♦ practice and reinforcement of the general education curriculum, provided generally by the extension teacher and/or teaching assistants assigned to the extension center; and

♦ classes that all students must take, such as social studies, science, foreign language, Drug Abuse Resistance Education (DARE), and/or computer lab.

This chapter outlines four possibilities for how school personnel might staff the extension center. Each of the proposed plans rests on a different rationale and staff configuration. Plan I involves reassigning a base teacher from one or more grade levels to assume the role of extension teacher; this generally is possible only in larger schools with relatively low pupil–teacher ratios, although sometimes in a smaller school that is contemplating a split-grade homeroom (such as a second and third grade mix), the additional teacher can be assigned as an extension teacher. In Plan II, selected support teachers, such as special education teachers, ESL teachers, or Title I instructors, may be assigned to work as extension staff. In Plan III, additional specialized staff, such as a foreign language teacher or science lab instructor, serve as extension teachers. Finally in Plan IV, we utilize features of Plans I to III to create a combination plan. We

conclude the chapter with Bonnie Dudley's detailed description of the operation of her extension center, which has been in operation at Hollis Hand Elementary School in Troup County (La Grange), Georgia, for more than a decade.

Plan I: Assign a Homeroom Teacher to Serve As an Extension Teacher

In large elementary schools with four or more teachers at a grade level and relatively low class sizes, it often is possible to use one of those teachers as the extension teacher. Imagine a grade level with four homerooms of 20 students each (80 pupils in all). We could reassign one homeroom teacher to the role of extension teacher, redistributing students to form three homerooms with 26 or 27 students each. Of course, such assignments need to be permitted by or negotiated according to union contracts and/or state class size limitations, and this change needs to occur before school begins and before parents and students are notified of any regular homeroom assignments.

Figure 7.1 (p. 222) illustrates a basic schedule for Plan I. The grade 2 extension teacher (2D) typically "extends" the work of the base teachers by providing supervised practice, reinforcement, and enrichment activities that are very difficult for self-contained teachers to juggle with direct instruction. Today, however, especially in the upper elementary grades, it would not be uncommon for the extension teacher (2D) to teach social studies during the morning LA/reading block and science during the afternoon math/science block and also to integrate a great deal of writing, language and "hands-on" activities into those classes. In this plan, the three core teachers focus on teaching reading, language arts, and math. In states where students are tested in science and social studies, we find students in this scheduling arrangement show improvement in science and social studies, especially in science test scores.

In Figure 7.1 (p. 222), we can follow a second-grader (George, say) for a day. After his 20-minute homeroom time, George remains with teacher 2C for his RWG 3 reading/writing group while the parallel group (RWG 6) goes to extension, staffed by teacher 2D (originally assigned to grade 2 as a base teacher). In most schools, a locally funded teaching assistant (TA) also would be assigned to assist with extension activities, including pick-up and delivery of groups. Others working in the extension room might include a special education teacher, an ESL teacher, or selected reading and math specialists, depending on which students have been scheduled during various extension periods.

In Plan I, all grade 2 base teachers have two periods each day for reading/writing instruction and two periods each day for math/science instruction, in each case with approximately half their class, an average of 13 students. This plan helps reduce the need for teachers to prepare the typical seatwork activities. Over the years we also have learned that fewer classroom management problems occur when elementary students spend less time engaged in independent activities.

When George goes to extension at 9:10, he may be assigned to work with the ESL teacher for a designated number of days per week. On the other days, he works with the regular extension teacher and/or the extension room TA. During period 3 (10:00–10:50), George returns to his base teacher for whole-group language arts/social studies instruction.

During period 4 (10:50–11:40), George eats lunch with his homeroom (teacher 2C) for the first 20 to 30 minutes and then has a supervised recess of 20 to 25 minutes. Following lunch and recess, George attends his encore classes (period 5, 11:40–12:30) while all grade 2 base teachers, along with the grade 2 extension and support staff, have individual and (on designated days) team planning time. This common planning period, if used correctly and purposefully, will contribute to the development of a learning community for all grade 2 teachers and students (DuFour & Eaker, 1998). It is during this time that grade 2 base teachers, extension personnel and all support staff who provide services through the extension program reach decisions on how they will coordinate lesson plans and supplemental instruction for all grade 2 students.[1]

During the three-period math/science afternoon block (12:30–3:00), George will spend period 6 with his homeroom teacher in a small math group and period 8 with his total homeroom group involved in math or science activities. In between (period 7), he engages in extension center activities that could include computer lab (CL) or time with a resource/support teacher, such as an ESL teacher or reading/math support teacher.

In Figure 7.2 (p. 223), we illustrate a similar plan for a larger school having seven base teachers assigned to grade 1 (with a

---

1 See chapter 3 for schedules that provide an occasional extended planning period (every five or six days, 80 minutes or more).

total of 126 students). In this case, teacher 1G serves as a Language Arts/Reading extension teacher for that grade level. Ideally, this teacher should be a reading specialist with at least a master's degree in reading—an educator in a position to diagnose, coordinate, and supervise the reading program for all students in grade 1, as well as to compensate for instructional weaknesses that may exist in particular classrooms because of attitude, attendance, and competency shortcomings that exist among most any group of teachers.

In this example of Plan I, the extension center occupies the classroom space originally assigned to teacher 1G as a homeroom teacher. Here, teacher 1G provides extension services to half the grade 1 teachers (A, B, C) during periods 1 to 3, while teachers 1D, 1E, and 1F have mathematics, social studies and/or science. During periods 6 to 8 in the afternoon, the slots are reversed. In most elementary schools today, teacher G would be assisted by several types of support teachers during various periods of the day. Under the Plan I extension model, teacher G is in a position to best coordinate all support services for students in that grade level.

In Figure 7.3 (p. 224), we adapt Plan I to show a situation in which one teacher serves as extension for grades 1 and 2. We often suggest this model when a school has an uneven number of students in two consecutive grade levels, or when enrollments change during a school year and a teacher is added. Sometimes it may cause fewer interruptions and parent complaints if the new teacher starts as an extension teacher rather than pulling students from the six original homerooms to create a new group.

In this adaptation, the extension teacher serves RWGs 1 to 6 (grade 1) during the first three periods, has two periods for planning and lunch, and then serves RWGs 7 to 12 (grade 2) in the afternoon. It is important that the extension teacher be available to plan with both grade-level groups. In this example, the extension teacher's planning period and lunch, scheduled back to back, can be switched to allow meeting with one group or the other on designated days.

In Figures 7.1 (p. 222), 7.2 (p. 223), and 7.3 (p. 224), we have illustrated various configurations of the Plan I extension model. In each case, relatively low pupil–teacher ratios made it possible for one base teacher to serve full time as the extension teacher for one or more grade levels. Whenever possible, we prefer the Plan I model. With support personnel in the building working with extension teachers to serve special needs students, we find that this model maximizes coordination of instructional programs while minimizing stigmatization of students and fragmentation of school programs. It also may be the best way to make certain all students with special needs, particularly those who are not exempt from the state testing program, receive full access to the general education curriculum and additional specialized support.

In Plan I, if a few students must be pulled for services (such as speech therapy), we strongly suggest taking them from the extension time—*not* from the base teacher's instructional time. For students receiving multiple services, we recommend parceling them out during assigned extension periods; for example, a speech therapist might schedule four students from their RWG extension period on Tuesdays and Thursdays; then those students might be assigned to work with the extension teacher or with the ESL teacher Mondays, Wednesdays, and Fridays. Other students in the same extension session might work daily with the

Title I reading specialist during their reading/language arts extension period.

When a base teacher becomes the extension teacher for a specific grade level, other support teachers often work selected periods of the day in the various extension rooms. For example, some students with disabilities might meet with their teachers during one or both of their extension periods on a daily or rotating basis. Likewise, depending on numbers and available space, talented and gifted (TAG) students might stay in the extension room or travel to another room for TAG instruction. If TAG students meet in the extension center space, some schools encourage other strong students to join them for selected activities. This practice is more likely to occur where the primary focus of the TAG program is not so much to "sort, select, and label" as to raise expectations for all students and provide school-wide opportunities for the application of higher-order thinking skills.

We have illustrated Plan I models with three-, four- and seven-teacher adaptations. Later in this chapter, Bonnie Dudley, a grade 4 extension center teacher for the past 11 years at Hollis Hand Elementary School in Troup County, Georgia, details a case study of an extension center classroom serving four grade 4 teachers.

Plan II: Assign Support Teachers as Extension Teachers

In Plan II, selected support teachers are assigned to work as extension center staff. The major argument in favor of this plan is that greater inclusion of students identified as needing support services occurs when the support teachers can work with both identified and non-identified students through the extension program. Such a plan reduces fragmentation in the school program and schedule, and proponents of Plan II also contend students are less stigmatized when the extension concept is implemented. As shown in Figure 7.4 (p. 225), schools having large numbers of special needs students and accompanying staff may, for example, assign ESL, reading resource teachers, and/or Title I teachers as extension teachers at various grade levels.

In this model, locally funded teaching assistants (TAs) may be assigned to the extension center, and for legal and funding purposes, some of the support teachers also may have a percentage of their salaries paid from local funds; some of the regular base teachers then could have a portion of their salaries paid from one of the support service funding sources. Using this funding distribution formula yields two benefits: greater flexibility in the assignment of various types of support personnel, and (because part of the general education teachers' salaries is paid through categorical funds) greater ownership taken by homeroom teachers for students served by these programs. Other support teachers (special education teachers, TAG teacher(s), speech therapists, technology specialists) also might be assigned to the center.

School personnel who implement this model believe that the best way to raise the level of achievement for the greatest number of students is *not* to fragment the school day with multiple pull-out programs and personnel but, instead, to provide strong support for base teachers. Proponents contend that special-needs students often have little or no support at home; therefore, the most critical person in their lives during the school year is their base teacher. They spend most of their time in school with that teacher, who must become both their anchor and advocate. In schools and states that have high-stakes testing and accountability programs, supporters of this model also believe that if special needs students are held to the same rigorous standards as other students, they must be taught the same curriculum. In the Plan II model, base teachers maintain control of the curriculum for all the students for whom they are accountable.

The rationale for Plan II views base teachers as somewhat like primary care physicians in medicine. They determine when and how the support teachers work with special needs students. In some schools in the past, the support teachers built their schedules and then expected the base teachers to fill in around the edges—a practice that often splintered programs in every classroom, leaving base teachers feeling like traffic cops and complaining of the tail wagging the dog. Plan II consolidates the schedule and maximizes the role of base teachers.

Plan III: Assign Enrichment Teachers as Extension Teachers

In Plan III, illustrated in Figure 7.5 (p. 226), the instructional programs of various enrichment teachers, such as science or foreign language specialists, may be scheduled as extension programs; obviously this plan is possible only in schools staffed with such positions. When enrichment staff members are scheduled as extension center staff, students do not receive instruction in those programs in homeroom groups. Under the parallel block schedule shown in Figure 7.5, two RWGs or MGs at a time pair up to form a Spanish class or science group, for example, leaving two base teachers with smaller groups for reading/writing or math instruction during the same period. In this example, the foreign language teacher is needed only for periods 1 to 3 in grade 4 and could be assigned to work at another level, say grade 5, during the afternoon. Similarly, the social studies and science teacher who serves as the extension teacher for grade 4 during the afternoon could work in grade 5 during morning periods.

Figure 7.5 (p. 226) shows a daily period of Spanish; however, it would be much more typical for elementary foreign language to be scheduled every other day. In a school with three sections of each grade level, adding computer/writing lab to the three morning extension periods in grade 4 and alternating that with foreign language instruction would enable one foreign language teacher and one technology person to accommodate students in four grade levels.

Let's follow the flow in Figure 7.5 (p. 226), focusing on teacher 2A. After a 20-minute homeroom session, she works with RWGs 1 and 4 from 8:20 to 9:10 on language arts. Following the whole-group work, RWG 1 stays for a period of teacher-directed reading/writing instruction, while RWG 4 goes to the extension center for instruction or assistance. At 10:00, the two reduced groups switch places.

After lunch/recess and encore classes during periods 4 and 5, grade 2 students begin their mathematics/science/social studies block at 12:30. The pattern is familiar: Teacher 2A works with her whole homeroom group (MGs 1 and 4) for 50 minutes. During period 7, teacher 2A keeps the MG 1 students for additional teacher-directed math instruction, while MG 4 students go to the science/social studies teacher. The science/social studies teacher might alternate work in these two subjects every other day, quarterly, or by semester.

During period 8, teacher 2A completes the day by working with MG 4 students in a directed math lesson while MG 1 students have science/social studies. If schools need some time for dismissal beyond the minutes shown in this schedule, they might reduce the homeroom time by five minutes or trim the afternoon periods by two or three minutes and create a dismissal period of five to ten minutes at the close of the day.

Using enrichment teachers and their programs in this fashion can do much to support base teachers in their desire to work with reduced groups in reading and mathematics without having to prepare seat work or spend so much time managing (some call it policing) small groups. The schedule presented in Figure 7.5 (p. 226) also reduces fragmentation of programs and of the school day for students assigned to multiple support and enrichment programs.

When schools provide teacher planning time with encore teachers and schedule reduced groups in both reading/language arts and mathematics with enrichment teachers, they typically use foreign language and writing labs to reduce groups in reading/language arts, in line with the common belief that these programs have greater instructional integration and correlation possibilities. Likewise, they usually arrange for reduced groups in mathematics through the services of the science lab teacher and/or a computer lab established exclusively for use in mathematics; again, the belief is that science/mathematics and technology have more shared curriculum content and activities. Depending on state or school district regulations, computer labs may be operated by a technology teacher, a teaching assistant, or a paraprofessional trained as a computer technician.

Plan IV: Combine Plans I to III

Plan IV, illustrated in a master schedule format in Figure 7.6 (p. 227), involves a combination of all of the above three plans.

For example, in Figure 7.7 (p. 228) in grades K–1, because each of the four kindergarten and four first grade sections had fewer than 18 students assigned, we collapse one homeroom into the remaining three at each grade level and assign that teacher to provide extension services. Although homeroom size now increases to an average 24 in those grades, we would argue that the benefits attained are worth this tradeoff. The kindergarten and first grade base teachers would spend two-thirds of their instructional time with small groups in language arts and/or mathematics. The kindergarten extension program allows base teachers to provide a double dose of small-group literacy time (ELGs) in a group of eight or less. The grade 1 extension center teacher allows us to provide small-group instruction in both literacy and mathematics daily in groups of 12 or fewer.[2]

---

2   In Plans I to IV, all students receive more teacher-directed instruction and spend less time working independently, which can be a major benefit for lower-achieving students and younger children (Fogliani, 1990; Hopkins, 1990; Wenglinsky, 1997).

In that same school, extension for grades 2 and 3 might be provided by various support staff members, such as Title I reading specialists, special education, ESL and TAG teachers, as shown in Figure 7.8 (p. 229). Meanwhile, teachers and students in grades 4 and 5 might arrange reduced groups in reading and math by relying on the computer lab, science or foreign language program, or a combination of such programs scheduled on a rotating basis, as illustrated in Figure 7.9 (p. 230). In Figure 7.10 (p. 231), we offer a schedule for the encore rotations that provides all teachers common planning time by grade level. Note that the planning period is consistent each day. This design will help elementary teachers develop relatively long blocks of protected teaching time each day and reduce the fragmentation of the school day for both teachers and students.

A Final Note on Staffing and Scheduling the Extension Center

Staffing levels in elementary schools across our nation differ dramatically. In some poorly funded schools, we find barely enough teachers to cover homeroom classes and provide an occasional encore class for students and a planning period for base teachers. Other schools with better funding often have so many encore, enrichment, and special service providers that they practically trip over each other trying to get access to students. Almost everywhere, however, we find that the principles of parallel block scheduling can focus our efforts to improve services to students. And almost always, this requires schools to rethink the roles of some staff members—often a very difficult change for many to accept.

We conclude this chapter with an in-depth description of the operation of Bonnie Dudley's fourth grade extension center in Troup County, Georgia.

Case Study: The Extension Center Classroom at Hollis Hand Elementary School, Troup County, GA[3]

Have you ever attended a school conference and walked away thinking, "That's an interesting concept?" That's the way a group of administrators and teachers from Troup County School System felt after attending a two-day conference where Robert Lynn Canady, the keynote speaker, explained how to implement Parallel Block Scheduling in the elementary school. Troup County Schools were going through a restructuring period, consolidating four small school systems into one large county system. Each school was encouraged to send representatives to learn about Parallel Block Scheduling and consider implementing it in the upcoming school year. I was lucky enough to be one of the three teachers representing my school.

---

3   This case study was written by Mary Bonnie Dudley. She can be contacted at dudleymb@troup.org.

We walked away so fired up that the next morning we met with our principal, Mrs. Sharon Alford, and asked if she would allow us to create a sample schedule and present it to our school council. Mrs. Alford saw how excited we were and let us go with it; and go with it we did. We sold our staff on this unique scheduling model, and the next step was to share our plan with our central office administrators and the Board of Education. The schedule was presented, accepted, and the rest is school history.

Our county has been using the parallel block scheduling model, including the "controlled heterogeneous" groupings described in chapter 6, for more than a decade. With the support, encouragement, and guidance of our elementary curriculum director, Dr. Pat Barton, each elementary school has taken the original parallel block model and revised it in order to meet the changing instructional needs of each school's student population. That's the beauty of PBS; it can be tweaked, modified and molded to allow a school to experiment with a variety of scheduling models. Each school's core curriculum goals rely heavily on the successful implementation of the parallel block schedule. Troup County Schools are very fortunate to have visionary administrators like Dr. Barton and Mrs. Alford who hear about unique educational ideas, encourage their teachers to implement them, and to make them better each year. Parallel block continues to be our scheduling model primarily because of support from our administrators, school board, teachers, and parents believing that this is the best scheduling model for Troup County's elementary students.

What do I hope you'll gain from reading this case study?

♦ A sense of how one school implemented parallel block scheduling,

♦ A detailed description of the organization and operation of an extension center,

♦ Instructional strategies that promote a creative learning environment, and

♦ Teacher planning activities that encourage teamwork, decision-making, risk-taking, and self-evaluation.

Parallel Block Scheduling and Extension Center Classrooms at Hollis Hand Elementary

At Hollis Hand Elementary, the principal and instructional specialist assign each student to a heterogeneous class to begin the school year. During the day, students receive on-grade-level instruction and grades in reading, math, language arts, social studies, science, and health from the regular classroom teacher. In addition to whole-group instruction, students also receive small-group instruction. Each classroom teacher forms two groups of students with nearly similar achievement levels (on grade level and approaching grade level). One group remains with the teacher for 50 minutes while the other group travels to the extension center classroom for accelerated, non-graded activities (see Figure 7.11, p. 232). The regular classroom teacher now has the opportunity to address individual student needs by working with a small group of students nearly homogeneously grouped. Very few student pull-outs occur during this protected time of small-group instruction.

Hollis Hand's administrators and teachers designed each extension center as a classroom where students are offered multiple ways to learn previously introduced concepts taught in the regular classroom. At the beginning of the school year, our principal, instructional specialist, and teachers schedule students from two different classrooms so that each extension group is heterogeneous. A certified teacher who plans with the regular classroom teachers operates the center. The center offers both extended and enriched curriculum activities that support the regular instructional program. The extension teacher does not give grades for extension work. The majority of special service pull-outs also occur during extension classes.

Role of the Extension Teacher

The following are expectations for extension center classroom teachers in the Troup County Schools:

- Demonstrates a contagious enthusiasm for teaching and learning.

- Has good classroom management and organizational skills but is not overly rigid.

- Has a high level of energy (at least most days).

- Can provide highly creative choices of instructional approaches and activities.

- Can manage cooperative learning groups as well as learning center activities.

- Enjoys working with students having a wide range of abilities.

- Enjoys teaming with colleagues and has the respect of other teachers.

- Prefers designing curriculum rather than being confined just to textbook strategies; seldom uses worksheets.

- Has the skills to evaluate student progress informally rather than relying solely on tests.

- Can excite students about learning without having to use grades as a motivator.

Doesn't this sound like a tall order? Even so, expectations have increased over the years. Today, each extension center classroom at Hollis Hand has six networked computers, so the teacher must be able to integrate technology into all units. Each team of teachers at Hollis Hand Elementary works together to develop the curriculum and themes they want included in the extension center. For example, the grade 4 team decided to place the fourth grade's laser disc player in the center; therefore, the lab teacher must be knowledgeable about all the social studies and science laser programs that extend the fourth grade curriculum. The center is where we produce our grade-level plays and large-scale puppet shows. The team also decided to place the school system's hands-on science kits in the extension center. When the extension teacher, support teachers, and regular classroom teachers combine their efforts in planning grade-level curriculum, students and teachers benefit, and the ultimate outcome has been higher student achievement.

Benefits of the Extension Center Classroom

- The extension center provides the regular classroom teacher time to work with small skill groups for extended periods of time throughout the school day. Instead of completing seatwork activities in the back of the room while their teacher works with another group, students work with a support teacher or in the extension room with a certified teacher working on accelerated activities.

♦ The extension teacher develops a curriculum that extends and enriches the core curriculum. This gives all students the opportunity to participate in enrichment activities daily. Providing accelerated activities that the extension teacher informally evaluates makes the center a nonthreatening classroom where students are willing to take risks.

♦ Students pulled for special instructional programs aren't missing lessons where they receive grades. When their group leaves the regular classroom to go to extension, some may go to their speech or resource classroom.

♦ Placing kits, active boards, and multiple computers in the extension center exposes all students to these resources equitably and is cost effective.

Organizing the Extension Center Classroom: Extension Center Classroom Space Arrangements

The physical arrangement of the extension center classroom is essential to this productive learning environment. The design offers students multiple ways of learning. It's a classroom that promotes teamwork on a daily basis and offers traditional

whole-group instructional lessons, small-group teacher-directed lessons, independent work areas, and independent learning centers. Figure 7.12 (p. 233) is a sample floor plan for fourth grade extension center classroom and Figure 7.13 (p. 234) is a sample floor plan for a primary grade extension center classroom.

Instructional Organization of the Extension Center Classroom

Begin Units with Whole-Group Instruction

Every language arts unit begins with whole-group activities. I use music, art prints, literature, dance, online video clips, and the supplementary instructional materials that accompany the regular classroom's curriculum, such as laser discs and transparencies. Students' textbooks, teachers' guides, teacher trade books, and Internet lesson plans also come into play, helping me extend objectives taught in the regular classroom. A great deal of communication takes place between the extension and regular classroom teachers to ensure that all activities taking place in the extension center classroom are enrichment and do not repeat activities used in the regular classrooms. This is one of the great advantages of common planning time. We develop the majority of our extension lab's themes by extending social studies and science units taught in the regular classroom. For example, when the grade 4 students studied the American Midwest, I taught a unit on the pioneers of the Midwest by using the Laura Ingalls Wilder novel *Little House on the Prairie*. When they studied the American Revolutionary War in the regular classroom, we created historical large-scale puppet shows in the center. I use cooperative learning group activities during whole-group instruction time. Students might work towards producing a group poem, song, letter, newspaper article, short story, PowerPoint slide show, or skit. After we've completed a few days of whole-group instruction, I divide the students between two learning stations: teacher-directed tables and learning centers tables (Figure 7.12, p. 233). Students remain in these stations for eight days and then switch stations for the next eight days.

What Happens at the Teacher-Directed Station?

This station is where I work with a small heterogeneous group of students. Depending on the number of students in the extension period, we try to keep these small groups no larger than 12 students. While students participate in a variety of activities, they primarily are engaged in vocabulary development, cooperative team projects, and individual writing assignments. I also like to read a variety of literature to students during this time. Students work on producing short skits, readers' theater, puppet shows, and plays, which they perform for the school and their families. They also create travel brochures, pop-up books, big books, Venn diagrams, outlines, and, eventually, the dreaded three-paragraph essay. The advantage of this extension organization is that it allows me to move constantly among small groups of students and do quick informal assessments of students' work or have brief group or individual mini-conferences. Students can make immediate changes to their work after conferencing. While students are working independently at the teacher-directed station, I take time to move among the students working in learning centers and do quick evaluations of their work.

What Happens at the Learning Centers Station?

Keeping the learning centers station simple and manageable is the only way I have controlled the "mess" that always accompanies centers. I have four learning centers in the fourth grade extension center classroom: Art Center, Research/Writing Center, Listening Center, and Computer Center. When creating a new unit, I always plan two to three independent activities for each station. Students are required to complete a minimum of one activity at each center, but most students try to do them all. They work two consecutive days at a center to complete the assignments. If they finish early they move on to the next center, but only after a teaching assistant or I have quickly checked their work and determined they have successfully completed the assignments at the center. Several periods daily, a teaching assistant works in the extension center classroom and supervises students working in learning centers. The assistant encourages students to stay on task, solves computer problems, and informally evaluates students' work. This valuable assistance allows the extension teacher to maximize instruction for students at the teacher-directed station.

One goal of the extension program is to help students develop self-evaluation skills for learning center products. I create a simple checklist for each language arts unit, which all students glue inside their theme booklets. Students check off each activity when they've completed it; this lets us know they are ready for their work to be evaluated. The checklist also provides a visual reminder of how many activities are at each station and allows us to scan quickly and determine if students are using their time wisely (example found in the unit "Learning to Be Me" in Appendix 1).

What Happens Near the End of the Unit?

After all students have worked eight days at the teacher-directed station and eight days rotating through the four learning centers, we have one or two wrap-up days called "Polish and Shine Day." This gives students a little extra time to polish up their center products plus time for the teacher assistant and me to move among students and evaluate theme folders. I skim through all theme folders, looking over completed center activities. I've already looked over work completed at the teacher-directed station. The students who have satisfactorily completed all assignments work on an independent activity during this time. Most choose to listen to a book on tape and take Accelerated Reader tests. Some bring their own books to read from home or the media center. Others choose to work in skill-based computer programs.

Classroom Management

Student Assignments

Hanging above each table is a large colored star made from poster board. The different colors help students locate their assignments in the center. Five tables are in the room, so there are five different colored stars.

- Teacher-directed table 1—red star
- Teacher-directed table 2—yellow star

- Art center—orange star
- Research/writing center—blue star
- Listening center—green star

As students enter the extension center classroom, they refer to a bulletin board to help them quickly locate their workstation. Students check the bulletin board titled "Stations" when they will be working in the teacher-directed station or learning centers (Figure 7.14, p. 235). If they will be working whole-group, they refer to the "Extension Teams" bulletin board (see Figure 7.16, p. 217). I have made two different laminated charts for each extension class.

Careful consideration goes into making up the cooperative, heterogeneously grouped teams. I like to wait until I have worked with the students one week at the beginning of the school year before making teams. I always make a few changes in order to make the teams diverse. Next, I write the students' names on the charts using an overhead transparency pen. This allows me to make changes when students withdraw, new students enter, or students move to the on-grade-level group or the approaching-grade-level group. Some extension teachers change teams every grading period or each semester. I like to change the grade 4 cooperative teams at the beginning of each new unit, which gives each student at least one opportunity to work with every student in their extension class during the school year.

The chart depicted in Figure 7.14 (p. 235) is posted on the bulletin board for each extension period when students work in the learning center station or at the teacher-directed station. This chart has saved my sanity. The students locate their class chart, find their names, look for their assignments, and go directly to their assigned workstation. I divide students into eight cooperative teams for the language arts extension classes. If there are more than 24 students in a class, some teams will have four students. The teacher station label and learning centers label are interchangeable. At the end of eight days, I pin the teacher station's label above teams E through H. Pinned above teams A through D is a learning centers' label. Pinned beside each team is a small colored star. The students go to the table with the matching colored star hanging above it. The stars on the bulletin board rotate to the right every other day. The computer center does not have a star; there, I hang a small laminated picture of a computer.

Management of Students and Activities
Managing Students' Work

How does a teacher keep up with 70 to 100 students' projects when they don't have their own desks to store work? During the first week of school, I distribute a pocket-file folder to each student. They write their names on the inside and return them to me. At the end of the day, I write their names and center class number with magic marker on the front of the folder. Students keep all of their work inside their folder. They use small Ziploc bags to store small parts of unfinished projects and place them inside their folder. As they are leaving the lab to return to their regular classroom, they place their folder in a stacked basket beside the door. The top basket is for students in extension class 1, the second basket is for extension class 2, and the bottom basket is for extension class 3. Students are responsible for keeping up with all of their work and placing it inside their folders. If I see any work or folders left on the tables, I place the work in a Lost and Found box.

When students enter the extension center the next day, I assign two student helpers to distribute the folders to the students. The grade 1 and 2 extension center teachers usually meet with their whole group on the carpet for the first ten to 15 minutes before students move to their assigned stations, and then they distribute the folders. Helpers return folders to me if a student is absent or has gone to the speech, resource, or gifted classrooms. I return those folders to the correct storage basket. If students can't find their folder or work, they know to look in the Lost and Found box. Occasionally a student's folder will end up inside another student's folder, but we always manage to find it quickly.

Managing Curriculum Materials

Keeping up with all of the "stuff" necessary to run the Language Arts and Math/Science centers is a huge challenge. I have two four-drawer file cabinets that help me organize my units, books on tapes, and thematic unit guides. Two large closets and an extra long sink counter are used for storing manipulatives, props for drama activities, and games. On shelves installed above the sink counter, I have placed several stack crates turned sideways and inserted file trays inside them. This provides extra shelving for sorting construction paper, tissue paper, paints, crayons, markers, sequins, glitter, and all materials necessary for the art center. Everything is visible for students to use.

Twelve large stack bins and a bookcase placed in the middle of the classroom provide visual separation between the teacher's direct instruction station and the learning centers station. The bookcase and stackable bins provide for additional storage of learning center materials. Two large concrete blocks with a long wooden plank has been placed under the dry-erase board to manage the science kits as they arrive throughout the year. It's low enough for the team captains to gather materials necessary for their table and high enough to store the large science kits underneath. Extra bookshelves are used for storing reference books, games, students' folders and teacher manuals.

During the first nine weeks of school, I'm assigned two fifth grade student assistants who help me get the centers organized every morning. These students usually arrive no later than 7:35. They make sure each table and learning center area is set up and ready for students. Our school provides several boxes of orange pencils labeled "Extension Center" for each extension center classroom. Students do not bring any supplies to extension unless requested by the extension teacher. Small two-sided carry buckets placed in the middle of each table hold pencils, scissors, and glue. Two containers filled with crayons are placed on each table. The student helpers turn on the computers, sanitize all the headphones, and set up the listening center with three cassette players. They also help primary grade students with the Accelerated Reader computer program between 7:45 and 8:05. The second grade is directly in front of the fourth grade extension room. It is very convenient for the teachers to send a few students to the fourth grade center early in the morning to take computer reading tests. It takes a couple of weeks for everything to run smoothly.

The students in the last language arts center class are responsible for putting away all the center materials in the correct storage area before leaving the extension classroom. The students working at each learning center know where to place all the materials for their center. Occasionally I remind students to clear the tables, but eventually they remember to do it on their own.

The stacked storage bins that divide the center into two learning stations conveniently contain the math extension materials. Five of the bins have a colored star hanging on the front. This helps the table captains know which basket to carry to their team. (Remember that each table has a large colored star hanging above it.) I have prepared the baskets with all the materials needed for each activity. We do have a few bulky math games that will not fit in the baskets. I place them on a bookshelf behind the stack baskets. For example, if the directions state to play one of the large board games, the captain gets the game from the shelf. This allows a teacher assistant or me to move from table to table and facilitate the activities at each table plus provide help at the computer center when necessary.

I provide directions for the computer center on neon-colored paper and place them beside each monitor. This way the students know which computer program to open. I use neon paper for math because I print the language arts extension's directions on white paper. This eliminates confusion about which directions the students must follow when working on computers. The captains of the last math class are responsible for putting materials back in the basket, returning games to the shelf, and shutting computers down. The younger the students, the longer it takes to teach them to help set up and run the various stations in the extension room, but the time spent ultimately provides excellent training for the students.

Successful Ways to Work with Students Who Participate in Pullout Programs

Before the school year begins, the exceptional education teachers, principal, and instructional specialist strategically place all students served in exceptional education programs. They try to cluster exceptional education students by placing them in two classrooms per grade level. This enables the exceptional education teacher to pull the majority of these students during their extension periods. The speech teachers also look at their students' extension schedule and make every effort to pull them during extension time. Some of these students do not participate in the language arts extension classes but do attend the Math/Science extension classes. Speech students usually miss 30 to 40 minutes of extension class two days each week.

Hollis Hand also uses a collaborative, co-teaching model, where the regular and special education teachers work together to teach students with and without disabilities in a shared classroom. Collaborative teaching occurs in extension centers and regular classrooms during the 50-minute instructional periods throughout the day. Both teachers are responsible for planning and teaching lessons, evaluating students' work, and maintaining discipline. Students receive appropriate academics, support services, and modified instruction as specified by the students' individualized education programs (IEPs). This model provides a minimum of scheduling problems, frequent communication between the regular and exceptional education teachers, and a lower student-teacher ratio. What occurs in each co-teaching segment is as unique as each learning disabled or speech student's IEP. Some classes divide into small groups while others teach the entire class. Teachers are working with small groups or circulating around the room providing immediate support or re-teaching (see chapter 4 for a discussion of co-teaching instructional models).

Cooperative groups are extremely beneficial in helping our special needs students achieve success in the extension center classroom. Encouraging students to work as a team enables all students to complete at least one project at each learning center. Most students are able to accomplish this because they spend two days at each center. The majority of our speech students usually receive service every other day, so they are able to complete one assignment. When students return to the extension center, they know how to locate their assigned workstation, get their folder, and begin working on an activity or continue working on an unfinished project. These students walk right into the extension center classroom and get busy. If they are at the teacher-directed station, they go to their assigned table and go to work. Many times we're working on a continuous project. Once in a while, the assistant or I will need to provide a few students with a little one-on-one help to get them started. Providing students who participate in pullout programs with an extension program that uses informal assessments allows them to miss some of the extension center's instructional activities. Special needs students can maintain better grades in their core subject areas when pullouts occur during the extension classes. The stigma of leaving the classroom no longer exists. Organizing full implementation of the parallel block schedule is an enormous task, but the results are very worthwhile.

Developing Curriculum for the Extension Center Classroom

Collaborative Planning with Grade-Level Team

I'm fortunate to work with a team of fourth grade teachers who truly teach as a team. Our team takes full advantage of common planning time, which is very evident during the spring of each school year when we plan together. Using the school system's calendar, we map the next school year. We decide what our grade-level play will be, our puppet show's theme, guest speakers, and field trips. We print up a revised version of our school supply list and turn it into the office. We also decide which novels and short stories we'll read aloud in the regular classroom and during extension time. We consider new projects we might want to use next year. We may decide to use some projects at the entire grade level, or perhaps only one or two teachers may try them. We provide a list of our units of study to the music, art, and physical education teachers so they can integrate several of their activities with our units.

We try to accomplish all of this by the first week of May. It is a wonderful sharing experience that I wish every teacher could experience. This provides me with a tentative curriculum map of when the classroom teacher will teach the grade 4 units. It also provides me with an excellent guide enabling me to extend the grade 4 curriculum in the extension center. We do not plan together every single day during our common planning period; however, we usually do plan together a minimum of once a week. Some meetings are brief, while others take the entire period. The common planning period is also a good time to meet with our administrators. In addition, we have parent conferences during this time and meet with visitors interested in observing our parallel block scheduling program.

Instructional Strategies for the Language Arts Extension Center Classroom

In the spring of the previous school year, I determine the themes to be taught in the fourth grade extension center classroom. I have copies of the fourth grade curriculum teacher editions and have studied them to develop a list of themes that I share with my grade-level team. I've been fortunate that my team felt all of the suggested units would extend the curriculum. We have, however, had some give and take on some of the activities that I wanted to use in the center because they wanted to use the same activities in their regular classrooms. That occurs throughout the year, especially when I'm working on a new unit or revising a unit. Whenever I'm ready to develop or revise a unit, I try to locate every resource book in my school that I can find. I look for a variety of accelerated activities that will meet the criteria for developing an accelerated unit. I look for a minimum of three introductory activities, four teacher-directed activities, and two activities for each learning center.

I write brief descriptions of the activities I've decided to use on lesson plan forms. This provides a skeleton model of the unit. Next, I write formal plans required by my principal and place them in a notebook. These plans include objectives, procedures and materials, and evaluations. I also use a chart created in a spreadsheet program which I insert into my lesson plans. (See blank lesson plan forms and a sample language arts unit in Appendix 1.)

Language Arts Lesson Plan Template

Figure 7.15 (p. 236) is a copy of the chart I insert into my lesson plans each week. I've saved this spreadsheet on my computer and change it weekly. It takes just a few minutes to open the file, make changes, and insert a copy. Teachers may choose to print a copy of the chart and tape it onto their lesson plans if they are not writing lesson plans on a computer. I refer to this chart at the end of each day to make sure I have placed the correct colored stars over each team's learning center assignment for the next day.

The Math/Science Extension Center Classroom

The fourth grade students return to the extension center classroom in the afternoon for a 40-minute block of math/science activities. Because there are four regular classroom teachers on my team, the students come to the extension center on a two-day rotation schedule (similar to the plan illustrated in Figure 6.7, p. 181). Some years, the grade 4 team has three classroom teachers, so students return to extension every afternoon for 40-minute periods (similar to the plan illustrated in Figure 6.5, p. 179).

The afternoon extension period supports the math and science programs taught in the regular classroom. I have a curriculum map of when the fourth grade math and science objectives will be introduced. I bookmark math website activities that support the units being taught in the classroom. Our school system has adopted the *Successmaker Math* computer program to supplement our math curriculum. The math activities can be used in a whole-group setting, cooperative group lessons, or learning centers.

Our school system has purchased excellent hands-on science kits to supplement the science objectives taught in the elementary grades. The grade 4 team decided to house and use the science kits in the extension center classroom. Each kit takes three to four weeks to teach when students come to extension every other day in the afternoon.

Whole-Group Activities in the Math/Science Center

I begin math and science units by introducing the bookmarked websites that support the objectives being taught in the classroom. Our extension centers have a 27" large-screen television for students to view an online lesson. During the second week of school, I divide the students into four teams (five if there are more than 24 students). The teams never have more than six students because the center has six networked computers.

When the students enter the extension center in the afternoon, they refer to the bulletin board titled "Extension Teams." The afternoon teams are different from the language arts teams, because the classes may not have the same students. Most of the exceptional education students participate in extension in the afternoon. Students who have a computer symbol above their team go directly to the computer center, log on, and read the math directions on neon-green paper. I have bookmarked their computer assignments so if they log off in the middle of an activity, then log on again, they return to the activity they left.

The teacher management system for *Successmaker Math* automatically scores students' computer assignments. I print the performance reports at the end of each week and document each student's progress. The other teams go to their assigned table and work with me. I use transparencies to teach math mini-lessons that cover standards tested on our state's criterion-referenced test. Lessons are about ten minutes. Lessons might include place value, estimation activities, solving word problems, calculator skills, reading and creating graphs, or speed tests covering the basic facts.

I use the chart illustrated in Figure 7.16 (p. 217) for the math/science center bulletin board and when we are working with the whole group. The title of the bulletin board is EXTENSION TEAMS. Each class has a laminated chart. I tack a small colored star above each team. The students go to the table with the matching star hanging above it. I also use a small picture of a computer to let each team know when they will be working in the computer center on math programs. The stars and computer symbol rotate to the right every time the class leaves the lab. I also stick a colored pushpin beside a student's name on each team designating who will be the captain for the week. The pushpin rotates down the list so that each student gets to be the team captain on a rotating basis.

Team Activities for Math

When the students have completed the whole-group mini-lesson, they usually work in partner activities. (Occasionally one group will have three students.) The math activities are games or performance tasks that help students master specific standards. One example from our math frameworks is "Place

Figure 7.16 Math/Science Extension Center Teams Chart

Extension Class 1				
Red Star	Blue Star	Yellow Star	Green Star	Computers
Team 1	Team 2	Team 3	Team 4	Team 5
1.	1.	1.	1.	1.
2.	2.	2.	2.	2.
3.	3.	3.	3.	3.
4.	4.	4.	4.	4.
5.	5.	5.	5.	5.
6.	6.	6.	6.	6.

Value Concentration." Each pair of students receives a Ziploc bag with cards that have numbers written in standard form and number word form (Figure 7.17). The students match numbers to number words. An answer key is provided inside each bag. I move among the groups and offer assistance, and computers provide help whenever needed.

Figure 7.17. Example of Game Piece

2,437,301	two million, four hundred thirty-seven thousand, three hundred one

Throughout the year we'll use traditional board games, math activities from school supply stores, math cards, and teacher-made activities. After explaining the center activities, I set up a rotational schedule. All math materials are placed in stack baskets. Each basket has a colored star hanging on its side. The captain of each team gets the basket with the matching colored star above the team's assignment. Each basket has one or two activities that each team completes. At the end of the period, the captain places all materials inside the basket and returns the basket to the storage area. The four math teams rotate through four stations over the next four sessions. One of the stations always includes the computer center.

Team Activities for Science

When I'm teaching a science unit using the school system's science kits, the students work cooperatively on hands-on science experiments. The kits have great lessons and supply most of the materials necessary for the many experiments. I prepare each lesson's materials by organizing all the materials in plastic tubs. The captain of each team gets a tub and returns to his table. I usually follow the procedures in the manual and the students conduct the experiments. Each experiment involves making predictions, a statement explaining their predictions, and what each team discovered. After each team has had an opportunity to discuss their findings with the class, the captains return the science materials to the shelf. The time goes by very quickly. I also use the science laser discs and online video clips that supplement our science curriculum during these classes. The manuals that accompany the laser disc program have excellent lesson plans and are a great resource for suggested extension activities.

Help for Developing Lesson Plans

I like to use spreadsheet charts when writing plans for the math/science extension center activities. They help me keep up with who comes to the extension center and the scheduled rotations of the various teams. I simply bring up my lesson plan file, make a few changes, and print a copy. Every teacher will come up with plans that work for him or her. The examples below are the charts that work for me.

Math/Science Extension Chart 1

I use this chart (Figure 7.18) every week. It shows which classes come to the extension center classroom in the afternoon. Rotation schedules can be a little tricky at first. Eventually the schedule runs very smoothly.

Math/Science Extension Chart 2

I use chart 2 (Figure 7.19) when the teams rotate through the computer center and the remaining three teams work on the same teacher-directed activities. It clearly states which team works at the computer center for the entire extension period.

Math Extension Chart 3

I use the chart illustrated in Figure 7.20 when each team works on a different cooperative group activity. The chart is for four teams of six students. The team captains transport their assigned basket to their tables and return the basket at the end of the period.

Figure 7.18. Math/Science Extension Chart 1

Schedule for Week 1					
Math/Science Extension Center Assignments					
Time	**Monday**	**Tuesday**	**Wednesday**	**Thursday**	**Friday**
1:00–1:40 Math/ Science Center	Lab 1 1st Rotation	Lab 2 1st Rotation	Lab 1 2nd Rotation	Lab 2 2nd Rotation	Lab 1 3rd Rotation
1:40–2:20 Math/ Science Center	Lab 3 1st Rotation	Lab 4 1st Rotation	Lab 3 2nd Rotation	Lab 4 2nd Rotation	Lab 3 3rd Rotation

Schedule for Week 2					
Math/Science Extension Center Assignments					
Time	**Monday**	**Tuesday**	**Wednesday**	**Thursday**	**Friday**
1:00–1:40 Math/ Science Center	Lab 2 3rd Rotation	Lab 1 4th Rotation	Lab 2 4th Rotation	Lab 1 1st Rotation	Lab 2 1st Rotation
1:40–2:20 Math/ Science Center	Lab 4 3rd Rotation	Lab 3 4th Rotation	Lab 4 4th Rotation	Lab 3 1st Rotation	Lab 4 1st Rotation

Figure 7.19. Math/Science Extension Chart 2

Computer Center Rotation for Math/Science Extension					
Assignment	**Directions**	**1st Rotation**	**2nd Rotation**	**3rd Rotation**	**4th Rotation**
Computer Center					
Teacher-Directed Activity					

Figure 7.20. Math Extension Chart 3

Computer Center Rotation for Math/Science Extension					
Learning Centers	**Directions**	**1st Rotation**	**2nd Rotation**	**3rd Rotation**	**4th Rotation**
Red Star Table					
Yellow Star Table					
Blue Star Table					
Computer Center					

A Final Word About Parallel Block Scheduling and Managing the Extension Center Classroom at Hollis Hand Elementary School

The implementation of parallel block scheduling (PBS), controlled heterogeneous groupings, and extension centers has helped Hollis Hand become a dynamic elementary school. Using the extension classroom concept is one of the primary reasons our students love school. The extension teacher has become a facilitator, a resource person, and an educator who teaches in the true sense of the word. When we first implemented PBS, our students were not working toward receiving a passing grade in the extension center. It was a place where students became totally involved in learning experiences without the fear of receiving a failing grade. They showed great enthusiasm, responsibility, and individual initiative.

With the passage of the No Child Left Behind Act, the high accountability of Adequate Yearly Progress (AYP), and the implementation of the Student Achievement Pyramid of Interventions, our school has made revisions to each grade level's schedule and the extension center's curriculum. Recently, Hollis Hand's administrators and teachers decided that the extension teachers in the second, third, and fourth grades would teach the social studies and science standards and give numerical grades. This would give the regular classroom teachers two 50-minute periods for English/Language Arts instruction. The fourth and fifth grade teams currently are departmentalized, and the fifth grade extension teacher provides all instruction for the math standards. We also modified our second through fifth grades' afternoon schedules to provide one 50-minute period of on-grade-level math with the regular classroom teacher plus an additional 50-minute instructional period in the extension centers to help students who are performing below grade level in math. This enabled us to meet the Early Intervention Program (EIP) guidelines for approved delivery models in Georgia. By using PBS, we're able to implement two approved EIP delivery models: a reduced-class model in the morning and a pullout model in the afternoon. Our extension center teachers also have one 50-minute Intervention class every day during which we provide extensive individualized interventions, assessments, and progress monitoring for target students.

Our first grade teachers lost their full-time extension teacher because of budget cuts a few years ago; however, we were able to obtain funds to hire two part-time assistants to staff the first grade extension center for four 45-minute instructional periods. We are fortunate that most of these assistants have been certified teachers or college graduates who have chosen to work part time. That enabled our first grade teachers to protect their small reading groups, which they have come to cherish.

Recent budget cuts have eliminated all of our valuable teacher assistants who were assigned to work in extension labs. In spite of changing financial constraints and imposed accountability mandates, our extension programs, although modified from the original concepts Dr. Canady described to us more than a decade ago, continue to be places where students engage in active, exciting learning activities. We continue to use the PBS model the entire school day for each grade level. The social studies and science standards taught in our extension centers are extremely challenging units of study and are integrated with all subjects, including music, art, and physical education. During the small-group reading periods, teachers support our science and social studies curriculum by using leveled guided readers to differentiate instruction.

Even though the extension center program has changed from the original model, we know our students continue to be enthusiastic learners when we hear them say, "I love coming to extension." If you were to ask teachers at Hollis Hand if they would ever want to stop using the parallel block scheduling model, they would emphatically answer, "No!" The significant increases in our test scores through the years and the accolades our school has received for impressive improvements seem to support why our administrators and teachers continue to believe that the parallel block scheduling model implemented at Hollis Hand provides our students with a positive, successful learning environment.

References

Teacher References

DuFour, R., & Eaker, B. (1998). *Professional learning communities at work: Best practices for enhancing student achievement.* Bloomington, IN: National Educational Service.

Fogliani, A. E. (1990). *A case study of parallel block scheduling: An instructional management study.* Unpublished dissertation, University of Virginia, Charlottesville, VA.

Hopkins, H. J. (1990). *A comparison of the effects of pull-out programs in a parallel block scheduled school and a traditionally scheduled school.* Unpublished doctoral dissertation, University of Virginia, Charlottesville.

Computer Software References

Accelerated Reader Version 6.2 (2002). Wisconsin Rapids, WI: Renaissance Learning.

Successmaker Math (2007). Upper Saddle River, NJ: Pearson Digital Learning.

Fiction Books

Brown, M. W. (1949). *The important book.* New York: Harper and Row.

Conway, J. (1977). *Will I ever be good enough?* Chicago: Raintree Publishers Limited.

Estes, E. (1944). *The hundred dresses.* New York: Harcourt Brace Jovanovich.

Peet, B. (1982). *The luckiest one of all.* Boston: Houghton Mifflin.

Music and Art Resources

Hart, C., Pogrelin, L.C., Rodgers, M., Thomas, M. (Eds.). (1974). *Free to be…you and me.* New York: McGraw-Hill.

Klee, P. (1922). *Senecio (going senile).* Available at: www.barewalls.com.

Figure 7.1 Plan I: Four Teachers at a Grade Level; One Base Teacher (2D) Serves as the Extension Teacher (School Day Divided into 5-Minute Increments)

Periods	HR	Period 1	Period 2	Period 3	Period 4	Period 5	Period 6	Period 7	Period 8
Teacher 2A	HR (20)	LA/SS 1,4 (50)	RWG 1 (50)	RWG 4 (50)	Lunch/ Recess (50)	Encore/ Plan (50)	Math/SC 1,4 (50)	MG 1 (50)	MG 4 (50)
Teacher 2B		RWG 5 (50)	LA/SS 2,5 (50)	RWG 2 (50)	Lunch/ Recess (50)	Encore/ Plan (50)	MG 5 (50)	Math/SC 2,5 (50)	MG 2 (50)
Teacher 2C		RWG 3 (50)	RWG 6 (50)	LA/SS 3,6 (50)	Lunch/ Recess (50)	Encore/ Plan (50)	MG 3 (50)	MG 6 (50)	Math/SC 3,6 (50)
Extension Teacher 2D		LA Extension			Lunch/Plan (100)		Math Extension		
		RWGs 2,6 (50)	RWGs 3,4 (50)	RWGs 1,5 (50)			MGs 2,6 (50)	MGs 3,4 (50)	MGs 1,5 (50)

Note: RWG = reading-writing group; LA = language arts; MG = math group; SS = social studies; SC = science

Figure 7.2 Eight-Period Parallel Block Schedule: Grade 1 Language Arts with Extension; Seven Base Teachers with One Assuming the Role of Extension Teacher

		8:00	9:00	10:00	11:00	12:00	1:00	2:00	3:00

Periods	HR	Period 1	Period 2	Period 3	Period 4			Period 5	Period 6	Period 7	Period 8
Teacher 1A		LA 1,4 (50)	RWG 1 (50)	RWG 4 (50)	D1 PE	D2 Art	D3 Mu	Lunch/ Recess (50)	Math/Social Studies/Science (150)		
Teacher 1B	HR (20)	RWG 5 (50)	LA 2,5 (50)	RWG 2 (50)	D1 MU	D2 PE	D3 Art	Lunch/ Recess (50)	Math/Social Studies/Science (150)		
Teacher 1C		RWG 3 (50)	RWG 6 (50)	LA 3,6 (50)	D1 Art	D2 Mu	D3 PE	Lunch/ Recess (50)	Math/Social Studies/Science (150)		
Extension Teacher 1G		**LA Extension**			Lunch/Plan (100)				**LA Extension**		
		RWGs 2,6 (50)	RWGs 3,4 (50)	RWGs 1,5 (50)					RWGs 8,12 (50)	RWGs 9,10 (50)	RWGs 7,11 (50)
Teacher 1D		Math/Social Studies/Science (150)			Lunch/ Recess (50)	D1 PE	D2 Art	D3 Mu	LA 7,10 (50)	RWG 7 (50)	RWG 10 (50)
Teacher 1E	HR (20)	Math/Social Studies/Science (150)			Lunch/ Recess (50)	D1 MU	D2 PE	D3 Art	RWG 11 (50)	LA 8,11 (50)	RWG 8 (50)
Teacher 1F		Math/Social Studies/Science (150)			Lunch/ Recess (50)	D1 Art	D2 Mu	D3 PE	RWG 9 (50)	RWG 12 (50)	LA 9,12 (50)

Note: RWG=reading-writing group; LA=language arts; PE=physical education; MU= general music. In this schedule students receive a 50-minute period of language arts extension or special services every day.

7.1
7.2

Figure 7.3 Eight-Period Parallel Block Schedule: Grades 1 and 2 Language Arts with Extension

Periods	HR	Period 1	Period 2	Period 3	Period 4	Period 5	Period 6	Period 7	Period 8
Teacher 1A		LA 1,4 (50)	RWG 1 (50)	RWG 4 (50)	Encore/ Plan (50)	Lunch/ Recess (50)	Math/Social Studies/Science (150)		
Teacher 1B	HR (20)	RWG 5 (50)	LA 2,5 (50)	RWG 2 (50)	Encore/ Plan (50)	Lunch/ Recess (50)	Math/Social Studies/Science (150)		
Teacher 1C		RWG 3 (50)	RWG 6 (50)	LA 3,6 (50)	Encore/ Plan (50)	Lunch/ Recess (50)	Math/Social Studies/Science (150)		
Grades 1 and 2 Extension Teacher		Grade 1 LA Extension			Lunch/Plan (100)		Grade 2 LA Extension		
		RWGs 2,6 (50)	RWGs 3,4 (50)	RWGs 1,5 (50)			RWGs 8,12 (50)	RWGs 9,10 (50)	RWGs 7,11 (50)
Teacher 2A		Math/Social Studies/Science (150)			Lunch/ Recess (50)	Encore/ Plan (50)	LA 7,10 (50)	RWG 7 (50)	RWG 10 (50)
Teacher 2B	HR (20)	Math/Social Studies/Science (150)			Lunch/ Recess (50)	Encore/ Plan (50)	RWG 11 (50)	LA 8,11 (50)	RWG 8 (50)
Teacher 2C		Math/Social Studies/Science (150)			Lunch/ Recess (50)	Encore/ Plan (50)	RWG 9 (50)	RWG 12 (50)	LA 9,12 (50)

Note: RWG=reading-writing group; LA=language arts. In this schedule students receive a 50-minute period of language arts extension or special services every day.

Figure 7.4 Plan II: Three Teachers at a Grade Level; Special Needs Teachers Provide Extension Services

Periods	HR	Period 1	Period 2	Period 3	Period 4	Period 5	Period 6	Period 7	Period 8
Teacher 2A		LA/SS 1,4 (50)	RWG 1 (50)	RWG 4 (50)	Lunch/ Recess (50)	Encore/ Plan (50)	Math/SC 1,4 (50)	MG 1 (50)	MG 4 (50)
Teacher 2B	HR (20)	RWG 5 (50)	LA/SS 2,5 (50)	RWG 2 (50)	Lunch/ Recess (50)	Encore/ Plan (50)	MG 5 (50)	Math/SC 2,5 (50)	MG 2 (50)
Teacher 2C		RWG 3 (50)	RWG 6 (50)	LA/SS 3,6 (50)	Lunch/ Recess (50)	Encore/ Plan (50)	MG 3 (50)	MG 6 (50)	Math/SC 3,6 (50)
Extension	Language Arts Extension (Reading Specialist, ESL Teacher, LD Teacher)			Lunch/Plan (100)		Math Extension (Math Specialist, Computer Lab and LD Teacher)			
	RWGs 2,6 (50)	RWGs 3,4 (50)	RWGs 1,5 (50)			MGs 2,6 (50)	MGs 3,4 (50)	MGs 1,5 (50)

Note: RWG = reading-writing group; LA = language arts; MG = math group; SS = social studies; SC = science

7.3
7.4

Figure 7.5 Plan III: Three Teachers at a Grade Level; Enrichment Personnel Provide Programs

Periods	HR	Period 1	Period 2	Period 3	Period 4	Period 5	Period 6	Period 7	Period 8
Teacher 2A		LA 1,4 (50)	RWG 1 (50)	RWG 4 (50)	Lunch/ Recess (50)	Encore/ Plan (50)	Math 1,4 (50)	MG 1 (50)	MG 4 (50)
Teacher 2B	HR (20)	RWG 5 (50)	LA 2,5 (50)	RWG 2 (50)	Lunch/ Recess (50)	Encore/ Plan (50)	MG 5 (50)	Math 2,5 (50)	MG 2 (50)
Teacher 2C		RWG 3 (50)	RWG 6 (50)	LA 3,6 (50)	Lunch/ Recess (50)	Encore/ Plan (50)	MG 3 (50)	MG 6 (50)	Math 3,6 (50)
Extension		Spanish Teacher			Lunch/Plan (100)		Social Studies/Science Teacher		
		Spanish RWGs 2,6 (50)	Spanish RWGs 3,4 (50)	Spanish RWGs 1,5 (50)			SS/SC MGs 2,6 (50)	SS/SC MGs 3,4 (50)	SS/SC MGs 1,5 (50)

Note: RWG = reading-writing group; LA = language arts; MG = math group; SS = social studies; SC = science

Figure 7.6 Plan IV: Master Block Schedule

		8:00	9:00	10:00	11:00	12:00	1:00	2:00	3:00
Kinder.	HR (15)	Morning Activities; Center Time; M/SC/SS (45)	Early Literacy Groups and Language Arts (105)		L/R (50)	Encore/Plan (50)	Early Literacy Groups and Language Arts (105)		Afternoon Activities; M/SC/SS (40)
Grade 1	HR (15)	Language Arts, Social Studies, LA Extension (150)			R/L (50)	Math, Science, Math Extension (100)		Encore/Plan (50)	Math, Science, Math Ext. (50)
Grade 2	HR (15)	Language Arts, Social Studies, LA Extension (150)			Math, Science, Computer Lab (50)	L/R (50)	Math, Science, Computer Lab (100)		Encore/Plan (50)
Grade 3	HR (15)	Math, Science, Computer Lab (150)			Encore/Plan (50)	R/L (50)	Language Arts, Social Studies, LA Extension (150)		
Grade 4	HR (15)	Language Arts, Social Studies, Spanish (100)		Encore/Plan (50)	Language Arts, SS, SP (50)	Math and Science (50)	L/R (50)	Math and Science (100)	
Grade 5	HR (15)	Math and Science (50)	Encore/Plan (50)	Math and Science (100)		Language Arts, SS, SP (50)	R/L (50)	Language Arts, Social Studies, Spanish (100)	
Read. Spec. & 2-3 LD	HR (15)	Grade 2 RWGs 2,6 (50)	Grade 2 RWGs 3,4 (50)	Grade 2 RWGs 1,5 (50)	Encore/ Plan (50)	Lunch/Duty (50)	Grade 3 RWGs 2,6 (50)	Grade 3 RWGs 3,4 (50)	Grade 3 RWGs 1,5 (50)
Comp. Lab.	HR (15)	Grade 3 RWGs 2,6 (50)	Grade 3 RWGs 3,4 (50)	Grade 3 RWGs 1,5 (50)	Grade 2 RWGs 2,6 (50)	Lunch/Duty (50)	Grade 2 RWGs 3,4 (50)	Grade 2 RWGs 1,5 (50)	Encore/ Plan (50)
Spanish	HR (15)	Grade 4 RWGs 2,6 (50)	Grade 4 RWGs 3,4 (50)	Encore/Plan (50)	Grade 4 RWGs 1,5 (50)	Grade 5 RWGs 2,6 (50)	Lunch/Duty (50)	Grade 5 RWGs 3,4 (50)	Grade 5 RWGs 1,5 (50)
Science	HR (15)	Grade 5 RWGs 2,6 (50)	Grade 5 RWGs 3,4 (50)	Encore/Plan (50)	Grade 5 RWGs 1,5 (50)	Grade 4 RWGs 2,6 (50)	Lunch/Duty (50)	Grade 4 RWGs 3,4 (50)	Grade 4 RWGs 1,5 (50)
Arts/PE		Plan (50)	Grade 5	Grade 4	Grade 3	Kinder.	Lunch/Duty (50)	Grade 1	Grade 2

Key: RWG = reading-writing group; SP = Spanish; SS = social studies; SC = science

7.5
7.6

Figure 7.7 Plan IV: Grades K and 1 (Teachers KD and 1D Assigned as Extension Teachers)

		8:00	9:00	10:00	11:00	12:00	1:00	2:00	3:00
KA		HR (15)	Morning Activities; Center Time; M/SC/SS (45)	ELG 1 (35)	ELG 4 (35)	ELG 7 (35)	L/R (50)	Plan (50)	ELG 1 (35)	ELG 4 (35)	ELG 7 (35)	Afternoon Activities; Center Time; M/SC/SS (45)	
KB		HR (15)		ELG 8 (35)	ELG 2 (35)	ELG 5 (35)	L/R (50)	Plan (50)	ELG 8 (35)	ELG 2 (35)	ELG 5 (35)		
KC		HR (15)		ELG 6 (35)	ELG 9 (35)	ELG 3 (35)	L/R (50)	Plan (50)	ELG 6 (35)	ELG 9 (35)	ELG 3 (35)		
KD (Ext.) & 2 Aides	Duty		Morning Activities; Center Time; M/SC/SS (45)	Language Arts Extension			L/R (50)	Plan (50)	Language Arts Extension			Afternoon Activities; Center Time; M/SC/SS (45)	
				ELGs 2,3,4,5,7,9 (35)	ELGs 1,3,5,6,7,8 (35)	ELGs 1,2,4,6,8,9 (35)			ELGs 2,3,4,5,7,9 (35)	ELGs 1,3,5,6,7,8 (35)	ELGs 1,2,4,6,8,9 (35		
1A		HR (15)	LA/SS 1,4 (50)	RWG 1 (50)	RWG 4 (50)	R/L (50)	M/SC 1,4 (50)	MG 1 (50)	Plan (50)	MG 4 (50)	
1B		HR (15)	RWG 5 (50)	LA/SS 2,5 (50)	RWG 2 (50)	R/L (50)	MG 5 (50)	M/SC 2,5 (50)	Plan (50)	MG 2 (50)	
1C		HR (15)	RWG 3 (50)	RWG 6 (50)	LA/SS 3,6 (50)	R/L (50)	MG 3 (50)	MG 6 (50)	Plan (50)	M/SC 3,6 (50)	
1D (Ext.)	Duty		Language Arts Extension			R/L (50)	Math Extension		Plan (50)	Math Ext.	
			RWGs 2,6 (50)	RWGs 3,4 (50)	RWGs 1,5 (50)		MGs 2,6 (50)	MGs 3,4 (50)		MGs 1,5 (50)	

Key: ELG=early literacy group; RWG=reading-writing group; LA/SS=language arts/social studies; MG=math group; M/SC=math/science; SC=science

Figure 7.8 Plan IV: Grades 2 and 3 (Reading Specialist, LD Teacher, ESL Teacher, and Computer Lab Assigned as Extension Teachers)

		8:00	9:00	10:00	11:00	12:00	1:00	2:00	3:00
2A	HR (15)	LA/SS 1,4 (50)	RWG 1 (50)	RWG 4 (50)	M/SC 1,4 (50)	Recess/ Lunch (50)	MG 1 (50)	MG 4 (50)	Plan (50)
2B	HR (15)	RWG 5 (50)	LA/SS 2,5 (50)	RWG 2 (50)	MG 5 (50)	Recess/ Lunch (50)	M/SC 2,5 (50)	MG 2 (50)	Plan (50)
2C	HR (15)	RWG 3 (50)	RWG 6 (50)	LA/SS 3,6 (50)	MG 3 (50)	Recess/ Lunch (50)	MG 6 (50)	M/SC 3,6 (50)	Plan (50)
Grade 2 Ext.	Duty	Read. Spec., Gr. 2-3 LD, and ESL — RWGs 2,6 (50)	RWGs 3,4 (50)	RWGs 1,5 (50)	Comp. Lab — MGs 2,6 (50)	Recess/ Lunch (50)	Computer Lab — MGs 3,4 (50)	MGs 1,5 (50)	Plan (50)
3A	HR (15)	M/SC 1,4 (50)	MG 1 (50)	MG 4 (50)	Plan (50)	Lunch/ Recess (50)	LA/SS 1,4 (50)	RWG 1 (50)	RWG 4 (50)
3B	HR (15)	MG 5 (50)	M/SC 2,5 (50)	MG 2 (50)	Plan (50)	Lunch/ Recess (50)	RWG 5 (50)	LA/SS 2,5 (50)	RWG 2 (50)
3C	HR (15)	MG 3 (50)	MG 6 (50)	M/SC 3,6 (50)	Plan (50)	Lunch/ Recess (50)	RWG 3 (50)	RWG 6 (50)	LA/SS 3,6 (50)
Grade 3 Ext.	Duty	Computer Lab — MGs 2,6 (50)	MGs 3,4 (50)	MGs 1,5 (50)	Plan (50)	Lunch/ Recess (50)	Read. Spec., Gr. 2-3 LD, and ESL — RWGs 2,6 (50)	RWGs 3,4 (50)	RWGs 1,5 (50)

Key: ELG=early literacy group; RWG=reading-writing group; LA/SS=langugage arts/social studies; MG=math group; M/SC=math/science; SC=science; LD=LD resource; ESL=English as a Second Language; Read. Spec.=reading specialist

7.7
7.8

Figure 7.9 Plan IV: Grades 4 and 5 (Science Teacher and Spanish Teacher Assigned as Extension Teachers)

		8:00	9:00	10:00	11:00	12:00	1:00	2:00	3:00
4A	HR (15)	LA/SS 1,4 (50)	RWG 1 (50)	Encore/ Plan (50)	RWG 4 (50)	M/SC 1,4 (50)	Lunch/ Recess (50)	MG 1 (50)	MG 4 (50)
4B	HR (15)	RWG 5 (50)	LA/SS 2,5 (50)	Encore/ Plan (50)	RWG 2 (50)	MG 5 (50)	Lunch/ Recess (50)	M/SC 2,5 (50)	MG 2 (50)
4C	HR (15)	RWG 3 (50)	RWG 6 (50)	Encore/ Plan (50)	LA/SS 3,6 (50)	MG 3 (50)	Lunch/ Recess (50)	MG 6 (50)	M/SC 3,6 (50)
Grade 4 Ext.	Duty	Extension-Spanish		Plan (50)	Ext.-Spanish	Ext.-Science	Lunch/Duty (50)	Extension-Science	
		RWGs 2,6 (50)	RWGs 3,4 (50)		RWGs 1,5 (50)	MGs 2,6 (50)		MGs 3,4 (50)	MGs 1,5 (50)
5A	HR (15)	M/SC 1,4 (50)	Encore/ Plan (50)	MG 1 (50)	MG 4 (50)	LA/SS 1,4 (50)	Recess/ Lunch (50)	RWG 1 (50)	RWG 4 (50)
5B	HR (15)	MG 5 (50)	Encore/ Plan (50)	M/SC 2,5 (50)	MG 2 (50)	RWG 5 (50)	Recess/ Lunch (50)	LA/SS 2,5 (50)	RWG 2 (50)
5C	HR (15)	MG 3 (50)	Encore/ Plan (50)	MG 6 (50)	M/SC 3,6 (50)	RWG 3 (50)	Recess/ Lunch (50)	RWG 6 (50)	LA/SS 3,6 (50)
Grade 5 Ext.	Duty	Ext.-Science	Plan (50)	Extension-Science		Ext.-Spanish	Lunch/Duty (50)	Extension-Spanish	
		MGs 2,6 (50)		MGs 3,4 (50)	MGs 1,5 (50)	RWGs 2,6 (50)		RWGs 3,4 (50)	RWGs 1,5 (50)
Spanish and Science Teacher Schedules (derived from extension groups shown above)									
Spanish	HR	SP Grade 4 RWGs 2,6 (50)	SP Grade 4 RWGs 3,4 (50)	Plan (50)	SP Grade 4 RWGs 1,5 (50)	SP Grade 5 RWGs 2,6 (50)	Lunch/Duty (50)	SP Grade 5 RWGs 3,4 (50)	SP Grade 5 RWGs 1,5 (50)
Science	HR	SC Grade 5 RWGs 2,6 (50)	SC Grade 5 RWGs 3,4 (50)	Plan (50)	SC Grade 5 RWGs 1,5 (50)	SC Grade 4 RWGs 2,6 (50)	Lunch/Duty (50)	SC Grade 4 RWGs 3,4 (50)	SC Grade 4 RWGs 1,5 (50)

Key: RWG = reading-writing group; LA/SS = language arts/social studies; MG = math group; M/SC = math/science; SC = science; SP = Spanish

Figure 7.10 Encore Rotations

8:15-9:05		Encore Planning		
		Day 1	**Day 2**	**Day 3**
9:05-9:55	5A	PE	Art	Music
	5B	Music	PE	Art
	5C	Art	Music	PE
		Day 1	**Day 2**	**Day 3**
9:55-10:45	4A	PE	Art	Music
	4B	Music	PE	Art
	4C	Art	Music	PE
		Day 1	**Day 2**	**Day 3**
10:45-11:35	3A	PE	Art	Music
	3B	Music	PE	Art
	3C	Art	Music	PE

		Day 1	**Day 2**	**Day 3**
11:35-12:25	KA	PE	Art	Music
	KB	Music	PE	Art
	KC	Art	Music	PE
12:25-1:15		Encore Lunch/Duty		
		Day 1	**Day 2**	**Day 3**
1:15-2:05	1A	PE	Art	Music
	1B	Music	PE	Art
	1C	Art	Music	PE
		Day 1	**Day 2**	**Day 3**
2:05-2:55	2A	PE	Art	Music
	2B	Music	PE	Art
	2C	Art	Music	PE

7.9
7.10

Figure 7.11 Sample Formation of Extension Center Groupings

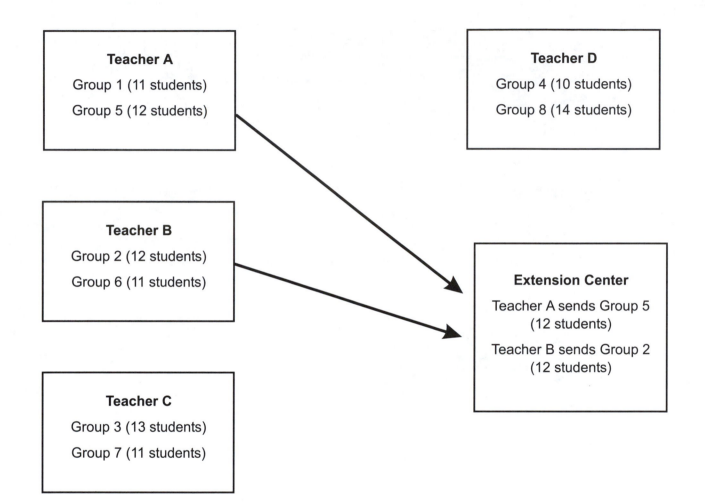

Teacher A

Group 1 (11 students)

Group 5 (12 students)

Teacher B

Group 2 (12 students)

Group 6 (11 students)

Teacher C

Group 3 (13 students)

Group 7 (11 students)

Teacher D

Group 4 (10 students)

Group 8 (14 students)

Extension Center

Teacher A sends Group 5
(12 students)

Teacher B sends Group 2
(12 students)

Figure 7.12 Floor Plan 1: Fourth Grade Extension Center Classroom

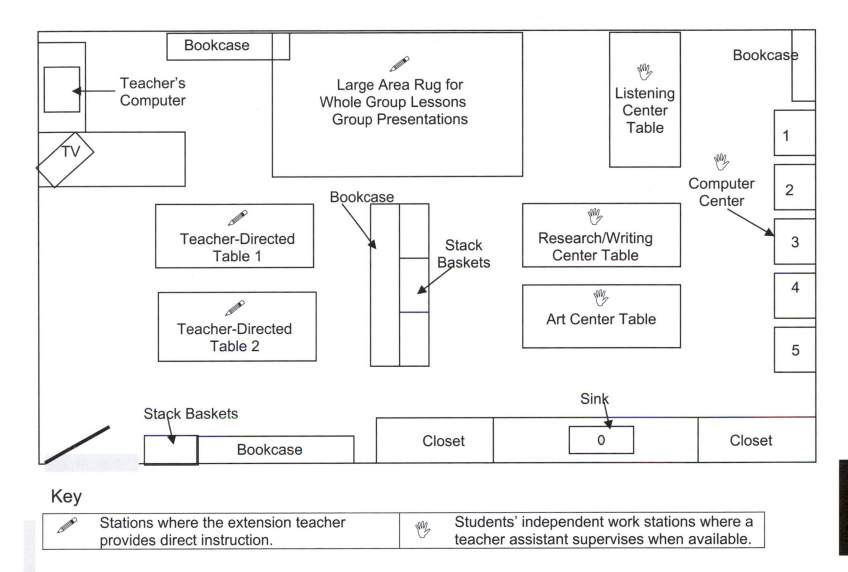

Bookcase

Teacher's Computer

TV

Large Area Rug for Whole Group Lessons Group Presentations

Listening Center Table

Bookcase

1

2

Computer Center

3

4

5

Teacher-Directed Table 1

Bookcase

Stack Baskets

Research/Writing Center Table

Art Center Table

Teacher-Directed Table 2

Stack Baskets

Bookcase

Closet

Sink

0

Closet

Key

	Stations where the extension teacher provides direct instruction.		Students' independent work stations where a teacher assistant supervises when available.

7.11
7.12

Figure 7.13 Floor Plan 2: Primary Grade Extension Center Classroom

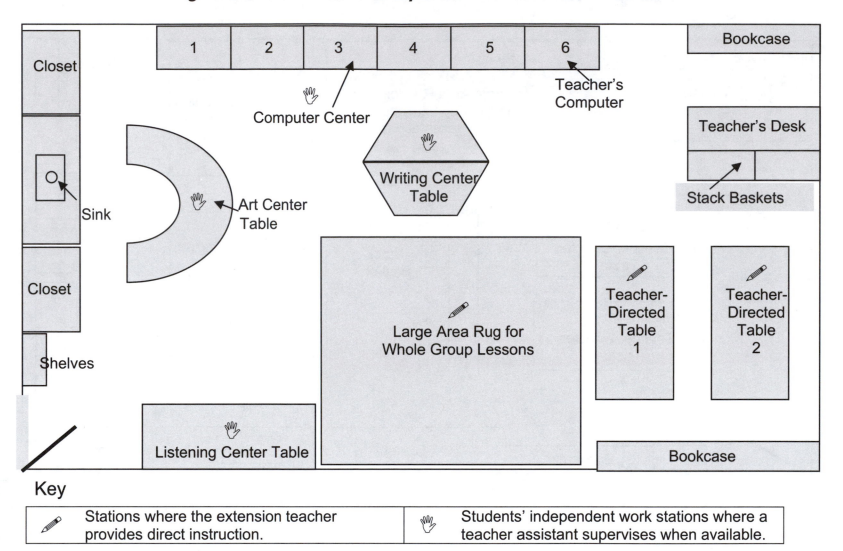

Key

	Stations where the extension teacher provides direct instruction.		Students' independent work stations where a teacher assistant supervises when available.

Figure 7.14 Stations Bulletin Board

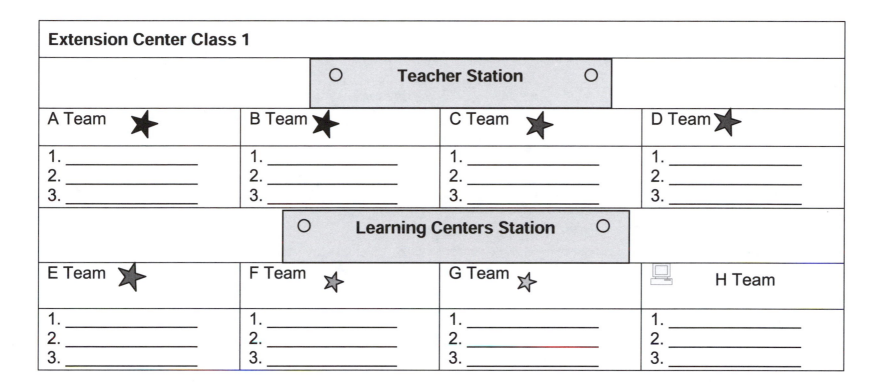

7.13
7.14

Figure 7.15. Copy of Lesson Plan Chart

LEARNING CENTER ROTATION FOR LANGUAGE ARTS GROUPS					
Date:					
CENTER	**MONDAY**	**TUESDAY**	**WEDNESDAY**	**THURSDAY**	**FRIDAY**
Orange Star Art Center	A Team	A Team	D Team	D Team	C Team
Blue Star Research Center	B Team	B Team	A Team	A Team	D Team
Green Star Listening Center	C Team	C Team	B Team	B Team	A Team
Computer Center	D Team	D Team	C Team	C Team	B Team
TEACHER-DIRECTED CENTER					
	MONDAY	**TUESDAY**	**WEDNESDAY**	**THURSDAY**	**FRIDAY**
See lesson plans notebook	Teams E, F, G, H	Teams E, F, G, H	Teams E, F, G, H	Teams E, F, G, H	Teams E, F, G, H
	Activity 1	Activity 2	Finish Activity 2	Activity 3	Activity 4

8

Elementary Mathematics Scheduling Variations

This chapter explores alternative scheduling models for the delivery of the elementary mathematics curriculum. In chapter 6, we describe the "traditional" parallel block scheduling (PBS) approach to providing instruction in mathematics. In those models, the base teacher works with students twice daily in mathematics—typically once in a regular-size class and once in a reduced-size math group, while the other half of the class participates in a mathematics extension class, special services, or science and/or social studies. Because of the sequential nature and structure of mathematics, this chapter describes variations on the parallel block scheduling theme for mathematics: the Concept-Mastery model (two plans) and the Acceleration model.

The Concept-Mastery and the Acceleration Models

In many elementary schools that implement PBS, homeroom teachers provide all their assigned students instruction in the core subjects: reading/language arts, social studies, mathematics and science. An increasing number of schools, however, have begun to adapt the basic PBS plan, creating variations on the self-contained, homeroom teacher model. For example, in chapter 6 we demonstrate how in some cases the extension teacher for the primary grades may be responsible for providing basic instruction for science and/or social studies (see Figures 6.4 [p. 178], 6.5 [p. 179], 6.6 [p. 180], 6.7 [p. 181], 6.9 [p. 184], and 6.10 [p. 185]), and we also detail various PBS models for the intermediate grades with varying degrees of departmentalization.

This chapter focuses on mathematics and offers two alternatives to the self-contained-classroom model of instructional delivery. Both models provide time for intervention and either enrichment or acceleration throughout the school year. We have found that these alternatives can be helpful especially in grades 3–5 in schools with low achievement in mathematics. The Concept-Mastery plans are appropriate for schools with large numbers of students who need extended learning time to master the content required to pass rigorous district- or state-mandated grade-level examinations. For schools having large numbers of students who may be able to complete the required curriculum at an accelerated pace, we suggest the Acceleration model described later in this chapter.

The Concept-Mastery Model

In the sections that follow, we develop two variations of the Concept-Mastery model of instruction in mathematics (Plans A and B); both plans may be used to reduce dependence on the homogeneous grouping and tracking of students in mathematics that often results because of the building-block structure of mathematical concepts.

Implementing the Concept-Mastery model requires significant advance preparation and collaboration among participating teachers. The model employs a structured approach to curriculum, instruction, and assessment, which includes at its heart five components: a common curriculum, taught at a common pace, with common formative assessments, a collaborative monitoring team, and common time for interventions and enrichment (I/E).[1]

◆ Common Curriculum—Before the school year begins, all teachers involved in the model (typically a grade level) must agree on the common topics or curriculum to be taught during the school year. There are several different ways to divide mathematics curricula into manageable units. Mathematics textbooks often are divided conveniently into chapters that can serve as the basis for concept topics. Given that 49 of 50 states have mandated standards, deciding on the overall curriculum goals for the year should not be difficult.

◆ Common Pacing—Teachers also must agree to a common division of the curriculum into units of instruction, a determination of the time length of each of these units, and sequencing of these topics. Generally this is delineated on a document called a "pacing guide" that is designed collaboratively by the group of teachers before the school year starts.

◆ Common Formative Assessments—Similarly, the team of teachers must create or adopt a set of common formative assessments designed to measure students' mastery of the content of each unit. These assessments typically are administered to all students at the same time upon completion of each unit. For example, Measures of Academic Progress (MAP, available through the nonprofit Northwest Evaluation Association) are research-based, state-aligned computerized adaptive formative assessments (Northwest Evaluation Association, 2000).

---

1 A detailed description of this process is the substance of Rettig, M. D., McCullough, L. L., Santos, K. E., & Watson, C. R. (2004). *From Rigorous Standards to Student Achievement: A Practical Process.* Larchmont, NY: Eye On Education.

- Collaborative Monitoring System—Once data from these assessments are available, the teachers meet to discuss and determine ways for addressing the needs of small groups and individual students who need instructional intervention and/or enrichment.

- Common Time for Interventions and/or Enrichment—Finally, a schedule must be devised that temporarily regroups students to provide time for instructional interventions and enrichment. (See chapter 4 for additional suggestions on planning for effective use of the I/E period.) Once time has been provided for these activities, students return to their original instructional grouping and begin the cycle again with a new unit.

The Concept-Mastery model of mathematics provides a systematic plan and a schedule to facilitate the process described above. The plan involves the division of instruction for mathematics into two different groupings (Concept groups and Mastery groups), two different time periods, and two different instructional approaches. We propose a dual system for the delivery of instruction: basic grade-level instruction in the Concept class, followed by interventions and/or enrichments in a Mastery class. We believe that if all students at a grade level are expected to take the same end-of-year tests, it is critical that they all receive instruction in the required curriculum; this essential instruction is provided in the Concept class. Moreover, when state and federal accountability systems have high-stakes consequences for both students and school personnel, it is morally, ethically, and legally imperative that students experiencing difficulty receive support to achieve required curriculum mastery;

one vehicle for providing this support is the built-in and scheduled Mastery class. We also can provide extended learning time for students through the I/E period.

Concept Groups in Mathematics

During the Concept math group, each teacher is assigned a heterogeneous group of students (controlled heterogeneity may be advisable sometimes; see chapter 6 for details). Membership in Concept groups tends to remain constant for the entire school year. The Concept teacher's charge is to give basic, on-grade-level instruction to all students. During the Concept class, students are instructed through a variety of teaching models. In addition to teacher-directed instruction, peer tutoring may be used; with controlled heterogeneous groups, student pairs often work well; and the use of manipulative materials is encouraged. During the Concept class, practice and reinforcement activities are conducted by using a variety of instructional strategies. Teaching assistants, volunteers, and resource teachers, if available, also can assist students having difficulty. Because of the wide range of ability in the Concept groups, efforts should be made to avoid self-esteem-defeating comparisons among students. We suggest that tests be administered in Concept groups only to provide the teacher with feedback for diagnostic purposes and to serve as a basis for the creation of the Mastery groups, not for grading.

Mastery Groups in Mathematics

Mastery groups are created from each Concept group; Mastery groups usually range in size from 10 to 15 students. With the smaller Mastery groups, teachers design instruction to meet the needs of students in their group as identified by formative assessments for a particular unit. Depending on their performance on the unit assessment, students may be assigned to a group that has mastered all aspects of the topic, needs remediation in a few areas, or requires significant intervention. Teachers differentiate instruction with a variety of approaches, including the use of math manipulatives, math games, problem-solving activities, and computer-assisted instruction, if available in individual classrooms or computer labs. Appropriate homework and/or guided practice could be assigned and monitored.

Scheduling the Concept-Mastery Model Plan A

Figure 8.1 (p. 253) illustrates a schedule for Plan A of the Concept-Mastery model in its simplest form. Plan A of the model is easier to schedule and to implement than Plan B. In our illustration, the third grade mathematics curriculum is divided into nine units (parts 1 to 9). A pacing guide is designed for each part and a formative assessment is created to measure the mastery of each part. In this example, a 60- to 70-minute time block is carved out of the master schedule daily for mathematics instruction (see Figure 8.2, p. 254, periods 7 and 8). Teachers instruct the grade-level curriculum to their heterogeneous Concept group for a period of about 17 days,[2] closely following the pacing guide. On day 17, all four third grade teachers administer the formative assessment for part 1 of grade 3 mathematics. The team meets to analyze the assessment results and to regroup students temporarily (for the next three days) into Mastery groups (Figure 8.1, p. 253) for interventions or enrichment activities. During these three days, perhaps additional personnel—a math specialist, a Title I teacher, an ESL teacher, a computer lab specialist, and/or a teacher of the learning disabled—can be added to provide interventions and enrichment, thereby reducing group size.

Mathematics could be scheduled during a different time block and/or on a varying rotation cycle for each grade level to allow support personnel to be shared easily among several grade levels. If two or more grade levels schedule math at the same time, students could be regrouped across grade levels. Students may work in several different small groups to receive remediation and/or enrichment depending on the areas of weakness and strength identified by the formative assessments. At the conclusion of the three days, students return to their Concept groups for instruction in part 2 of grade level instruction (17 days as shown in Figure 8.1, p. 253). If it is determined that three days of mastery, intervention and enrichment do not suffice, the model could be changed, for example, to a 15-day, 5-day rotation; that is, provide 15 days of concept work and then regroup for 5 days of mastery and enrichment. The plan would vary from school to school and/or by difficulty of content. Some units of work typically would need more time than others. If additional intervention time is needed for some students, the I/E period (see chapter 4) could be used if it has been implemented as part of the master schedule.

---

2 Obviously, 17 days is an arbitrary division; the curriculum needs to be divided into short enough segments to allow timely interventions when students are struggling. See Rettig & Canady (2000) for a middle-school version of this model.

Scheduling the Concept-Mastery Model Plan B

In Figure 8.3 (p. 255), we illustrate a more complex version (Plan B) of the Concept-Mastery model, in which Concept groups and Mastery groups meet on a four-school-day rotation during math from 1:20 until 2:30. The basic grade-level curriculum topics on which students will be tested are taught during Concept classes for two consecutive days. This is followed by one day of instruction in a small-group Mastery class with their homeroom teacher, who provides interventions and/or enrichments, and one day of practice, reinforcement, and/or enrichment in the computer lab or with support teachers. Because this plan offers more frequent opportunities for interventions, we believe it is more responsive to students' immediate instructional needs; but for the same reason, it is more difficult to organize and to implement. For schools with significant numbers of students needing timely intervention, the additional effort needed to implement Plan B may be worthwhile.

As detailed in the shaded portion of Figure 8.3 (p. 255), a student in math group 5 (MG 5) is assigned to teacher 3A's homeroom. During instruction in mathematics from 1:20 until 2:30 for days 1 and 2 (D1, D2) the student meets for the Concept class with the entire homeroom (MGs 1 and 5); on day 3, students in MG 5 may work with support teachers or in the computer lab using various software to enrich or to strengthen the skills taught in the Concept groups on days 1 and 2. On day 4 students in MG 5 are with their base teacher for the Mastery class. At the end of the four-day rotation, all groups begin another four-day rotation that continues throughout the school year.

The Concept-Mastery models gain even more power when special service personnel are available to provide support. With sufficient staff and a well-crafted master schedule, special education teachers in the elementary school can be limited to working with students in just two grade levels in a variety of service delivery models, including co-teaching during inclusion times and pre-teaching and/or re-teaching during I/E periods. Essentially, we recommend that students with special needs

♦ receive pre-teaching two or three days before their Concept group receives similar instruction from their base teacher;

♦ then be co-taught during the Mastery group and,

♦ when needed, be re-taught during the I/E period following the co-teaching periods.

This format ensures that all students with special needs are taught the full curriculum, but also that they are provided various levels of support. Including support teachers as co-teachers should keep them well connected with the curriculum content, which often did not occur with traditional pullout programs.

In Figure 8.4 (p. 256), we show a full-day elementary school schedule including a special education teacher who provides services to both second and third grade students. In this example, the special education teacher starts the day providing inclusion services in language arts for 45 minutes to each grade level. Then she spends the next hour working in third grade mathematics to support their implementation of the Plan B Concept-Mastery model. After lunch, she supports her second grade students during the I/E period, and then for the next hour she assists the second grade's implementation of the Concept-Mastery model in math. After her planning period, she provides assistance during the grade 3 I/E period. This same type of schedule can be designed for ESL, Title I, TAG, and other support service teachers; depending on the number of special service providers in a particular area (e.g., Title I), teachers may be shared with more than two grade levels, or perhaps work in only one grade level.

Figure 8.5 (p. 257) offers an expanded version of the grade 2 Concept-Mastery math period (scheduled at 12:15–1:15 in Figure 8.4, p. 256) to show how Plan B might be implemented for three base teachers, with support from the special education teacher and computer lab personnel. Six Mastery math groups have been formed from the three base teachers' Concept classes. Such groups could have been formed by following the principles of controlled heterogeneity described in chapter 6. Most likely many of the students receiving special education services have been placed primarily into the three lower Mastery groups (1, 2 and 3). The special education teacher is assigned to co-teach with a general education teacher with each of these lower groups, as indicated in the shaded and asterisked periods in Figure 8.5. Notice that the special education teacher works collaboratively with teacher 2C to instruct Mastery MG 3 on days 1 and 4, with teacher 2B to instruct Mastery MG 2 on days 2 and 6, and with teacher 2A to instruct Mastery MG 1 on days 3 and 5. This plan allows the special education teacher to pre-teach and re-teach during the I/E period and then co-teach during the Mastery math period. Following this design should lead to greater integration and coordination of support services.

A few years ago, we would have recommended that the co-teaching occur during the Concept sessions, which have larger class size than Mastery sessions; however, that version of co-teaching did not produce great results. Too often one of the two teachers taught while the other teacher observed or, at the most, moved about the room and asked students if they needed any assistance. The plan we offer can produce better results in terms of student achievement if *both* teachers assume responsibility for raising the math achievement of all students in the lowest three groups. This means the base teacher has to be primarily responsible for determining and coordinating instruction for all students in those groups. The support teacher must be willing (and allowed by policy) to work with some students who are not classified to avoid stigmatizing the classified students. Some days, for example, the base teacher may want one of the two teachers to work with three students who have been absent for several days and need to catch up. In this case, the other teacher works with the remaining students. When co-teachers work with each of the three lowest groups, we recommend that the instruction and groupings be data-driven and vary according to the changing needs of the students (see chapter 4 for a detailed discussion of Friend and Cook's [1996] co-teaching models.).

Obviously not all schools have three or four teachers per grade level as illustrated in Figures 8.3 (p. 255) and 8.5 (p. 257). If there are six teachers at a grade level, the schedule might be built around two three-teacher teams; if eight, two four-teacher teams. If a school has two teachers in grade 4 and two in grade 5, a four-teacher team might be developed and work with students across the two grade levels.

Grading Issues in the Concept-Mastery Model

The Concept-Mastery models can help schools with a wide range of student achievement raise math scores; however, this dual approach to grouping and instruction can create issues related to grading and reporting students' performance to parents. If we were to assign grades based only on students' performance in the heterogeneous Concept class, many students for whom the grade-level content and instructional pace is a stretch would receive low grades and very likely become discouraged. On the other hand, if we were to assign grades (and report to parents) based only on students' performance in the Mastery group, parents of the same students might interpret a higher grade incorrectly. Our challenge is to devise a system that rewards students for working, learning, and improving, so they stay motivated and continue to work, learn and improve, but which also provides parents with a realistic view of their child's relative standing among peers and mastery of grade-level content.

One recommendation might be to create a dual reporting system, with one grade based on work during the Mastery group and the second reflecting work in the Concept group. Historically, dual reports have had some success; for example, writing teachers sometimes give one grade for mechanics and another for content. However, such plans can cause confusion with parents; dual reporting tends to work best if each report has a different design and format and if parents truly understand what the two reports convey and why both are important. In general, the grading report needs to answer three questions for parents: (a) How is my child doing? (b) What does that grade mean? and (c) Do I need to be concerned?

For example, in the Mastery class students might receive a letter grade based on their improvement during the grading term. The Concept report, though, might present a graphical representation of students' progress on a curriculum continuum for the grade level. Major concepts for the entire year would be shown in a sequential format. At the end of each grading period, students and parents receive a graphic display of where the student "has been" (the concepts on the continuum mastered to date) and where the student currently is working. As a point of reference, it also might be wise to note on the graphic where the "average"[3] student fell in terms of curriculum mastery.

To position students for success on district- or state-mandated tests, the Concept class report would illustrate graphically the remaining objectives a student needs to master before the date of this assessment. If schools have no choice about when students must take high-stakes tests, and if some students have more curriculum left to master than is reasonably possible given the remaining allotment of time, it would be wise to try to accelerate the lower Mastery groups by providing them more time and support in mathematics. Additional time to learn can be provided in a variety of formats:

- ◆ Extra periods of math each week in place of some other activity;

---

3 Depending on the assessments administered, "average" could mean average for the class, grade level, school, district, state, or nation.

- A daily Intervention/Enrichment (I/E) period;

- A before- or after-school program;

- A Saturday school program; or

- An extended-year program, such as summer school or the extra days/weeks provided in many year-round schooling models.

In the context of the Concept-Mastery models, extended time does not imply the traditional "took course/failed course/repeat course" format; rather, extended time gives students a chance to continue to progress until the full curriculum has been taught and mastered by all students.[4]

The Concept-Mastery models discussed in this chapter use the Concept groups to make certain all students have access to the full math curriculum and the Mastery group to provide support to help students learn the material. To significantly raise student achievement, schools must raise the bar for students for whom low expectations traditionally have been set. If schools, however, lack a plan for helping these students actually attain higher standards, both students and schools will experience frustration and failure.

Goals and Benefits of the Concept-Mastery Models

The major goals and benefits of the Concept-Mastery models of instruction are as follows:

- To improve or insure access to the full, grade-level curriculum (Concept groups) for students who sometimes have languished in low groups. With accountability testing at various grade levels, this is a critical issue. Schools must find ways to give all students access to the full curriculum on which they will be tested and to help students experiencing difficulty obtain a high level of mastery.

- To provide scheduled extended learning time for struggling students and enrichment for students who have achieved mastery, a plan which can help schools address a wide range of achievement levels in mathematics.

- To maintain stability for students throughout the school year; each student's homeroom teacher typically instructs the Concept group, which meets yearlong.

- To allow opportunities for teachers on the team to group and regroup on a temporary basis to help a greater number of students reach a high level of mastery with selected critical topics.

- To organize pullout programs as integral parts of the instructional schedule. In the Concept-Mastery models, teachers of compensatory and enrichment programs can become valuable assets during Mastery groupings. The services of support teachers must be built into the schedule so they do not frag-

---

4 That is, all but the most severely challenged students with disabilities.

ment core instructional time, but permit resource personnel to become a critical resource in improving math achievement for a large percentage of students.

- To improve the success rate for students assigned to heterogeneous classes by reducing the practice of comparison grading.

- To provide a mix of heterogeneous and homogeneous groupings in mathematics that is instructionally practical, politically acceptable, and supported by research (Slavin, 1986, 1987).

Concerns and Issues for the Concept-Mastery Models

The major concerns and issues for the Concept-Mastery models of instruction in mathematics are these:

- The Concept-Mastery models require significant collaboration among teachers; therefore, teachers must have common planning time to design curriculum, assessments, intervention and enrichment activities, and to construct Mastery groups. Schools that do not adequately provide planning time for these critical activities risk failure.

- For the Mastery groups to function properly, teachers must diagnose what individual students and groups need during the Mastery sessions (see chapter 11 for suggestions). Teachers without adequate training in mathematics may have difficulty accurately diagnosing students' learning problems; if so,

they will have trouble prescribing appropriate groupings and instruction for the Mastery periods. Sometimes teachers will know children are failing their tests, but they may not know how to diagnose and plan instruction so failure is not as likely to occur on the next test of similar content. It is critical that the Mastery groups do not deteriorate into "slow" and "fast" groups or into study halls. Mastery group membership and instruction must be data-driven by diagnostic assessments!

The Acceleration Model

A key aspect of the Concept-Mastery models is that students essentially progress at the same rate through the grade-level curriculum. Both Plan A and Plan B provide interventions for students who are struggling and enrichment for those who are not, but they make no provisions for acceleration. The Acceleration model allows some students to progress through the mathematics curriculum more quickly than others. This model is useful particularly in schools having a large number of students who may be expected to accelerate into Algebra I sometime during middle school. For example, if a school district establishes a goal of having 85 percent of the district's students complete Algebra I by the end of grade 8, acceleration may need to begin in grades 4 and 5 to reach such a goal.

A major difference between the Concept-Mastery and the Acceleration models is that in the former, the Concept groups typically are taught by each student's homeroom teacher, thus providing an element of stability and consistency for the students; only the Mastery groups in Plan A may change instructors, and then only temporarily. In the Acceleration model, however, a student's instructional group and mathematics teacher may change every 4½ to 9 weeks; therefore, we recommend considering this model only for implementation in the upper elementary grades. Often schools and/or school districts delay acceleration opportunities—and the tracking that can result with such models—until middle school.

To implement the Acceleration model, we suggest that the master schedule include a period of time for mathematics of not less than 60 minutes and preferably 70 to 90 minutes, as shown in Figure 8.2 (p. 254; periods 7 and 8). The model probably cannot be implemented without at least three teachers at a grade level. In Figure 8.6 (p. 258), we show four teachers in grade 4 who are willing to work collaboratively during the same period of time. In some small schools, it may be possible to have teachers team across two grade levels to provide at least four teachers; this is necessary to provide services for the various groups as students become accelerated and/or need intervention.

Much preparation is required prior to implementation of the Acceleration model. As shown in Figure 8.6 (p. 258), the school year is divided into eight quarters, four each semester (Q1 to Q8); depending on the structure of the school calendar, each quarter is 4½ to 5 weeks in length. Similar to the Concept-Mastery models, the common curriculum is divided into distinct units. As shown in Figure 8.6, grade 4 math is divided into four parts, as is grade 5 math. For each part of the course, a pacing guide delineates the duration of each topic and a formative assessment measures students' mastery. At the completion of each part, after data from the

formative assessments are gathered, all teachers on the collaborative team come together to analyze the data.

This is the point where Acceleration and the Concept-Mastery models begin to differ. The Concept-Mastery models provide several days for instructional interventions and enrichment in somewhat homogeneous groups, and then students return to their more heterogeneous Concept group and resume the instructional schedule as defined by the pacing guide. In the Acceleration model, regroupings provide some students with more time to learn and others are permitted to progress at a faster pace.

As illustrated in Figure 8.6 (p. 258), each of the four teachers is assigned a heterogeneous group of students and proceeds to teach part 1 of fourth grade math according to the jointly developed pacing guide. After 4½ weeks, the 4.1 assessment is administered to all students; based on their mastery, students are regrouped according to those who need more time and those who can move ahead. In this hypothetical example, because 75 percent of the students have attained the predetermined mastery level on part 4.1, three of the four teachers (4A, 4B, and 4C) move on to instruct part 4.2 of the course, while teacher 4D works with the students who need more time to master part 4.1. (Occasionally, students who have yet to master all material in a specific part are encouraged to progress to the next part, if they are not deficient in any essential sequential skills.)

During this block of time, it also may be beneficial to have support personnel join the team. Special education teachers, Computer Lab personnel, teaching assistants (TAs), student tutors from the high school, Title I and English as Second Language (ESL) teachers could collaborate with teacher D to address specific identified needs (deficits) of the students who have not mastered the critical content of part 4.1. At the end of part 4.2, students working with teachers A, B, and C take the part 4.2 assessment; students working with teacher D take a second form of the part 4.1 assessment. Based on these results, students again are regrouped. It is important to note that the size of the groups each quarter will vary with the number of students attaining mastery (or not).

This system continues throughout the year. In the example shown, one group completes both fourth and fifth grade mathematics; a second group completes half of the grade 5 curriculum. Two groups spend the entire year mastering fourth grade mathematics, although one finishes a bit earlier than the other (see Figure 8.6, p. 258). Although this chart shows the slower-progressing students working with teacher D each quarter, this is not necessary; teaching assignments can be exchanged up and down the columns. For the group that ends up with teacher 4C during Q8, it may be advisable to spend time reviewing fourth grade math concepts and vocabulary, rather than proceeding into the fifth grade curriculum for just 4½ to 5 weeks. In Figure 8.7 (p. 259) we illustrate how instruction continues at the beginning of fifth grade, and we delineate a potential continuation of the model throughout that year.

One of the benefits of the Acceleration model is that *all*[5] students are given an opportunity to attempt part 1 of the course; no predetermination is made for any significant number of students that they will not be able to handle the content and should, therefore, start out in a "lower" group. Expectations are universally high. In addition, time becomes a variable that we manipulate by offering the possibility of completing two years of work in one school year for the most able students and providing additional learning time for those whose performance indicates they need additional time and support.

In Figure 8.8 (p. 260), we show a similar model for a team of six teachers. If the school is large, these six teachers might all be at the same grade level; in smaller elementary schools, the six-teacher team might be three teachers from each of grades 4 and 5.

Grading Issues in the Acceleration Model

Several grading issues arise out of the Acceleration model. We recommend that students only receive a summative grade to be reported to parents after the completion of a "part" or unit of the grade level curriculum. The ramifications of this recommendation can be illustrated using Figure 8.6 (p. 258). At the end of the first nine-week grading term, the groups with teachers 4A and 4B would have completed parts 4.1 and 4.2; these students would receive a grade for each of these parts of the course (two grades). The students with teacher 4D at the end of nine weeks would have completed only part 4.1; therefore, they would receive one grade. Students with teacher C would have completed part 4.1, but would have just been assigned to additional instructional/learning time for part 4.2. These students would receive a summative grade for part 4.1 and the grade of "work in progress" (WIP) for part 4.2, which would be changed once

---

5 Again, we mean all but the most severely challenged students with disabilities.

completed. (Some schools use "I" for incomplete; "E" for extended time needed; or possibly "NY" for not yet!).

The report card, therefore, would need to list the various parts of the math course; those parts completed would be assigned a grade. In addition, it would be wise to note, perhaps through the use of a graphic math continuum, how far the "average" student had progressed to date. This would allow parents to see how far their children had progressed through the curriculum, how well they had done in the work completed, and how each child's progress compared to the average.[6]

Benefits of the Acceleration Model

The major benefits of the Acceleration model of instruction in mathematics are as follows:

♦ As in the Concept-Mastery models, teachers at a designated grade level or across two grade levels work as a team during the math period/block to construct curriculum, design innovative instructional strategies, create objective assessments and regroup students within limits of the scheduling format (Iverson, 2003). If some teachers are not as skilled in teaching mathematics as others on the team, or if they do not have a strong preference for teaching math, rotations can be made so no group of students has the same teacher throughout the year.

♦ All students are provided equal opportunity. Movement to the next unit of work is based on objective assessments and attainment of learning goals.

♦ Students who fall behind do not flounder for the balance of the year, which is a major instructional problem in a sequential subject like mathematics. Students who need tutorials and/or extended learning time can receive such assistance at least every 4 to 5 weeks.

♦ A variety of placements are available for transfer students; this can be very valuable for schools with a high transience rate during the school year.

Implementation Issues and Concerns for the Acceleration Model

The major concerns and issues for the Acceleration model of instruction in mathematics are these:

♦ Intervention for students experiencing difficulty is not as immediate as in the Concept-Mastery models, unless it is provided during the I/E period.

♦ Professional staff development time will be necessary to decide on curriculum "parts" and to design common assessments. This crucial task must be

---

6 The truth is that the Acceleration model implies a radical rethinking of student grading. When we allow some students more time to learn and accelerate others, comparison grading at any point in time is inappropriate. At the very least, schools and districts must move towards standards-based grading that allows different kinds of grades to be reported for students at various times during the year. Students do not "arrive" at the same place at the same time in these models.

completed and institutionalized before implementing the plan.

♦ Staff development time also is needed to address instructional practices in longer class periods (Canady and Rettig, 1996).

♦ There is no guarantee that class sizes after each regrouping will remain the same after assessments; some classes may be larger than others, which may be a problem in schools with class size restrictions in the union contract. Even without such a contract, we strongly suggest placing controls on class sizes and regroupings. For example, we would hope no class, even for 4½ weeks, would have 35 to 40 students while others have 5 to 10. Obviously, the class size issue must be determined within the confines of personnel available. It may be possible to provide additional resources during such crunch times. In some schools, for example, a Title I teacher might teach one group as a regular member of the team, a plan that would provide greater flexibility in adjusting the size of classes; in other schools, such a practice might not be permitted or preferred. If students in the extended time sections were assigned to the computer lab as a base and if small groups were served by the designated math teacher(s) and also by other resource personnel, it may be possible to assign a larger number of students to these intervention classes.

♦ Some will argue that in the proposed Accelerated model, regrouping is simply another form of tracking. We contend that the regroupings are based on performance and that students have multiple opportunities to complete the grade-level content in a timely fashion. Also, early in the program, groupings are temporary, and regrouping based on goal attainment is institutionalized. Our experience with the model suggests that significantly larger numbers of students master the required content than in typical organizational formats. At the same time, some students are not slowed down or "held back" to wait while others receive the extended learning time they need.

Table 8.1 (p. 250) compares traditional, Concept-Mastery, and Acceleration scheduling models for mathematics instruction.

Table 8.1. Comparison of Scheduling Models for Mathematics Instruction

	Traditional	Concept-Mastery	Acceleration
Curriculum	Individual teacher	Common for all students	Common for all students
Pacing	Individual teacher	Common for all students	Common for all students in the same unit
Formative assessment	Independently designed and administered	Common for all students; prepared prior to instruction	Common for all students in the same unit; prepared prior to instruction
Data analysis, diagnosis, and decision-making	Independent	Collaborative	Collaborative
Response to formative assessment data	Independently designed and structured instructional interventions, enrichment, and/or acceleration	Collaboratively structured instructional interventions or enrichment	Collaboratively structured instructional interventions or acceleration
Responsibility for students' performance on high-stakes summative assessments	Individual	Individual and shared	Shared
Staff development	Individual	Embedded in collaborative team to build capacity	Embedded in collaborative team to build capacity

A Comment on Instructional Grouping in Mathematics

In this chapter, we have referenced three forms of grouping used in instructing elementary students in mathematics: Concept groups, Mastery groups, and Accelerated groups. Because of the generally accepted belief that the discipline of mathematics is highly structured and sequential, many educators believe that some forms of grouping are needed if *all* students in a typical, diverse elementary school are to be served adequately.

Research on within-class grouping supports the forms of grouping we have proposed. Specifically, Slavin (1986) summarized this research as follows:

> Research on within-class ability grouping is unfortunately limited to mathematics in upper elementary school. However, this research clearly supports the use of within-class grouping (approximate median ES=+.34), especially if the number of groups is small. Achievement effects of within-class ability grouping are slightly higher for low than for high or average achievers.

In addition to the conclusions about the effects of particular grouping strategies, several general principles of ability grouping were proposed on the basis of the experimental evidence. The following are advanced as elements of effective ability grouping plans:

1. Students should remain in heterogeneous classes at most times, and be regrouped by ability only in subjects (e.g. reading,

mathematics) in which reducing heterogeneity is particularly important. Students' primary identification should be with a heterogeneous class.

2. Grouping plans must reduce heterogeneity in the specific skill being taught (e.g. reading, mathematics).

3. Grouping plans must frequently reassess student placements and be flexible enough to allow for easy reassignment after initial placement.

4. Teachers must actually vary their level and pace of instruction to correspond to students' levels of readiness and learning rates in regrouped classes

5. In within-class ability grouping, numbers of groups should be kept small to allow for adequate direct instruction from the teacher for each group. (pp. 75–76)

In addition, we believe the following factors also should be considered when deciding to employ a particular grouping plan for the instruction of mathematics:

1. How wide is the range of diversity in terms of mathematics achievement in the school and/or particular grade level?

2. Is the district mandating that a certain percentage of students successfully complete Algebra I in middle school? If so, some acceleration in mathematics needs to begin in the upper elementary grades.

3. How skilled are the teachers in providing differentiated instruction to meet the varying needs of students?

4. Is the school serving a relatively large number of special needs students? Do those students typically need support beyond what the ordinary classroom teacher can provide?

5. Is the school located in a district or state with high-stakes accountability tests and consequences that go with such measures?

6. Do teachers have the skills, knowledge base, and instruments to diagnose adequately the changing instructional needs of students in mathematics?

7. Do teachers have the support needed (i.e., planning time) to confer with their peers when analyzing formative assessment results and considering the reassignment of students to the flexible groups?

8. Have the teachers been provided the necessary curricula guides and assessments to appropriately determine the various groupings— for example, Mastery groups—suggested in this chapter? It is critical that such groupings do not deteriorate into "tracked groups."

Based on our combined 80+ years in education, we, too, support the forms of grouping suggested in this chapter, if they are used appropriately. By "appropriate use" we mean that the groups are data-driven and flexible, and that whatever grouping is used, all students are taught the full grade-level curriculum. Grouping structures alone, however, are not sufficient to serve fully the needs of a diverse student population. Following initial instruction, we advocate providing support through the use of the I/E period, and when necessary, extended learning time. By following the various models for delivering instruction in mathematics to elementary students described in this chapter, we believe we can increase mathematics achievement for all students.

We believe that all students can learn, but we also know that all students do not learn at the same rate. In the past, the design of elementary school schedules has not institutionalized this notion; managing the varying rates of student learning has typically depended on the energy level, motivation, and creativity of individual teachers, which often means that students in the same school experience very different learning environments.

We also know that in subjects with a sequential curriculum, such as mathematics, student mastery of critical skills or concepts is crucial to prevent frustration and failure for teachers and students alike. In the Concept-Mastery and the Acceleration math models presented in this chapter, we have offered various scheduling designs that make time, not achievement, the key variable.

References

Canady, R. L., & Rettig, M. D. (Eds.) (1996). *Teaching in the block: Strategies for engaging active learners.* Larchmont, NY: Eye On Education.

Friend, M., & Cook, L. (1996). *Interactions: Collaboration skills for school professionals.* White Plains, NY: Longman Publishers.

Iverson, N. R. (2003). *Staff development and kindergarten reading achievement.* Unpublished doctoral dissertation, University of Virginia, Charlottesville.

Northwest Evaluation Association (2000). *Measures of academic progress.* Retrieved September 5, 2007 from http://www.nwea.org/.

Rettig, M. D., & Canady, R. L. (2000). *Scheduling strategies for middle schools.* Larchmont, NY: Eye On Education.

Slavin, R. E. (1986). *Ability grouping and student achievement in elementary school: A best evidence synthesis. Report 1.* Baltimore, MD: Center for Research on Elementary and Middle Schools. (ERIC Document Reproduction Service No. ED348174)

Slavin, R. E. (1987). Ability grouping and student achievement in elementary school: A best evidence synthesis. *Review of Educational Research, 57,* 328.

Figure 8.1 Concept Mastery Math Team Schedule (Plan A): Grade 3 (60–90 Minutes Daily)

	17 Days	3 Ds	17 Days	3 Ds	17 Days	3 Ds	17 Days	3 Ds	17 Days	3 Ds	17 Days	3 Ds	17 Days	3 Ds	17 Days	3 Ds	17 Days	3 Ds
Teacher 3A	Concept Class Math 3, Part 1	Mastery Class: Interventions and Enrichment	Concept Class Math 3, Part 2	Mastery Class: Interventions and Enrichment	Concept Class Math 3, Part 3	Mastery Class: Interventions and Enrichment	Concept Class Math 3, Part 4	Mastery Class: Interventions and Enrichment	Concept Class Math 3, Part 5	Mastery Class: Interventions and Enrichment	Concept Class Math 3, Part 6	Mastery Class: Interventions and Enrichment	Concept Class Math 3, Part 7	Mastery Class: Interventions and Enrichment	Concept Class Math 3, Part 8	Mastery Class: Interventions and Enrichment	Concept Class Math 3, Part 9	Mastery Class: Interventions and Enrichment
Teacher 3B	Concept Class Math 3, Part 1		Concept Class Math 3, Part 2		Concept Class Math 3, Part 3		Concept Class Math 3, Part 4		Concept Class Math 3, Part 5		Concept Class Math 3, Part 6		Concept Class Math 3, Part 7		Concept Class Math 3, Part 8		Concept Class Math 3, Part 9	
Teacher 3C	Concept Class Math 3, Part 1		Concept Class Math 3, Part 2		Concept Class Math 3, Part 3		Concept Class Math 3, Part 4		Concept Class Math 3, Part 5		Concept Class Math 3, Part 6		Concept Class Math 3, Part 7		Concept Class Math 3, Part 8		Concept Class Math 3, Part 9	
Teacher 3D	Concept Class Math 3, Part 1		Concept Class Math 3, Part 2		Concept Class Math 3, Part 3		Concept Class Math 3, Part 4		Concept Class Math 3, Part 5		Concept Class Math 3, Part 6		Concept Class Math 3, Part 7		Concept Class Math 3, Part 8		Concept Class Math 3, Part 9	

Figure 8.2 Parallel Block Schedule for Four, Grade 3 Homeroom Teachers and Extension Center for Language Arts, Social Studies, Science, and the Concept-Mastery or Acceleration Models (School Day Divided into 5-Minute Increments)

Periods		Period 1	Period 2	Period 3	Period 4	Period 5	Period 6	Period 7 (70)	P8 (30)
Teacher 3A RWGs 1,5	Homeroom Activities (20)	LA/SS/SC RWGs 1,5 (100)		RWG 5 (50)	RWG 1 (50)	Lunch/ Recess (50)	Encore Classes and Teacher Planning Time (50)	Concept-Mastery or Acceleration Models (See Figures 8.1, 8.5-8) (70)	Foreign Language, Silent Sustained Reading, Etc. (30)
Teacher 3B RWGs 2,6		LA/SS/SC RWGs 2,6 (100)		RWG 2 (50)	RWG 6 (50)				
Teacher 3C RWGs 3,7		RWG 3 (50)	RWG 7 (50)	LA/SS/SC RWGs 3,7 (100)					
Teacher 3D RWGs 4,8		RWG 8 (50)	RWG 4 (50)	LA/SS/SC RWGs 4,8 (100)					
Extension Center* Teacher		LA Extension							
		RWGs 4,7 (50)	RWGs 3,8 (50)	RWGs 1,6 (50)	RWGs 2,5 (50)				

* For language arts extension, the center could be staffed by a Title I teacher and one or more resource teachers, such as LD, reading, ESL, or Technology.

Figure 8.3 Concept-Mastery Model (Plan B) for Mathematics with a Four-Day Rotation for Whole Group and Small Group Mathematics with Computer Lab

8.2
8.3

		Period 1	Period 2	Period 3	Period 4	Period 5	Period 6	Period 7 (70)				P8 (30)
Teacher 3A RWGs 1,5	Homeroom Activities (20)	LA/SS/SC RWGs 1,5 (100)		RWG 5 (50)	RWG 1 (50)	Lunch/ Recess (50)	Encore Classes and Teacher Planning Time (50)	D1 / MG 1,5	D2 / MG 1,5	D3 / MG 1	D4 / MG 5	Foreign Language, Silent Sustained Reading, Etc. (30)
Teacher 3B RWGs 2,6		LA/SS/SC RWGs 2,6 (100)		RWG 2 (50)	RWG 6 (50)			D1 / MG 2,6	D2 / MG 2,6	D3 / MG 6	D4 / MG 2	
Teacher 3C RWGs 3,7		RWG 3 (50)	RWG 7 (50)	LA/SS/SC RWGs 3,7 (100)				D1 / MG 3	D2 / MG 7	D3 / MG 3,7	D4 / MG 3,7	
Teacher 3D RWGs 4,8		RWG 8 (50)	RWG 4 (50)	LA/SS/SC RWGs 4,8 (100)				D1 / MG 8	D2 / MG 4	D1 / MG 4,8	D2 / MG 4,8	
Extension Center* Teacher		LA Extension						Computer Lab				
		RWGs 4,7 (50)	RWGs 3,8 (50)	RWGs 1,6 (50)	RWGs 2,5 (50)			D1 / MG 4,7	D2 / MG 3,8	D3 / MG 2,5	D4 / MG 1,6	

* In the afternoon on a four-day rotation students have whole group math for two days, the reduced-size MG one day, and go to the computer lab one day. Key: RWG-Reading-writing Group; MG-Math Group; D1-Day 1; D2-Day 2, etc.

Figure 8.4 Master Schedule Showing a Special Education Teacher Assigned to Inclusion Language Arts, Invervention/Enrichment (I/E) and Concept-Mastery Mathematics for Grades 2 and 3

	8:00	9:00	10:00	11:00	12:00	1:00	2:00	3:00
Kinder.	HR	Language Arts (150)		Lunch/ Recess (50)	Math (50)	Encore/ Plan (50)	I/E (50)	SS/SC (50)
Grade 1	HR	Language Arts (140)		Math (60)	Lunch/ Recess (50)	I/E (50)	Encore/ Plan (50)	SS/SC (50)
Grade 2	HR	Language Arts (140)		Recess/ Lunch (50)	I/E (50)	Math (60)	SS/SC (50)	Encore/ Plan (50)
SPED 2/3		Inclusion LA 2 (45)	Inclusion LA 3 (45)	Concept-Mastery Math 3 (60)	Lunch (40)	Grade 2 I/E (50)	Concept-Mastery Math 2 (60)	Plan (50)	Grade 3 I/E (50)
Grade 3	HR	Language Arts (90)	Math (60)	Encore/ Plan (50)	Recess/ Lunch (50)	LA (50)	SS/SC (50)	I/E (50)
Grade 4	HR	Math (50)	I/E (50)	Encore/ Plan (50)	Language Arts (100)	Lunch/ Recess (50)	Math/SS/SC (100)	
Grade 5	HR	Math (50)	Encore/ Plan (50)	I/E (50)	Language Arts (100)	Recess/ Lunch (50)	Math/SS/SC (100)	
I/E		Plan (50)	Grade 4	Grade 5	Lunch/ Duty (40)	Grade 2	10	Grade 1	Kinder.	Grade 3
Arts/PE Teachers		Plan (50)	Grade 5	Grade 4	Grade 3	Lunch/Duty (50)	Kinder.	Grade 1	Grade 2

Figure 8.5 Grade 2 Concept-Mastery Model (Plan B)
12:15-1:15 p.m. for 3 Base Teachers, 1 Special Education Teacher, and a Computer Lab

	Day 1 (M)	Day 2 (T)	Day 3 (W)	Day 4 (Th)	Day 5 (F)	Day 6 (M)
Teacher 2A	C-MG 1,4	C-MG 1,4	M-MG 1	M-MG 4	M-MG 1	M-MG 4
Teacher 2B	M-MG 5	M-MG 2	C-MG 2,5	C-MG 2,5	M-MG 5	M-MG 2
Teacher 2C	M-MG 3	M-MG 6	M-MG 6	M-MG 3	C-MG 3,6	C-MG 3,6
SPED Teacher	M-MG 3	M-MG 2	M-MG 1	M-MG 3	M-MG 1	M-MG 2
Computer Lab	MG 2,6	MG 3,5	MG 3,4	MG 1,6	MG 2,4	MG 1,5

Key: C-MG=Concept Math Group; M-MG=Mastery Math Group; Highlighting and Asterisks signify Progress Math groups co-taught by the base teacher and the special education teacher.

Figure 8.6 Acceleration Model for Four Teachers (Year 1)

	Q1	Q2	Q3	Q4	Q5	Q6	Q7	Q8
Teacher 4A	Part 4.1	Part 4.2	Part 4.3	Part 4.4	Part 5.1	Part 5.2	Part 5.3	Part 5.4
Teacher 4B	Part 4.1	Part 4.2	Part 4.3	Part 4.3	Part 4.4	Part 4.4	Part 5.1	Part 5.2
Teacher 4C	Part 4.1	Part 4.2	Part 4.2	Part 4.3	Part 4.3	Part 4.4	Part 4.4	*
Teacher 4D	Part 4.1	Part 4.1	Part 4.2	Part 4.2	Part 4.3	Part 4.3	Part 4.4	Part 4.4
Special Assistance		After Q1 special assistance may be provided to students needing more time to master Part 4.1 by a variety of support personnel such as a computer lab teacher, math specialist, LD teacher, ESL teacher, Title I teacher, peer tutors, etc.						

Key: Q1 = Quarter 1 (4½ to 5 weeks); Part 4.1 = About ¼ of the Grade 4 Curriculum

Figure 8.7 Acceleration Model for Four Teachers (Year 2)

	Q1	Q2	Q3	Q4	Q5	Q6	Q7	Q8
Teacher 5A	Part 6.1	Part 6.2	Part 6.3	Part 6.4	Part 7.1	Part 7.2	Part 7.3	Part 7.4
Teacher 5B	Part 5.3	Part 5.3	Part 5.4	Part 6.1	Part 6.2	Part 6.3	Part 6.3	Part 6.4
Teacher 5C	Part 5.1	Part 5.2	Part 5.3	Part 5.3	Part 5.4	Part 6.1	Part 6.2	Part 6.2
Teacher 5D	Part 5.1	Part 5.1	Part 5.2	Part 5.2	Part 5.3	Part 5.3	Part 5.4	Part 5.4
Special Assistance	Special assistance may be provided to students needing more time to master a specific part of the curriculum by a variety of support personnel such as a computer lab teacher, math specialist, LD teacher, ESL teacher, Title I teacher, peer tutors, etc.							

Key: Q1 = Quarter 1 (4½ to 5 weeks); Part 6.1 = About ¼ of the Grade 6 Curriculum

Figure 8.8 Acceleration Model for Six Teachers

	Q1	Q2	Q3	Q4	Q5	Q6	Q7	Q8
Teacher 4A	Part 4.1	Part 4.2	Part 4.3	Part 4.4	Part 5.1	Part 5.2	Part 5.3	Part 5.4
Teacher 4B	Part 4.1	Part 4.2	Part 4.3	Part 4.4	Part 5.1	Part 5.2	Part 5.3	Part 5.4
Teacher 4C	Part 4.1	Part 4.2	Part 4.3	Part 4.3	Part 4.4	Part 4.4	Part 5.1	Part 5.2
Teacher 4D	Part 4.1	Part 4.2	Part 4.3	Part 4.3	Part 4.4	Part 4.4	Part 5.1	Part 5.2
Teacher 4E	Part 4.1	Part 4.2	Part 4.2	Part 4.3	Part 4.3	Part 4.4	Part 4.4	*
Teacher 4F	Part 4.1	Part 4.1	Part 4.2	Part 4.2	Part 4.3	Part 4.3	Part 4.4	Part 4.4
Special Assistance		After Q1 special assistance may be provided to students needing more time to master Part 4.1 by a variety of support personnel such as a computer lab teacher, math specialist, LD teacher, ESL teacher, Title I teacher, peer tutors, etc.						

Key: Q1 = Quarter 1 (4½ to 5 weeks); Part 4.1 = About ¼ of the Grade 4 Curriculum

Part III

Instruction and Planning

9

The Road to Becoming Literate: Instruction in Kindergarten Through Grade Three

Ruth Short[1]

All children deserve the best instruction possible in the early grades regardless of their experiences prior to entering school. Thinking of children who have had few experiences with print, books, and stories as "inexperienced" learners creates a different view of their instructional needs than does thinking of them as "slow," "language impaired," or any of the other labels often assigned children who enter school inexperienced in literacy activities. The critical need of providing children with a print-rich, story-rich, book-rich classroom becomes clear when we take this view. In kindergarten classrooms, the major literacy goal should be to stimulate both formal and informal reading and writing encounters that many children have experienced before entering school. Students who participate in these literacy experiences generally gain an understanding that reading and writing

1 Ruth Short is an associate professor in the Department of Curriculum and Instruction at the University of Wisconsin–Milwaukee. Dr. Short's current focus is on early intervention programs for children in grades K–3 in urban communities who are at risk of reading failure. She may be contacted at rashort@uwm.edu.

are very important activities that "big people" do, and they want to learn how to do them because they want to be "big."

In the late 1980s, the view of reading readiness as being requisite to beginning reading instruction was challenged. Researchers and teachers moved toward the concept of emergent literacy (Strickland & Morrow, 1989; Teale & Sulzby, 1986). This view proposed that for all children in a literate society, learning to read and write begins very early in life, rather than at age 5 or 6. Literacy development was viewed as a more appropriate term than reading readiness because it was determined that children develop as readers and writers, and that reading, writing, and oral language develop simultaneously and are interrelated rather than sequential. Meaningful and purposeful bases of early literacy are a critical part of learning to read and write and must be emphasized in the curriculum. With this "informed thinking" as the lens through which we view literacy, let's look at "good" instruction in the primary grades.

Foundations of Literacy Development

A successful early literacy program must include the following components: comprehension instruction, a multifaceted word study program, writing, reading fluency, and "real reading" of connected text.

Comprehension

A core component of all instruction must be comprehension. Comprehension instruction should be a central part of teaching young children how to read from the beginning. It should not be delayed until after children have learned how to decode. In kindergarten, before children can read conventionally from print, comprehension instruction typically involves children's understanding of stories read to them. Teachers read aloud from different genres, including poems, informational texts, and stories. Through shared reading experiences, children are invited to make predictions about what the text might be about before the teacher reads aloud. They are invited to predict what might happen next during the reading of the story and to verify or change their predictions as the story unfolds. In addition to predicting the story, children are often invited to tap into their prior knowledge and discuss the reading while making personal connections between the story and their own lives. They may respond to stories and readings through art, dramatic activities or music. In these varied ways, children learn about written language, its syntactic patterns, vocabulary, and text structure. By the time children are ending their kindergarten year, they should be able to retell stories on their own, create art work or writing that demonstrates comprehension of text that has been read aloud to them, and make sensible predictions about a story as it is being read.

As children move through kindergarten and first grade and become able to read on their own, comprehension strategies should be taught in the context of reading. By using both narrative and informational texts, comprehension instruction will strengthen and build children's background knowledge and comprehension skills. Teachers can support children in developing and using strategies in two ways: (a) through modeling and demonstrating strategy use, and (b) by creating classroom environments that encourage wide and varied opportunities to read

(Gambrell & Dromsky, 2000). Helping children become strategic readers should be every teacher's goal. Such strategies as KWL (what I *K*now, what I *W*ant to know, what I *L*earned; Ogle, 1986), retelling, and using text clues (either listed as words or provided as visual or manipulative clues) are examples of techniques that enhance understanding of text. These strategies engage the children in making personal connections between text and their prior knowledge; they also support the development of higher-order thinking skills, and they help develop an awareness of narrative and expository text structures (Gambrell, Koskinen, & Kapinus, 1991).

Comprehension goals for second and third grade students include the skills of summarizing what has been read; answering comprehension questions; discussing informational texts; responding to literature through writing, art, oral expression, or drama; and developing an understanding of story structure and story grammar (Teale & Yokota, 2000). Just as in kindergarten, teachers need to model and demonstrate strategy use while encouraging wide and varied opportunities for children to read.

Word Study

A multifaceted word study program is critical to any balanced literacy program. Word study promotes decoding, vocabulary growth, structural analysis, sight word recognition and spelling. For primary grade children, decoding is the most talked about part of word study. Children need to know how letters, letter combinations, and sounds relate to one another in a systematic way. Several good models for helping children engage in word study in meaningful ways are available for teachers (see Cunningham, 2000; Gaskins, 1996; Bear,

Invernizzi, Templeton, & Johnston, 2004; Donat, 2003). Doing picture sorts, rhyming activities, and phonemic awareness activities are just a few ways teachers can engage children in decoding-related activities.

Oral language activities such as read-alouds, discussions, and written language experiences help develop children's knowledge of words and their meanings. Because vocabulary development is the single biggest factor in enhancing a child's reading comprehension (Blachowicz & Fisher, 1996), primary grade classrooms need to be "print-rich, word-rich" places. Activities that help children learn important words from stories and content areas, such as science and social studies, should be meaningful rather than worksheet oriented or measured through weekly tests of ten to 15 new words.

Writing

Writing enhances young children's literacy development in many ways, and research has shown a strong connection between reading and writing. As children compose, they put ideas together in a variety of ways and for a variety of purposes. When creating stories, they apply what they have learned about story structure and the elements of story, such as character, setting, plot, events, and resolution. They also may experiment with expository writing or tying writing to comprehension strategies, such as writing their own KWLs. Writing reinforces what they have learned through reading.

In kindergarten, teachers should provide a wide variety of writing materials, such as pens, markers, lined and unlined paper, blank overhead transparencies, colored paper, self-inking stamps, and stencils. Allowing children to choose their own writing instruments can be very motivating. Teachers can model different purposes for writing, from making lists to writing letters and notes. The important thing to remember for kindergarten children is the developmental nature of literacy development. First attempts at writing may be in the dramatic play area or labeling items in the classroom. These writings need to be accepted and celebrated. The focus should be on scaffolding children's learning by encouraging the use of invented spelling while guiding them toward conventional writing.

First, second, and third grade students also need the opportunity to write for a variety of purposes, including responding to literature. A common approach to teaching writing in the primary grades is known as process writing. When engaged in process writing, children learn and are supported during each step—from prewriting to drafting ("sloppy copy"), revising, editing and proofreading, and publishing. One should keep in mind that in grades one and two, revisions are minimal, but children need to be introduced to them. As children attempt to create their own writing, invented spelling should be encouraged. Not only will children write more when they use invented spelling, but they also will show what they know about sound–symbol correspondences. Teachers who really want to provide high-quality phonics instruction will include a great deal of writing experiences throughout the primary grades.

Fluency

Research has indicated a strong link between reading fluency and comprehension (Pinnell, Pikulski, Wixson, Campbell, Gough, & Beatty, 1995). Fluency occurs when children are reading conventionally on their own, especially in grade two.

Prior to grade two, children typically are learning how to decode and comprehend text. Teachers can do a great deal to help students become fluent readers. As with many aspects of teaching, modeling plays a significant role in children's literacy development. Teachers model fluency through read-alouds and guided reading. Hearing a fluent reader read helps children to hear the cadence and expression of language. Another way of helping children become more fluent in reading is through repeated readings (Samuels, 1979/1997). There are now packaged programs available for classroom use, such as "Read Naturally" and "Quick Reads." While packaged programs may be convenient, repeated reading can be accomplished through engaging, creative means such as Readers' Theater. Of course, one of the best ways to help children develop their fluency is by making sure every child in every class has texts they can read at an independent level. Multiple opportunities to practice with easy reading material is a useful method of fluency instruction.

Real Reading

Reading, reading, reading! In a quality early literacy program, a priority is to provide ample opportunities for children to be engaged with stories, magazines, informational texts, and other print resources. Studies conducted by Anderson, Wilson, and Fielding (1988) and Taylor, Frye, and Maruyama (1990) show a positive correlation between reading competency and time spent reading connected text. In fact, data from Anderson et al. (1988) suggest that if children spend at least 15 minutes a day reading, it makes a significant difference in their reading ability.

An emergent literacy approach that includes the core features of comprehension instruction, word study, writing, reading fluency, and real reading will help ensure that all children, including those students entering our schools with many literacy-related experiences and those who are inexperienced with literacy, will get a successful start to becoming literate. What does such a literacy program look like when we mesh a quality emergent literacy approach with parallel block scheduling? To illustrate, let's follow Andrea, the student we followed throughout the day in chapter 6.

A Day in the Life of Andrea: Literacy Instruction in Kindergarten

Andrea is a kindergarten student in Emergent Literacy Group[2] (ELG) 3, Figure 6.2 (p. 176). From 8:00 to 9:00, Andrea is with teacher C, her homeroom teacher, for opening activities that follow the same routine each day. For the first 20 minutes, children are allowed to choose a center as long as there is space at that center. As the children are arriving at different times, it is a good decision to allow free choice of centers. The teacher spent a good deal of time at the beginning of the year modeling and demonstrating what children could and could not do at each center. This initial investment of time has paid off, and there are seldom problems with behavior or routines.

During center time, the teacher circulates among the centers, greeting each child and helping start the day with a positive experience. Some of the children are drawing at one of the writing centers. As the teacher visits with these children, one child "reads" his picture to her. The teacher notes this in her anecdotal record notebook with the day's date and encourages him to "keep writing." Another child is in the reading center. Although he is unable to read the text, he is creating a story to match the illustrations. The teacher notes this in his record, and she compliments the child's use of dialogue.

At 8:20, the teacher goes to the rocking chair where the children will gather for the day's opening, calendar, and morning message. The children clean up their centers and join the teacher at the rocking chair. The teacher begins the whole-group activity, as she always does, by asking: "What day is it today? What day was yesterday? What day will tomorrow be? What is today's date? What is our weather like today? How many days have we been in school?" As the children answer each question, they find the appropriate word cards (Tuesday, Monday, Wednesday, November 18, rainy) to complete the sentences on the sentence strips in the pocket chart. They count the nine bundles of "tens" (10, 20, 30, etc.) and nine "ones" (ninety-one, ninety-two, ninety-three) to indicate the number of days they have been in school this year, and put them in a pocket chart used to teach place value.

Next, the teacher uses a marker and writes the morning message as the children watch. She doesn't talk as she did at the beginning of the year. She writes as the students quietly read

---

2 While we use the label "Early" Literacy Group throughout chapter 6, Ruth Short used the label "Emergent" Literacy Group in this chapter. We agree that "Emergent" is more descriptive than "Early" in this context.

"Dear Class." She begins the morning message by writing what day it is. As she writes, the children read "Today is Tuesday." She asks them how to spell *today*, *Tuesday*, and *is*. Most of the children know how to spell these words, and those who don't or who are unsure look back at the pocket chart. The teacher writes three more sentences: "We are going to visit the hospital tomorrow. What do we know about hospitals? What do you want to learn about hospitals?" She finishes by writing "Love," and her name.

When the teacher completes the day's beginning routines, she asks the children to read the morning's message with her as she points to the words. She asks Andrea to take the pointer and point to the words as they read it once more. This practice allows the teacher to observe Andrea's ability to track the words as she reads. Teacher C ends this portion of the day by starting a KWL chart about hospitals. This helps prepare the children for the next day's field trip and allows her to model a comprehension strategy. As the children offer information, she records it on another chart.

The children have been sitting for 20 minutes, so the teacher invites them to stand and stretch as tall as they can, to make themselves as wide as they can, as skinny as they can, and as small as they can before having them sit back down. She then takes the next 15 minutes to share the book *Curious George Goes to the Hospital* by H. A. Rey. Since this book is too long to read in the time remaining before students move to their ELGs, she will read the first half of the story now and finish it at the end of the day when she has her homeroom back together.

She begins by introducing the book's title and the names of the author and illustrator. She then invites children to make predictions as to what the story will be about. She encourages them to predict based on the cover's artwork and the title. She turns to the title page and asks for more predictions. Before reading the story, she tells the children to listen carefully to see if any part of the story matches what they already know (from the KWL chart) and to see if they can learn anything about hospitals from the story. This sets a purpose for listening and may help with comprehension.

She then rereads the cover and title page and begins reading the story. She keeps student comments to a minimum in order to model fluent reading while taking a moment to discuss any words the children may not understand. Before finishing the first half of the story, she asks students to predict what will happen in the rest of the story. Their predictions will be an indication of how well they comprehend the story so far. At 8:55, she has the students return to their seats so they will be ready to transition when a teaching assistant arrives to escort them to the first period of their ELG block. Andrea will be going to the Story Area (9:00–9:35).

When the students arrive at the extension area, they are greeted by teacher D and two teaching assistants (TAs). For the next 35 minutes, Andrea's group (ELG 3) and one other group (ELG 5) from another homeroom will be working with the teacher in a shared reading activity. The teacher has selected a nonfiction big book that relates to the upcoming kindergarten field trip. She, too, introduces the book by drawing the children's attention to the cover, the title, and the author and illustrator. They make predictions about the story, based on the title and pictures. The students join in and share the reading of the big book with the teacher, as she prompts them to read the repetitive phrases.

Before turning to the last page, the teacher asks the students to make predictions about the ending. She turns the page and the students are excited because their prediction was correct. They discuss the book and, if time permits, they read and enjoy the book one more time. The teacher then has the students move from the story area to small tables, where they will draw a picture of their favorite part of the story. While they are drawing their pictures, the teacher goes from child to child and helps each student label the picture with words like *hospital*, *doctor*, and *nurse*.

Andrea has been working hard, and at 9:35 her group will move to centers. The TAs supervise the centers where students are working; they also monitor free play of other groups in the room. Centers include a pocket chart center where students will match pictures with initial consonants, a writing center stocked with a variety of writing tools and paper, a computer with headphones for playing an emergent reader game, a listening center where students can use headphones to hear a book on tape, and the dramatic play area. For the past two weeks, in anticipation of the field trip, the dramatic play area has been set up to resemble a doctor's office. The teacher modeled the use of props in the center, including taking phone messages, scheduling appointments, reading magazines while waiting for the doctor, and using a stethoscope to listen to a patient breathe.

Andrea chooses to go to the writing center. While at the writing center, she uses markers and ink stamps to make a birthday card for one of her friends. She looks through greeting cards and finds one that says "Happy Birthday." Then she copies these words on the card she is making, adds her friend's name, and signs it "Love, Andrea." She can spell the word Love on her own since her classroom teacher signs the morning message with that word every day. Her teacher also calls attention to the punctuation so that the children are aware of why these marks are included. Andrea then uses ink stamps, markers and a little glitter to finish decorating the card.

At 10:05, one of the TAs escorts Andrea's group back to their homeroom. Teacher C will work with Andrea's ELG from 10:10 to 10:45. Since she has just the one small group, Andrea's teacher will provide instruction that is designed especially for Andrea's performance level. The teacher initially will have the students engage in picture sorts for beginning consonants b and c, by using the picture cards provided in *Words Their Way* (Bear et al., 2002). The teacher will discuss the pictures, naming any pictures the children are unsure of, before having them place the card with the letters *Bb* and *Cc* on the table in front of them. The students individually then will place the corresponding pictures under the correct initial consonant. In light of the research of the National Reading Panel (2000), attention will be given to both the sound the letters make and how they look.

While the pictures are being sorted by initial consonant, the teacher will be recording the words on a chart, also categorized by initial consonants. For example, under the heading *Bb* the teacher will record the words *bug, book, belt, bed,* and *bat.* Under the heading *Cc* the teacher will record the words *cup, cow, can, car,* and *cat.* The teacher also has a picture next to *Bb,* such as a *boat,* and next to *Cc,* such as a *cap.* Later on, these words and pictures can be used in a matching game, which will have the children listening and matching both beginning and ending consonants.

At 10:50, the other children in Andrea's homeroom return to the classroom. They will be going to lunch and then recess from 10:50 to 11:40. At 11:40, all the kindergarten teachers will have planning time. It is during this time that they meet once or twice a week to plan together with the extension room teacher. By carefully planning the topics/areas/skills to be addressed, the teachers make sure the students will receive multiple exposures to specific material. The extension room team is an integral part in the overall instructional design for helping all the students become successful readers and writers. They offer students extra support in extension lessons and opportunities to engage in enrichment activities.

The afternoon work begins at 12:30, with Andrea's group going back to the extension activities. Initially, Andrea will engage in 30 minutes of free play, monitored by one of the assistants. If this activity has to take place in the extension room when the extension teacher is sharing a book with other students, Andrea's group will be expected to use "indoor voices" while they play games, play in the blocks area, or read with a partner in the "book nook" area of the room. This area is well stocked with books of various genres and levels, including wordless books and big books. This is a favorite area of the students because they are allowed to self-select their reading materials. As you can imagine, many students select books that were shared either by the homeroom teacher or the extension room teacher. At 1:05, Andrea's group goes to assigned centers. Since Andrea was in the writing center in the morning, she will be going to the computer center for 30 minutes in the afternoon.

Andrea knows what to do when she sits at the computer. She places her headset on her head, logs in, and begins to play the emergent reader game. This game has the students follow along with a story as the words are highlighted on the computer. The students hear the story and see the words as the yellow highlight box moves across the screen. Andrea is being exposed to concepts about print that are so important to becoming a reader. She is learning about directionality, concept of word, and punctuation. She is hearing a fluent reader read, exposing her to reading rate, phrasing, and expression—all important elements of becoming a fluent reader. Andrea enjoys the computer time and often will listen to the same story twice. She joins in on her favorite parts and the aide needs to remind Andrea to use a quiet voice when reading along.

Andrea goes back to teacher C, her homeroom teacher, from 1:40 to 2:15. During this time period, the teacher again works only with students in the ELG 3 group. The teacher reviews beginning consonant sounds of *Bb* and *Cc* and involves the students in writing activities by using words from the morning word sorts. The teacher thinks aloud about what she might write. As she writes, she models invented spelling by saying a word slowly and writing down the letters to represent the sounds she hears. In this way the teacher demonstrates for the students many different levels of writing, and shows them that all the levels are acceptable. On this day, the teacher writes the sentence *I uz my bat to hit basebalz*. She talks about the need for an upper case *I* at the beginning of the sentence and the period at the end, and she models using spacing between words.

Then the children review the pictures from the picture sort and individually decide what to write. The teacher also refers back to the chart of words from the morning lesson and helps the children "read" them. Andrea wants to write the sentence *My cat is yellow* and produces the following sentence: *mi cat iz ylo*. The teacher is able to monitor the children's writing because the group is small. She reminds them to start with a capital letter and end with a period. Each child has an alphabet strip to refer to, and Andrea is able to locate the upper case *M*. She corrects her writing and includes the period. The teacher is able to help the children read their sentences aloud to each other. The targeted instruction and activities make children in this group feel like readers and writers.

From 2:15 to 3:00, the teacher meets with her entire homeroom group for activities and unit time. She takes a few minutes for the children to share what they did in extension, and then she returns to *Curious George*. She reads the KWL chart to them as a reminder of the morning's discussion. She asks the children to tell her what had happened in the story so far and invites predictions about what will happen next and how the story will end. She reads the story, stopping before the ending to allow the children to revise their predictions (if they choose to revise) and then finishes reading the story.

The children discuss the story and respond to prompts from the teacher. Then they go back to the KWL chart to discuss anything they might want to add. Someone might say that he knew that ambulances take people to the hospital but he forgot to say that in the morning. The teacher adds that information to the "What I *Know*" column. As other students discuss the story, the teacher decides to have them act out a favorite scene. Two children volunteer to "be Curious George and the doctor" when the doctor takes George's temperature. Others want to show how George looked when he swallowed the puzzle pieces. Their enjoyment of the story is very obvious. The teacher ends the day

with getting the children to think about what they want to *Learn*. The teacher records their questions and tells them what great thinkers they are, and then she has them prepare for dismissal.

Andrea has had a full day of active engagement in her learning. The teachers have successfully coordinated instructional plans and provided both reinforcement and enrichment activities. Andrea and her classmates are well on their way to becoming literate. With over half the year left for instruction, the students should be ready for first grade with a solid beginning in reading and writing.

Literacy Instruction in Grade 2

While we followed Andrea's day, other children were receiving instruction across the school. Figure 6.3 (p. 177) illustrates a schedule for three grade 2 homeroom teachers scheduled with an extension center. Let's follow reading/writing group 3 (RWG-3) through their morning instruction, keeping in mind the basic components of a balanced approach to literacy: comprehension instruction, a multifaceted word study program, writing, reading fluency, and "real reading" of connected text. Student motivation and engagement underlie such an approach.

As you can see from Figure 6.3 (p. 177), all students in grade 2 are with their homeroom teachers from 8:00 to 8:20. This brief but needed time period allows the teachers to take attendance and lunch count, hear morning announcements, and share an opening to the day. In some schools this may include a moment of silence or the Pledge of Allegiance.

As students enter the classroom each morning, they open their journals and begin writing. Their writing can be in response to a teacher prompt written on the board, or it can be a free write. As the teacher completes the initial record keeping, he goes to individual children's desks to check on their writing. Some children may have specific questions, while others may need encouragement to begin writing.

Just before the children prepare to move to the first period of the day, the teacher reads a poem from one of the children's favorite poets, Shel Silverstein. Because the teacher is trying to encourage recreational reading at home while also tying into the poetry unit the second grade students are doing, he reads "Jimmy Jet and His TV Set" from *Where the Sidewalk Ends* (1974). The children then are escorted to their first period class (8:20–9:10), with students in RWG-3 remaining with teacher 2C.

After greeting the 10 students in RWG-3, their homeroom teacher has the students open their poetry folders. They have been reading a wide range of poems, including haikus and concrete poems. The students particularly enjoy the concrete poems, and today they will be asked to begin to write their own poetry. The teacher leads the students in a brainstorming session regarding possible topics and the shapes those topics could take. He then has five of the children join him at the reading table. Even though there are only ten children in the entire group, the teacher knows that there are different levels of instructional need and performance. He wants to provide reading instruction that is fast-paced and at their instructional level. The students have been reading leveled books, and five students in RWG-3 are reading slightly ahead of the other five. The teacher is good about systematically taking running records of the children's

oral reading and moving them through the book levels accordingly. During guided reading today, he reinforces the children's use of cueing strategies. In particular, he observes the children's use of semantic (determining meaning through text and pictures), syntactic (having knowledge of sentence structure and grammar), and graphophonic (understanding symbol-sound correspondence) cueing systems.

To begin the lesson, the children reread a familiar text. The text is at their independent level, so the rereading takes about three minutes. This rereading serves as a warm-up to the reading work to come while providing an opportunity for fluency building and instilling a confident attitude within the young readers. Then the teacher introduces a new book.

Because students in RWG-3 are reading fairly close to grade level, and because they have been working together for almost three months, the teacher leads the children through a modest introduction to the story. At the beginning of the year, the teacher provided a rich introduction, including a picture walk, vocabulary discussion, and predictions about the story. Now the children take picture walks on their own, with the pictures providing less support to the reader. This is why the teacher wants to reinforce the idea of cross-checking cueing systems—strategic readers use all three systems. The teacher asks the students to read the first two pages of the story silently, thus allowing them the opportunity to practice the strategies they've been taught. When the children are done, the teacher asks a couple of questions to check comprehension, and then the students are asked to read silently again.

Following the silent reading, the teacher has the students chorally read the first page together. He draws their attention to an error they all made; they all substituted the word *planet* for the word *planets*. He re-reads the sentence the way the children read it and asks if it "sounds right." Syntactically, it should not sound right since they have been reading about Mars and Earth. He asks if it "looks right." The children respond with, "Yes, it looks right." The teacher now asks the students to look at the ending of the word *planets*. The children notice the ending and then correct their reading. The teacher is able to reinforce their learning by using two cueing systems—graphophonic and syntactic—to correct their reading.

Next the students reread the sentence aloud, with the teacher emphasizing the need to determine if things "look right," "sound right," and "make sense." As these leveled reading materials are getting a bit lengthy, the students will read the second half of the story the following day. The five students who have been working at their seats are invited to join the teacher at the reading table while the students who have just completed their teacher-directed reading instruction return to their seats to begin work on their concrete poems. At the end of the second half of the period, the students in RWG-3 go to Language Arts extension, where they will be from 9:10 to 10:00.

In the extension room, RWG-3 students are joined by students in RWG-4. According to the parallel block grouping pattern for six RWGs, these groups would be functioning at about grade level. The extension staff is able to provide supplemental instruction for all 20 students. Extension personnel will involve the students in whole-class, small-group and individual activities. Because the classroom teachers plan with the extension staff, during extension time students will be provided both enrichment and intervention activities. Enrichment activities for some students most likely will correspond to the poetry unit; at the same time, depending on how the extension program has been staffed, other students may work in individual and small groups that address identified basic reading and writing skills.

The students are partner-reading Sharon Creech's *Love That Dog,* a story about a young boy's coming to grips with the death of his dog. It is written in prose style, and the students in the story also are studying poetry. Before having the children partner-read, a member of the extension staff reads a chapter from Kate DiCamillo's Newberry Honor book *Because of Winn-Dixie*. She has the students reconstruct the story thus far before beginning her read-aloud. Afterward, she has the students retrieve their literature logs and free-write any reactions to the chapter just read, encouraging them to make personal connections to the story whenever possible.

After 15 minutes, she asks eight students to join her at a table where they will begin completing a Venn diagram that compares and contrasts the main characters from the two books. They will brainstorm ideas with the teacher, who records the ideas on a chart while they fill in the Venn diagram. Later, the students will be asked to find specific examples from the texts to support their character descriptions. This is just one example of involving students in rereading text and developing fluency.

While the teacher is working with eight students, four are sharing two computers, looking for author information at the website of author Creech (www.sharoncreech.com) and the website for *Winn-Dixie* (www.winndixie.com)—information they will present to the rest of the students in RWG-3 and RWG-4. Three sets of partners are reading *Love That Dog* in various spots around the room. When the teacher calls the next group to the table, the students will rotate assignments, with some students going to the *Winn-Dixie* website to find a recipe for a special punch while others engage in partner-reading. Because the extension staff has these same students every day for 50 minutes, the rotations will continue the next day.

At 10:00, RWG-3 and RWG-6 return to teacher 2C, their homeroom teacher, for 50 minutes of whole-group instruction in social studies and language arts. For the past few days, the teacher has been running a Writers' Workshop, with students writing about personal artifacts, in response to teacher prompts, and self-selected topics based on their instruction from both social studies and language arts. The teacher has been coaching the students through the writing process by modeling prewriting (brainstorming), writing rough drafts (sloppy copy), peer conferencing, revising, editing, and publishing. At the second grade level, revisions are minimal but students are introduced to the concept. Publishing can be done informally by sharing writing during author's chair (Graves, 1995) or posting pieces in the room, or more formally by creating a bound book for the classroom or school library.

Writing facilitates young children's literacy development in two main ways. First, teaching writing helps students develop skills about composing and strategies that are critical for success in school (and life). Composing involves creating descriptions, characters, stories, and expository writing. Students learn how to combine ideas in a variety of ways for many purposes. Second, research indicates that there is a strong connection between reading and writing. Shanahan (1984) found that for second graders, there was a high correlation between phonic knowledge in reading and spelling knowledge. Additionally, encouraging students to use invented spelling allows teachers to observe what children know about sound–symbol relations. The Writers' Workshop offers daily opportunities for the teacher to provide mini-lessons on any number of topics, ranging from capitalization and punctuation to vocabulary and word study.

Following their reading/language arts block (8:20–10:50), the teachers and students in our sample grade 2 schedule (Figure 6.3, p. 177) go to lunch/recess or recess/lunch. Then they move into their mathematics/science block (11:40–3:00), broken by their encore classes (1:20–2:10). In some schools, the core teachers (2A, 2B, and 2C) teach math and science when they have their two combined math groups (MGs), while in other schools a science specialist teaches the combined groups in what Figure 6.3 shows as math extension groups. For example, if a science specialist staffed the extension center from 11:40–3:00, MGs 2 and 6 would receive science instruction during period 5, MGs 3 and 4 during period 6, and MGs 1 and 5 during period 8.

Combining math groups from the various homerooms for science instruction allows all grade 2 students one period of math in a combined group and one in a reduced-size group each day. (See chapter 8 for details on using the Concept-Mastery model with this grouping pattern.) When each of the core second grade teachers teaches science in the combined groups, the extension staff provides intervention and enrichment during the extension periods. In these schools, extension during the math block might include computer lab time in addition to small, rotating, data-determined intervention groups taught by math specialists, special education, teacher assistants, ESL and TAG personnel. In a few schools, usually depending on accountability factors present in the primary grades, both science and social studies might be offered during the math extension time, but we typically find this arrangement to be more prevalent in the upper grades than in the lower grades.

The students in this second grade classroom are in a very supportive educational environment. Their homeroom teachers make maximum use of small-group guided reading and writing strategies, and they use such activities as Writers' Workshop, Readers' Theater, partner reading, and other activities to connect and consolidate instruction. Their common planning time with the extension staff enables the three grade 2 teachers to engage their students throughout the day in a very active, integrated learning environment, and students have multiple opportunities to participate in both enrichment activities and interventions, when needed.

The homeroom teacher, extension teacher, and support staff are able to offer instruction that reinforces, enhances, and enriches concepts taught across the school day. Whether children are in kindergarten or second grade, reducing class size for even a portion of the school day, choosing sensible grouping options and using parallel block scheduling creates positive experiences for children and primary grade teachers.

References

Anderson, R. C., Wilson, P., & Fielding, L. G. (1988). Growth in reading and how children spend their time outside of school. *Reading Research Quarterly, 23,* 285–303.

Bear, D. H., Invernizzi, M., Templeton, S., & Johnston, F. (2004). *Words their way: Word study for phonics, vocabulary, and spelling instruction.* (3rd ed.). Upper Saddle River, NJ: Merrill.

Blachowicz, C., & Fisher, P. (1996). *Teaching vocabulary in all classrooms.* Englewood Cliffs, NJ: Merrill.

Creech, S. (2001). *Love that dog.* New York: HarperCollins.

Cunningham, P. M. (2000). *Phonics they use: Words for reading and writing.* New York: HarperCollins.

DiCamillo, K. (2001). *Because of Winn-Dixie.* Cambridge, MA: Candlewick Press.

Donat, D. J. (2003). Reading their way: A balance of phonics and whole language. Lanham, MD: Scarecrow Press.

Gambrell, L. B., & Dromsky, A. (2000). Fostering reading comprehension. In D. S. Strickland & L. M. Morrow (Eds.), *Beginning reading and writing* (pp. 145–153). Newark, DE: International Reading Association.

Gambrell, L. B., Koskinen, P. S., & Kapinus, B. A. (1991). Retelling and the reading comprehension of proficient and less proficient readers. *Journal of Educational Research, 6,* 356–362.

Gaskins, I. (1996). Word detectives: Benchmark extended word identification program for beginning readers. Media, PA: Benchmark Press.

Graves, D. H. (1995). *A fresh look at writing.* Portsmouth, NH: Heinemann.

National Reading Panel. (2000). Teaching children to read: An evidence-based assessment of the scientific research literature on reading and its implications for reading instruction. Washington, DC: National Reading Panel.

Ogle, D. (1986). K-W-L: A teaching model that develops active reading of expository text. *The Reading Teacher, 39,* 564–570.

Pinnell, G. S., Pikulski, J. J., Wixson, K. K., Campbell, J.R., Gough, P. B., & Beatty, A. S. (1995). *Listening to children read aloud: Oral fluency.* Washington, DC: U. S. Department of Education, National Center for Educational Statistics.

Samuels, S. J. (1979/1997). The method of repeated reading. *The Reading Teacher, 32/50,* 403–408/376–381.

Shanahan, T. (1984). Nature of the reading-writing relation: An exploratory multivariate analysis. *Journal of Educational Psychology, 76,* 466–477.

Silverstein, S. (1974). *Where the sidewalk ends.* New York: Harper & Row.

Strickland, D. S., & Morrow, L. M. (Eds.). (1989). *Emerging literacy: Young children learn to read and write.* Newark, DE: International Reading Association.

Taylor, B. M., Frye, B. J., & Maruyama, G. M. (1990). Time spent reading and reading growth. *American Educational Research Journal, 27,* 351–362.

Teale, W.H., & Sulzyb, E. (Eds.). (1986). *Emergent literacy: Writing and reading.* Norwood, NJ: Ablex.

Teale, W. H., & Yokota, J. (2000). Beginning reading and writing: Perspectives on instruction. In D. S. Strickland and L. M. Morrow (Eds.), *Beginning reading and writing* (pp. 3–21). New York: Teachers College Press.

10

Language Arts Instruction in Grades 3, 4, and 5: Planning for the Parallel Block Schedule

Karen Broaddus[1]

Overview of Language Arts Instruction in a Parallel Block Schedule

Parallel block scheduling (PBS) in the elementary language arts program provides a flexible setting in which teachers can group students for explicit instruction. Reading, writing, listening, and speaking activities are embedded across the language arts schedule in whole-class activities, small-group instruction, and extension work. This chapter describes one way to organize language arts in PBS to make optimal use of the teacher's instructional time with the whole class and with small groups. To demonstrate how time is structured in PBS, extended examples will be provided of whole-class time during a week in Ms. Naylor's third grade class, small-group lessons in Ms. Padilla's

1 Karen Broaddus teaches English at Woodberry Forest School in Virginia. She is a former college professor in reading. Her research interests include reading comprehension, engagement, and writing instruction. Dr. Broaddus may be contacted at Karen_Broaddus@woodberry.org.

fifth grade class, and extension time with Ms. Hope for one of the small groups from Mr. Edward's fourth grade class. In addition, short examples will be provided for whole-class and small-group instruction at each grade level to describe instruction and grouping in each setting during the same week. Resources are listed for further information on specific techniques and materials.

This model outlines one effective way to support student learning in the language arts. In PBS, the classroom base teacher takes primary responsibility for assessment and explicit instruction in comprehension, fluency, word knowledge, and writing during whole-class and small-group meetings. The extension class expands the time students have for guided practice in reading and writing. The extension teacher supports engaged reading and writing activities that provide students with the time to develop fluency by using the skills introduced and practiced in the classroom.

These organizational decisions need to be made by a planning team that includes both administrators and teachers at the local school site. Initially, the team should examine curricular guidelines and the school district's goals for meeting state and national standards in the language arts. Next, the team should consider the types of expertise that both classroom and extension teachers bring to the teaching of reading and writing. With careful attention to these two critical areas of instruction, realistic adaptations can be made to the model presented in this chapter to meet curricular goals and to address the varying needs of students in a particular grade or school setting. Before beginning this discussion, it will be important for the instructional team to consider the areas in which explicit teaching, guided

learning, and independent practice are essential in language arts instruction.

Essential Elements of Language Arts Instruction

Language arts instruction in grades 3, 4, and 5 needs to be grounded in clear, modeled instruction in four areas: word knowledge, fluency, comprehension, and writing. Using a parallel block schedule allows the classroom teacher to provide explicit instruction at developmentally appropriate levels to small groups of students or to individual students in a workshop setting. To understand why using this type of varied grouping is important for language arts instruction, consider what we know about evidence-based teaching in each of the four instructional areas.

Word Knowledge

Instruction in word knowledge includes the modeling of word analysis through spelling and vocabulary activities. In the elementary grades, students use their knowledge of letter sounds, word patterns, and meanings or derivations to read and spell words (Bear & Templeton, 1998; Henderson, 1990). Word analysis certainly is not an end in itself; however, this base of knowledge about how words work provides a foundation for building other language arts skills. Fluency in reading (e.g., development of sight words and decoding skills), comprehension of text (e.g., understanding of vocabulary words), and fluency in writing (e.g., ability to spell) all depend on word knowledge. Since learning about words is developmental, the best setting for this instruction is during small-group time when the teacher is able to work with developmental word-study groups to examine appropriate features about words. However, word study need not be limited to this type of leveled group work. It also is important to include instructional activities with the whole class that encourage language play and the examination of word meanings. For example, close text analysis can be modeled by the teacher after a class read-aloud. One approach would be to demonstrate how to create poetry from strong nouns and verbs in a passage; another approach would be to model how to analyze quotes in a double-entry journal (Worthy, Broaddus, & Ivey, 2001, pp. 175–185).

Fluency

The second area of focus, reading fluency, is a complex notion in the elementary grades: "Like music, it consists not only of rate, accuracy, and automaticity, but also of phrasing, smoothness, and expressiveness. Fluency gives language its musical quality, its rhythm and flow, and makes reading sound effortless" (Worthy & Broaddus, 2001/2002, p. 334). Since fluency and engagement go hand in hand with reading comprehension, this is a central component of language arts instruction. As expectations increase for students in the upper elementary grades to comprehend independent, silent reading of varied types of text, the need for explicit instruction becomes apparent. Perhaps the best time for teachers to provide effective coaching in fluency is in the small-group setting when students are able to practice reading individually or in pairs; however, fluency also can be supported in the whole class setting through teacher modeling during class read-alouds with direct explanation of the finer points of fluent reading. Because scripts include varied reading levels, teachers can direct the rehearsal and performance of Readers' Theater scripts in heterogeneous groups during whole-class time (Worthy et al., 2001, pp. 125–135). This type of fluency practice, which focuses on meaning through oral interpretation, paves the way for strategic reading.

Comprehension

When the demands of content-area reading increase in third, fourth, and fifth grades, comprehension takes on a central role in the language arts. Now students must learn to be strategic in their silent reading. As the team sets up language arts instruction in a parallel block schedule (PBS), time must be provided for teachers to learn about individual students as readers. Bomer (1999) describes this type of one-on-one work as "running alongside" the reader, or using deliberate coaching to support a student in making sense of text. Small-group time with the classroom teacher is ideal for this type of expert coaching, which allows the teacher to model the mental processes of reading and to demonstrate explicitly how a good reader makes decisions about text (Duffy, Roehler, & Herrmann, 1988). Because engagement is so closely linked to understanding text, another key decision in PBS is creating settings that encourage and support comprehension in whole-class, small-group, and extension time. Guthrie notes, "…engaging classroom contexts are observational, self-directed, strategic, collaborative, self-expressive, and coherent" (1996, p. 436). Inquiry is a key component in creating these contexts, which naturally links strategic reading with meaningful writing experiences. Students not only need plenty of time to read, but they also need access to varied reading materials and designated times to research and write about interesting topics (Ivey & Broaddus, 2000).

Writing

As students continue to enhance their writing skills in the upper elementary grades, there should be opportunities to develop both fluency in drafting and expertise in employing different forms of writing. This is where the foundation is laid for using different forms of exposition such as cause/effect, description, or problem/solution. In particular, upper elementary students need instructional support in how to find and record the information from content trade books as they conduct independent research on writing topics (Harvey, 1998; Swan, 2003). Writing instruction is ideal for PBS; workshop time can be orchestrated easily within whole-class time. In this approach, the teacher demonstrates writing techniques in focused mini-lessons and then guides students as they draft, conference, and share their writing (Fletcher & Portalupi, 2001). Extension time provides a place where students can continue to experiment with new forms of writing and develop fluency with these techniques in their learning logs or writers' notebooks (Harwayne, 2001, pp. 41–79).

Expert Teaching

"Good teaching is always a passionate and personal accomplishment" (Allington & Johnston, 2002, p. 4). In PBS, maintaining a focus on the essentials—word knowledge, fluency, comprehension, and writing—remains only part of the challenge. Deciding how to support teacher expertise is just as important. As PBS is being implemented, consider what Allington (2002) calls the "6 Ts" of effective instruction: *time, texts, teach, talk, tasks*, and *test*. In his work with expert elementary literacy teachers, Allington found that having adequate *time*

designated to reading and writing was essential. In exemplary classrooms, students spent half of their school day in engaged reading and writing activities. *Texts* also played a key role. Good teachers provided interesting, diverse materials for their students in a collection that included plenty of easy reading and also adequate complexity of texts for all levels of students. Explicit *teaching* demonstrations with expert instructional *talk* made certain that students understood how good readers handle text. *Tasks* for students were substantial and allowed for individual choice, and *testing* emphasized teacher evaluation of student work and improvement over time. PBS allows teachers to organize their time with students in a way that optimizes expert instructional time while including the extension setting for guided practice in language arts activities.

The Role of the Classroom Teacher

Initial Assessments

The classroom teacher carries primary responsibility for assessing students' reading and writing skills, designing instruction, and recording student progress. As the school year begins, initial sessions of small-group time need to include assessments that allow the teacher to get to know learners and that gather information about students' comprehension, fluency, word identification, and writing (Worthy et al., 2001, pp. 21–52). In these early weeks, teachers make use of instructional approaches that allow them to begin to know students. Surveys administered to the whole class provide information on individual students' reading and writing attitudes and preferences (pp. 291–293). An informal writing project, such as keeping student–teacher dialogue journals (pp. 28–30), provides useful data about students' writing fluency, the structure of writing, vocabulary usage, and interests. Assigning this type of independent writing task also provides time for the teacher to assess individual students' reading skills.

Whole-Class Instruction Focused on Comprehension and Writing

Comprehension and writing are the primary areas of focus for whole-class work. Both areas require that the teacher explicitly demonstrate techniques and guide students as they apply new learning. Mini-lessons allow the teacher to introduce new information through brief but content-rich lessons on approaches that students are ready to use in their work (Atwell, 1998). Sometimes a mini-lesson might be on a topic directed toward the entire class (e.g., how to write a lead in a newspaper article), while at other points special topics might be addressed to a smaller group ready to learn or review specific information during workshop time (e.g., how to use quotation marks and tags in dialogue). Explicit instruction is followed by writing workshop time, when the teacher individualizes instruction to meet varied student needs. Mini-lessons include the study of literary elements and grammar; students apply new understandings of writing techniques and editing approaches to their own writing in the workshop sessions. In general, mini-lessons last between 15 and 20 minutes; the rest of whole-class time is used for interactive writing or guided, individual practice with students.

An extended example follows of how Ms. Naylor covers required content in her third grade class in PBS; then shorter examples follow of whole-class instruction in grades 4 and 5 classrooms. Table 10.1 provides an overview of sample topics covered in PBS for each grade during this weekly schedule.

Table 10.1. Sample Instructional Plans in a PBS for Grades 3, 4, and 5

PBS Groups	Grade 3: Ms. Naylor	Grade 4: Mr. Edwards	Grade 5: Ms. Padilla
Whole-class mini-lessons and workshop	Persuasive and descriptive letters about content	Science poetry and the research process	Biographical writing and interviews
Small-group reading and writing	Writing and performing Readers' Theater scripts from books used to study first- and third-person perspectives	Independent research in science trade books; written entries in learning logs	Paired reading of biographies; selecting quotes from reading for analysis in double-entry journals
Small-group word knowledge	Word wall work and word-study groups	Content vocabulary and word-study groups	Word-study groups using word sorts, word hunts, and writing sorts
Extension	◆ Independent reading/writing ◆ Teacher read-alouds ◆ Book talks ◆ Performance reading		

Writing Persuasive Letters in a Grade 3 Classroom

Ms. Naylor uses whole-class time to cover specific reading and writing standards set by her state in the English language arts. In reading, these guidelines include the use of specific comprehension strategies. In writing, the standards contain items on writing descriptions, letters, and simple explanations with different types of content. This week during her whole-class time, Ms. Naylor wants to be certain that all her students are comfortable with the format used for letter writing. As a group, they also will explore different purposes for writing letters.

♦ *Setting the stage.* Across the school week, Ms. Naylor and her students work through the following procedures together to learn more about writing effective letters. At the beginning of the school year, she introduced her students to the conventions of letter writing with dialogue journals. These informal letters to the teacher allowed the students to gain fluency in writing by concentrating on topics about themselves. In these initial letters back and forth with students in their dialogue journals, Ms. Naylor supported her students in the use of clear descriptions and narrative structure in their writing by modeling storytelling in her own letters. In this week's focus on letter writing, Ms Naylor wants to extend her students' understanding of how to use persuasive writing and description in their letters. To meet the state standard of using different writing forms across content areas, she plans to examine how historical and scientific information can be presented in letters.

♦ *Engaging students' interest and examining the form of writing.* First, to engage her students in the topic, Ms. Naylor begins with a read aloud of Mark Teague's hilarious picture book, *Dear Mrs. LaRue: Letters from Obedience School* (2002). She wants her students to think carefully about why Teague chooses to show letters penned by Ike, a "bad" dog who finds himself sent away to the Igor Brotweiler Canine Academy to learn how to behave. To support students' development of comprehension strategies, she uses a "think aloud" technique as she reads, demonstrating how a good reader connects text to what s/he already knows, makes predictions, uses images to understand text, monitors his/her own comprehension, and fixes that comprehension (Worthy et al., 2001, pp. 87–89). As students model how they think through text as readers, she invites students to join the conversation and discuss how Ike is using letters to attempt to persuade Mrs. LaRue to let him come home.

♦ *Considering connections to prior learning about writing.* After the read-aloud, Ms. Naylor asks her students to revisit two books that they had compared in an earlier mini-lesson about using perspective in writing. *I Am the Dog, I Am the Cat* (Hall, 1994) is written in the first-person perspectives of a dog and a cat, whereas *Hondo and Fabian* (McCarty, 2002) is written in third-person perspective. These books present similar plotlines about the daily lives of a dog and a cat that live together. Using an overhead, Ms. Naylor returns to examine the first two pages of Teague's book about Ike. First, a newspaper article reports the dog's enrollment in obedience school, then a letter from Ike describes the school as a prison. Students are asked to identify the different perspectives taken in the newspaper article and in the letter. One student reads a line from *I Am the Dog, I Am the Cat* and shows how it uses the same first-person perspective as Teague uses in the first line of the letter composed by Ike. The text of *Hondo and Fabian* is compared to the news article on the first page. Ms. Naylor also asks the students to find several different ways that Teague has made *Dear Mrs. LaRue* humorous. Students point out how Ike exaggerates in his letters. The black and white, prison-like sketches also make his situation seem desperate; however, color illustrations on the same page reveal that obedience school is not that bad after all.

♦ *Interactive writing to explore the form of a letter.* As a wrap-up for the whole-class lesson, Ms. Naylor and the class extend Ike's story by composing one last letter from the dog to Mrs. LaRue. Writing on a chart, Ms. Naylor points out the format for the letter used by Teague in his book. Together, the class decides on the date the dog might write to convince Mrs. LaRue that he must remain at home. Even though Ike had escaped from obedience school, he did save Mrs. LaRue's life in the process. Ms. Naylor models how she writes the first line of the letter from the dog's perspective; Ike argues that he needs to stay home in order to protect Mrs. LaRue. Next, she invites students to suggest what should come next in the letter. They discuss the dog's purpose for the letter, and they decide that it is to convince Mrs. LaRue to never send Ike away to obedience school again. Together, they brainstorm a list of reasons why the dog needs to be at home; then Ms. Naylor guides the students in shaping the rest of the letter and the closing.

♦ *Teacher modeling and student writing time.* The next day Ms. Naylor introduces her students to a resource book they can consult as they write: *Messages in the Mailbox: How to Write a Letter* (Leedy, 1991). She does a book talk as she walks through the text by reading aloud several short excerpts. She points out how the format of the book and specific headings help her find answers to her questions about how to set up different types of letters. She stops on the section on persuasive writing, and by engaging the whole class, she compares the guidelines for persuasive writing with the letters that they read together yesterday in *Dear Mrs. LaRue*. On the board, she creates a quick outline for writing her own letter. Ms. Naylor has decided to request that a traffic light be added at an intersection close to her home; she lists three reasons for her request with accompanying examples. On the overhead, Ms. Naylor shows how she drafts her letter, using the business form from the Leedy book and referring back to the information on her outline on the board. After a few minutes of modeling, she puts down her pen and asks students to help her list other good topics for persuasive letters. One girl wants to request that the school sponsor a soccer team for girls. Another girl says that she will try to convince her parents that their family should have an aquarium at home. A boy decides to ask the PTO for picnic tables outside the cafeteria. The students begin their own graphic organizers, which are charts that organize brief descriptions in boxes of the reasons for the letter, several examples of supporting evidence, and a reasonable solution (Worthy et al., p. 288). Ms. Naylor provides individual assistance to students as they use their graphic organizers to begin their drafts of persuasive letters.

◆ *Extending letter writing to historical and scientific content.* As students gain competence during the week with persuasive writing about familiar topics, Ms. Naylor begins to introduce geography, history, and science books that use correspondence to describe content information. First, they read several of the letters written by a traveling teacher that are sent back to her class in the picture book *Around the World: Who's Been Here?* (George, 1999). They also look at collections of postcards that describe children's trips, such as *Postcards from France* (Arnold, 1996) and *Stringbean's Trip to the Shining Sea* (Williams, 1988). They consider a few letters in books on familiar historical topics, such as the portrait of life on a wagon train in *Dear Levi: Letters*

from the Overland Trail (Woodruff, 1994) or the description of seeing slavery for the first time in *Nettie's Trip South* (Turner, 1987). Last, they look together at how scientific description is used in *Postcards from Pluto: A Tour of the Solar System* (Leedy, 1993). Next week, Ms. Naylor will guide her students to use trade books to collect information for their descriptive letter writing. They will collect their information on a graphic organizer that highlights four key characteristics of a topic with lists of specific details (Worthy et al., p. 283). After writing several drafts on different topics, students and their peers will select one final letter or postcard to edit for publication in the history, geography, or science collections in the classroom library.

Content-Area Poetry in a Grade 4 Classroom

In Mr. Edwards' class, students are using whole-class time to learn about the research process and how an author uses scientific detail in writing. In pairs, they examine texts about different animals and record facts in their learning logs (Broaddus & Ivey, 2002, p. 149). To highlight the use of specific detail, Mr. Edwards guides students in how to use these scientific observations in their learning logs to form poems (Chancer & Rester-Zodrow, 1997, pp. 89–91; Cullinan, Scala, & Schroder, 1995, pp. 65–71). Beginning with models of observational poems from Fletcher's *Ordinary Things: Poems from a Walk in Early Spring* (1997), he and his students rehearse and perform readings. This type of repeated reading allows students to examine Fletcher's use of detail in this free-verse poetry and to consider the author's line breaks. To familiarize students with how to organize their learning logs to collect information for their poems, Mr. Edwards shares published field journals. Books such as Wright-Frierson's *A North American Rain Forest Scrapbook* (1999), Cole's *On the Way to the Beach* (2003), and Arnosky's *Field Trips: Bug Hunting, Animal Tracking, Birdwatching, Shore Walking* (2002) show how scientists collect information in drawings, labels, and descriptions. Next week, as students are collecting observations from their reading, Mr. Edwards plans to do a mini-lesson on the use of strong verbs (Portalupi & Fletcher, 2001, p. 73) and scientific vocabulary to help students focus on specific language. Students will use the facts collected in their writer's notebooks to form "quick write" descriptions of each observation; then they will use the technique of found poems (Worthy et al., pp. 181–183) to harvest the specific words for their final poems. A content editing checklist will allow the teacher to evaluate each stage of their research and writing (Worthy et al., p. 299).

Writing Biographies in a Grade 5 Classroom

Ms. Padilla's class has been studying biographical writing. This week, students are focusing on how to conduct a personal interview about a specific event in order to write a brief incident biography. On the board, Ms. Padilla and the class brainstorm a list of specific topics that would work well for a focused interview with a family member, a neighbor, or a member of the school community. They generated topics for an interview such as a memory of severe weather (e.g., hurricane, tornado) or an experience during a historical event (e.g., nurse during the Gulf War). As a model for research, Ms. Padilla shares a book that contains actual interviews conducted by a fifth grade class during their project on civil rights. She and a student perform one of these interviews from *Oh, Freedom! Kids Talk about the Civil Rights Movement with the People Who Made It Happen* (King & Osborne, 1997) as a demonstration of how to ask questions and how to take notes on responses. The class discusses which questions proved most effective, and they brainstorm other questions that might be appropriate for an interview of someone they know. In conclusion, Ms. Padilla goes over guidelines for interviewing that she developed from *Nonfiction Matters: Reading, Writing, and Research in Grades 3–8* (Harvey, 1998, pp. 108–115), and her students leave with a sample interview form from her demonstration. When students return with their own interview notes and are ready to begin on their first drafts, Ms. Padilla plans to do a mini-lesson on how to use quotations in nonfiction writing (Portalupi & Fletcher, 2001, p. 91).

Small-Group Instruction in Word Knowledge and Reading Fluency

In PBS, whole-class sessions provide time for each teacher to cover required content with all the students in the class. Individual practice is supervised during workshop sessions. Small-group sessions complement whole-class instruction by providing daily time for students to work together at appropriate levels. Because successful instruction in word knowledge and reading fluency depends on working with students at appropriate stages of development, these areas work well as points of focus for small-group sessions.

Small-Group Instruction in a Grade 5 Classroom

We will examine how Ms. Padilla sets up word study and fluency practice in her fifth grade classroom. Word study work typically lasts for 15 minutes during the small-group period, and reading fluency is the focus for the remainder of the period. Here is how Ms. Padilla organizes her classroom for small-group work:

♦ *Setting up word-study groups.* Initially, Ms. Padilla administers a qualitative spelling inventory (Bear, Invernizzi, Templeton, & Johnston, 2004, pp. 296–327) to her whole class in order to determine each student's developmental knowledge of word features. This quick developmental assessment allows the teacher to set up word-study groups that focus on varied topics such as learning about phonetic spelling, examining the vowel patterns in words, analyzing multisyllabic words, and studying word derivations. In addition to what students learn about spelling, the strategic study of words by sound, pattern, and meaning also supports students' development of strategies for decoding words and for understanding new vocabulary.

Ms. Padilla found that her students were working on four basic levels. Two of the groups were in her first small-group section, and two of the groups were in the second small-group section. Her instructional approach included the same weekly schedule for word study for all of these groups: introduction and analysis of new word patterns, research and practice using the new words, applications of this word-study feature to current reading and writing, sorting word cards for automaticity and review, and assessment of the feature studied (Worthy et al., 2001, pp. 210–211). When a group completes the study of a new feature, the feature is added to a list on students' editing checklists in their writing folders. Students are responsible for editing and correcting spelling errors for all of the features listed after a draft is completed.

♦ *Word analysis activities at the phonetic and vowel pattern level.* In her first small group, Ms. Padilla has a group of students who are able to spell beginning and ending consonant sounds in words, but occasionally they have problems representing initial consonant blends (e.g., *gr*, *sw*, *bl*) and consonant digraphs (e.g., *ch*, *sh*, *th*). In addition, they occasionally make errors in representing the short vowel sounds in the middle of words. These students have been studying word families with a flip chart that allows them to change the beginning sound (e.g., s*at*, ch*at*, fl*at*), and they are becoming more confident reading and writing using these patterns. Several of her students are English language learners and need additional support with vocabulary development. Today, Ms. Padilla assigns this group of students to work in pairs on "word hunts" for words that begin with consonant digraphs. Each student enters a new word in a personal alphabet book with a small drawing and a sentence. Students look for words in magazines they find easy to read, such as *Spider*, or in books they have already read in class.

Ms. Padilla's second word-study group has mastered short vowels and consonant blends and digraphs, but they are inconsistent in representing long vowel patterns in their spelling. These students sort word cards to gain automaticity by distinguishing long and short "a" vowel patterns. First they sort by sound into two columns (e.g., short "a" vs. long "a") and then by vowel pattern into four columns (e.g., p*a*t, c*a*ke, r*a*in, h*a*y). After completing the sort several times for speed and accuracy, the students enter their words in these columns in their word-study notebooks for the teacher to check at a later time.

♦ *Word analysis activities at the syllable and derivational level.* In her second small-group class, Ms. Padilla has a group of students studying at the syllable level who are learning about how inflectional endings such as "ed" and "ing" are added to words. These students have been comparing words with "o" vowel patterns in which the consonant doubles when an ending is added (e.g., hopping, plotting) with words that lose the final silent "e" (e.g., coping, smoking). Today, they are doing a writing sort. The teacher has given them a list of base words (e.g., hope, shop, vote), and they have been asked to write the word with the "ing" ending under one of the following exemplars, "hopping" or "smoking." Next, they try a new sort with additional "o" patterns (Worthy et al. 2001, p. 204).

The second group in this class is working on word derivations by looking at prefixes that have negative meanings (e.g., non-, un-, dis-) and base words. Today, they are dividing up in teams to do some dictionary work to collect 20 to 25 known words for each prefix on index cards. After posting these cards on a bulletin board, each team selects two favorite "challenge" words to highlight without accompanying information; other students in the class will try to guess the definitions from derivational clues in the words.

♦ *Fluency practice.* Word knowledge work takes about 15 minutes daily of each small-group time period. Some teachers prefer to set aside a more extended time on alternating days, such as a 30-minute period two days a week. The rest of small-group time is designated for reading fluency practice with a focus on comprehension. This morning, both of Ms. Padilla's small groups of students are reading aloud in pairs from biographies and recording quotes for analysis in their double-entry journals (Worthy et al., 2001, pp. 178–181). As she works with each pair of readers, Ms. Padilla keeps anecdotal notes on her observational chart for the small group. She records the text used, the reading fluency of each student, and how comprehension strategies are employed. The students are considering the different forms a biography can take. They have studied how authors write about a person's lifetime, a phase in the person's life, or a single incident. In particular, Ms. Padilla supports student pairs as they select quotes to analyze how an author reveals character motivation. She first helps each pair to coach each other during their reading, then guides them in the selection and analysis of quotes.

To support the fluency of diverse readers, Ms. Padilla has provided a wide range of formats for biography at different levels of difficulty. For example, *Freedom River* (Rappaport, 2000) looks at one incident in John Parker's life, a harrowing escape on the Underground Railroad. *Carver: A Life in Poems* (Nelson, 2001) uses poetry "snapshots" to provide detailed portraits of points in George Washington Carver's life. *Mountain Men: True Grit and Tall Tales* (Glass, 2001) combines a collection of short-incident biographies with the tall tales connected with the actual men. Later in the week, each pair creates a graphic chart to organize the biographical information in the book they read together. The book on slavery works well in a narrative graphic, while the information in the Carver book fits best on a timeline with dates and headings about important events. The pair of students working on the mountain men may decide to compare the short biographies on a chart. The pairs will present their graphic charts and a rehearsed reading of favorite quotes to their group.

Small-Group Time in Grade 3

Word knowledge work at the grade 3 level also includes work in word-study groups. In addition, Ms. Naylor reinforces the learning of sight words with a word wall of high-frequency words (Cunningham, 2000) to help less-practiced readers gain fluency in reading and move toward more conventional spelling. This week fluency practice in Ms. Naylor's class is focused on writing and performing Readers' Theater scripts (Worthy & Broaddus 2001/2002). The final performances will take place in the extension class with a new audience. Ms. Naylor typically includes two or three rehearsal groups in small-group time to be sure that each student has plenty of practice reading. The students have created their scripts from the books about pets that

they used to study first and third person perspectives. The first group takes one short chapter with lots of dialogue from *A Bit More Bert* (Ahlberg & Briggs, 2002) to create a performance script. They found that "Bert's Dog Again" includes reading parts for six performers: two narrators, Bert, a policeman, a policewoman, and a sergeant. The second group uses short poems or stanzas from *Love That Dog* (Creech, 2001) to set up a series of first-person readings.

Small-Group Time in Grade 4

In addition to their work in word-study groups, Mr. Edwards uses his small-group time in grade 4 to help his students learn more about the content vocabulary that they will need to use in their poems about animals. He also wants his students to learn new techniques for finding information in science trade books. In particular, one priority in Mr. Edwards' small-group time is to provide individual coaching for students during silent, independent reading. This is key instructional time for supporting less-skilled readers, teaching new skills to individual students, and monitoring progress (Worthy et al., 2001, pp. 107–118). In this setting, Mr. Edwards can model the appropriate selection of reading materials and then fine-tune fluency and comprehension instruction for the reader. He keeps anecdotal notes, which are observational records of these conferences, with written goals set for each student.

To help students keep a record of the creatures they are examining in their reading, he demonstrates how to set up learning logs modeled after the *Snakes, Salamanders, and Lizards (Take-along Guides)* (Burns, 1995). Each page of the log has a header for the name of the creature, then boxes for tips on how to find it, what it looks like, what it eats, where it lives, and a place at the side for interesting facts. There is a box at the bottom of the page for students to write down the title and pages of the book in which they located this information. These learning logs not only guide the students to read for specific information, but they also provide a record of reading and a source of information for future writing. As a group wrap-up after independent reading, he and his students add new content vocabulary words to their bulletin board, grouping new terms under exemplars such as "habitat" or "species."

The Role of the Extension Teacher

Extension time is focused on student engagement in the language arts of reading, writing, listening, and speaking. This daily period provides practice time for students to extend the skills introduced by the classroom teacher during whole-class and small-group instruction. There are three activities around which extension time should be organized. First, the top priority for each week is to set aside uninterrupted time for sustained, silent reading in high-interest materials. Second, the extension time needs to include activities in which students can fine-tune their listening and speaking skills through teacher read-alouds, teacher and student book talks, and reading performances. Speaking skills also are developed during whole-class and small-group book discussions. Last, the extension period is a time for free-choice writing in personal journals, through letters to pen-pals, or in group publications such as a classroom newspaper.

An efficient way to structure extension time is to provide a weekly schedule for sustained reading and writing activities. For a sample schedule, look at the example in Table 10.2. A 50-minute extension period could be set up the following way: Monday, Tuesday, and Wednesday are days for independent reading (30 minutes), teacher read-alouds (10 minutes), and book talks and performances (10 minutes). Thursdays and Fridays are independent writing days (30 minutes) with time for teacher instruction with read-alouds (10 minutes) and student sharing of work (10 minutes). An alternate schedule could be to set up as a daily reading/writing workshop with flexible times for reading and writing activities (40 minutes) and discussion and sharing (10 minutes).

Table 10.2. Sample Schedule for Extension with a Focus on Sustained Reading and Writing

Time	Monday	Tuesday	Wednesday	Thursday	Friday
10 minutes	Teacher read-aloud: Introducing a text set	Teacher read-aloud: Think aloud	Teacher read-aloud: Class book discussion	Teacher demonstration: Journal writing	Teacher demonstration: Poetry journals
30 minutes	Independent reading	Independent reading	Independent reading	Independent writing	Independent writing
10 minutes	Teacher book talks from text set	Student book talks	Student performances of rehearsed reading	Peer conferences on writing	Author's chair

Independent Reading

Time to Read

Independent reading is a key component of instructional time in extensions. This can be set up on a minimum as a daily 20-minute reading time or as a 30-minute period three times weekly. The extension teacher serves as an individual coach and record keeper as students pursue periods of silent reading. This teacher monitors students' entries in reading logs, helps students select appropriate and diverse books, and guides them as they set reasonable, yet challenging goals for varied reading. To track reading progress, students keep records of both the fiction/nonfiction materials that they prefer to read and the fiction/nonfiction books that they choose to expand their horizons (Worthy et al., 2001, p. 106). In addition to this type of basic reading log, extension time can be used to practice learned techniques for writing about reading, such as keeping double-entry journals or composing literary letters. The extension teacher also is responsible for monitoring students' self-selected reading completed at home.

Access to Varied Materials

One of the most important roles of the extension teacher is to provide students with access to an extensive collection of books in a quiet, comfortable area that is conducive to sustained reading. Classroom teachers may want to circulate some of the books used in their whole-class and small-group instruction in this extension collection. Including rotating collections of books from school and public libraries provides variety. This extension library represents all levels of materials, from repetitive pattern books for emergent readers to sophisticated fiction and nonfiction for skilled readers. The collection also varies in format (e.g., question and answer books, case files, novels in poems, historical letters), genre (e.g., folk tales, science fiction, mysteries), and style of presentation (e.g., photo documentary with primary sources, bilingual books).

Independent Reading in a Grade 4 Classroom

For the fourth grade groups, the extension teacher, Ms. Hope, has focused on providing books that engage student interest in reading independently at school and at home. Keeping in mind the curricular goals for this year, she has focused her book collection for independent reading on the following areas:

- *Information books*. Accessible reading on high-interest topics is important, and, for this reason, information books are a key part of the collection. For example, the fourth graders are intrigued by illustrated versions of historical conflicts, such as the description of waiting for combat in *Patrol: An American Soldier in Vietnam* (Myers, 2002) or of a slave's escape along the Eastern shore in *Barefoot* (Edwards, 1997). Illustrated science books about animals, like *Coyote at Pinon Place* (Dennard, 1999) or *Nutik, the Wolf Pup* (George, 2001), provide a place for students to practice their content reading skills introduced in whole and small-group settings. Students need access to biographies about diverse individuals, such as *Talkin' about Bessie: The Story of Aviator Elizabeth Coleman* (Grimes,

2002). Other information books on sports, adventure, computers, and mathematics round out the collection. Comics, joke and riddle books, magazines, scary stories, mysteries, and series books are important to have available for checkout to encourage independent reading outside of school hours.

♦ *Text sets or topical collections.* Ms. Hope also has worked to collect high-interest text sets for the fourth grade. This type of topical collection supports the development of content knowledge and vocabulary, and the grouping of texts encourages students to expand their reading in new genres. For example, photographs and an engaging format of questions and answers makes *Everything Dog: What Kids Really Want to Know about Dogs* (Crisp, 2003) a book that the students want to pick up and read. The fourth grade text set on dogs includes humorous information books such as *How to Talk to your Dog* (George, 2000) or real-life adventure stories such as *Dog to the Rescue II: Seventeen More True Stories of Dog Heroism* (Sanderson, 1995). Historical adventure stories with a dog hero such as *The Great Serum Race: Blazing the Iditarod Trail* (Miller, 2002) or *Togo* (Blake, 2002) introduce unusual content vocabulary. *Max Goes to the Moon: A Science Adventure with Max the Dog* (Bennett, 2003) extends the topic of interest to science content. Simple picture books such as *The Stray Dog* (Simont, 2001) or *A Day in the Life of Murphy* (Provenson, 2003), and short novels about dogs such as *Sable* (Hesse, 1994) or *Because of*

Winn-Dixie (DiCamillo, 2000), provide accessible fiction for students to explore the topic independently. In addition to high-interest topics, text sets should be created to expose students to topics covered in the curricular standards in different content areas during that academic year.

Teacher Read-Alouds, Book Talks, and Reading Performances

A weekly schedule in the extension class includes designated time for students to listen to the teacher read aloud, to practice and perform their own reading, and to share their reactions to the books that they have read. This is an excellent way to begin or conclude an extension period. These activities promote book discussions that lead to engaged, independent reading.

Ms. Hope focuses on the following areas during this week in extension class:

♦ *Reading aloud to introduce books and to support comprehension.* Initially, Ms. Hope used read-alouds to expose students to a wide range of reading materials. By reading aloud, a teacher is able to demonstrate what is interesting in the most accessible materials. For example, the easy-to-read and humorous picture book about friendship and soccer, *Willy and Hugh* (Browne, 1992) has a worthwhile message that deserves a classroom discussion on theme. In a more complex read-aloud, Ms. Hope focuses on making the reading understandable. This might include demonstrating ways to think through text such as *The Grapes of Math: Mind-stretching*

Riddles (Tang, 2001) in which students must figure out mathematical riddles. At times, Ms. Hope chooses to read a full-length book aloud in daily segments in order to provide access for all students to specific curricular content. For example, a read-aloud from entertaining historical fiction about American Indians, such as *The Birchbark House* (Erdrich, 1999) or *Sees Behind Trees* (Dorris, 1996) helps students build background knowledge and content vocabulary for studies in American history.

♦ *Modeling how to talk about books.* Ms. Hope also introduces students to different types of materials through book talks. She provides a model of how to present a book in an interesting way; one purpose for her book talks is to teach students how to talk to each other about their own books. In the fourth grade, these book talks usually happen two or three times weekly. Sometimes Ms. Hope spends a little more time with an individual book, reading a portion of the text out loud and sharing the illustrations with the class. She usually introduces related books after a book talk. This ensures that a variety of reading materials are readily available for students who are interested in a particular topic. For example, when Ms. Hope prepared a book talk on a new book *The Zoo on You: Life on Human Skin* (Breidahl, 2001) from the Life in Strange Places series, she also included a book display with *There's a Zoo on You!* (Darling, 2000), *Micromonsters: Life Under the Microscope* (Maynard, 1999), and *Hidden*

Worlds: Looking Through a Scientist's Microscope (Kramer, 2001). Over the course of the academic year, Ms. Hope's students gradually take more responsibility for preparing classroom book talks for their peers. These presentations often include pairs or small groups of students who present books in a series, such as Sill's guides for children on amphibians, reptiles, and fish (1999, 2001, 2002).

♦ *Readers' Theater.* In addition to supporting the students in developing presentation skills through book talks, Ms. Hope also guides them in the rehearsal and performance of Readers' Theater scripts and poems that have been scripted for performance. This performance time is alternated with book talks. Sometimes these scripts are student written and come from small-group work during classroom time. Extension provides an opportunity for a focused rehearsal for a new audience, which can be a group from another classroom. Ms. Hope uses website resources as well as published collections for scripts (see Appendix 2). Because the fourth grade students have been writing poetry this week, Ms. Hope includes poetry performance as part of extension time. First, students begin with rehearsed readings by groups of four from Fleischman's *Big Talk: Poems for Four Voices* (2000); this book provides a model for creating poetry scripts for multiple readers. Next, they highlight different voices in poems to create scripts from poetry books that feature students' perspectives such as *Fearless Fernie: Hanging Out with Fernie* and *Me* (Soto, 2002) and *Visiting Langston* (Perdomo, 2002). This type of preparation for a performance activity encourages wide reading in materials that students might not otherwise consider because they want to find the perfect poem for a performance script.

Personal Writing and Classroom Publications

Writing Fluency

Extension provides the ideal time for students to develop increased fluency in writing through sustained, personal writing in journals and letters. This is also a place that students can serve as mentors for younger children by exchanging letters with reading/writing buddies and publishing short books for them to read. Pen pals from other schools provide real reasons for correspondence. If computer access is available, conversations can take place online with students in a different school or even another country. Other fluency exercises, such as interactive writing in which students share the pen (e.g., dialogue writing), encourage quick, competent writers.

Formats for Writing

As fluency becomes more developed, extension time can provide the setting for students to practice forms of writing introduced in the classroom. Students can employ creative ways of writing about books that they have read, such as creating simulated journals from the perspectives of characters from a historical time period. Ms. Hope is using extension time in the fourth grade class to help interested students write poetry in a performance format. Using models of scripted poems they have performed for extension and books they have used for paired reading, such as *Joyful Noise: Poems for Two Voices* (Fleischman, 1988), Ms. Hope assists students as they draft and edit performance poems. These students will compile these performance poems in a script book for rehearsed readings. Classroom publications, such as newspapers or literary magazines, also allow students to experiment with personal reasons for using different styles of writing. Persuasive writing (e.g., letters to the editor, editorials) and feature articles on people (e.g., biographical writing through interviews) are just two of the ways students can contribute. Different forms, such as advice columns, comic strips, advertisements, and public notices, all allow students of differing abilities to contribute to a final product. The focus in extension should be on engagement by setting up the types of literate opportunities that will encourage students to continue reading and writing at home.

Final Thoughts on Orchestrating Language Arts Instruction Across the Parallel Block Schedule

In their study of the common characteristics of exemplary fourth grade teachers, Allington and Johnston note that "…the variations we observed also convinced us that effective teaching can only be nurtured within a framework that celebrates the unique qualities and capacities of individual teachers" (2002, p. 33). PBS provides the organizational structure for teachers to be explicit through the use of instructional talk and specific models. Whole-class instruction is extended in work with individual students, student pairs, and small groups. Teachers have time to fine-tune language arts instruction to appropriate levels for their students. This framework is ideal for inquiry-based learning that promotes the engaged reading and writing of content materials such as Concept-Oriented Reading Instruction, CORI (Guthrie,1996; Swan, 2003). In the end, good teaching matters, and the PBS framework provides teachers with the instructional time and various groupings to do their best instruction with students.

References

Allington, R. L., & Johnston, P. H. (2002). *Reading to learn: Lessons from exemplary fourth-grade classrooms.* New York: Guilford.

Atwell, N. (1998). *In the middle: New understandings about writing, reading, and learning* (2nd ed.). Portsmouth, NH: Heinemann.

Bear, D. R., Invernizzi, M., Templeton, S., & Johnston, F. (2004). *Words their way: Word study for phonics, vocabulary, and spelling instruction* (3rd ed.). Upper Saddle River, NJ: Pearson, Merrill, Prentice Hall.

Bear, D. R., & Templeton, S. (1998). Explorations in developmental spelling: Foundations for learning and teaching phonics, spelling, and vocabulary. *The Reading Teacher, 52*(3), 222–242.

Bomer, R. (1999). Conferring with struggling readers: The test of our craft, courage, and hope. *The New Advocate, 12*(1), 21–38.

Broaddus, K., & Ivey, G. (2002). Surprising the writer: Discovering details through research and reading. *Language Arts, 80*(1), 23–30.

Chancer, J., & Rester-Zodrow, G. (1997). Moon journals: Writing, art, and inquiry through focused nature study. Portsmouth, NH: Heinemann.

Cullinan, B. E., Scala, M. C., & Schroder, V. C. (1995). *Three voices: An invitation to poetry across the curriculum.* York, ME: Stenhouse.

Cunningham, P. (2000). *Phonics they use: Words for reading and writing* (3rd ed.). New York: HarperCollins.

Duffy, G. G., Roehler, L. R., & Herrmann, B. A. (1988). Modeling mental processes helps poor readers become strategic readers. *The Reading Teacher, 41,* 762–767.

Fletcher, R., & Portalupi, J. (2001). *Writing workshop: The essential guide.* Portsmouth, NH: Heinemann.

Guthrie, J. T. (1996). Educational contexts for engagement in literacy. *The Reading Teacher, 49*(6), 432–445.

Harvey, S. (1998). *Nonfiction matters: Reading, writing, and research in grades 3–8.* York, ME: Stenhouse.

Harwayne, S. (2001). *Writing through childhood: Rethinking process and product.* Portsmouth, NH: Heinemann.

Henderson, E. H. (1990). *Teaching spelling* (2nd ed.). Boston: Houghton Mifflin.

Ivey, G., & Broaddus, K. (2000). Tailoring the fit: Reading instruction and middle school readers. *The Reading Teacher, 54*(1), 68–78.

Portalupi, J., & Fletcher, R. (2001). *Nonfiction craft lessons: Teaching information writing K–8*. Portland, ME: Stenhouse.

Swan, E. A. (2003). *Concept-oriented reading instruction: Engaging classrooms, lifelong learners*. New York: Guilford.

Worthy, J., & Broaddus, K. (2001/2002). Fluency beyond the primary grades: From group performance to silent, independent reading. *The Reading Teacher, 55*(4), 334–343.

Worthy J., Broaddus, K., & Ivey, G. (2001). *Pathways to independence: Reading, writing, and learning in grades 3–8*. New York: Guilford.

Children's Books

Ahlberg, A., & Briggs, R. (2002). *A bit more Bert*. New York: Farrar, Straus & Giroux.

Arnold, H. (1996). *Postcards from France*. Orlando, FL: Steck-Vaughn.

Arnosky, J. (2002). *Field trips: Bug hunting, animal tracking, birdwatching, shore walking*. New York: HarperCollins.

Bennett, J. (2003). *Max goes to the moon: A science adventure with Max the dog*. Boulder, CO: Big Kid Science.

Blake, R. (2002). *Togo*. New York: Philomel.

Breidahl, H. (2001). *The zoo on you: Life on human skin* (Life in Strange Places series). Brookfield, CT: Millbrook Press.

Brown, D. (2000). *Uncommon traveler: Mary Kingsley in Africa*. Boston: Houghton Mifflin.

Browne, A. (1992). *Willy and Hugh*. Cambridge, MA: Candlewick Press.

Burns, D. L. (1995). *Snakes, salamanders, and lizards (Take-along Guide)*. Ill. L. Garrow. Chanhassen, MN: North Word Press.

Cole, H. (2003). *On the way to the beach*. New York: Greenwillow.

Creech, S. (2001). *Love that dog: A novel*. New York: HarperCollins.

Crisp, M. (2003). *Everything dog: What kids really want to know about dogs*. Chanhassen, MN: North Word Press.

Darling, K. (2000). *There's a zoo on you!* Brookfield, CT: Millbrook Press.

Dennard, D. (1999). *Coyote at Pinon Place*. Ill. J. P. Genzo. Norwalk, CT: Soundprints.

DiCamillo, K. (2000). *Because of Winn-Dixie*. New York: Candlewick.

Dorris, M. (1996). *Sees behind trees*. New York: Hyperion Books.

Edwards, P. D. (1997). *Barefoot*. Ill. H. Cole. New York: HarperCollins.

Erdrich, L. (1999). *The birchbark house*. New York: Hyperion Books for Children.

Fleischman, P. (1988). *Joyful noise: Poems for two voices*. New York: Harper & Row.

Fleischman, P. (2000). *Big talk: Poems for four voices*. New York: Candlewick.

Fletcher, R. (1997). *Ordinary things: Poems from a walk in early spring.* Ill. W. L. Krudop. New York: Atheneum.

George, J. C. (2000). *How to talk to your dog.* New York: HarperCollins.

George, J. C. (2001). *Nutik, the wolf pup.* Ill. T. Rand. New York: HarperCollins.

George, L. B. (1999). *Around the world: Who's been here?* New York: Greenwillow.

Glass, A. (2001). *Mountain men: True grit and tall tales.* New York: Doubleday.

Grimes, N. (2002). *Talkin' about Bessie: The story of aviator Elizabeth Coleman.* New York: Orchard Books/Scholastic.

Hall, D. (1994). *I am the dog, I am the cat.* Ill. B. Moser. New York: Dial.

Hesse, K. (1994). *Sable.* New York: Henry Holt.

King, C., & Osborne, L. B. (1997). *Oh, freedom! Kids talk about the Civil Rights movement with the people who made it happen.* New York: Knopf.

Kramer, S. (2001). *Hidden worlds: Looking through a scientist's microscope.* Boston: Houghton Mifflin.

Leedy, L. (1991). *Messages in the mailbox: How to write a letter.* New York: Holiday House.

Leedy, L. (1993). *Postcards from Pluto: A tour of the solar system.* New York: Holiday House.

Maynard, D. (1999). *Micromonsters: Life under the microscope.* New York: DK Publishing.

McCarty, P. (2002). *Hondo and Fabian.* New York: Henry Holt.

Miller, D. S. (2002). *The great serum race: Blazing the Iditarod Trail.* Ill. J. Van Zyle. New York: Walker & Company.

Myers, W. (2002). *Patrol: An American soldier in Vietnam.* New York: HarperCollins

Nelson, M. (2001). *Carver: A life in poems.* New York: Front Street.

Perdomo, W. (2002). *Visiting Langston.* New York: Macmillan.

Provenson, A. (2003). *A day in the life of Murphy.* New York: Simon and Schuster.

Rappaport, D. (2000). *Freedom River.* New York: Hyperion Books.

Sanderson, J. (1995). *Dog to the rescue II: Seventeen more true tales of dog heroism.* New York: Scholastic.

Sayre, A. P. (2001). *Dig, wait, listen: A desert toad's tale.* New York: Greenwillow.

Sill, C. (1999). *About reptiles: A guide for children.* Atlanta, GA: Peachtree.

Sill, C. (2001). *About amphibians: A guide for children.* Atlanta, GA: Peachtree.

Sill, C. (2002). *About fish: A guide for children.* Atlanta, GA: Peachtree.

Simont, M. (2001). *The stray dog.* New York: HarperCollins.

Soto, G. (2000). *Fearless Fernie: Hanging out with Fernie and me.* New York: Putnam Juvenile.

Tang, G. (2001). *The grapes of math: Mind-stretching riddles.* New York: Scholastic Press.

Teague, M. (2002). *Dear Mrs. LaRue: Letters from obedience school*. New York: Scholastic.

Turner, A. (1987). *Nettie's trip south.* Ill. R. Himler. New York: Simon & Schuster.

William, V. (1988). *Stringbean's trip to the shining sea.* New York: Scholastic.

Woodruff, E. (1994). *Dear Levi: Letters from the overland trail.* New York: Knopf.

Wright-Frierson, V. (1999). *A North American rain forest scrapbook.* New York: Walker.

11

Providing High-Quality Mathematics Instruction in Elementary Schools

Laura L. McCullough[1]

The mathematical concepts, connections and skills that students acquire in the elementary grades not only provide a foundation for their further learning but also develop the habits of mind with which students will approach mathematics in the future. Will they perceive mathematical puzzles and problems as interesting, engaging, and challenging? Will they decide that anything related to math is confusing, abstract, and incomprehensible? Will they look forward to math time as a part of their day that is full of variety, interaction, and a sense of accomplishment? Or will they associate math class with a series of worksheets and workbook pages that must be navigated each day—day after day, with more of the same for homework that night?

---

1 Laura L. McCullough is the Director of Instruction for the Waynesboro City Schools in Virginia. She is a former elementary school principal and teacher, whose areas of interest include mathematics instruction and best practices in assessment. Dr. McCullough may be contacted at lmccullough@waynesboro.k12.va.us.

This chapter uses examples of classroom practices and activities to describe and illustrate elements of high-quality math instruction. These elements apply in any type of schedule or grouping pattern, although certain settings capitalize on particular instructional elements. For example, students who are finding multiple ways to solve an open-ended problem need to describe and discuss their strategies, including which strategies work, which don't, and why. This discussion not only aids learning, but it also gives the teacher a window into student thinking, as well as valuable formative assessment information. Given the option, most teachers would choose to conduct this type of discussion in a small group, where several students can share ideas and listen to each other, and the teacher can hear everyone's ideas.

Earlier (chapter 4), schedules that include an intervention/enrichment period were detailed. This chapter provides recommendations regarding the types of models and activities that engage and instruct students best for these purposes. Examples demonstrate how assessment data can be used to diagnose students' needs, select students for small groups, and plan intervention/enrichment activities.

In parallel block schedules (chapter 6), students have opportunities to learn in various combinations of whole-group, small-group, and extension center settings. This chapter recommends instructional methods that are most effective in each of these venues and clarifies how their purposes are different, yet complementary, in meeting students' learning needs. In addition, guidelines for choosing appropriate extension activities to make the most productive use of this learning time are shared.

Finally, the chapter shows how these instructional recommendations might be applied through the following illustrations:

♦ Whole-group instruction with an intervention period for a struggling student (based on the schedule shown in Figure 4.12, p. 124);

♦ Whole-group instruction with an enrichment period for a high-achieving student (based on the schedule shown in Figure 4.6, p. 116);

♦ A parallel block schedule for a second grader (based on the schedule shown in Figure 6.3, p. 177); and

♦ A Concept-Mastery schedule in which students are regrouped based on assessment information (based on the schedule shown in Figure 8.1, p. 253).

Elements of High-Quality Math Instruction

"Teaching for understanding" is a phrase often bandied about among educators in their discussions of math instruction. Of course when we teach, we hope the result is that students understand; but in order to plan effective math instruction, we must be clear about what we mean when we say "understanding." In this chapter, understanding means a child's way of picturing, representing, communicating, and connecting mathematical ideas. When students understand concepts in these ways, then the strategies and procedures that follow (such as adding three-digit numbers, simplifying fractions, or writing an equation to solve a word problem) make sense, have meaning, and can be learned more efficiently and remembered longer. To illustrate this idea, consider the sentence shown below. What do you think it means?

PZTOH VB K

Although you might have some random guesses, it is unlikely that these groups of letters have any meaning to you, because they are not words you recognize. If one of the letter groups said FISH or FLOWER, you would get a picture in your head that you understand. Not all of us would conjure up the same picture. For example, a child who has an aquarium in his classroom might have a different concept of FISH than his mother, who is at the market shopping for a dinner entree. Nonetheless, they each have a clear picture. Consider the next sentence, shown below.

12 + 33 = 45

Students in elementary grades who have conceptual understandings of these groups of symbols might, for example, picture the number twelve as one bundle of ten sticks and two single sticks. Perhaps they picture the number in its position on a number line. Maybe the picture of this sentence in a child's head looks like the image shown at the top of the next column.

Most of the time, students who struggle in math have no mental picture (or at least not a clear one) that matches the numbers and mathematical symbols they see on a page. For these children, the number sentence above has no more meaning than the series of nonsense words. So for these students, "practice" of

skills for which they have little or no conceptual basis is wasted time. Even worse is the likelihood that over time, these children learn that math makes no sense. They become frustrated, eventually give up, and have high failure rates in middle and high school (Jordan, 2007).

Of course it is important for students to be able to perform operations and to practice so they can use procedures efficiently and accurately. There also is a role in every elementary math classroom for rote memorization of certain facts (such as every kid's nightmare—the multiplication table!). These three components—understanding concepts, demonstrating skills, and remembering facts—are appropriate goals in math classrooms at every grade level, but they are not the ultimate goal. Uppermost in every teacher's mind when planning a math lesson should be the same question we often hear from students: "Why are we doing this?" Whether the focus is concepts, skills, or recall of facts, every math lesson should have problem solving as its ultimate goal. The National Council of Teachers of Mathematics has developed process standards to guide decisions about what and how students should learn about mathematics. Their problem-solving standard is summarized as follows:

> Solving problems is not only a goal of learning mathematics but also a major means of doing so. It is an integral part of mathematics, not an isolated piece of the mathematics program. Students require frequent opportunities to formulate, grapple with, and solve complex problems that involve a significant amount of effort. They are to be encouraged to reflect on their thinking during the problem-solving process so that they can apply and adapt the strategies they develop to other problems and in other contexts. By solving mathematical problems, students acquire ways of thinking, habits of persistence and curiosity, and confidence in unfamiliar situations that serve them well outside the mathematics classroom. (National Council of Teachers of Mathematics, 2000, p. 4)

Concepts, skills and facts, kept in their proper proportions and taught in a problem-solving context, give students the tools and experiences they need to become mathematical thinkers. It is distressing to us that we sometimes hear students describe themselves as "just not good at math." We believe that one of the most positive and powerful gifts elementary teachers can give their students is the knowledge that everyone has a math brain. The difference between people who like and are good at math and those who dislike and avoid it is simply the strength of their conceptual understanding—how often and how easily they retrieve and manipulate those pictures they have carried in their heads since learning them. The degree to which students can "see" mathematically, compute mentally, and solve problems strategically depends largely on the instruction they have in the elementary grades. These skills are learned, not inherited.

The following sections describe and give examples of several elements of math instruction that are important to teaching for understanding in an elementary classroom. The elements we have chosen are the following:

1. Representing ideas with models;
2. Asking open-ended questions;
3. Talking and writing about math;
4. Focusing on patterns and connections;
5. Providing practice with feedback; and
6. Integrating technology.

Element 1: Representing Ideas with Models

Models show us the mental pictures upon which we base our understanding of mathematical concepts and procedures. Generally, models take the form of either concrete manipulative materials or graphics such as pictures, tables, or diagrams. When introducing students to new concepts, it generally is advisable to build sequences of lessons that move from concrete representations to graphic, and then later to using symbols to record responses.

For example, Ms. Jefferson is teaching beginning multiplication concepts. She wants her students to see a variety of representations that help them understand what multiplying means.

In one activity, each pair of students chooses a kind of pattern block to use. Pattern blocks may have three, four, or six sides. Marie and her partner have chosen the four-sided square. Their handful of pattern blocks, arranged in a line, looks like this:

Their question is something like "How many sides do you have on your blocks altogether?" Marie and her partner might figure this out by counting all the sides, starting at 1 and counting to 28. They might think about counting by twos or fours (skip counting is one way to multiply). Ms. Jefferson asks Marie and her partner to explain how they got their answers and calls their attention to the fact that they got the same answer two different ways. She provides them with a blank table and asks them to see if they can figure out the answer a third way.

How many squares?											
How many sides?											

The students' completed table looks like this.

How many squares?	1	2	3	4	5	6	7	8	9	10	11
How many sides?	4	8	12	16	20	24	28	32	36	40	44

Marie and her partner only have seven squares, but because they used a model and discovered a pattern, they could continue picturing more squares and "adding on" or counting by fours until they filled all the boxes on the table. Some students in this situation would count only what they see and not go further. These students should be encouraged to add more actual blocks to their row and continue counting, or to predict what the next number might be, and then add the block and count to confirm. Other students will go further, filling not only the boxes in the table but the whole paper with multiples of four. This is one way students might construct the fours' row of a multiplication table. The next challenge for these students might be to figure out how they would make this table if their shape had been a pentagon. Suppose that in their set of blocks, they have no pentagon; some students will skip over the need for a model by now and simply construct their chart by counting by fives and writing in the multiples of five. Others will need to draw a row of five-sided shapes, and count the sides of their drawings just as they did with their blocks. By working with other shapes and patterns, these students invent the entire multiplication table themselves.

This activity includes the use of concrete (blocks) and graphic (picture) models as well as another kind of representation—the representation of data using a table. All of these are ways that children organize information so that they can work with it mentally. Teachers often wonder whether students at certain grade levels are "developmentally ready" for particular concepts and skills. As this activity illustrates, children at a range of developmental and skill levels can attack (and solve) the same problem as long as they can access models, tools and strategies that make sense to them. As children move towards mastery of concepts and skills, their strategies for solving problems become more efficient, and they rely less on concrete manipulatives. We caution teachers about removing manipulatives too early; students should know how and be able to use them as problem-solving tools whenever they choose.

Additionally, teachers should not assume that because they have taken the time to use concrete models to teach one concept, students will transfer that mental picture to the learning of a new concept. Most teachers find that it is helpful (even necessary) to begin the concrete—graphic—symbolic sequence over again with the introduction of each new concept.

Some teachers worry that if they introduce the use of concrete materials in their math classes, management difficulties will result. We offer these suggestions for managing the use of manipulatives:

◆ Allow students time to explore using the materials before starting a structured activity where they are expected to use their manipulatives in specific ways. Good manipulative materials are designed to be attractive and engaging for students to use, and to invite many creative ways of sorting, building, and experimenting with them. These activities are an important step in the learning process and should not only be allowed, but also be encouraged. Open-ended questions that invite exploration (How many ways can you sort those blocks? How can you make a pattern using all the colors?) can add value to this otherwise unstructured time. If teachers are wary about providing this exploration time in a whole-group setting or in a center where students will not be closely supervised, then the small-group setting provided in the parallel block schedule provides a good opportunity to introduce students to new manipulatives.

◆ Be clear with children about why and how these materials are to be used. We want math to be fun, but math materials are tools, not toys. By reinforcing that these materials are tools for learning math and sticking to a few basic rules (the same ones that would be appropriate for any other classroom materials), teachers generally find that children are very capable of using manipulative materials appropriately. One specific suggestion is to introduce one type of manipulative at a time, and give students practice with it before adding another type.

◆ Create an organizational system and hold students responsible for using it. Some math programs (such as *Math Their Way*) that are heavily manipulative-based recommend particular ways of storing and organizing materials so that they can be accessed, managed, and put away by children—even young children. For example, math materials often are stored in tubs on low shelves, with picture labels as well as written labels. For young children, the process of matching materials to their spots is a sorting activity that has merit for their learning. Whatever the organizational plan, it is important that students learn routines for getting out and putting away their materials. (Chapter 7 has a detailed description of the organizational plan for one extension center.)

Models, whether they are concrete or graphic, are most effective when they provide a reference for a whole sequence of skills. Consider our friend Mrs. Condry. For many years, she has had a large square piece of plywood leaning up against the front wall of her classroom beside the chalkboard. Mr. Condry, a supportive and patient husband, hammered one hundred nails into that piece of plywood long ago, in ten straight and even rows of ten each. On each nail Mrs. Condry has hung a round key tag, and each key tag is labeled with a number between 1 and 100. This hand-made hundred board (shown below) looks like the hundred charts in many classrooms, which are manufactured in a variety of materials, sizes, and forms.

1	2	3	4	5	6	7	8	9	10
11		13	14	15	16	17	18	19	20
21	22	23	24		26	27	28	29	30
31	32	33	34	35	36		38	39	40
41	42	43	44	45	46	47	48	49	50
51	52	53		55	56	57	58	59	
61	62	63	64	65	66	67	68	69	70
72	73	74	75	76	77	78	79	80	
81	82	83	84	85	86	87		89	
91	92		94	95		97	98	99	100

Some days, Mrs. Condry claims to have misplaced several of her key tags, and students use the patterns in the chart to figure out what the missing numbers are. Some soon discover that "stepping" one square to the right is the same as adding one or counting up one. Mrs. Condry asks, "Then what would happen if you stepped left?" Someone notices that stepping down means adding ten. Soon thereafter Mrs. Condry makes her next instructional move—teaching mental addition and subtraction of numbers to 100. Students have worked with tens and ones using a variety of models, including the hundred chart. Guided by the teacher's questions and with plenty of time to talk with each other, they see that by stepping down twice and then once to the right from any number, they can add 21 (two tens = two steps down and one = one step to the right). Soon the children can put their fingers on any number and add or subtract any other number by moving their fingers in the correct pattern—down and right for adding, up and left for subtracting. Over time, they progress to the point where they don't need to physically place their fingers on the board. Just looking at it from their seats, they can picture the steps and get the answer.

The National Council of Teachers of Mathematics (2000) includes "Representation" as one of its "Process Standards." These standards reflect important ways that students "acquire and apply" math content. An introduction to the Representation Standard states:

Mathematical ideas can be represented in a variety of ways: pictures, concrete materials, tables, graphs, number and letter symbols, spreadsheet displays, and so on. The ways in which mathematical ideas are represented is fundamental to how people understand and use those ideas. Many of the representations we now take for granted are the result of a process of cultural refinement that took place over many years. When students gain access to mathematical representations and the ideas they express and when they can create representations to capture mathematical concepts or relationships, they acquire a set of tools that significantly expand their capacity to model and interpret physical, social, and mathematical phenomena. (p. 4)

Element 2: Asking Open-Ended Questions

The power of questioning to influence classroom interaction and the level at which students process information cannot be underestimated. When planning lessons, we encourage teachers to take the time to decide some of the key questions they will ask and at what point in the lesson those questions will be asked. Classroom questions are used for a variety of purposes, and it is important that the type of question fit the purpose. If we want students to explore, investigate, notice patterns, and analyze mathematical relationships, then questions need to be open-ended so that they stimulate students to look at a problem in a variety of ways. It is true that in math many problems have one and only one correct answer; however, these answers usually can be found in a variety of ways. Learning only one method (generally the teacher's method) will enable most students, at least those who remember, to get the right answer. Investigating multiple paths to a solution, however, teaches students much more—to reason, to make and justify decisions, to assess the reasonableness of their results, and to apply flexible strategies rather than memorized steps for problem solving. Open-ended questions can be used to spark curiosity and give students a *beginning* point for a task, as the following examples show.

- How many different ways can you find to make the number 35?

- The whole third grade is going to a play next week! How can we figure out how many buses we need?

- How might you sort these buttons?

Open-ended questions also are used *during* a discussion or task to focus, guide, and extend thinking, as in these examples.

- Would drawing a picture help you solve this problem?

- How could you use a chart to record what you've done so far?

- What is the next step in your plan for solving this problem?

- How could you discover which of these is heavier?

- Can you find another way to get this answer?

As students come to the *end* of their work on a problem or task, responses to open-ended questions can provide valuable formative assessment information about their thinking processes. Listening to children describe their reasoning is an easy, direct way to pinpoint their misconceptions or errors—much easier than analyzing written work! Perhaps the best assessment question is the simplest: "How did you figure out this answer?" Other examples of informal questions that provide this kind of assessment information include the following:

- How could you explain this to another student?

- Why is your answer different from Talley's?

♦ Show me how you did that.

Of course not all questions in math class can be open-ended. The area of a 7×8-inch rectangle is not open to interpretation, and there always will be 20 nickels in a dollar. Still, teachers who structure more discussion around open-ended questions find that they get more student participation, higher levels of engagement in the task, and higher-quality thinking on the part of students.

Element 3: Talking and Writing About Math

As students become more accustomed to responding to open-ended questions, teachers can create many opportunities for them to communicate mathematically. Most teachers know that during reading class, it is important for students to generate questions, share ideas, and articulate their thinking in writing as they respond to what they are reading. We see journals, literature circles, book clubs, and reading buddies all organized to prompt children to talk about what they read. The primary reason for engaging in all this talking and writing is to aid comprehension—understanding, if you will.

The same is true in developing understanding in math. How many of us can remember an example of a concept or skill that we never truly understood until we had to teach or explain it to someone else? Activities in which students describe, articulate, summarize, question, and share their math thinking help them to organize their thinking and to mentally review it. Communicating contributes to understanding. Hearing or reading what other students have to say also can increase math learning, as students compare their own understanding, ideas and procedures to those

of their classmates. A summary of the NCTM Communication standard states:

> Mathematical communication is a way of sharing ideas and clarifying understanding. Through communication, ideas become objects of reflection, refinement, discussion, and amendment. When students are challenged to communicate the results of their thinking to others orally or in writing, they learn to be clear, convincing, and precise in their use of mathematical language. Explanations should include mathematical arguments and rationales, not just procedural descriptions or summaries. Listening to others' explanations gives students opportunities to develop their own understandings. Conversations in which mathematical ideas are explored from multiple perspectives help the participants sharpen their thinking and make connections. (National Council of Teachers of Mathematics, 2000, p.4)

Element 4: Focusing on Patterns and Connections

Mathematics is largely a study of patterns. An awareness of these patterns and the relationships among them supports children's understanding of math. When these patterns are not evident to students, they learn math as a series of isolated, disconnected skills. Then it is harder (if not impossible) for them to make sense of or to remember what they have learned. A common complaint of elementary teachers is that students don't always come to them with the prerequisite skills their teachers might expect. Fourth and fifth grade teachers often are overheard to say things like, "I don't know what they learned last year. I would have thought they'd have seen this before, but I'm finding that I have to start from the beginning." If a teacher from the previous grade level is within earshot, he will often respond, "They knew that when they left me last spring! I assessed every one of them myself, and I know they could do it."

Research into how the brain learns supports the emphasis on patterns and relationships rather than discrete bits of knowledge:

> Education is about increasing the patterns that students can use, recognize and communicate….Whenever new material is presented in such a way that students see relationships, they generate greater brain cell activity and achieve more successful long-term memory storage and retrieval. (Willis, 2006, p. 15)

Consider the ongoing struggle with which all elementary teachers and students are familiar—the process of memorizing the basic addition, subtraction, multiplication, and division facts. If we were to count all the facts using the digits 0 to 9, beginning with addition and ending with the division table, we would have a list of 390 separate facts, shown in Figure 11.1 (p. 321).

Although no teacher would ever attempt to have students memorize all these facts at once, almost every teacher, beginning in about first grade, expects students to know some subset of these facts. By the upper elementary grades, we assume that students know them all and can retrieve them quickly. Generally we find that students who are good at this retrieval process have learned some important patterns. For example, skip counting by threes can be helpful when multiplying or dividing by three.

Similarly, adding nine to a number always increases the tens' place by one and decreases the ones' place by one.

Students who are good at basic facts also use their understanding of important relationships. For example, division is the inverse of multiplication, so a student who remembers most of the multiplication facts can use those to determine the answers to division facts. Multiplication also can be thought of as repeated addition. So a student who remembers that $7 \times 8 = 56$ but can't remember 7×9 may know that this answer can be determined by adding 7 more to 56 (7×8 can mean "8 sevens" and 7×9 can mean "9 sevens"; so it's just one more seven).

The understanding and use of patterns and relationships doesn't mean that students shouldn't practice their basic facts with memorization as the goal. It does mean that those facts will be remembered longer if the student knows how they are connected with each other and, as we discuss later, practice always should come after understanding. Imagine being a child faced with the memorization of 390 isolated facts and not knowing how to get from one to another by using patterns and relationships. It's easy to see how these facts might be forgotten during the summer!

Connections among mathematical ideas help children understand and retain information, as do connections between math and the real world in which children live. Many children are fascinated to discover the mathematical patterns found in nature, for example. Often, the earliest experiences children have with "real-world math" involve the collection, organization, representation and analysis of data. Classrooms where rich math environments have been established display data everywhere. For example, consider a typical morning in Mrs. Taylor's class. As children arrive at school, they record their lunch choices for the day on a graph posted on the wall. One morning, the graph looks like the chart shown here:

Terrance		
Aida		
Peter		
LaKeisha		Devon
Emily		Sam
Amadi	Kate	Maggie
Lainie	Josh	Tammy
Pizza	**Salad**	**Pack**

As part of her opening circle time, Mrs. Taylor asks a combination of closed and open-ended questions about the graph, varying the difficulty of the question in order to provide support for struggling students and challenges for high achievers. Some of her questions are:

♦ What did most people select for lunch?

♦ How can you tell?

♦ How many people packed their lunch today?

♦ If the same number of people in our class and Mrs. Bedford's class ordered salads, how many salads will there be in the two classes? How do you know?

♦ How many people who are here today have not put their name on the graph yet?

♦ How many more people ordered pizza than salad?

♦ Look at our graphs from today, yesterday, and Monday. What can you say about the lunch choices we have made?

Element 5: Providing Practice with Feedback

Practice is an important component of any math program and is necessary to learn skills. When practice is used at the right time and in the right ways, it can support and "cement" new learning, or serve as reinforcement and review of prior learning. When used ineffectively, practice can be frustrating, demoralizing, and detrimental.

In light of ongoing research on learning and the brain, the traditional quote, "practice makes perfect," is often revised to read "practice makes permanent." The role of practice is to repeat a process already learned, so that it becomes automatic. Practice alone does not help students learn a skill. When students are practicing a skill, they need close monitoring and frequent corrective feedback. When students don't completely understand what they're doing but drill and practice anyway, they can end up practicing errors that deter rather than advance learning. John Van de Walle (2001) argues that "what needs to become automatic is the use of an effective strategy." In other words, students should be practicing *the ways they think* about facts and procedures, rather than relying on rote memory alone. Van de Walle goes on to make four suggestions for practice:

◆ Keep practice short. Fifteen minutes three or four times a week is much better than any full class period of practice.

◆ Individualize practice so that students actually are practicing the things they need to practice. Nothing is more pointless than repetitive drill of a mastered skill.

◆ Provide conceptual help. Students who are experiencing difficulty in a practice setting are not going to be aided by more practice. A conceptual deficit is nearly always the root of a skill deficiency.

◆ Help students understand that the purpose of practice is to become quick yet flexible. Practice of meaningful skills allows them to be used with greater ease. With this in mind, try to avoid practice students will not need to use, such as long division with three-digit divisors. (p. 445)

Homework can be effective for practice as long as the guidelines above are followed. It is essential that the teacher has already checked for understanding before assigning homework so that students who are confused are not practicing incorrectly. It follows, then, that not all students in the class would have the same homework assignment at the same time. Generally, it is wise to keep homework short but assign it frequently to allow misunderstandings to be revealed and corrected.

The results of ineffective practice are easy to observe in a classroom. One of the most common examples involves regrouping or "borrowing" in subtraction. Take, for example, the two subtraction problems as shown here:

$$\begin{array}{r} 578 \\ -321 \\ \hline \end{array} \qquad \begin{array}{r} 578 \\ -399 \\ \hline \end{array}$$

The problem on the left can be done easily using either the traditional algorithm or another strategy; either way, regrouping is not necessary. The problem on the right requires regrouping to arrive efficiently at a solution (a child could solve this problem, for example, by counting up from 399 to 578, which is not very efficient). Teachers often find that once students have learned a procedure for regrouping, they apply it all the time, whether the problem requires it or not. This is frustrating for teachers but predictable if students have been involved recently in lengthy drill and practice using regrouping repeatedly without any attention to thinking through the problem. It is not uncommon to see children writing, regrouping, erasing, and correcting on their papers in order to find the difference in the problem shown below:

$$\begin{array}{r} 500 \\ -499 \\ \hline \end{array}$$

Simply using mental math or counting would provide a quick and accurate answer here. Students who have been trained to follow rote procedures, however, rather than to think and select a strategy first, often plow ahead, dealing unnecessarily with "borrowing across zeroes." As Van de Walle (2001) states:

Lengthy drills of algorithmic skills tend to diminish flexibility and reflective thought. Often teachers want to drill skills in preparation for a standardized test. The result is that when students confront a computation on the test, they respond as they have been drilled to do: They begin immediately to perform the indicated algorithm. Often a mental computation, estimation, or a nonstandard approach would be twice as fast, especially when the format is multiple-choice. The distracter choices on standardized tests are designed to match the typical errors that students make in mindless application of the algorithms. Students who have practiced thinking are much less likely to make these errors and will actually be able to complete these tests more quickly. (p. 445)

Short, regular periods of practice with monitoring and corrective feedback can be delivered easily during extension time. Through the sample schedules described later in this chapter, we show where in each type of schedule practice with feedback fits best.

Element 6: Integrating Technology

If we accept the premise that school experiences should prepare students to succeed outside of school, then it follows that technology integration is an important component of every classroom. Anyone who has seen a fifth grader hold a calculator in both hands and push the buttons with two thumbs (as if texting on a cell phone) knows that students are already users of technology. Electronic tools such as computers and calculators are as basic to classroom instruction as textbooks were a generation ago. As we have emphasized all along, how to use a strategy or tool is only part of what students need to learn. Understanding when that strategy or tool is needed is the more important learning goal. A few of the technology applications that are most closely related to the elementary math curriculum are listed below, with descriptions and examples to guide their use.

Calculators in the classroom do not replace paper and pencil computation. They are a supplement to it. When people need to compute in real life, they may wonder: Do I need a calculator? In answering this question, they are quickly and automatically assessing a range of options:

- ♦ Can I do this quickly in my head?

- ♦ If not, will an estimate do in this situation?

- ♦ Which will be quicker—doing this with a pencil or a calculator?

Students need to learn to make these decisions so they can benefit from problem situations where these questions are discussed. For example: You go to the grocery store with a $10 bill. Your mom has asked you to get a carton of milk and to be sure to bring back at least $5.00 in change. The milk costs $2.79. You'd like to buy a pack of gum for 79 cents. You know there is sales tax on food. Can you get the milk and gum and still bring your mom at least $5.00 in change? A good question for children to think about in relation to a problem like this is "Would I use a calculator in this situation even if I had one?" By assessing various problems and situations, children learn when they need a calculator and when they don't.

It is true that without sufficient guidance, some children may become overly dependent on a calculator to the detriment of their paper/pencil computational skills. This may indicate insufficient understanding of the procedure rather than too little practice or just plain laziness. Teachers should be aware that what these students need may be further instruction to understand the skill.

For most of us, calculators come in handy in certain common situations, such as when we have to do a long series of computations, a computation that involves many numbers in a series, a calculation involving very large numbers, or one in which it is important to be accurate to several decimal places. We believe these situations are the ones in which children should learn to use calculators as well. Consider this problem:

> The students in Mr. Marshall's class wanted to buy a video iPod for their classroom, so they decided to sell hot dogs at the high school football game on Friday night. The cost of the iPod was $279.00. Half of the $1.50 they charged for each hot dog was profit, and one third of the 840 people at the game bought a hot dog. Did the students have enough profit to buy the iPod? If not, how much more money do they need?

This problem has several steps, and it would be easy for children to lose track of their strategy as they navigate their way through the computations with pencil and paper. Providing a calculator as a tool in situations like this one may allow students to find a strategy and solve a problem successfully that would otherwise be beyond their grasp.

Virtual manipulatives are computer graphics that children can control on-screen to help them develop concepts and solve problems. These graphic but interactive representations provide a useful link between the use of hands-on materials and the move to drawing diagrams or pictures on paper. Because they are interactive, they closely mimic real manipulatives. Because they are two-dimensional, they correspond to graphic representations of the concepts being studied. The National Library of Virtual Manipulatives (Utah State University, 2007) is an excellent online resource for these representations.

Spreadsheets and data-gathering tools allow children to collect, organize, sort, and work with data in ways they never could by hand. Imagine, for example, a project for third graders in which they and another third grade class in a different part of the country collect weather data using handheld instruments to measure temperature, humidity, and wind speed. These data can be automatically downloaded into a spreadsheet which is shared between the two classes so that comparisons between their locations can be made. The data most likely would be communicated back and forth via e-mails, to which students easily could attach digital pictures taken at their location.

Even the most basic spreadsheet programs generate a variety of graphs. So rather than spending time struggling to draw basic graphs with a pencil, students can devote their time and attention to selecting which kind of graph best represents particular data, what the scales and labels should be, and what inferences and conclusions can be made based on the data.

School Scheduling and High-Quality Mathematics Instruction

School schedules support learning in a variety of ways. Schools serving students across a wide variety of achievement levels might choose a parallel block schedule in order to provide the most time possible for students and core teachers to be together in small-group settings. Schools with significant populations of high-achieving students may be searching for ways to keep these children challenged each day without leaving others behind, and, therefore, might choose an acceleration model for their schedule. Regardless of the ways time and staffing are structured, the elements of math instruction discussed in this chapter should be built purposefully into the program. Where they occur, which teacher takes primary responsibility for making sure they occur, and who plans for them are all functions of the schedule. The following sections provide several examples.

Whole-Group Instruction with an Intervention Period for a Struggling Student

Note: The following material is based on the schedule shown in Figure 4.12 (p. 124).

As discussed in chapter 4, some schools build intervention/enrichment periods into their schedules in order to provide differentiated services to students who need more time to learn skills or whose level of performance shows that they would benefit from a more challenging activity linked to what they have already done in class. The intervention/enrichment period is generally staffed by a combination of specialists (and sometimes teaching assistants) who monitor student progress and plan with classroom teachers in order to target services to children at the times they can be most beneficial. In the following example, the first grade intervention/enrichment period is staffed by the three first grade teachers, along with five others (a special education teacher, an ESL teacher who serves this school part-time, a Title I teacher, a Title I aide, and a gifted resource teacher).

Marcus is in first grade. By following the first grade line in Figure 4.12 (p. 124), we see that he begins the day with a language arts block of over two hours, during which he participates in a whole-group lesson, a small-group guided reading activity, and a word-study group. Next, Marcus has math with Mrs. Friend, his homeroom teacher, for an hour. Today's lesson focuses on measurement skills. Mrs. Friend models and students practice measuring length with two nonstandard units (an unsharpened pencil and a glue stick). The teacher emphasizes measuring techniques, such as placing the end of the measuring tool at the edge of the object to be measured, measuring length along one edge, lining up units (pencils or glue sticks) end to end, and carefully counting the number of units. Students work in pairs to conduct their first measurements, and they soon discover that their units are not exactly the right length to measure the objects. Mrs. Friend pulls the class back together to discuss how they might record a measurement when the length of an object doesn't "come out right." Students suggest a variety of strategies, which they then test in a follow-up activity.

Mrs. Friend observes as the students are working and notices that Marcus and Julie are not using the targeted skills correctly. As the children clean up and get ready for lunch, Mrs. Friend adds Marcus and Julie to a list of students who will continue work on the process of measuring accurately in future intervention/enrichment periods.

When the intervention/enrichment period begins, several of Mrs. Friend's students are working with specialists. The Title I teacher is working with a reading group, two students are with the speech therapist, and the TAG teacher is guiding several students through the completion of a piece of writing they began yesterday. Mrs. Friend is working with a group of first graders (some from her class, some from the other two classes) to build upon the measurement activity they all did that morning. She demonstrates measuring the same object with two different nonstandard units and asks students what they noticed about the results. They make predictions and test their predictions by measuring. Mrs. Friend's goal is to begin exposing students to the need for standard units, but she is not directly teaching this concept yet. Meanwhile, Marcus and Julie are with a smaller group across the hall in Mr. Coltrane's room. Here, students use Cuisenaire rods to measure a series of lines taped to the floor. Mr. Coltrane guides them through the process step-by-step the first few times; then they take their Cuisenaire rods outside, where five lines are drawn in chalk on the sidewalk. Mr. Coltrane watches these eight students carefully, and when they have arranged their Cuisenaire rods and are ready to count, he listens to them count aloud and corrects them as needed.

The daily intervention period allows Marcus and other students to benefit from the additional modeling and guided practice; by following this procedure teachers will discover whether or not students understand the concepts before they are expected to practice independently or to move ahead to another skill. This timely intervention is especially important in math, where so many skills build upon each other. Marcus' mastery of this measurement skill is important not only for today's and tomorrow's lessons, but for a whole sequence of subsequent skills.

Whole-Group Instruction with an Enrichment Period for a High-Achieving Student

Note: The following material is based on the schedule shown in Figure 4.6 (p. 116).

The I/E period is so named because enrichment is its purpose in addition to intervention. We do not recommend that this period be used to accelerate students by moving them through the curriculum objectives or from book to book at a faster rate. Rather, enrichment suggests that students will deepen their understanding of the concepts they are learning in class, participate in activities that reveal many connections among math concepts and ideas, and foster creative approaches to mathematical problem solving.

In a school environment where particular staff, such as a "teacher of the gifted," might be assigned to an identified caseload of students, it is important to remember that enrichment groups are designed to be flexible. Special educators often serve students who are not "identified," but who need extra support with one topic or skill area. In the same way, the staff (whether classroom teachers or specialists) who work with enrichment groups must be alert to the interests and capabilities of all children and make sure that all students who are ready for the enrichment activities are included. Almost all teachers deal at some time with students who are hard to engage, reluctant to participate, and likely to avoid completing work. Generally, the assumption is that these students need extra help in order to understand the content. Sometimes, however, teachers find children with these behaviors respond best to enrichment, rise to the challenge when it is put before them, and enjoy the interaction with other highly capable students.

Consider the example of Maribel, a fourth grader. Her teacher, Mrs. Shackleford, is using visual representations to help students learn to write number sentences. For example, given the picture shown below, students wrote number sentences like $5 + 5 + 5 = 15$, $10 + 5 = 15$, and $3 \times 5 = 15$.

Maribel remains quiet in the back of the room. The teacher knows that Maribel's math performance is uneven. She arrived from Peru last year, and though she catches on to new concepts quickly, there are gaps in her prior knowledge. Mrs. Shackleford calls on Maribel, who comes forward and writes $30 \div 2 = 15$ and $\frac{1}{2} \times 30 = 15$. This response shows Mrs.Shackleford that Maribel has experience multiplying and dividing by two; it also appears that she connects division by two with multiplication by one half.

The next day during the enrichment period, six students from Mrs. Shackleford's class and three from Ms. Ivy's class play a game using doubles and halves of numbers. Some of the students can do this in their heads. Keeping manipulatives available for use as needed and modeling with a paper-folding activity, Mrs. Shackleford leads students in an investigation of doubles and halves using even and odd numbers.

Sometimes teachers have specific plans for what will occur during the enrichment period following any lesson. There are particular aspects of a concept they want students to build upon or important connections to be made by students who are ready to make them. Occasionally, as in the example above, students themselves generate the ideas upon which enrichment is built. The enrichment period can give students opportunities to show their peers the kinds of thinking they are doing, and with a skilled teacher guiding this, it can be a powerful learning experience for the whole enrichment group.

A Parallel Block Schedule for a Second Grader

Note: The following material is based on the schedule shown in Figure 6.3 (p. 177).

We believe that all students need and deserve *both* exposure to the full curriculum and targeted work at their levels of performance. Struggling students do benefit from exposure to the curriculum in heterogeneous groups, even in situations where they do not yet fully grasp the concept. Familiarity with the vocabulary, models, and concepts creates a base upon which students can build as they work towards mastery. Parallel block schedules (described in chapter 6) support these needs by providing a combination of whole-class instruction in a heterogeneous group, small-group instruction in a leveled group, and an extension center where students can practice and reinforce their skills at their individual levels.

Dustin is a second grader whose assessments indicate that he is slightly below grade level in math. He often needs more time and some extra help to fully understand concepts. However, his teacher, Ms. Reid, generally finds that with some assistance he can keep up with the class. It is early in the year, but Mrs. Reid already knows how important it is to keep Dustin engaged and motivated, so that he will be willing to make the extra effort needed in order to achieve at grade level. She works with the other two second grade teachers as well as resource teachers to plan activities that will hold the interest of Dustin and others as they move from large group to small group to extension center.

Dustin is in math group 3 (refer to Figure 6.3, p. 177). After lunch, he and the other eight students in his group meet with Ms. Reid while the rest of the students go to the extension center. Second grade is working on comparing numbers today, and the teacher wants to spend some time with Dustin's group reviewing the place value concepts they'll need for the activity they will be doing later this afternoon. As a warm-up activity, the nine students play a game in which they order numbers from smallest to largest and largest to smallest using place value concepts.

Ms. Reid notices that Dustin is slower to get the numbers in the correct order than the other students in his group and that he often waits, listening for someone to mention the answer, and then raises his hand. During the second round of the game, Ms. Reid stops for a few minutes to sit with Dustin's group. She has a place value chart with her, which includes pictorial representations of tens and ones on ten frames. She cues Dustin to think about the numbers in terms of how the ten-frame representation of each number would look. She knows that Dustin has worked successfully with the ten-frame model in the past, and that this is a representation very likely to make sense to him.

The students put away their game materials and join Ms. Reid on the rug, where she demonstrates the use of base ten blocks to compare numbers larger than 100. Working in pairs, students use the blocks to build a variety of numbers. They compare how many hundreds, tens, and ones are in each number, and then students determine which number is larger and which is smaller. They record their answers and respond to open-ended questions such as: "If my hundreds place digit is larger than yours, is my number always larger?"

Later in extension, Dustin begins by using a computer software program to review simple addition and subtraction computation. Several students are pulled out of extension for LD, speech, and ESL work. There are 18 students here, and each has the use of a computer. The Title I teacher is monitoring this practice session—checking for effective strategy use by spending a few minutes with each student, asking questions like: "How did you get that answer?" and "Can you draw that one for me?" or "Could you show me that using blocks?"

After about 10 minutes of this practice, the students are divided into three groups that work at three different centers in the extension room. These centers change periodically, but they always reinforce previously taught skills. Dustin and a partner spend about 15 minutes playing a game, and then they choose another center where they work together at a computer manipulating a set of "virtual" base ten blocks to build numbers between 1 and 999. Before he leaves the extension center, Dustin spends about five minutes writing in his math journal.

After his encore class, Dustin goes to whole-group math. Today's lesson starts with a warm-up game of "Between," in which children practice comparing numbers. After about 10 minutes of the game, Ms. Reid gets out the estimation jar—a large (about half gallon) jar which she fills with various objects at various times during the year. She uses the jar as a model to teach concepts of proportion ("Which could I fit more of into the jar—M&M's or Starbursts?") and estimation, as well as other mathematical connections. Today, she asks students to estimate how many Life Savers (individually wrapped) are in the jar. Guesses are recorded on a place-value chart and then ordered from smallest to largest. The chart includes a place for the children to write about their comparisons, which helps them articulate their understanding and also serves as an informal assessment of their thinking process.

After some discussion, the students record their new estimates in their math journals and write about how they adjusted to get a closer estimate. The class period ends with children counting the Life Savers into groups of hundreds, tens, and ones.

When small-group, whole-group and extension center activities are available daily, all students are able to access the full curriculum and still have opportunities to work at their own levels as well as have time for monitored practice activities. The small-group time may provide preparatory work before the whole-group lesson, as in the example above, or it may be used for extra reinforcement after the lesson or for extension/enrichment.

A Concept-Mastery Schedule for a Student Performing at Grade Level Who Has a Specific Skill Deficit

Note: The following material is based on the schedule shown in Figure 8.1 (p. 253).

Plan A of the Concept-Mastery schedule builds in time for intervention and remediation, not daily as in a parallel block model, but periodically during the year for a concentrated period of a few days. Classroom teachers build daily time into their routines for immediate intervention when students are struggling. Although this is helpful, it does not always provide sufficient time for students to thoroughly master skills and concepts that may be missing or shaky. The Plan A mastery schedule allows the entire grade level to take a "time out" of sorts every few weeks to bring together groups of students with similar instructional needs and address those needs more systematically.

The third grade teachers in Emilio's school like to plan together while being as efficient as they can. At the end of the school year in June, they take the time to review their pacing guide while the notes they made during the year are still fairly fresh in their minds. Based on their students' test results from this year, they determine that they want to change the sequence of two of their units and lengthen one unit that seemed to be the most difficult for children across all four classes. They update the guide as a preliminary plan for next year, knowing that as the year goes along, they will make adjustments.

It is early October when the team comes together to plan their fractions unit, which is scheduled to begin in about a week.

This unit is scheduled to last 17 days, as shown in Figure 8.1 (p. 253), with three days of mastery class to follow. The length of each unit and the amount of time to be set aside between units for remediation/intervention will vary depending on the content and the students' needs. The pacing guide provides an estimate for the length of each unit based on the amount and the difficulty of the content to be included.

Because these teachers have worked together for the past two years, they know each others' strengths well. It does not take them long to decide that Mr. Duncan and Ms. Garland will plan the lessons for the first eight days of the unit. These lessons focus on fractions concepts. By the beginning of the third week, they will be moving on to simple addition and subtraction of fractions. Mrs. Farmer and Mrs. Dorsey will work together to plan the instruction for these seven days. As they are planning, both pairs of teachers will gather activities, materials, and ideas for re-teaching and reinforcing their lessons. These will be organized and ready when it is time for mastery classes. All the teachers agree on fraction strips and pattern blocks as the basic models they will use to introduce concepts and skills during this unit. Although other visual representations will be included (who can study fractions without pizza?), fraction strips and pattern blocks will appear most often. These are models that seem to make the most sense to students, and all four teachers have plenty of these materials.

A few days later the teachers come together again. Mr. Duncan and Mrs. Garland share a draft of the lesson plans for the first ten days of the unit, and the other two teachers describe their ideas for the other seven days. Title I and resource teachers hear the ideas and, in several cases, make suggestions that they think will help the lesson connect with students on their case loads. Some changes are made in the plans as all the teachers around the table remember strategies that worked best last year, as well as some ideas that weren't very successful. Each teacher has his or her own ideas about exactly how the lessons will be implemented; there is no expectation that every teacher will do exactly the same thing every day. Still, in order to be ready for mastery groups to begin meeting in 17 days, it is important that all teachers teach the scheduled objectives in the time available. This collaborative planning structure provides clarity for everyone on what is to be taught and equips teachers with a set of lessons they can use as a framework but are free to adapt and modify as they assess their students' needs.

Nearing the end of the third week in the fractions unit, the teachers devote one of their planning times to creating student groups for mastery classes. They have administered several assessments along the way, including written quizzes, observation of children working with manipulatives, and short interviews with each of their students. They also gave a short multiple-choice test designed to mimic the types of fractions questions children will see on the state test. For ease and efficiency, they all have recorded their assessment data on a chart, a portion of which is shown below:

	Model/ Write a Fraction	Compare Fractions	Compare in Word Problems	Add Fractions	Add Fractions in Word Problems
Sylvia	MPS	MPS-?	?	MPS-E	?
Ted	M	M-?	?	MPS-?	?
Lynn	MPS	MPS	MPS	MPS-E	?
Mike	MP	M-R	R	MPS-?	?
Dwight	M	M-R	R	MP-?	?

Key: M = with manipulatives; ? = inconsistent, needs practice; P = with pictures; R = needs reteaching; S = with symbols; E = needs enrichment

The teachers spend about 45 minutes grouping students for the upcoming three-day mastery class based on the assessment information in their chart. One group, which includes Lynn, will be working in a variety of short project and problem-solving situations. The problems will be more complex and less routine than those already seen in the concept class, and these students will use fractions concepts along with information from other content. The second group, which includes Ted, will have more time to work with the fractions skills already taught, mostly using pictures and symbols. For the most part, these students understand fractions concepts if they can directly work with them using concrete materials, but they have not made the connection to paper and pencil. Making this connection will be the focus of this group.

The third group, of which Mike and Dwight are members, will spend the first two of the three days in lessons where comparison of fractions will be taught using different models and

methods than those that were used initially. Most of these students caught on fairly well to addition of fractions, but their comparison skills are not strong. The skill of "comparing" needs to be re-taught; otherwise, these students will have difficulty with all subsequent fractions content.

The fourth group includes Sylvia. These are students who are well on their way to mastery of all the concepts and skills so far; in fact, they are ready to take on more complex problems and to work with fractions with higher denominators. At the same time, they still need more practice in order to become consistent and confident with the skills already learned. During the three days of mastery class, these students will alternate between frequent short periods of practice and enrichment activities that push their skills to a slightly higher level.

The Mastery schedule illustrated in this example has different advantages than the other schedules. Students are not regrouped for intervention and enrichment daily, and so the ongoing differentiation that students need must be provided in the context of the regular classroom or through an I/E period. Providing a longer period of sustained time in Mastery groups between each unit, however, creates a practical opportunity to form instructional groups guided by assessment data.

A Final Word

It is often said that "good instruction is good instruction." Learning can occur at any time of day, with any materials, in almost any environment. Great teaching is what engages and inspires students. The tools (such as materials and technology) and the structures (such as student groups and their schedules) aren't magic. They don't produce student learning. Only good teachers can do that. These tools and structures can, however, make a significant difference. Though it is true that students can learn in any schedule, some schedules capitalize on the available time better than others.

For students to be most successful as mathematics learners, they need a variety of activities so they can see concepts in multiple ways, thereby enabling them to make the connections that are so important to mathematical thinking. If students are to think mathematically rather than just repetitively perform rote skills, they also need flexibility in learning time. For any particular student, some concepts and skills will require more effort to learn than others. Some will be easier to remember, while others will require more modeling and re-teaching. The schedules described in this book provide the flexibility in learning time that is necessary for teachers to meet the needs of students with a range of abilities and skills.

References

Baratta-Lorton, M. (1995). *Mathematics their way.* New York: Addison Wesley.

Jordan, N. C. (2007, October). The need for number sense. *Educational Leadership, 65*(2), 63–66.

National Council of Teachers of Mathematics (2000). *Principles and standards for school mathematics: Executive summary.* Reston, VA: Author.

Utah State University (2007). *National library of virtual manipulatives.* Retrieved October 15, 2007 from http://nlvm.usu.edu.

Van de Walle, J. A. (2001). *Elementary and middle school mathematics: Teaching developmentally.* New York: Longman Addison-Wesley.

Willis, J. (2006). *Research-based strategies to ignite student learning: insights from a neurologist and classroom teacher.* Alexandria, VA: Association for Supervision and Curriculum Development.

Figure 11.1 Basic Math Facts

0+1=1	2+7=9	5+2=7	7+7=14	15-9=6	7-7=0	8-4=4	9-1=8	0×8=0	3×4=12	6×0=0	8×6=48	48÷8=6	35÷5=7
0+2=2	2+8=10	5+3=8	7+8=15	14-9=5	15-6=9	7-4=3	8-1=7	0×9=0	3×5=15	6×1=6	8×7=56	40÷8=5	30÷5=6
0+3=3	2+9=11	5+4=9	7+9=16	13-9=4	14-6=8	6-4=2	7-1=6	1×0=0	3×6=18	6×2=12	8×8=64	32÷8=4	25÷5=5
0+4=4	3+0=3	5+5=10	8+0=8	12-9=3	13-6=7	5-4=1	6-1=5	1×1=1	3×7=21	6×3=18	8×9=72	24÷8=3	20÷5=4
0+5=5	3+1=4	5+6=11	8+1=9	11-9=2	12-6=6	4-4=0	5-1=4	1×2=2	3×8=24	6×4=24	9×0=0	16÷8=2	15÷5=3
0+6=6	3+2=5	5+7=12	8+2=10	10-9=1	11-6=5	12-3=9	4-1=3	1×3=3	3×9=27	6×5=30	9×1=9	8÷8=1	10÷5=2
0+7=7	3+3=6	5+8=13	8+3=11	9-9=0	10-6=4	11-3=8	3-1=2	1×4=4	4×0=0	6×6=36	9×2=18	63÷7=9	5÷5=1
0+8=8	3+4=7	5+9=14	8+4=12	17-8=9	9-6=3	10-3=7	2-1=1	1×5=5	4×1=4	6×7=42	9×3=27	56÷7=8	36÷4=9
0+9=9	3+5=8	5+10=15	8+5=13	16-8=8	8-6=2	9-3=6	1-1=0	1×6=6	4×2=8	6×8=48	9×4=36	49÷7=7	32÷4=8
1+0=1	3+6=9	6+0=6	8+6=14	15-8=7	7-6=1	8-3=5	9-0=9	1×7=7	4×3=123	6×9=54	9×5=45	42÷7=6	28÷4=7
1+1=2	3+7=10	6+1=7	8+7=15	14-8=6	6-6=0	7-3=4	8-0=8	1×8=8	4×4=16	7×0=0	9×6=54	35÷7=5	24÷4=6
1+2=3	3+8=11	6+2=8	8+8=16	13-8=5	14-5=9	6-3=3	7-0=7	1×9=9	4×5=20	7×1=7	9×7=63	28÷7=4	20÷4=5
1+3=4	3+9=12	6+3=9	8+9=17	12-8=4	13-5=8	5-3=2	6-0=6	2×0=0	4×6=24	7×2=14	9×8=72	21÷7=3	16÷4=4
1+4=5	4+0=4	6+4=10	9+0=9	11-8=3	12-5=7	4-3=1	5-0=5	2×1=2	4×7=28	7×3=21	9×9=81	14÷7=2	12÷4=3
1+5=6	4+1=5	6+5=11	9+1=10	10-8=2	11-5=6	3-3=0	4-0=4	2×2=4	4×8=32	7×4=28	81÷9=9	7÷7=1	8÷4=2
1+6=7	4+2=6	6+6=12	9+2=11	9-8=1	10-5=5	11-2=9	3-0=3	2×3=6	4×9=36	7×5=35	72÷9=8	54÷6=9	4÷4=1
1+7=8	4+3=7	6+7=13	9+3=12	8-8=0	9-5=4	10-2=8	2-0=2	2×4=8	5×0=0	7×6=42	63÷9=7	48÷6=8	27÷3=9
1+8=9	4+4=8	6+8=14	9+4=13	16-7=9	8-5=3	9-2=7	1=0=1	2×5=10	5×1=5	7×7=49	54÷9=6	42÷6=7	24÷3=8
1+9=10	4+5=9	6+9=15	9+5=14	15-7=8	7-5=2	8-2=6	0×0=0	2×6=12	5×2=10	7×8=56	45÷9=5	36÷6=6	21÷3=7
2+0=2	4+6=10	7+0=7	9+6=15	14-7=7	6-5=1	7-2=5	0×1=0	2×7=14	5×3=15	7×9=63	36÷9=4	30÷6=5	18÷3=6
2+1=3	4+7=11	7+1=8	9+7=16	13-7=6	5-5=0	6-2=4	0×2=0	2×8=16	5×4=20	8×0=0	27÷9=3	24÷6=4	15÷3=5
2+2=4	4+8=12	7+2=9	9+8=17	12-7=5	13-4=9	5-2=3	0×3=0	2×9=18	5×5=25	8×1=8	18÷9=2	18÷6=3	12÷3=4
2+3=5	4+9=13	7+3=10	9+9=18	11-7=4	12-4=8	4-2=2	0×4=0	3×0=0	5×6=30	8×2=16	9÷9=1	12÷6=2	9÷3=3
2+4=6	4+10=14	7+4=11	18-9=9	10-7=3	11-4=7	3-2=1	0×5=0	3×1=3	5×7=35	8×3=24	72÷8=9	6÷6=1	6÷3=2
2+5=7	5+0=5	7+5=12	17-9=8	9-7=2	10-4=6	2-2=0	0×6=0	3×2=6	5×8=40	8×4=32	64÷8=8	45÷5=9	3÷3=1
2+6=8	5+1=6	7+6=13	16-9=7	8-7=1	9-4=5	10-1=9	0×7=0	3×3=9	5×9=45	8×5=40	56÷8=7	40÷5=8	18÷2=9

12

Creating a Planning, Implementation, and Training Process to Support an Elementary School Schedule Change

Susan W. Golder[1]

The positive impact of our work today includes the fact that district and school leaders, teachers and parents have come together to focus on the issue of instructional time for students and professional time for teachers. It's been refreshing and energizing to share our thoughts on scheduling and to develop a plan for creating a model that suits our particular needs.

An Elementary Teacher

---

[1] Susan W. Golder is a former Director of Curriculum, Instruction, Assessment and Professional Development. Dr. Golder works as an educational consultant with a focus on training and support for effective instruction, systemic change, and leadership development. She can be reached at woodsgolder@gmail.com.

This testimony at a scheduling committee workshop in a Pennsylvania school district mirrors many reactions I've received when engaging district and school staffs in a process to prepare them for changes in their approach to scheduling. Paying careful attention to the structure of elementary scheduling as a powerful tool to bring about instructional change has, traditionally, been overlooked in reform efforts. All too often, the task has been viewed as a technical, school-based challenge undertaken primarily by busy principals. Thankfully, in response to the pressures of increasing student achievement, districts have begun to devote time and resources to the complex issue of elementary scheduling. This chapter outlines effective "before, during, and after" reform steps for districts to consider and offers a sequential planning, implementation, and support process that complements the technical tasks involved in a major schedule change. When I led my former school district through a yearlong collaborative process to inform and accompany Michael Rettig's master schedule design, the combined results made a positive difference for students and teachers. Since then, I've focused on consulting with districts that opt for a collaborative and systemic approach to ensure a smooth transition to a new way of addressing the concept of time.

While one may think that staff would welcome any improvements to the school schedule, the fact is that what one faculty member sees as an improvement, another may view as a compromise, or even a negative change. What one principal views as an optimal time allocation for recess, for example, another may see as limiting. What one parent sees as an ideal time for a child's instrumental music lesson, another may see as an inconvenience. By engaging stakeholder groups, including superintendents, boards, central office staff, principals, teachers, and parents in a yearlong study and planning process, districts can realize the optimal results of a district-wide schedule that truly supports staff and student needs. Table 12.1 summarizes the recommended components of the process, which include setting clear expectations, formulating plans, establishing guidelines for data collection, analyzing data, decision making, communicating and conducting training.

Table 12.1. Suggested Study and Planning Process

Month	Tasks	Participants
August	Establishing parameters Setting budget	Designated board member Superintendent District project coordinator
September	Conducting planning sessions Developing project plan, intended outcomes, and timeline	District project coordinator Consultant
October	Providing overview of the initiative Exploring issues and goals Conducting needs assessment Discussing transition management Creating communication plan	District project coordinator Central office staff Elementary principals Consultant

Month	Tasks	Participants
November	Developing common guidelines Collecting and comparing schools' schedules Clarifying district and school decision making Identifying variations among schools	District project coordinator Elementary principals Consultant
December–February	Conducting onsite school focus groups	Faculties of each district school Consultant Principal (optional)
March–April	Analyzing focus group data Formulating report outlining key district issues and concerns Compiling recommendations for change Completing draft schedules	Consultant
March–May	Completing phone-a-thon and/or e-interviews Meeting for guided debrief	Selected committee members Consultant
June	Providing training and support: effective use of intervention/extension time; effective use of collaborative planning time in professional learning communities Completing final schedules	Consultant Teacher leaders

Month	Tasks	Participants
August	Providing training and support: effective use of intervention/extension time; effective use of collaborative planning time in professional learning communities	Teacher leaders All elementary staff

Planning and Implementation Process

Getting Started

In approaching the opportunity and the challenge of leading their district through a systemic process in schedule reform, how do district leaders organize for success? Before formulating a committee of district and school representatives to work collaboratively on the process, it is important for superintendents, curriculum directors, and boards to meet together and to set parameters for the upcoming reform. The level of school board understanding of the initiative and its potential impact on students and/or taxpayers undoubtedly will influence the resources they are willing to devote. Preliminary discussions with the board by the senior leadership team are imperative. Beginning dialogue early in the process will allow the cross-district committee to be launched with a set of common understandings, such as "there will be no furloughs of staff as a result of this reform," or "the board will support the committee's recommendations provided they are budget neutral." Such parameters, when communicated up front to committee members, produce strong vertical articulation, and, further, help teachers focus on the potential benefits of the change rather than a set of anxiety-producing concerns, real or imagined.

Once preliminary direction is set and boundaries established, I suggest that school districts convene two committees. The first is the Leadership Steering Committee, usually comprised of all the district's principals and those members of the central office leadership team whose areas of responsibilities are instructionally based. Assistant superintendents, curriculum directors, and special education supervisors have specific needs and provide multiple perspectives at the project table. Their collaboration in laying out the tasks and timeline for the study/planning year and the transition, along with the communication plan, is invaluable to the reform's success and depends in part on their traditional norms for interaction.

When working with schools and districts on a reform such as the elementary scheduling change, one of the factors I look for is the clarity leaders have about their roles, responsibilities, and decision-making capacity with respect to the initiative. In my experience, administrators tend to operate on "spin cycle" these days as they rotate from one responsibility to another. It is vitally important to use early Leadership Steering Committee time to organize a responsibility diagram and decision-making ladder for future work. Attending to clarifying questions, such as those listed below, fosters efficiency and signals "with-it-ness" to the wider stakeholder group.

- Will there be a district-wide approach to scheduling into which school-based needs will be accommodated?

- To what degree will principals be decision makers about shared staff, about time allocations for classes, or about scheduling meetings with teachers during collaborative planning time?

- What aspects of the reform will be determined centrally before the nuts-and-bolts scheduling work unfolds?

- Who will determine how often principals can meet with teachers during their collaborative planning time?

- To what degree will the teachers' union be invited to work with human resources on changes regarding, for example, lunch and non-teaching duties?

The second committee to be assembled early in the study/planning year is the Cross-District Study and Planning Team. This group—generally composed of representatives from each school and grade level, encore teachers, special service providers, and union leaders—closely mirrors the composition of a typical faculty in its ratio of academic to encore and specialist representatives. Principals and some central office staff also participate in this team. Parents occasionally are included as well, although their function is to serve as key communicators to other families, rather than as decision-makers. The responsibilities of this group include meeting three or four times with the Leadership Steering Committee to analyze problems with the current schedule, set goals for improvement, investigate possible solutions, and make recommendations for change.

Committees at Work

When working with committee members in a "before" reform workshop, I start with an exercise called "Making the Case for Change." During this individual reflective activity, I invite everyone in the room to consider and describe their current reality with respect to the elementary schedule and then to brainstorm positive changes they can imagine. Invariably, responses center on common constraints, such as frequent interruptions of instruction, excessive pull-outs, and lack of collaborative planning time. When participants imagine the possibilities of an ideal scheduling structure, they often mention extended time for intervention and enrichment, sufficient time to meet with colleagues, and blocks of uninterrupted instructional time. Writing about personal challenges and hopeful choices honors individual perspectives and allows committee members to begin the important process of contributing to data collection during the "before" reform stage. Individual reflections are the first steps in an empowering process that culminates in subsequent school-based focus groups.

Usually, after a few facilitated work sessions, stakeholders from across the district are validated by the consistency of their individual concerns, hopes, and dreams for the upcoming reform. It's always challenging, though achievable, to have them agree *as a group* on a series of common guidelines to direct the work of the "during" reform stage. Moving to consensus, then, is our next logical step. Meeting in mixed job groups, participants work through a facilitated exercise during which they respond to and evaluate a set of worthy guidelines—ones that, if agreed upon, will assist future decision-making. Affirmations, such as the examples that follow, signal that the group's thinking

has merged and confirm their focus on making things better for students.

"We are open to examining and adjusting time allocations across the content areas."

"We are committed to the establishment of an intervention/enrichment period."

"We agree not to personalize the options presented."

If—through show of a majority of hands, dot votes, or table-to-table consensus counts—committees can come together on the majority of guidelines presented, their agreement tends to be a strong predictor of how full faculties will later embrace the change.

When working with school districts, I always suggest that the "before" reform work culminate in a published list of "talking points" for full district distribution. As Bridges (2003) states, "one of the most important leadership roles during times of change is that of putting into words again and again what will be left behind and what is to come" (p. 33). Frequently communicating goals and points of progress to all who will be impacted by the change must be a primary function of those who lead the charge. Imagine the comfort and clarity lent to potentially anxious teachers in one district when they received an e-mail update from their committee following the first Effective Scheduling Meeting, one paragraph of which read:

Our goals throughout the process will be to

♦ gain a clear understanding of the benefits and shortcomings of our current approach to scheduling;

- discover ways other schools have structured their school days to best meet current instructional needs;

- make a decision about which scheduling model will best suit our needs;

- plan for the implementation of an improved schedule for our elementary schools at the start of the next school year.

Collecting and Analyzing Data

Once a district's Leadership Steering Committee and Cross-District Study and Planning Committee complete the initial phase of their work, the next step is to conduct a wider-scale needs assessments through focus groups at each school. I typically ask that principals plan creatively to free faculties so that all teachers' voices can be heard and their data about scheduling concerns recorded. The ideal way to structure focus groups is to rotate substitutes from grade to grade for approximately 40 minutes apiece while grade-level teachers meet with me or the district project facilitator. Many times, principals sprinkle special education teachers, encore teachers and special service providers into the grade-level meeting mix. Sometimes, depending on encore teachers' schedules, principals schedule an "all encore" teachers' session at the end of the day. Occasionally, principals find focus groups cumbersome to organize and opt to hold data collection sessions before school or during lunch-time meetings. Both of these forums are less productive, because they tend to be rushed. If tightly structured, though, they, too, can elicit valuable data.

Conducting focus groups can be inspiring and productive. Teachers are grateful for the opportunity to share their individual concerns and glad for the information flow with colleagues. They appreciate the fact that I will note their scheduling challenges in an unabridged report to the district's Leadership Steering Committee. While grade-level teachers from the *same* school generally share similar concerns like excessive pull-outs, frequent interruptions in instructional time (particularly for language arts and math), and lack of collaborative planning time, I often observe interesting and significant variations among teachers' concerns *across* schools in the same district. These issues, when brought to the forefront, can lead to constructive conversations among the leadership team, better alignment of programs, and increased consistency in services to students. Table 12.2 illustrates a sampling of school-specific concerns and their impact occurring in one, but not all, schools in a district.

Table 12.2 School-Specific Concerns and Impact

Situation	Impact
Students in one school were studying up to three instruments at a time; thus, they were leaving academic classes three times per cycle for lessons, and they missed class even more if they received special services.	Fragmented instructional time; overextended students
Half-day kindergarten students were having multiple encore classes on one day and none on other days.	Loss of consistency in academic delivery; lack of predictability/routine for students
Physical education classes were offered to two different grade levels in the same gymnasium with different start and stop times.	Excessive distractions to teachers and students; compromised integrity of PE program
4th grade students in one school were having a special at 10:55, followed by 15 minutes of core instruction, then recess for 30 minutes, followed by 10 more minutes of core instruction, then lunch.	Cumbersome planning required for teachers; wasted instructional time
In one school, children were admitted to their classrooms 20 minutes earlier and dismissed 10 minutes later each day than in other schools across the district.	30 minutes per day discrepancy in instructional time across schools in the district; unequal teacher workloads

Principals assert that the data from faculty focus groups present valuable opportunities to uncover and resolve issues that can significantly improve alignment of instruction, curricular programs, and student services. Furthermore, the Cross-District Study and Planning Team and the Leadership Steering Committee need the qualitative information about the benefits and short-comings of teachers' schedules to complement the hard data of numbers of students, classes, teachers, specialists, itinerants, and others. Putting the spotlight on classroom-to-classroom commentaries about ineffective scheduling practices will challenge administrators to commit themselves to keeping the instructional needs of students and the professional needs of teachers in the forefront as they ready themselves to design the schedules.

Partnering with Other Schools or Districts for Student Success

As the revision process begins to take shape and stakeholders get a sense of its potential positive impact, it's only natural for them to experience a level of ambivalence or reservation. It is precisely at this point in the "during" reform stage that I establish connections between staff from the district that is *about* to modify its schedule and one that has recently undergone a scheduling overhaul. Often, because of time and distance consideration, this connection is achieved through phone or e-mail interviews, rather than in face-to-face conversations. Teachers and principals always are eager to hear first-hand about the "wows" and "whoops" of large-scale reform in districts similar to their own. Similarly, in districts where collaboration is an established norm, folks are eager to share what's been successful and what's still a work in progress. Interviewers ask a uniform set of questions of counterparts who have agreed to participate. Questions such as those below lead to rich conversations, add to the pool of perspectives on change, and, sometimes, grow into partnerships over time.

- What were some of the scheduling limitations your school was experiencing before the change, and what were your goals in creating a new schedule?

- What are the most significant benefits for students and teachers since the schedule at your school has changed?

- To what degree has the quality of instruction improved since the scheduling change?

- Were there any personal compromises you made for the collective good of the scheduling reform?

- Can you describe the way the intervention/enrichment period works? What does it look like in your school?

Teachers, principals and central office staff who participate in phone-a-thons or e-interviews bring data from their conversations to a subsequent committee meeting during which they create a list of "lessons learned" to carry them into the implementation phase of the scheduling revision. Bridges (2003) contends that successful change takes place when employees have a purpose, a mental picture, a plan for change, and a part to play. In short, successful change takes place only when employees are "on board" with it (p. 60). Engaging in a collaborative process over the course of the study and planning nurtures global thinking, promotes informed decision-making and increases the likelihood that the reform will be received enthusiastically and conscientiously implemented.

Providing Training and Support for the Change

Once a scheduling template is in place and teachers begin to settle in to the luxury of uninterrupted blocks of instructional time and collaborative planning time, they soon begin to wonder and worry about incorporating the Intervention/Enrichment period, one of the hallmarks of the Canady-Rettig model, into their daily routine. So as not to let this valuable addition of dedicated time to meet student needs become either a concern or an afterthought, I strongly suggest that districts include training for teachers on how to effectively use intervention/enrichment time as an integral part of their reform process. Establishing a professional learning community of teacher leaders and supporting their growth as future trainers for all staff can facilitate the transition to the differentiated instructional setting that I/E provides. Growing school-based leaders who can serve as ambassadors of best practice and liaisons for colleagues with ideas or concerns is critical. Continuous on-site support as faculties proceed through instructional transformations during the implementation year should be nonnegotiable parts of the reform plan.

In the conclusion to this chapter, I share the story of a Pennsylvania school district that successfully integrated a training and sustained support model, and struck an effective balance (Lieberman & Miller, 1999) between the content of their reform and the process of changing the culture, between teacher and student need and between reflection and action. I urge the reader to appreciate the scheduling reform and the institution of the Intervention/Enrichment period for what they are—unmistakable opportunities to nurture instructional change and to foster among faculties the growth of professional learning communities strongly centered on student needs.

A Perspective on Supporting the Intervention/Enrichment Period

I paused after facilitating a recent professional development workshop on effective use of I/E periods and noted the sense of confidence and positive expectation permeating the room. The teachers who participated in this summer leadership forum to prepare for the upcoming year's roll-out of the elementary I/E period appeared energized at the end of a hard day's work. They came to the workshop excited by the adoption of a new schedule that would result in more productive learning environments for children, yet apprehensive about their upcoming responsibilities as I/E teachers attending to individual learning needs. The group was composed of a cross-section of grade-level teachers and specialists from the district's four elementary schools who would be charged in the future with providing training to their colleagues. They came together in a professional learning community to understand the purpose and function of the I/E period; to share strategies for a successful implementation; and to develop a plan for communicating, informing and encouraging colleagues in the effective use of the new "window" of intervention and enrichment time.

This end-of-school-year workshop marked the culmination of a yearlong scheduling study and revision process begun to "confront the brutal facts" (Collins, 2001, p.13) about the limita-

tions of an outdated schedule, and ending with a series of good decisions for students and teachers. Imagine the degree of ambivalence teachers brought to the table as they began their dialogue on what would be different the following year. They were pleased with the reform's obvious benefits, which included

- ◆ large uninterrupted blocks of instructional time;
- ◆ common grade-level planning time;
- ◆ significantly reduced travel time for shared staff;
- ◆ revised and "authentic" time allocations for instructional programs;
- ◆ uniform allocations of time for encore subjects;
- ◆ new and improved plans for the delivery of special services across the district; and
- ◆ the institution of an I/E period for practice, reinforcement, intervention and enrichment of skills.

This day, however, their concerns focused on one aspect of the change—the Intervention/ Enrichment period. The following questions surfaced early in the day and helped frame intended outcomes:

- ◆ How will I manage the flow of students in the classroom from day to day?
- ◆ How will I establish positive expectations for learning in this need-based environment?
- ◆ How will I hold students accountable for their core extension tasks?

- How will I organize the I/E program to maximize time and maintain my sanity?

- What instructional structures and strategies will provide the best support to my students?

- What other support personnel will be working with me and my students and how will we share responsibilities?

In his discussion of preconditions for sustainability of change, Michael Fullan (2005) talks about the critical importance of lateral capacity building that expands traditional learning communities *within* teams and schools to the broader context of learning teams *across* schools. The Intervention/Enrichment leadership event was a vitally important forum to access perspectives of stakeholders across the district, to "increase their identification with the larger piece of the system" (p. 70), to capitalize on teachers' arsenal of instructional tools, and to foster a meaningful and intentional approach to I/E planning. "While the teachers have been an integral and essential part of the planning, they are also the ones who have to fully implement and live with the changes," said Great Valley (PA) Superintendent Rita S. Jones. "It is critical that this implementation period is flexible in that it provides opportunities for many conversations and then additional tweaks and adjustments."

When school districts tackle substantial reforms, such as the revision of the elementary schedule, the weight of the process sometimes can steer resources toward the nuts-and-bolts of the revision. Technical issues—counting students and staff, determining numbers of sections and students in them, allocating staff, assigning core and encore personnel—can consume time and talent. I argue, however, that the impact of the changes on teachers and students must not be minimized, and, certainly, never ignored. Adequate preparation for new learning environments and continuous monitoring of the I/E period must be integral and non-negotiable parts of the reform plan. Districts that fail to provide continuous doses of support and accountability to teachers over the first few years of I/E implementation run the risk of fragmented programming and marginal student performance gains.[2]

Picture, if you will, a sampling of some skills required by teachers to effect a successful transition to the I/E period:

- Opening one's classroom door and welcoming other staff into the room and the routine;

- Learning to diagnose, plan and instruct in a collaborative environment;

- Aligning student need with instructional technique;

- Incorporating differentiated instruction into one's practice;

- Mastering the management of small and dynamic learning groups;

---

2 While the author of this chapter refers to the I/E period here because of her personal experience with that scheduling innovation, many of her observations also apply to the implementation of the "extension center" in schools that adopt parallel block schedules (see chapters 6 and 7).

◆ Using formative assessments and authentic data to drive I/E planning;

◆ Grouping and re-grouping students for content and skill reinforcement and enrichment.

Given the sophistication of skills required to bring about exemplary models for I/E instruction, it is clear that school district leaders must plan and budget for training and professional development as they establish their I/E programs.

In this Pennsylvania school district, the professional learning community began with a focus on implementing the I/E period in a manner that reflected DuFour, DuFour, Eaker, and Karhanek's (2004) principles for successful intervention. The teachers left the workshop that June day as ambassadors of a school district that takes a systems approach to their work. They left gratified by the dialogue that had begun, confident in its continuation, and committed to the discoveries of the year ahead.

References

Bridges, W. (2003). *Managing transitions*. Cambridge, MA: Perseus Books Group.

DuFour, R., DuFour, R., Eaker, R., & Karhanek, G. (2004). *Whatever it takes*. Bloomington, IN: National Educational Service.

Collins, J. (2001). *Good to great*. New York: HarperCollins.

Fullan, M. (2005). *Leadership and sustainability*. Thousand Oaks, CA: Corwin Press.

Lieberman, A., & Miller, L. (1999). *Teachers—transforming their world and their work*. New York: Teachers College Press.

Appendix 1
Forms, Lesson Plans, and Strategies

created by
Bonnie Dudley,
extension center teacher,
Hollis Hand Elementary School,
Troup County, Georgia

Lesson Plan Form for Introductory Activities

Unit: _____

Introductory Activity 1:

_____
_____
_____
_____
_____

Introductory Activity 2:

_____
_____
_____
_____
_____

Introductory Activity 3:

_____
_____
_____
_____
_____

Lesson Plan Form for Teacher-Directed Activities

Unit: _____

Teacher-Directed Activity 1:

_____

_____

_____

Teacher-Directed Activity 2:

_____

_____

_____

Teacher-Directed Activity 3:

_____

_____

_____

Teacher-Directed Activity 4:

_____

_____

_____

Teacher-Directed Activity 5:

_____

_____

_____

Lesson Plan Form for Learning Centers

Unit: _____

Art Center (Orange Star)

Activity 1:

_____
_____
_____
_____

Activity 2:

_____
_____
_____
_____

Research/Writing Center (Blue Star)

Activity 1:

_____
_____
_____
_____

Activity 2:

_____
_____
_____
_____

Computer Center

Activity 1:

_____

_____

_____

_____

Activity 2:

_____

_____

_____

_____

_____

Listening & Accelerated Reader Center (Green Star)

Books on Tape:

_____

_____

_____

_____

_____

Sample Language Arts Unit Taught at the Beginning of the Year

"Learning to Be Me"

Introductory Activities—Whole Group

Activity 1: Self-Portrait

♦ *Objectives:*

1. Students will use their creativity to complete a self-portrait drawing.

2. Students will increase their skills in drawing facial features in correct proportions.

♦ *Procedure:* Review feature placement. Demonstrate how to draw an oval face. Review where to place the eyes. (Draw them in the center from top to bottom.) Draw small egg shapes for the eyes and draw a "u" shape inside each eye and place a dark pupil in the center. Draw a nose from the eyes halfway to the chin. Draw only one side and the bottom of the nose. Show how to draw the mouth halfway between the bottom of the nose and the chin. The mouth is as wide as the pupil in the eyes. Draw the mouth to show both lips. Demonstrate how to draw different versions of hair. Add neck, shoulders and a simple shirt. Students color their portrait by using color crayons. Cut out the portrait and glue on the front cover of theme booklets, "Learning to Be Me."

♦ *Evaluation:* Completed self-portraits and teacher observation

Activity 2: You and Me

♦ *Objective:* Students will compare and contrast themselves with the teacher.

♦ *Procedure:* Teach the song "Free to Be You and Me" by Stephen Lawrence and Bruce Hart. Next, distribute paper to students. Place two large round coffee can lids on each table. Demonstrate how to draw a Venn diagram comparing and contrasting two people. The left circle will describe the teacher, while the right side will describe the student. The overlapping section will list how you are the same. Use a decorated box that contains items that will help students develop a more rounded picture of who the teacher truly is. Use pictures of your family, home, and pets. Include favorite color and food. Show your pictures and pull out a card with your age. Pull out a map of your state and country and then pull out a globe. Use all of the information shared to complete the Venn diagram. Draw an enlarged sample on the board and ask students to list ways you are the same. Fill in the middle section with their responses. Next, complete the teacher's side. Last, allow the students to complete their section. Provide assistance where needed. Place diagram inside folders.

♦ *Evaluation:* Teacher observation and completed Venn diagram

Activity 3: Head of a Boy/Girl

♦ *Objectives:*

1. Students will study abstract art by observing a head of a person influenced by an artist's style.

2. Students will create an abstract drawing using warm or cool colors.

♦ *Procedure:* Display the art reproduction poster "Senecio" by artist Paul Klee. Share information about the artist. Discuss the technique and style used by the artist. Distribute 11" × 14" white drawing paper, large paper plates, and rulers to students. Demonstrate how to trace the paper plate for a round head. Add the neck and shoulders. Add details to complete the drawing. Show how to draw a 3- or 4-inch grid on top of the drawing. The grid lines do not need to be exactly 3 or 4 inches. Students determine whether they want to use cool or warm colors. Color in every "enclosed" area. They should change colors when they come to a line. They need to make sure they do not have the same

color side by side. Students sign their work in permanent marker and place inside their folders.

♦ *Evaluation:* Completed drawings and teacher observation

Learning to Be Me: Teacher-Directed Station Activities

(Each activity takes approximately two 45-minute periods)

Activity 1

♦ *Objectives:*

1. Students will respond to oral questions.

2. Students will listen and respond to a story.

3. Students will write an imaginative paragraph.

♦ *Procedure:* Lead a group discussion on self-esteem using the following questions:

- What does self-esteem mean?

- Do all people feel good about themselves most of the time?

- How can you help someone feel good about them self?

- What is the purpose of communication?

- What qualities are important to you in a friend?

Read *Will I Ever Be Good Enough* by Judith Conway. Discuss that most people have doubts about trying new things. Review how the girls in the book learned how to do new things. Explain that achieving goals is a step-by-step process. Use examples from the book. Copy the following sentences on the board:

- If I could be an animal, I would be a/an _____ because _____.

- If I could be a color, I would be _____ because _____.

- If I could meet a famous person, I would choose _____ because _____.

- If I could star in a TV show, I would choose _____ because _____.

- If I could change one thing about my looks, it would be _____ because _____.

Have students complete a framed paragraph using the above sentences. Review indenting a paragraph, using margins, and skipping lines on notebook paper. Explain how to justify a paragraph by using the margins. Assist where needed. Have students share their papers. Demonstrate how to stand, hold a paper, make eye contact, project their voice so everyone in the group can hear, and read fluently. Place in folders at end of activity.

♦ *Evaluation:* Teacher observation and completed paragraphs.

Activity 2

♦ *Objectives:*

1. Students will listen and respond to a story.

2. Students will work cooperatively to generate a list of twenty items students appreciate.

3. Students will prioritize an individual list of ten items each student appreciates.

♦ *Procedure:* Have a brief discussion on ways that people wish they could change something in their lives. (Examples: Wish they had a bigger house, a swimming pool, longer hair, bigger muscles.) Read *The Luckiest One of All* by Bill Peet. Discuss how no one appreciated their situation and wished they could change. Make sure students are aware of the irony of the beginning and ending in this book. Convey the message that it's important we learn to appreciate the things we have, such as a place to sleep, food to eat, a relative to take care of us. Have each table brainstorm 20 items that they are grateful for. A designated writer writes the team's list. Encourage all team members to contribute to the list. Give about five minutes. The "reader" for each team takes turns sharing one item from their list until the teacher has them all listed on chart paper. Students turn to a blank page in their theme booklets and title it "10 Things I Appreciate." They get ten precut neon paper squares and number them 1 to 10. Each student must pick the top ten items from the chart that they are grateful for and rank them in order of importance. They randomly glue the blocks on their page and decorate with art supplies. Take a few minutes at the end of class to have a few students share their prioritized list. Ask the class if they thought prioritizing was easy or difficult? Why?

♦ *Evaluation:* Teacher observation, team lists, each student's prioritized list and discussion of prioritized list.

Activity 3

♦ *Objectives:*

1. Students will follow multiple oral directions.

2. Students will entertain peers by performing a readers' theater group presentation.

♦ *Procedure:* Demonstrate how a stage is divided into nine areas by drawing the following layout on the board.

(Back of Stage)

Up Right	Up Center	Up Left
Center Right	Center Stage	Center Left
Down Right	Down Center	Down Left

(Audience)

Explain how some raked stages (tilted) gave the audience a better view of the action taking place over the entire stage. This design particularly was true when the audience stood on a level floor and the stage was above the heads of the audience. Have students use rulers to draw the layout drawn on the board. The teacher may choose to give specific measurements and demonstrate various measurement procedures. Make sure students understand the role of the director. He/she gives directions according to the right and left of the actors when they are facing the audience. Students will need to copy the stage directions on their paper. Divide the classroom carpet into the stage areas using masking tape. Select two or three students to take "center stage" and follow stage commands given by the teacher. Repeat until all students at the teacher station have had an opportunity to participate.

Distribute copies of a four- or five-stanza poem glued on black construction paper to each student. Explain the readers' theater activity. Students at each table will present two stanzas. They must decide how they will read it, where and how they will stand, if they will use body motions and/or sound effects. Allow a short time for students to practice. (If possible, practice quietly in the hall so the remainder of the class will see only the final performance.) Before the performance, the groups must decide how they will enter the stage, if they will use any props, how they will introduce the group and how they will make their final bow. Provide assistance where needed. When ready, they perform for the remainder of the class.

- *Evaluation:* Teacher observation. Teacher informally critiques when students return to tables/groups. Rubrics can be provided to students before presentations. However, this unit was designed to be used at the beginning of the school year and some teachers choose to wait a few weeks before using rubrics. This would be a good activity to demonstrate how students will be evaluated on the Listening, Speaking, Viewing standards.

Activity 4

- *Objectives:*

  1. Students will write a personal narrative.

  2. Students will write a first draft, revise, edit and publish a final copy of a composition.

- *Procedure:* Read *The Important Book* by Margaret Wise Brown. Discuss how each page follows a specific format. Bring to students' attention how the first and last lines of each page are exactly the same. Write the following framed paragraph on the board:

  The important thing about me is _____. It is true that when I was a baby I _____. Now I am _____. I hope that I will _____. But the important thing about me now is _____.

Students will write a first draft on notebook paper, proofread, revise, edit, and make a final copy using erasable ink. The extension teacher has mini-conferences with students to help students through the writing process. The teacher may choose to do peer editing during the writing process. Demonstrate how to use erasable ink to prevent smudges. Assist where needed. Students will decorate their final copy by drawing a picture in pencil, outlining with thin permanent black marker, and painting with watercolor paints.

◆ *Evaluation:* Teacher observation of the writing process, mini-conferences, students reading their paragraph, and final copy of students' written paragraphs.

Learning to Be Me:
Learning Station Center Activities

ORANGE STAR TABLE: Art Center

♦ *Objectives:*

1. Students will read and follow multiple written directions.

2. Students will communicate respect for self and others.

Activity 1

♦ *Procedure:* Students will design a coat of arms following written directions from *Connecting Rainbows,* pp. 69–70. Students will use materials from the art center to create their coat of arms.

♦ *Evaluation:* Completed coat of arms

Activity 2

♦ *Procedure:* Students will create a poster titled "Learning to Be Me." It will demonstrate qualities about themselves. They'll use words and pictures. They are to include family, friends, school, books, hobbies, talents, sports, anything important to them.

♦ *Evaluation:* Completed poster

BLUE STAR TABLE: Research Center

♦ *Objectives:*

1. Students will use a dictionary to identify appropriate word meaning.

2. Students will determine which resource to use to locate specific information.

Activity 1

♦ *Procedure:* Students will use the dictionary to identify definitions of new vocabulary words on a teacher-made worksheet. Vocabulary words will be character education words.

♦ *Evaluation:* Completed worksheet

Activity 2

♦ *Procedure:* Students will use the encyclopedia, atlas, and nonfiction books to complete a teacher-made chart. The chart will show food, places, and friendly animals not commonly found in America, using the letters in the word FRIENDS.

♦ *Evaluation:* Completed chart

GREEN STAR TABLE: Listening Center

- *Objective:* Students will listen to and comprehend a variety of literature.

- *Procedure:* Students will listen to books on tape and take the *Accelerated Reader* tests.

- *Required book: The Hundred Dresses*

- *Optional books:* Students select books on tape from the leveled book baskets.

- *Evaluation: Accelerated Reader* test scores.

COMPUTER CENTER

- *Objective:* Students will use technology to assist in writing content-area pieces.

Activity 1

- *Procedure:* Students will use a word processor program to complete "That's What Love Means to Me" from *Building Self-Esteem*, p. 24.

- *Evaluation:* Printed passage

Activity 2

- *Procedure:* Students will use a word processor program to complete "The Colors of My Rainbow" from *Connecting Rainbows,* p. 56.

- *Evaluation:* Printed passage

Student's Checklist

All students receive a copy of the unit's checklist and glue it inside the front cover of their theme book. They check off each activity when completed. This helps them keep up with what they need to work on, especially on "Polish and Shine" days. The checklist allows me to see who has used time wisely, if directions have been followed, and if students successfully demonstrated the self-evaluation process of their work.

EXTENSION CENTER PROGRESS CHART: LEARNING TO BE ME		
Name	**Check when you have completed activity**	**Teacher's Evaluation**
TEACHER-DIRECTED STATION ACTIVITIES		
1. Wrote a paragraph: "What Would I Choose"		
2. "I Appreciate" chart		
3. Venn diagram		
4. Self-portrait glued on front of booklet		
5. Wrote short essay: "The Important Thing"		
6. Modern art drawing: "Head of a Boy/Girl"		
7. Stage directions		
8. Vocabulary book		
LEARNING CENTER STATION ACTIVITIES		
1. Computer Center: Wrote "That's What They Mean to Me"		
2. Computer Center: Wrote "The Color of My Rainbow"		
3. Computer Center: Worked in Cornerstone Program (optional)		
4. Listening Center and Accelerated Reader		
AR score – The Hundred Dresses _____		
Write the titles of other AR books you heard and completed test		

a.		
b.		
5. Research Center: Completed dictionary worksheet		
6. Research Center: Looked up "Unusual Friendly Favorites"		
7. Art Center Activity 1: Made a coat of arms		
8. Art Center Activity 2: Made "Learning to Be Me" poster		

Appendix 2
Extension Center Activities

created by
Harriet J. Hopkins,
former elementary principal and
coordinator of elementary programs,
Fairfax County Schools, Fairfax, Virginia

Reading Activities

Children must learn many skills when they begin to read for information in the content areas. Vocabulary, comprehension of what is read, remembering, organizing, generalizing, and pacing are a few of the areas where students need instruction as they become sophisticated readers. Frequently, little instruction in content reading is given. Extension center teachers make a valuable contribution to learning if they teach reading skills for content subjects. Suggestions include the following:

♦ Use extension center time to build a strong, formalized independent Sustained Silent Reading (SSR) program. According to *Becoming a Nation of Readers* (Center for the Study of Reading, 1984), elementary students read fewer than eight minutes a day and middle school students fewer than four! Opportunities for free reading provide students with additional practice in their skills and reading fluency.

♦ Read aloud to students every day to share in the joy of reading. Introduce new authors, and acquaint them with different genres to inspire them to read independently.

♦ Engage younger students in choral reading, repeated reading, and pattern books as a means of increasing their reading expression and speed.

♦ Engage students in Readers' Theater where students read the parts of various characters. Small groups of students may engage appropriate audiences.

♦ Provide reading time, guidance, and a large selection of trade and reference books related to topics being studied in health, science, and social studies.

♦ Teach vocabulary words from science, social studies, and health texts using the Cooperative Learning Teams, Games, Tournament format developed by Robert Slavin. This will help students in reading comprehension as well as test preparation.

♦ Use Inspirations software with older elementary students or Kidspirations software with younger elementary students to organize material they have read or are preparing to write.

Writing Activities

Just as students learn to read by reading, children learn to write by writing. Students tend to spend much of their time in the traditional classroom circling, underlining, matching, filling in blanks, and checking correct items rather than creating text. As with sustained reading, the extension center is an ideal place for teaching creative and expository writing. Below are some suggested activities.

♦ Assist young students to construct and maintain word banks. Structure activities so students work in small groups conducting word sorts, composing sentences, and learning vocabulary. Older students may maintain personal dictionaries on computer discs.

- Provide small mailboxes for all extension center students and allow students to communicate with each other through notes and letters placed in these mailboxes. Students may collect and deliver mail only on entering or leaving the Center. To ensure that all students receive mail, have students select secret pals to whom they must write weekly. As an extra incentive, e-mail can be used as a means of communicating with classmates. Secret pals may be changed periodically.

- Have students rewrite familiar myths, legends, or fairy tales in a modern setting.

- Ask students to keep a daily record of classroom activities and assignments. Students who have been absent can learn what they missed, and everyone can check the record to see what they might have forgotten.

- Encourage students to write their book reports online! That way other students who are considering reading a book can go online to see what other students say about it. In addition, it creates a wonderful audience for students' writing.

- After sharing patterned stories, have students create their own verses. Use of appropriate desktop publishing software can allow students to illustrate and create covers for their stories.

- Following the language experience model developed by Stauffer, have students create and record class or small-group stories that may be collected, bound into book form, and distributed to other children.

- After instructing children in various poetry forms, establish a poetry center where students may write and illustrate concrete poetry, haiku, senryu, tanka, cinquain, and diamanté, for example.

- In a separate poetry center, allow students to compose other forms of poetry "when the mood hits." Encourage them to occasionally set their poetry to music.

- Conduct writing conferences with students as a pre-writing stimulus. These conferences may be conducted by older student helpers or parent volunteers as well as the extension center teachers.

- Read accounts of well-known historical events and have children write themselves into the story by preparing first-person accounts of the incident as they "witnessed" it.

- Use the local newspaper for teaching how to read the daily paper and other newspaper activities. Have students write, publish, and distribute *The Extension Center News,* which includes advertisements for student services such as school-wide plays and assemblies.

- Rewrite or audiotape new endings to stories or books. Published unfinished stories are available to support this activity.

- Use a digital camera to take pictures around the school and scan them into the computer. Use the pictures for children to write stories on the computer about what they have recorded. These can be printed for a class book!

- Have students "adopt" a tree on school grounds. Using the digital camera, they can take pictures of the tree at different times during the year. They can scan in their pictures to record changes or non-changes of the tree throughout the school year and write about what they observed.

- Permit students to write on transparencies, projecting their work on a wall or screen as they write. This activity motivates many students to write and allows them the opportunity to edit easily with water-soluble writing pens. Some students who have difficulty finding errors when writing on notebook paper become successful editors when their work is projected.

- Have students write journal entries, keeping a log of thoughts, feelings, and reflections on their daily activities. This activity may be the first exercise of the day as children enter the extension center from various classes.

- Students can create their own pattern books on the computer using word processing software such as HyperStudio. Use students in other classes and extension centers as audiences from time to time.

- Encourage students to write and publish stories to share with younger students periodically. In addition to improving oral reading skills, this exercise should engender confidence, and it is an excellent way to aid students in becoming comfortable appearing in front of an audience. Students *must* be well rehearsed! Some schools even place student-published books in the library for other students to read!

- Teach computer keyboarding skills and word processing so that students may easily edit their written work. Many students increase their writing output dramatically after learning word processing. Computer software programs are available for teaching keyboarding. Hint: by placing a shoebox with one long side removed over the keyboard, students can learn without looking at the keys!

- Conduct editing workshops so that students may become proficient editors of their own and others' work. After obtaining a child's permission, copy his writing on an overhead transparency and project it for his peers to read and edit. Ask students to describe the *positive aspects* of the writing. After compiling a list of attributes, ask the students to offer *one* suggestion for improving the manuscript. Then coach the child and his classmates in incorporating the editorial advice into his writing. When students become comfortable with the format, allow them to work in small groups to conduct their own editing workshops.

- Teach note-taking skills. Help students learn to identify critical elements of their content area textbooks by learning simple note-taking abbreviations and recognizing written "markers." Use of "webs" to outline and organize information from texts around topics is an excellent strategy. The fishbone and bubble webs are frequently-used formats.

- Use extension center time for teaching writing strategies in support of homeroom content assignments. For example, if students are assigned essays, books reports, or research papers, spend time demonstrating how these papers are composed. Offer corrective feedback and editing for works in progress.

- Have students listen to a story and either audio- or videotape their retelling of the story. Next, have other students listen to the retold story and tape their version. After a third or fourth group has repeated this activity, replay the original story for comparison.

- Have students create a database of classroom library books. Include comments from others who have read each book so students can see what their friends think of the book. Students also can "check out" books online so that recordkeeping is kept to a minimum.

Using Technology to Enhance Content Area Learning

There are many software packages on the market that can help students learn. The current thinking, however, is to integrate technology into the learning process to help students create, discover, process, and apply their learning.

The leading association in this field is the International Society for Technology in Education (ISTE), which promotes technology use and integration into the teaching and learning process. ISTE's Website, www.iste.org, provides a wealth of ideas. At the left-hand side of the homepage, click on Educator Resources to find ideas for technology integration, curriculum and lesson plans, and assessment programs and strategies. Below are some activities and other Websites, by content area, that offer activities for students and resources for teachers.

General Activities

- Have students use the computer to conduct research related to their topic. Also, "teacher-bookmarked" Websites are an invaluable tool for allowing students the opportunity to research (and read!) material. Students also can create their own Websites of information on identified topics.

- Have students conduct research using "Web Quests" from the University of San Diego Website. Teachers love this structured approach to finding information from the Internet, which can serve as a framework for reports.

- Have students use PowerPoint to create presentations for their classmates on reports they have written. By writing text and scanning pictures from the Internet or from photos, students are able to illustrate their publication. Having an audience for their work also increases its quality.

- Use Movie Maker software from Microsoft to create movies from videos and still digital photography. Students can record activities, science experiments, field trips, and so on to download into a PowerPoint presentation for the class.

- Have students create databases as a means of organizing information they are gathering on a topic. Information about Native Americans, U.S. presidents, or other famous people in history—where they were from, what they ate, what they wore—can be organized using a data base. K-W-L information (Know, Want to Know, Learned) can be completed online as a class activity when studying a unit. Thus, all students in a classroom can have the opportunity to contribute to this information.

Social Studies

- National Geographic Society: www.nationalgeographic.com. Resources and activities for children; an educators' section with lesson plans and activities for all ages and grades.

- The History Channel: www.history.com. Many resources for students to conduct research.

- U.S. Library of Congress: www.loc.gov. Resources for students and teachers.

- U.S. Department of Education: www.ed.gov. Resources for teachers, including activities, simulations, and primary documents for students to use in their research.

Science

- National Science Foundation: www.nsf.gov. Classroom resources for teachers in a broad list of curriculum subjects.

- U.S. Department of Energy: www.doe.gov. Resources for science teachers.

- National Aeronautics and Space Administration: www.nasa.gov. Games and activities for kids and resources for students and teachers.

- National Wildlife Federation: www.nwf.com. Resources, articles and information about global issues.

Mathematics

- National Council of Teachers of Mathematics: www.nctm.org. Resources for elementary teachers, Title I teachers, and students.

Additional Enrichment Activities

Often classroom teachers do not have time to complete all the activities in the teacher's manual. The extension center teachers can implement some of these creative and exciting enrichment or remedial activities, which include reading, writing, art, drama, and other creative projects.

Here is but a small selection of the innumerable possibilities.

- Organize cooperative learning groups for students to coach and drill each other prior to major tests and examinations.

- Demonstrate book-making for children; permit them to bind and "publish" many of their works as a basis for an extension center library of children's writings. Attractive book covers may be made from wallpaper samples.

- Write Trivial Pursuit questions based on science, health, and social studies content. Also use the Jeopardy format for content review and Wheel of Fortune for teaching vocabulary, idioms, clichés, and common expressions. The questions can be put on a computer and projected on a screen for the entire class to play.

- Permit students to make posters advertising favorite books, short stories, poems, films, filmstrips, videotapes, and records.

- After organizing an extension center art center, encourage individuals or small groups of students to make dioramas, paintings, or murals inspired by their readings.

- Dramatize favorite stories using puppets, mime, and improvisation.

- Using information from the *Extension Center News*, local newscasts, and newspapers, produce a daily or weekly school news program for the entire school following the nightly news television format and starring extension center students. Have a lunch-hour broadcast once a week in the school cafeteria.

- Maintain records of each child's completed readings along with a teacher's or parent volunteer's positive reactions and comments.

- Use trade books to teach and illustrate concepts for young children. For example, abstract words such as *big, handicapped, old, beyond*, may be more easily understood from the context of a good children's book.

- Have students illustrate their writing. Using software such as KidPix, students can create covers and pictures for the stories they create on the computer.

- Provide an art and materials center to support the preparation of projects and other assignments. This is essential for those students who may not have such support available in their homes.

- Allow one group of students, in a cooperative learning group, to select and design a reading lesson following the basal reader model. After choosing a story to teach, students select vocabulary words to be introduced. Next, they write an introduction to the story, construct questions for checking for understanding, and develop worksheets for guided and independent practice. Lastly, children may develop enrichment activities to be used as follow-up assignments. Working in groups of four or five students, this project requires several days for development. When completed, each group member teaches this story to a small group of peers. Repeat the activity with each class group.

♦ Another source of learning activities is Paula Rutherford's book *Instruction for All Students,* written for teachers in an easy-to-read format. The author provides teachers with ideas for lesson and unit design, presentation modes, and ideas for colle-gial collaboration. In addition, there are many learning activities designed for specific purposes—active learning strategies, activities to support higher-level thinking skills, practical ways to differentiate instruction, and ideas for assessing student learning in multiple ways.

References

Center for the Study of Reading (1984). *Becoming a nation of readers.* Washington, DC: National Academy of Education.

Rutherford, P. (2002). *Instruction for all students.* Alexandria, VA: Just ASK Publications.

Stauffer, R. G. (1980). *The language experience approach to the teaching of reading.* New York: Harper & Row.

Appendix 3
Prince William County Public Schools Regulation

Elementary Instructional Day

This regulation describes the organization of the 6.5 hour, elementary instructional day, with guidelines and descriptions of instructional blocks of time, including time allocations, remediation, and teacher planning time.

I. Definitions

    A. **Core** – Instruction in reading/language arts, mathematics, science, and social studies.

    B. **Core Extension** –Needs-based extended instruction, not new instruction, in reading/language arts, mathematics, science and/or social studies. This shall include remediation and/or enrichment, strings, and special services as appropriate. This may include instruction in other encore areas, based upon individual school needs.

    C. **Special Services** – Resource services such as special education, Title I, gifted education, and English for Speakers of Other Languages (ESOL).

    D. **Encore** – Instruction in art, music, physical education, and other subjects outside the core.

    E. **Rotation** – The scheduling of encore classes.

II. Organization of the School Day

The elementary schedule shall provide consistency in the instructional day and in the implementation of the Prince William County curriculum, and shall maximize instructional time for curriculum delivery. The schedule shall provide opportunity for remediation during the school day, and daily individual and grade level planning time for teachers.

The schedule allows for flexibility in the scheduling of lunch, recess, and the encore subjects.

III. Daily Core Content Instruction*

	Reading/ Language Arts	Mathematiecs	Science and Social Studies
Kindergarten	60 minutes	45 minutes	45 minutes
Grades 1 and 2	120 minutes	90 minutes	45 minutes
Grades 3, 4, 5	90 minutes	75 minutes	90 minutes (45 minute each)s

*These times include travel time

IV. Use of Core Extension

Core Extension shall be 30–45 minutes for students in grades 1–5. Core Extension in kindergarten shall be alternated with instruction in Encore. Students who have failed the SOL tests in reading/language arts and/or math and students who are below grade level in those subjects shall receive remediation according to Regulation 649–1.

Time allotments for specific resource programs follow:

Special Education – A student's Individual Education Plan (IEP) should determine time allotments for services.

ESOL (English for Speakers of Other Languages) – A student's English proficiency level, academic needs, and program screening results should determine time allotments for services ranging from 45 minutes to three hours daily commensurate with the most appropriate support level. Instructional support may be provided by pull out (Level 1 and 2) or inclusion (Levels 3 and 4).

Gifted Education – A student's grade level should determine minimum time allotments for START and SIGNET services.

Kindergarten	45 minutes every other week
Grades One and Two	45 minutes each week
Grade three	90 minutes each week
Grades Four and Five	225 minutes each week These minutes may be provided on-site or in an off-site center.

V. Use of Encore

Instructional time in art, music, physical education, and other encore subjects (as determined by the school) for grades 1–5 shall be 45 minutes. Schools shall schedule art, music, and physical education to meet at least once in six days. These classes may meet more frequently, every three, four, or five days. Half-day kindergarten students shall receive instruction in art, music, and physical education as part of the rotation block with half the frequency of grades 1–5.

VI. School Closings

When school is closed for holidays or due to inclement weather or other unscheduled reasons, the rotation shall resume the next day of student attendance (i.e., if school is closed due to inclement weather on day three of the rotation, the next day that school is in session would be day three). However, strings and START programs shall follow their designated schedule.

VII. Teacher Planning

A daily, unencumbered, standard block of planning time will be provided within the instructional day for all teachers. This shall include both individual and team planning.

The principal and area associate superintendent are responsible for implementing and monitoring this regulation.